A Student's Guide to Hearsay
REVISED 4th Edition

(2011–Pub.748)

A Student's Guide to Hearsay

REVISED 4th Edition

Clifford S. Fishman
Professor of Law
The Catholic University of America

CAROLINA ACADEMIC PRESS
Durham, North Carolina

Revised 4th edition ISBN 978-0-7698-4696-5

ISBN 978-1-4224-9366-3 (softbound)

Library of Congress Cataloging-in-Publication Data

Fishman, Clifford S.
A student's guide to hearsay / Clifford S. Fishman. — 4th ed.
p. cm.
Includes index.
1. Evidence, Hearsay. I. Title.
KF8969.F57 2011
347.73'64 — dc23

2011024228

Carolina Academic Press, LLC
700 Kent Street
Durham, NC 27701
Telephone (919) 489-7486
Fax (919) 493-5668
www.caplaw.com

Printed in the United States of America
2018 Printing

PREFACE

"I've already spent a ridiculous amount of money on a casebook and separate rules pamphlet. There are hornbooks and manuals that cover all of evidence. Why should I buy a book that only deals with hearsay?"

Good question. Here are my answers:

1. Hearsay is an important subject. It is a major component of your evidence course; it is one of those subjects that every lawyer should understand.

2. Hearsay is one of the most difficult bodies of law you will ever encounter in law school. The basic concept is a tricky one; once you've mastered that, you have to deal with dozens of technical exceptions, written and unwritten.

3. This book will help you learn it.

Let me expand a little on each of these reasons.

1. Hearsay is an important subject.

Hearsay pervades everything a lawyer does in a courtroom; it is impossible to try even the simplest case without encountering it. The leading evidence casebooks devote anywhere from 20-40 percent of their length to the hearsay rule and its exceptions; professors spend an equivalent percentage of classroom time covering the subject.

2. Hearsay is a difficult subject.

The hearsay rule is simple enough; hearsay is not admissible unless any of the following provides otherwise:

a federal statute;

these rules; or

other rules prescribed by the Supreme Court.

The legal profession has struggled for more than a century just to come up with a basic *definition* of hearsay. Even though hearsay is now defined by statute — thank goodness for the Federal Rules of Evidence! — there are numerous "unwritten exceptions" to the definition, as well as eight statutory exceptions to the definition, each of which creates a category of evidence that fits the definition (or appears to), but is classified as *non*-hearsay. in addition, there are 29 statutory exceptions to the hearsay rule,[1] each of which creates a category of evidence that is hearsay but is nevertheless admissible over a hearsay objection. Each of these statutory exceptions has its own requirements, procedural wrinkles, legislative history, and judicial gloss.

To learn this body of law and apply it correctly is a major challenge. Suppose, for example, I want to call W, a witness who will testify, "On March 1, X said to me, 'I'm going out with Frank tonight,'" Under some circumstances, what X said to W is not hearsay; under some circumstances it fits the basic definition of hearsay but is not hearsay because what X said fits within an exception to the hearsay definition; under other circumstances what X said is hearsay but fits within an exception to the hearsay rule; in still other circumstances, it is

---

[1] There are 23 exceptions codified in Fed. R. Evid. 803, five exceptions in Fed. R. Evid. 804, and a "residual" exception in Fed. R. Evid. 807.

hearsay and does not fit within any exception; and yet in other circumstances, it is hearsay but judges disagree as to whether it fits within an exception to the hearsay rule.

Additional complicating factors include constitutional considerations (in particular, the Fifth Amendment privilege against self-incrimination and the Sixth Amendment Confrontation Clause), as well as the concept of multiple hearsay.

To repeat the basic point: hearsay is a difficult subject.

3. This book will help you learn it.

This book will help you learn hearsay because it breaks down each element of the hearsay definition, and each exception to the definition or to the rule, into its component parts. For example, for each hearsay exception, this book:

- Outlines the policies underlying the provision
- Lists and explains the requirements that must be satisfied for the evidence to fit within the exception
- Explains additional issues that have arisen or are likely to arise
- Explains how a rule interacts with other rules of evidence
- Spells out the procedural and tactical considerations that must be understood to appreciate how the rule "plays" in the courtroom
- Gives review questions and answers so you can test and apply what you've learned

Has an associated website, http://law.cua.edu/Fac_Staff/FishmanC/ studentguidetohearsay-.cfm, which will post updates on major developments in hearsay law.

Don't misunderstand: you are not getting a simplified, comic book version of hearsay. This book will help you learn hearsay as you want to learn it, to do well on your final, the bar exam, and in practice.

Along the way, I also explain the hearsay significance of: a ham sandwich, Humpty Dumpty, the Greek god of wine, Tim McGraw, dog saliva, IBM's computer and Jeopardy champion "Watson," my wife Betty, William Shakespeare, the Chicago Cubs, 1950's TV shows, peat moss, a squeaky boot, Leondardo DiCaprio, the French Army, the speed of sound, and the way criminals treat their girlfriends. As a bonus, I even tell you a little big about what "love" means.

I've been teaching evidence for 35 years, to an average of 80 or so students each year. (Before that, I was a prosecutor in New York City for eight years.) The outlines, explanations, and questions in this book have been tested in the classroom. they work for my students; I'm confident they will work for you.

Clifford S. Fishman

The Catholic University of America

Washington, D.C. 20064

2011

DEDICATION

This book is dedicated, in ascending order of importance, to:

1. The Supreme Court, whose Confrontation Clause decisions, and the Advisory Committee, whose Restyled text of the Federal Rules of Evidence, made this Fourth Edition necessary.

2. My colleagues and friends at the Catholic University of America Law School.

3. My evidence students, who for the past 35 years have helped me learn how to teach, and therefore how to write about, the law of evidence.

4. Betty; Rebecca, Brian, Sam and Yael; and Sarah and Luke.

TABLE OF CONTENTS

Chapter 1

THE HEARSAY RULE AND ITS RATIONALE

§ 1.1 INTRODUCTION

At 2:00 p.m. on February 1, a man wielding a revolver robbed a bank on 10th Street and Metropolitan Avenue. Three months later, on May 1, D was arrested and charged with the robbery. He has retained you to represent him. No one who was in the bank on the day of the robbery has positively identified your client as the perpetrator; the case against him is based on circumstantial evidence.

On October 1, the trial begins. A jury is selected and the government calls X, Y and Z. Each testifies that he or she was in the bank that afternoon and saw the robbery. Each testifies that the robber wore a three-piece navy blue suit and a ski mask, and stuffed the proceeds of the robbery into a black leather doctor's bag. They testify that D is roughly the same height and build as the robber, but none can identify him as the perpetrator.

Next, the government calls W. After W is sworn, he testifies as follows:

Q.   Do you recognize the defendant?

A.   Yes, I do.

Q.   When did you first meet him?

A.   At a party late in January. Someone introduced us, and we talked for a couple of minutes.

Q.   Did you see him again sometime thereafter?

A.   Yes.

Q.   When and where did you see him next?

A.   On February 1st, at five minutes after two in the afternoon. It was on Metropolitan Avenue between 8th and 9th Streets.

Q.   Describe what happened.

A.   I was walking toward 9th and he was walking from the direction of 9th toward 8th. When I saw him, I angled over toward him and stuck out my hand and said, "Hey, man, how're ya doin'?" He looked right at me like he was real upset and then went right by me, without saying a word.

Q.   Describe his physical appearance.

A.   Well, he was wearing a blue suit and he was carrying a black bag.

§ 1.2   QUESTION

Question 1. Is this testimony relevant? Why?

Ans. If W's testimony is accurate, D was walking downtown (from 9th Street toward 8th Street), away from the scene of the crime (10th Street), a few minutes after the crime was committed. Thus, it is circumstantial evidence that D was at the scene of the crime at the time the crime was committed. Like the robber, D wore a blue suit and carried a black bag. He was in a hurry and seemed upset that W saw (or recognized) him, which permits the inference that D was anxious to leave the area as quickly and unobtrusively as possible.

By itself, this testimony is not enough to convict; still, it is useful circumstantial evidence that (to paraphrase Fed. R. Evid. 401) "tend[s] to make it more probable" that D is the robber. It only has this "tendency," however, if the jury believes W.

§ 1.3   TESTIMONIAL INFERENCES

How does a juror decide whether to believe a witness? Jurors probably began to evaluate W from the moment he walked into the courtroom. They watched him take an oath to tell the truth. They observed his demeanor (eye movement, body language, tone of voice, etc.) as he testified.

A witness's testimony is relevant only if we can make four *"testimonial inferences"* about the witness, relating to perception, memory, narration, and sincerity.

1. Did the witness accurately *perceive* the events in question?

2. Has the witness *remembered* the events accurately from that day to this?

3. Has the witness accurately *narrated* what he or she perceived and remembers (i.e., do the witness's words mean the same to him or her as they do to us?)

4. Is the witness *sincerely* trying to testify accurately, or is there a reason why the witness might be deliberately lying, or subconsciously shading the truth?

Generally, the best opportunity to assess a witness's sincerity and the accuracy of his or her testimony occurs when the witness is tested by cross-examination. Effective cross-examination might expose weaknesses with respect to any or all of these *testimonial inferences*. Consider the following cross-examination of W in the robbery case:

Q.   What did you say D was wearing when you saw him on the street on February 1?

A.   A blue suit.

Q.   Three-piece? Two-piece?

A.   No, it was one piece. Y'know, with the big zipper up the front?

Q.   And he was carrying a bag?

A.　　　　　　Yeah, a black bag. Like if you buy something at a department store, they put it in one of those bags . . .

This testimony exposes problems in narration: when W said "blue suit" and "black bag," he meant something quite different than X, Y and Z meant when they used the same words to describe the robber.

The point is this: there are no guarantees, but sometimes cross-examination can dramatically reduce the impact of a witness's story.

§ 1.4　RATIONALE BEHIND THE HEARSAY RULE

Now suppose that instead of calling W as a witness, the prosecutor calls Police Officer Y. She is sworn and testifies as follows:

Q.　　　　　　Did anything happen on May 2 that relates to this case?

A.　　　　　　Yes. A man walked into the station house and identified himself as Mr. W. He said, "I read about the guy who was arrested yesterday for bank robbery; I have some information that might be helpful. I first met that guy at a party late in January. Then I saw him again on February 1 at 2:05 p.m. He was coming from the direction of 9th Street toward 8th Street on Metropolitan Avenue, wearing a blue suit and carrying a black bag. When I saw him then, I went up to him and said 'Hey man, how ya doin?' He looked right at me like he was real upset and went right by me without saying a word." That's what Mr. W told me on May 2.

Officer Y is under oath; the jury can watch and hear her testify; and you can cross-examine her to test the accuracy of her perception and memory, examine her choice of words, and probe whether she might have a reason to lie or subconsciously shade the truth. For example, you might ask Y whether W spoke with an accent which might have interfered with Y's ability to understand (perceive) what W was saying. You might test her memory of what W said by asking when (if at all) she took notes or wrote a memorandum about her conversation with him. Let us assume, though, that Y is an honest, efficient, conscientious officer. She had W write out his statement. Thus, we know precisely what W said to Officer Y, in W's own words. (Perhaps she even had W swear to his statement before a notary.) You proceed, therefore, to ask Officer Y the questions you otherwise would have asked W — designed to test *W's* perception, memory, narration and sincerity — and run into a stone wall, because Y's honest, efficient, conscientious response to virtually every question is, "I don't know."

You have just encountered hearsay. W's statement to Officer Y is hearsay, whether he made his statement orally or in writing, even if it was made in a sworn affidavit.[1]

And you have also just encountered the reason for the hearsay rule. W, not Y, is the real source of the information here. Yet, unless *W* comes to court and testifies, it is

---

[1] The major portion of the next chapter is devoted to defining hearsay. If at this point you don't know why W's statement to Officer Y is hearsay, don't panic — we haven't gotten to that yet. For now, just take my word for it.

difficult or impossible to test *W*'s perception, memory, narration, or sincerity. This is why the *"testimonial inferences"* that underlie the relevance of any witness's testimony are often referred to as the *hearsay risks*, because unless W takes the stand and is cross-examined, we run the risk the jury will rely on his hearsay statement without an opportunity to adequately assess whether he perceived accurately, remembered correctly, narrated clearly, and is sincerely trying to tell the truth.

You will encounter the phrases *testimonial inferences* and *hearsay risks* from time to time in this book, in court decisions, and in law review articles and treatises. Both phrases refer to the same thing: perception, memory, narration (sometimes referred to as "communication"), and sincerity (sometimes referred to as "veracity").

Since the end of the 17th century, hearsay has been considered such an inherently *untrustworthy* form of evidence that, as a rule, it is not admissible in a trial. W's statement to Officer Y illustrates the primary reasons the law distrusts hearsay evidence:

1. The typical hearsay statement was not made under oath.

2. The fact-finder does not have the opportunity to observe the demeanor of the person making the statement.

3. Most important, the party adversely affected by the hearsay has no opportunity to test, by cross-examination, the perception, memory, narration, and sincerity of the person who made the hearsay statement.

§ 1.5 THE HEARSAY RULE

Hence, hearsay is generally not admissible at trial. **Fed. R. Evid.** 802 sets forth the hearsay rule. As of December 1, 2011, that rule reads:

Rule 802. The Rule Against Hearsay

Hearsay is not admissible unless any of the following provides otherwise:

- **a federal statute;**
- **these rules; or**
- **other rules prescribed by the Supreme Court.**

[Prior to December 1, 2011, the rule read as follows:

> **Hearsay is not admissible except as provided by these rules, by other rules prescribed by the Supreme Court pursuant to statutory authority or by Act of Congress.**

The Federal Rules of Evidence were rewritten solely to make them easier to understand; the Advisory Committee did not intend to make any substantive change in the Rules. The text of the old rule may remain useful in reading court decisions that precede the revision of the rules. Thus, this edition of the Student's Guide provides the text of both the new and the old version of each relevant provision of the Federal Rules of Evidence.]

§ 1.6 THE FEDERAL RULES OF EVIDENCE; LEGISLATIVE HISTORY

This book analyzes Article VIII of the Federal Rules of Evidence, and the issues that have arisen or are likely to arise as courts apply the provisions of Article VIII. The Federal Rules of Evidence were enacted into law by Congress in 1975. Since then, the vast majority of the states have enacted or promulgated evidence codes based on the Federal Rules.

Because the Federal Rules of Evidence have been enacted as a statute, it is sometimes necessary to refer to the legislative history in analyzing a rule. Enactment of the Federal Rules of Evidence was the culmination of a lengthy process that began in 1965, when then Chief Justice Earl Warren appointed an Advisory Committee to draft rules of evidence for federal courts. A first draft was issued in 1969; a second draft was issued in 1971. In 1972, Congress decided to deal with the matter by legislation. The Judiciary Committees of the House and Senate each studied and debated the Advisory Committee draft. Some provisions were amended in committee; some were amended on the floor of the House; as to some provisions the House and Senate disagreed, and the dispute was reconciled in a Conference Committee made up of representatives of both houses of Congress. Ultimately, Congress enacted the rules into law, effective January 2, 1975. Since then, from time to time this or that provision of the Rules has been amended by Congress or by the judicial rule-making process. Nearly all of these amendments are discussed in Advisory Committee Notes, House, Senate or Conference Committee Reports, or floor debates in Congress. Where necessary, I refer to this legislative history. Finally, effective December 1, 2011, the Federal Rules of Evidence have been rewritten solely to make them easier to understand; the Advisory Committee did not intend to make any substantive change in the Rules. Because the text of the old rule may remain useful in reading court decisions that precede the revision of the rules, this edition of the Student's Guide provides the text of both the new and the old version of each relevant provision of the Federal Rules of Evidence.

Chapter 2

DEFINING AND RECOGNIZING HEARSAY

PART A:
INTRODUCTION

§ 2.1   IN GENERAL

Knowing that there is a rule against hearsay, students tend to form a mental equation: "Hearsay = inadmissible evidence." This equation is inaccurate. Much evidence that is hearsay is nonetheless admissible, as you will learn in Chapters 3–12. Conversely, much evidence that is not hearsay is inadmissible on a variety of other grounds (e.g., because it is irrelevant or prejudicial, is not properly authenticated, or is excluded by some other rule). As you study these materials and outline your answers to the problems, keep in mind that this chapter does not address whether a particular offer of evidence is admissible. Rather, the focus is on defining and recognizing hearsay.

§ 2.2   THE BASIC DEFINITION OF HEARSAY; "DECLARANT"

Fed. R. Evid. 801 Definitions That Apply to This Article; Exclusions from Hearsay
—

(c) Hearsay. "Hearsay" means a statement that:

(1) the declarant does not make while testifying at the current trial or hearing; and

(2) a party offers in evidence to prove the truth of the matter asserted in the statement.

[Prior to December 1, 2011, the rule read as follows:

"Hearsay" is a statement, other than one made by the declarant while testifying at the trial or hearing, offered in evidence to prove the truth of the matter asserted.

The Federal Rules of Evidence were rewritten solely to make them easier to understand; the Advisory Committee did not intend to make any substantive change in the Rules. The text of the old rule may remain useful in reading court decisions that precede the revision of the rules. Thus, this edition of the Student's Guide provides the text of both the new and the old version of each relevant provision of the Federal Rules of Evidence.]

The definition has three elements: (1) a "statement"; (2) that "the declarant does not make while testifying at the current trial or hearing," i.e., the declarant made it days, weeks, months, or years prior to "the current trial or hearing"; (3) "that a party offers in evidence to prove the truth of the matter asserted in the statement." Because the definition uses the term "declarant," we should also examine the definition of that term.

Fed. R. Evid. 801(b) defines "declarant" as follows:

(b) Declarant. "Declarant" means the person who made the statement.

[Prior to December 1, 2011, Fed.R.Evid. 801(b) provided:

(b) Declarant. A "declarant" is a person who makes a statement.

The Federal Rules of Evidence were rewritten solely to make them easier to understand; the Advisory Committee did not intend to make any substantive change in the Rules. The text of the old rule may remain useful in reading court decisions that precede the revision of the rules. Thus, this edition of the Student's Guide provides the text of both the new and the old version of each relevant provision of the Federal Rules of Evidence.]

The definition of "declarant" is straight-forward and rarely raises any issues.[1]

To avoid missing potential hearsay issues, every offer of evidence should be examined to ascertain whether the evidence fits this definition:

1. Is the evidence a "statement," as that term is defined in Fed. R. Evid. 801(a)?

2. When and where was it made?

3. Why is it being offered?

We will examine each element of the definition in detail. First, however, a brief overview might be helpful.

"Statement" is defined in Fed. R. Evid. 801(a) as "a person's oral assertion, written assertion, or nonverbal conduct, if the person intended it as an assertion." The key word in each part of the definition is "assertion." Because the Federal Rules of Evidence offer no definition of "assertion," we apply the everyday meaning: an assertion is something someone says or does in order to communicate a fact or opinion in the hope or expectation that it will be accepted as true or accurate. Obviously, many spoken or written remarks are not "statements" under this definition, because they are not "assertions." A man who turns to a woman as they are slogging along in a January blizzard and says, "I enjoy these sunny summer days," is not asserting, and does not expect the woman to believe, that it is summer, or that the weather is sunny, or that he is enjoying himself.

If words (or conduct) are spoken (or performed) by the declarant (or actor) with the intention of communicating a fact in the hope or expectation that it will be accepted as

---

[1] Concerning non-human "declarants," see § 2.19.

true, then we have an assertion (i.e., a "statement" as defined in Fed. R. Evid. 801(a)). Otherwise, we do not have a "statement"; and if we do not have a "statement," we do not have hearsay.

The third element of the definition — "that a party offers in evidence to prove the truth of the matter asserted in the statement" — requires us to focus on the purpose for which the evidence is offered. Why does the lawyer offering the evidence want the judge or jury to hear it? In other words, why, in the context of this particular lawsuit, is the evidence relevant? For example, suppose it is important to determine when a man and woman first met. She claims it was in January; he claims it wasn't until June. The woman is on the witness stand.

Q.   Describe when and how you first met him.

A.   It was in the middle of January. I had just gotten off a bus on my way home from work. It was a miserable day — snowing, windy. This man got off right behind me and said, "I enjoy these sunny summer days." I laughed and we struck up an acquaintance.

The woman is quoting the man, but not to prove that what he said was true. The attorney eliciting this testimony isn't trying to prove that it was a sunny summer day. Thus, we do not have to draw the "testimonial inferences" discussed in § 1.1 in order for the *man's* words to have probative value. The hearsay hazards are absent, because we are not relying on *his* perception or memory or choice of words; we are not relying on *his* sincerity. In this particular lawsuit, *what* the man said is not all that important. What *is* important is that he said something (anything) to the woman during a January blizzard, as a result of which they became acquainted. In this lawsuit, his comment to her would have been equally relevant if he had said "Twas brillig and the slithy toves did gyre and gimble in the wabe" (the opening line to "Jabberwocky" in Lewis Carroll's *Alice Through the Looking Glass*). The woman is testifying to the man's remark, *not* to prove the truth of what he said to her, but simply to prove that the words were said, because in this lawsuit, the mere saying of the words, regardless of whether they were "true," is relevant evidence of a fact of consequence in the lawsuit.[2]

Now consider the second element of the hearsay definition: "not [made] by the declarant while testifying at the current trial or hearing."

Assume we are trying a personal injury case involving a collision between a bus and an automobile in a Manhattan intersection. The plaintiff (P), the owner and driver of the automobile, calls a witness, who is sworn and testifies as follows:

Q.   What is your name?

A.   Winston Smith.

Q.   Where do you live?

A.   1984 Orwell Drive, New London, Connecticut, apartment 101.

Q.   What is your occupation?

---

[2] Needless to say, issues frequently arise as to whether a "statement" is being "offer[ed] in evidence to prove the truth of the matter asserted by the declarant," or whether it is being offered for some other relevant purpose. We will explore these issues in some detail later in this chapter.

A.   I'm a rat exterminator.

Q.   Where were you at one o'clock in the afternoon on April 4, 2011?

A.   I was at the corner of Broadway and 48th Street in Manhattan.

Q.   What was the weather like?

A.   Bright and cold.

All of Mr. Smith's answers are "statements," (i.e., they are "assertions"): he claims to be telling the truth, to be communicating accurate information, based on his own knowledge and perception. The attorney eliciting his answers hopes the jury will believe those answers, so Smith's testimony is being offered "to prove the truth of the matter asserted in [declarant Smith's] statement[s]." However, nothing Smith has said so far is hearsay, because Smith is making his statement "while testifying at the current trial or hearing." Defendant's attorney can test Smith's perception, memory, choice of words and sincerity by cross-examination. Thus, the hearsay hazards are absent.

P's lawyer continues to examine Smith:

Q.   Did anything unusual occur at that time and place?

A.   Yes. I was looking at a movie poster when I heard a woman shout, "Oh look, the bus is running the red light!" A second later I heard a crash.

Once Smith relates what someone else said, we enter the realm of hearsay. Why does P's attorney want Smith to tell the jury what the woman shouted? "To prove the truth of the matter asserted in the statement" (i.e., to prove that the bus ran the red light). Smith is not the source of this information: he has not testified that *he* saw the bus run the light. Rather, the woman is the source of that information. She, not Smith, is the "declarant." She made her statement (assertion of fact) out of court. Her statement is offered to prove the truth of what she asserted. Hence, her statement is hearsay.

Note that her statement poses most of the trustworthiness hazards that make hearsay objectionable.

1. *Perception*: perhaps the sunlight reflecting off the traffic light made it appear that the bus had a red light when actually it was green.

2. *Memory* does not seem to be much of a problem here. (It is unlikely that she forgot what she saw in the split second between seeing the event and making her statement.)

3. *Narration*: perhaps, in the excitement of the moment, she said "bus" when she meant "car."

4. *Sincerity*: perhaps what she said — or what she thought she saw — was colored by some bias against the bus company.

Since the woman is not on the witness stand, the defendant's attorney cannot cross-examine her about potential lapses in perception or narration or about the possibility of bias. Nor would it do much good to cross-examine Smith about them, because he did not see the accident or what caused it.

§ 2.3   A NOTE ON VOCABULARY; COMMON ABBREVIATIONS

The terms we use in discussing and analyzing hearsay problems are quite important. As used in this book, the words "witness," "declarant," "statement," "adverse party" and "testimony" each has a precise definition.

Adverse party is the party against whom the evidence is offered.

Declarant (often abbreviated "DL") is defined in Fed. R. Evid. 801(b) as "the person who made the statement." This includes someone who testified at a prior trial or proceeding, whose testimony is now being offered at the current trial.

Statement will be used as defined in Fed. R. Evid. 801(a): in essence, words or conduct intended to be an assertion.

Testimony will be used to mean what a witness says while under oath.

Witness (abbreviated as "W1, W2," etc.) will be used to mean a person who has taken the witness stand at the trial or proceeding currently in progress.

In sum, therefore, a "declarant" is someone who made a "statement," other than while testifying at the current trial or hearing. A "witness" gives "testimony." Often a "witness" is called to testify that he or she heard a "statement" made by a "declarant." This is sometimes described as *"hearsay testimony,"* because the witness is being asked to testify about the declarant's hearsay statement.

A person can be both a declarant and a witness: this occurs when a declarant is called to testify about something she herself said previously. When this occurs, I sometimes use the abbreviation, "DL/W."

PART B:
"OUT-OF-COURT"

§ 2.4   "A STATEMENT THAT THE DECLARANT DOES NOT MAKE WHILE TESTIFYING AT THE CURRENT TRIAL OR HEARING"

We begin our detailed examination of the definition of hearsay with the second aspect of the definition, which relates to when and where the statement was made. A commonly used shorthand definition of hearsay is "an *out-of-court* statement offered in evidence to prove the truth of the matter asserted in the statement." The phrase "out-of-court" is adequate to cover most situations, but not all. Hence the wordier, but more accurate, phrase contained in Fed. R. Evid. 801(c): "a statement that the declarant does *not make while testifying at the current trial or hearing.*" The lengthier phrase is necessary, because some "in-court" statements are also hearsay.

§ 2.5 QUESTIONS

Question 1. In the bus-auto collision case, assume that Smith testified at a pre-trial deposition as to the positions of the bus and auto in the intersection immediately after the collision, and then repeated this testimony at a trial that ended in a hung jury. Now, with the second trial about to begin, Smith cannot be located. P therefore seeks to introduce into evidence the transcript of the testimony Smith gave at the *pre-trial deposition.* Is it hearsay?[3]

Ans. Re-read Fed. R. Evid. 801(c). Smith's deposition testimony describing the accident scene is hearsay as defined in Rule 801(c), because that testimony was not given "at the *current* trial or hearing."

Question 2. P next seeks to introduce into evidence the transcript of Smith's *testimony at the first trial.* Is it hearsay?

Ans. Yes! That testimony was given at an earlier trial of the same case, but it was not given at "the *current* trial."

Question 3. One more aspect of the "out-of-court" element of the definition merits consideration. Again assume we're trying the bus-auto collision case. P calls Ms. Julia Albion as a witness. She testifies that she was on the corner of Broadway and 48th Street at 1 p.m.

Q.   And what, if anything, happened?

A.   I glanced out into the intersection and I shouted "Oh my gosh, the bus is running the red light!"

Is this hearsay?

Ans. The portion of Ms. Albion's testimony in which she quotes herself ("Oh my gosh, the bus is running the red light!") is a statement (i.e., an assertion). P is offering it in evidence to prove the truth of the matter asserted (i.e., to prove that the bus ran the red light). And when Ms. Albion originally made the statement, she was not "testifying at the current trial or hearing"; she was on the corner of Broadway and 48th Street. Thus, her prior statement *is* hearsay under Fed. R. Evid. 801(c). Ms. Albion may, of course, testify that she *saw* the bus run the red light; such testimony would not be hearsay. But once she repeats on the witness stand what she *said* on an earlier ("out-of-court") occasion, she is relating hearsay.

To recapitulate: whenever a witness seeks to testify to words that were spoken by anyone (including himself or herself) at any time other than while testifying during the current trial or hearing, those words fit the second element of the definition in Fed. R. Evid. 801(c) (and therefore must be classified as hearsay if those words also constitute a statement and are offered in evidence to prove the truth of the matter asserted).

---

[3] Take it as given that his deposition testimony consisted of assertions: "Here's what I saw at that intersection after I heard the collision"; and that P's lawyer hopes the jury will accept Smith's testimony as true; i.e., he is offering it to prove the truth of what Smith asserted at the deposition.

PART C:
"STATEMENT"

§ 2.6 IN GENERAL

Fed. R. Evid. 801(a) defines statement as "a person's oral assertion, written assertion, or person's nonverbal conduct, if the person intended it as an assertion." The Advisory Committee Note on this definition includes the comment: "The effect of the definition of 'statement' is to exclude from the operation of the hearsay rule all evidence of conduct, verbal or nonverbal, not intended as an assertion. The key to the definition is that nothing is an assertion unless intended to be one."

I have divided discussion of this definition into the following: spoken words (both "assertive" and "non-assertive"); written words (both "assertive" and "non-assertive"); conduct (both "assertive" and "non-assertive"); photographs and films; non-human "declarants"; and silence.

§ 2.7 INDIVIDUAL DECLARATION OR NARRATION AS A WHOLE

Cars driven by Falstaff and Fields collided as both were leaving a party hosted by Dion Ysius.[4] Describing the situation a few days later, Falstaff said, "That was quite an ending to quite a party. Ysius kept pouring and wouldn't take no for an answer. I had a couple of scotch sours before dinner, wine with, and a brandy afterward; and you should've seen Fields! He had half a bag on when he got to the party, then he had three martinis before we ate, wine *and* beer during dinner, and two full snifters of brandy afterward. And those cigarettes he was smoking sure looked and smelled funny!"

This might legitimately be considered a single statement — "What went on at Ysius's party." Or it might be considered to be several statements: (1) "Ysius kept pouring"; (2) what Falstaff drank at the party; (3) Fields's condition when he arrived at the party; (4) what Fields drank at the party; (5) what Fields smoked at the party. Which is the proper approach, when deciding the hearsay implications of what Falstaff said?

The answer depends upon the particular provision of Article VIII of the Federal Rules being applied. Most provisions within the hearsay definition and some of the hearsay exceptions require us to examine each assertion within the narrative.[5] Others may permit an examination of the narrative as a whole.

---

[4] "Falstaff" is a hard-drinking comic character in three of Shakespeare's plays. W.C. Fields was a comic actor who often played hard-drinking characters in numerous movies during the first half of the twentieth century. In Greek mythology, Dionysus was the god of fertility and wine. (This cultural note is brought to you by the author free of charge.)

[5] In *Williamson v. United States*, 512 U.S. 594, 600–601 (1994), the Supreme Court held that, when applying the declaration against interest exception (Fed. R. Evid. 804(b)(3)) in certain situations, "statement" meant "a single declaration or remark" (i.e., an individual factual assertion), rather than "overall narrative." (*See* § 9.12.)

When in doubt, it is better to examine a passage (or a document) clause-by-clause and phrase-by-phrase, to see which clauses, phrases, sentences, etc. are hearsay, and which ones aren't.

§ 2.8 ASSERTIVE SPEECH

When a person says something it is generally easy to determine whether his utterance is a "statement." Simply look at the words themselves. If they appear to be an assertion of fact (or opinion), they constitute a "statement" under Fed. R. Evid. 801(a), unless unusual circumstances clearly indicate that the declarant did *not* intend them to be an assertion of fact. "I enjoy these sunny summer days" appears to be an assertion of fact until we consider that it was spoken in the middle of a blizzard in January.

§ 2.9 NON-ASSERTIVE SPEECH

Much of what is spoken is not overtly assertive. When a person asks a question, generally the purpose is not to assert, but to obtain, information. "Did the Nationals win today?" "Have you eaten dinner yet?" "Who's at the door?"

Similarly, when a person states a direction or makes a command or request, generally her purpose isn't to assert; it is to direct, order or ask someone to do something. "Make the next left." "I'll take the red one in a size medium." "Don't forget to pick up my suit at the dry cleaner's."

Utterances are sometimes referred to as "non-assertive verbal conduct." Because they are non-assertive, they are not statements; and because they are not statements, they cannot be hearsay. And this makes sense. If the declarant did not intend to assert anything, we don't have to worry about whether he had some reason to lie or mislead; and this eliminates, or at least minimizes, the "sincerity" hearsay risk discussed in § 1.1.

§ 2.10 IMPLIED ASSERTIONS

Unfortunately, it often is not quite that simple, for several reasons. First, human speech is not always clearly divisible into assertions and non-assertions; sometimes people say one thing but mean another. Second, sometimes, even if the declarant really intends to ask a question or make a demand or request, a key fact is so implicit in what she says that, at least according to some courts and scholars, the utterance should be classified as an assertion.

To determine whether an utterance was an assertion, therefore, we apply a three-part test.

    1. Does the utterance look and sound like an assertion?

    2. Why (with what purpose or intent) did the declarant say what she said?

    3. Does the situation involve an "implied assertion"?

Discussing each part of this test:

1. Does the utterance look and sound like an assertion?

As § 2.8 explains, if words appear to be an assertion, they are, unless someone can convince the judge otherwise; and if the words do not appear to be an assertion, then they are not an assertion, unless someone can convince the judge that the words were in fact an assertion. The second and third parts of this test explain how an attorney might argue that what does not look like an assertion, was in fact an assertion.

2. Why did the declarant say what he or she said?

If declarant meant his or her words to be an assertion, we have to classify them as such, even though the words themselves seem to be non-assertive.

Sometimes it is easy to tell whether the declarant meant his or her apparently non-assertive words to be an assertion, sometimes not.

(A) After a long and intense romance, F told M that she did not want to see him anymore. This hit M pretty hard, but after a while, he thought he was getting over it — until he went to a party; and there was F, clinging to her new guy. The next day, M's friend W asked M, "Did it upset you to see F at the party?" M replied, "Does the sun rise in the east?"

Superficially, "Does the sun rise in the east?" looks like a question, but here, it is M's way of saying "Yes" (i.e., his way of saying, "I was upset to see F at the party"). If an issue later arises about how M felt on seeing F that night, W's question and M's response would be hearsay.

(B) A father says to his son: (1) "You left your @#$!$^%@*! bicycle in the driveway!"[6] This is a straightforward assertion (i.e., a "statement" per Fed. R. Evid. 801(a)). If this utterance is later offered at a trial to prove where the bicycle was at the time, it is hearsay.

Suppose instead the father says: (2) "How many times have I told you not to leave your @#$!$^%@*! bicycle in the driveway?" Superficially, this appears to be a question, but anyone who has ever been a parent — or a child — knows that the father is in fact asserting to his son that the bicycle is in the driveway. So this "question" is really an assertion, hence a statement.

Suppose instead the father says: (3) "Get your #$!$^%@*! bicycle out of the driveway!" Here, you could argue that the father doesn't intend to assert that the bike is in the driveway; he's just telling his son to move it. But that is a pretty lame argument, because the assertion that the bike is in the driveway is so clearly implicit in the father's demand. As a practical matter, there is no real difference between (1), (2) and (3); so there is no logical reason why the law of hearsay should treat them differently.

---

[6] "@#$!$^%@*!" probably is *not* the brand name of the manufacturer.

2. "Implied assertions."

Courts — and evidence professors — have spent a great deal of time debating "implied assertions"; it is a difficult issue, and how a court treats it can make the difference between admitting and excluding evidence.

We saw in the third bicycle example that some assertions are so implicit in what the declarant says that as a practical matter, we should treat the utterance as an assertion. On the other hand, you could make a logical argument that virtually every utterance contains implicit assertions. Consider the questions, directions, commands and requests I used as examples at the beginning of this section.

(1) "Did the Nationals win today?" Implicit in this question is the assertion that the declarant believes that the Nationals played today, and perhaps also that the declarant is a Nationals fan.

(2) "Have you eaten dinner yet?" Here the implied assertion is that it is more-or-less dinner time.

(3) "Who's at the door?" This implies, first, that there is a door, and second, that someone is at it, or, at least, that the declarant heard or saw something to make him think that someone was at it.

(4) "I'll take the red one in a size medium." This implies that the declarant, or someone she is shopping for, likes red and wears size medium.

(5) "Don't forget to pick up my suit at the dry cleaner's." This implies that the declarant owns a suit, that the suit is at a dry cleaner's, and that the person to whom declarant is speaking knows which dry cleaner declarant is referring to.

You may be thinking, "Some of these examples are a real stretch." Yes, they are; and that is precisely the point: if the "implied assertion" concept is taken too far, virtually every utterance could be called an assertion, which would vastly expand the impact of the hearsay rule.

So why the fuss? Because sometimes the hearsay risks *may* be significant even where the declarant does not intend to assert anything. Suppose an issue at trial is whether X came to the door of a particular home at 3 p.m., listened for a few seconds, and then left without ringing or knocking. W will testify that DL, her grandson, got home from school shortly before 3 p.m. She asked him, "How was school today?" Before he could reply, the phone rang, and she answered it. A few seconds later, she heard DL call out, "Who's at the door?" This is relevant to show that someone was at the door,[7] but only if we overlook the hearsay risks of perception and narration. Perception: we have to accept that DL saw or heard something which did in fact indicate someone was at the door — that he didn't misinterpret the sound of a lawnmower from across the street, or a shadow caused by a cloud briefly covering up the sun. Narration: we also have to accept that DL said what he meant to say; that he

---

[7] Even if DL said nothing to suggest that the person at the door was X, DL's utterance is relevant to show that *someone* came to the door; and if other witnesses testify that X was the only person who was walking on that block around 3 p.m., their testimony, plus X's statement, adds up to circumstantial evidence that X in fact came to the door.

didn't really mean to ask W, "Who's on the phone?" And of course there is always the possibility that DL made up the whole thing, for reasons we cannot guess (but which a skillful attorney might discover on cross-examination).

Courts and professors have suggested numerous approaches to the "implied assertion" question.

(1) Reject the idea altogether, applying the hearsay definition rigidly and literally. Very few people seriously advocate this approach.

(2) Place the emphasis on what the declarant intended: regardless of the form her words took, classify what she said as an assertion if that is what she probably intended. But if she did not intend to assert anything, it is not hearsay.

(3) Place the emphasis on the hearsay risks: if the relevance of the statement depends heavily on the declarant's perception, memory and narration, classify the utterance as an assertion even if the declarant did not intend to assert anything.

Needless to say, there are variations and spinoffs within the second and third approaches.

Which is the "right" approach? Whichever one your evidence professor prefers, of course. In the absence of a clear preference from your professor, I would suggest the second approach, which emphasizes the declarant's intent. If the words look like an assertion, that's how the judge should rule, unless the party arguing that the utterance is not hearsay can convince the judge that no assertion was intended. If the utterance does not look like an assertion, then it isn't, unless the party arguing that the utterance is hearsay can convince the judge that the declarant intended his utterance to be an assertion.

We will return to the "implied assertion" doctrine later, when we look at the third element of the hearsay definition, "that a party offers in evidence to prove the truth of the matter asserted by the declarant."

§ 2.11 QUESTIONS

Question 1. Which of the following are "statements" as defined in Fed. R. Evid. 801(a)?

Statement 1: "I'm looking for John Henry."

Ans. This is a statement.

Statement 2: "I'm looking for John Henry. Does anybody know where he is?"

Ans. The first sentence is an assertion, hence a statement. While the second sentence is not, it's so closely linked with the first that a judge is likely to consider the entire utterance as a unit.

Statement 3: "If you see John Henry, tell him I'm looking for him."

Ans. This is a directive but contains an assertion ("I'm looking for him") within it, and probably the assertive character predominates.

Statement 4: "Has anyone seen John Henry?"

Ans. This is not an overt assertion (unless DL said it in response to a question, "Who are you looking for?"). Whether it is an implied assertion that DL is looking for John Henry depends on your professor's position on implied assertions.

Question 2. Police officers are searching X's apartment for drugs. The phone rings, and PO1 answers.

Caller: Is X there?

PO1:   He's busy. What's up?

Caller: This is Freddy Big Hat. Tell X I want two ounces for tonight.

PO1:   I'll tell him.

Is Freddy's directive, "Tell X I want two ounces for tonight," as testified to by PO1, hearsay, if offered to suggest that X in fact sold drugs from his apartment?

Ans. Most courts classify a call like this as a non-assertion and therefore not hearsay. Freddy's main purpose in making the call was to arrange to buy drugs, not to assert anything, so if we take the "declarant's intent" approach to implied assertions, Freddy's call is not an assertion that X sells drugs. But if we take a "hearsay risk" approach, X's lawyer can argue that the evidence is relevant only if we rely on Freddy's memory (i.e., that he accurately remembered who he could buy cocaine from, and what that person's phone number was, and that he correctly dialed that number).

§ 2.12   THE WRITTEN WORD

Return to the collision between the bus and the auto in § 2.2. It just so happened that 25 out-of-town clergy were at the intersection that afternoon with their host, Rev. A. All except Rev. A saw the accident. Each immediately wrote down a description of what he or she saw (i.e., that the bus ran the light and collided with the car), signed it, and handed it to Rev. A. Unfortunately, by the time the case comes to trial, only Rev. A is still in New York.

§ 2.13   QUESTIONS

Question 1. Rather than incur the expense of bringing clergypersons B-Z back from the states and countries to which they have returned, P's attorney decides to offer the written accident descriptions into evidence. What must P's attorney do before offering the descriptions in evidence? How should he go about doing so?

Ans. P's attorney has to authenticate the descriptions. See Article IX of the Federal Rules of Evidence.

Question 2. Are the written descriptions statements?

Ans. The witnesses wrote the accident descriptions with the intent of asserting what they saw. Therefore, they are "statements."

Question 3. Re-examine Fed. R. Evid. 801(c). Are the statements hearsay?

Ans. The statements were made (written) out-of-court. P's attorney is offering them in evidence in the hope that the jury will accept them as true i.e., "to prove the truth of the matter asserted in the statement." Yes, they are hearsay.

Note that these statements don't present significant hearsay risks. It's highly unlikely that all 25 witnesses would misperceive, misremember or misdescribe who had the red light; it's even less likely that they would deliberately lie about what they saw. Nevertheless the statements are hearsay, because they fit the definition of hearsay.

This does *not* necessarily mean they will be excluded; it *does* mean that to secure their admission over a hearsay objection, P will have to find a provision within Fed. R. Evid. 801(d) (exceptions to the hearsay definition) or Rules 803, 804 or 807 (exceptions to the hearsay rule) in order to overcome a hearsay objection.

Written words may be assertive or non-assertive just as spoken words may be assertive or non-assertive. "Has anyone seen John Henry?" is presumptively non-assertive whether it is spoken or written.

§ 2.14 ASSERTIVE AND NON-ASSERTIVE CONDUCT

Recall the bus-auto collision. A minute after the collision, a police officer rushes to the scene. He calls out to the bystanders, "What happened?" Six or eight people immediately respond, "We saw it all. The bus ran the light!" At trial, P's lawyer calls the officer to the stand, and seeks to have him testify as to what the bystanders said. Is this hearsay?

Of course. The bystanders made out-of-court "statements" — assertions of fact. P is now offering those statements into evidence, through the police officer, to prove that what the bystanders asserted was true (i.e., to prove the bus ran the light). Hence, hearsay.

Change the facts slightly. By coincidence, the bystanders are all law students who have just begun to study hearsay. They don't want to get involved but they want to see that justice is done.

Q.   Tell us, officer, what happened when you arrived on the scene?

A.   There was a bunch of people standing there, and I asked them, "Did any of you see what happened?" Nobody said a word, but they all nodded their heads. Then I asked, "Did one of them run the light?" They all nodded again, and then they all walked over and pointed to the bus.

Defense counsel objects to this testimony as hearsay. P's lawyer responds that it can't be hearsay, because none of the bystanders said anything. Ruling?

Rule 801(a) provides: "Statement" means: a person's ... nonverbal conduct, if the person intended it as an assertion." The corresponding Advisory Committee Note comments, "The key to the definition is that nothing is an assertion *unless intended to be one.*" Applying these concepts to the problem, we ask: Why (with what intent) did the bystanders nod their heads and, a few seconds later, point to the bus?

They did those things to answer the officer's questions, i.e., to assert that they saw the bus run a red light and collide with the car. Nodding and pointing, in these circumstances, constituted *assertive conduct*, because the actors intended that conduct to be an assertion of fact. Thus, their conduct constituted out-of-court statements, which plaintiff is offering in evidence to prove the truth of the matter asserted. Hence, the nodding and pointing are hearsay.

In deciding whether conduct was intended to be assertive, the key factor is common sense. What's the *most probable* reason the actor did what he or she did? If the answer is, "To communicate or assert information," then the conduct is considered assertive and, therefore, a statement. If the answer is anything else, the conduct is considered nonassertive and, therefore, not hearsay. In doubtful and ambiguous situations, the law assumes that no intent to assert existed.

§ 2.15 QUESTIONS

Question 1. An important issue in a lawsuit is whether it was raining at 1 p.m. on a particular afternoon. W1 testifies that she looked out of her office window on the seventh floor at that time and noticed that many pedestrians on the sidewalk below were holding open umbrellas over their heads. How is this relevant?

Ans. When people hold open umbrellas over their heads, they generally do it to keep from getting wet. Therefore, we can logically conclude that it was raining.

Question 2. The adverse party objects, on the ground that the pedestrians' behavior constituted assertive conduct (i.e., hearsay). How should the judge rule?

Ans. When people hold open umbrellas over their heads, they generally do it to keep from getting wet in the rain. They are not trying to communicate anything; they're just trying to stay dry. Since they did not intend to assert anything, there's no "statement," and therefore, no hearsay.

Question 3. In the same lawsuit, W2 takes the stand, and testifies: "A friend and I were on our way out of the office building at one o'clock. He got to the door first and I asked him whether it was raining. He turned to me, pointed to his umbrella, and opened it." Objection: hearsay, on the ground that W2's friend's behavior constituted assertive conduct. Ruling?

Ans. W2's friend opened the umbrella and pointed as a dramatic way of answering W2's question about the weather. This was an "assertion." Objection sustained.

Suppose W2 had not asked his friend if it was raining. Let's say W2 testifies:

> . . . As my friend and I approached the door — he was a couple of feet in front of me — he turned to me and waved his hands to get my attention, and then pointed to his umbrella.

Even though W2 had asked no questions, his friend's conduct is nevertheless assertive: he was telling W2, through his actions, that it was raining.

Question 4. Return to the bus-auto collision suit. Plaintiffs call W3, who testifies, "I was standing near the intersection of Broadway and 48th at about 1 p.m., and noticed a young woman pushing a baby carriage on the sidewalk by the curb. She stopped at the corner for several seconds, looking in the direction of the traffic light. Then she started to push the carriage into the intersection, walking east on 48th Street. Suddenly I saw this bus barreling down Broadway right at her — if P's car hadn't pulled into the intersection going the same direction as the woman, the bus would've knocked her all the way to Times Square![8] Instead, the bus broadsided the car."

How is this relevant?

Ans. We don't *know*, for certain, why this woman was pushing a baby carriage at the intersection of Broadway and 48th that afternoon. Maybe her ex-boyfriend's suits were in the carriage, and she was wheeling them to the nearest trash bin. And maybe she was so spaced out on drugs that she couldn't even *see* the traffic light, let alone tell whether it was red or green. Or maybe she deliberately crossed against the light because she was hoping to tie up traffic to protest global warming. Anything is possible (particularly within a few blocks of Times Square).

Common sense and experience tell us, though, that the most likely reason she was pushing a baby carriage is that she had a baby in the carriage. If so, it's unlikely she would expose the baby to unnecessary danger. She didn't step into the street until after she looked at the traffic light for several seconds. Conclusion: she waited until the light was green for eastbound traffic and pedestrians on 48th Street before she entered the intersection. If all this is true, then since she was going in the same direction that P was, if she had the green light, so did P.

Question 5. Defendant objects on the ground that the woman's conduct was hearsay. Ruling?

Ans. What was her intent when she (and the carriage) left the sidewalk? Why did the woman cross the road? The most likely reason is, "to get to the other side." She didn't intend to assert anything, she just wanted to cross Broadway. Hence, no assertion; no hearsay.

Question 6. During a murder investigation, Detective W went to S's home and asked Mrs. S to give him the clothing her husband, the prime suspect, had been wearing on the day of the homicide. She handed the officer a knit shirt. At trial, the prosecutor seeks to have W testify about this event and then offer the shirt into evidence. (Once it is admitted, she will call T, a lab technician, who will testify that the shirt contained a blood stain with the victim's DNA.) D objects that W's testimony consists of hearsay. Ruling?

Ans. Objection sustained in part. When Mrs. S handed the shirt to W, she was answering W's question, asserting, in essence, "This is the shirt my husband wore that day." This assertive conduct occurred out of court and is offered to prove the truth of the matter asserted.

---

[8] Times Square is located at Broadway and 42nd Street, six blocks south of Broadway and 48th.

By the way, this could easily be a multiple choice question on an exam. The choices might be:

A)   The officer may testify that the wife gave him a knit shirt, but the shirt itself will not be admitted into evidence.

B)   The officer may not testify that the wife gave him a knit shirt, but the shirt itself will be admitted into evidence.

C)   The officer may testify that the wife gave him a knit shirt, and the shirt itself will be admitted into evidence.

D)   The officer may not testify that the wife gave him a knit shirt, nor may the shirt be admitted into evidence.

The correct answer is B).

Question 7. What should the prosecutor do at this point?

Ans. She has two options. First, she can call Mrs. S as a witness, and ask her if she recognizes the knit shirt as the one her husband had worn the day of the crime. This may not work, though. Mrs. S may assert a spouse's privilege not to testify against her husband (*see* Fed. R. Evid. Art. V); or she may no longer remember which shirt her husband had worn.

The second option is to have Detective W testify, "On such and such a date I went to S's home and obtained this shirt from the premises." This involves no hearsay, because it contains no assertion, by Mrs. S or anyone else, that S had been wearing the shirt on the day of the homicide. Ultimately, after T testifies, the prosecutor will argue that W's and T's testimony, taken together, constitute circumstantial evidence that S committed the murder (while wearing that shirt); still, in this sanitized version, no hearsay problems arise.

To repeat: to determine whether a person's conduct was assertive, so as to constitute a "statement" within Fed. R. Evid. 801(a)(2), we must discern the intent with which she acted, keeping in mind (as the Advisory Committee emphasizes) that "[t]he rule is so worded as to place the burden upon the party claiming that the intention existed; ambiguous and doubtful cases will be resolved against him and in favor of [classifying the conduct as non-assertive and therefore non-hearsay]."

§ 2.16 PHOTOGRAPHS, FILMS, VIDEOS

X lives in a third-story apartment directly across the street from the bank on 10th Street and Metropolitan Avenue. At 2:00 on February 1, he sees a man wearing a three-piece blue suit and a ski mask run out of the bank, glance quickly up and down the street, remove the mask, stuff it quickly into a black leather doctor's bag, and walk hurriedly away. D is later charged with the robbery. If X testifies as to what he saw, describes the man's facial features, and identifies D as the man he saw that afternoon, no hearsay is involved, because all of his statements about the event are being made in court, on the witness stand.

Now suppose instead X happened to be holding a camera with a telephoto lens that day, and managed to snap several shots of the man before and after he removed the mask. At trial, X testifies as to when and how he took the photographs, which are then offered into evidence. Just as in the previous paragraph, none of this involves hearsay. When X took the photographs, he wasn't "stating" anything; he merely preserved on a computer chip what he saw when he looked through the camera. As far as the law of evidence is concerned, the photos are simply another way for X to say, "Here's what I saw that day."

As a rule, therefore, a photograph, movie, video recording, etc. is not a "statement" (except perhaps in an artistic sense). It's simply the end-product of a series of electronic or chemical processes that begin when light enters a camera through its lens. If it would not be hearsay for a witness to take the stand and describe a certain scene or certain events, it would not be hearsay for that witness to take the stand and testify, "This is a photograph (movie, video recording) of what I saw that day."

If, on the other hand, the actions or scene portrayed in the photo, video recording, etc. were *posed or staged* with the primary purpose of *demonstrating or communicating* something, then we have photo, film or video recording of assertive conduct. Testimony describing assertive conduct raises hearsay problems; a video of that same conduct raises the exact same hearsay problems.

§ 2.17   QUESTIONS

Question 1. The day after he took the photographs, X read in the newspaper about the bank robbery, notified the police, gave the photographs to Detective Y, and explained when and how he took them. A trial, the prosecutor calls Det. Y to the stand. If permitted, Det. Y will testify, "X told me he took these photographs at 2 p.m. on February 1 from his apartment across the street from the bank." D objects: hearsay. Ruling?

Ans. Objection sustained. The photographs aren't hearsay, but X's statement to Det. Y is hearsay.

Question 2. The bank had an automatic camera that videorecorded the robbery. At trial the prosecutor calls a bank official who testifies how the camera works, then offers the video recording in evidence. D objects: hearsay. Ruling?

Ans. Objection overruled. In deciding whether the video recording is hearsay, we do *not* ask, "why was the video recording made"; we ask, "why did the people whose actions were captured on film do what they were doing at the time?" When the robber pointed a gun at a teller and demanded money, his purpose wasn't to make assertions, it was to commit robbery. Thus, the video recording is not hearsay even though it was *made* so it could be used as evidence at a trial.

Question 3. P claims she was injured in an industrial accident, and sues for damages, claiming that as a result of nerve damage, there is a constant tremor in her hands. At trial, to help illustrate the extent of her injuries, she testifies that her attorney hired C, a photographer, to come to her house and videorecord her as she went through her normal daily routine. P testifies that nothing was pre-arranged or rehearsed; when C arrived, she simply began filming P's activities. C testifies likewise.

The video recording shows P washing her face, brushing her teeth, pouring cereal and milk into a bowl, eating it. Because of the constant shaking in her hands, she has considerable difficulty doing each of these things. Then she turns to the camera and says, "Let me show you what happens when I try to put on lipstick." She walks to the bathroom and does so; the result is a garish smear. She wipes the lipstick off, walks into the living room, and, with difficulty, manages to put a compact disk into the player and push the play button.

Defendant objects that the video recording is hearsay. Ruling?

Ans. Objection sustained in part. The key question is not why the video recording was made; rather, we have to consider why P did the things she did that were captured on film. Presumably she washed her face, brushed her teeth, ate breakfast and listened to music for their own sakes: to be clean, to prevent tooth decay, to provide the body with sustenance and to soothe the soul (or to annoy her parents, depending on her age and the kind of music). As to these acts, therefore, the objection should be overruled.

But the objection should be sustained with regard to the lipstick, because that episode was a conscious "performance": "let me show you. . . ."

You may be wondering: how do we know that P wasn't faking, or exaggerating, the extent of her disability when she did the other things? We don't; but the jury will be able to view the video recording (except the lipstick episode) and watch P on the stand, and will be able to form a judgment about whether she was exaggerating.

§ 2.18 SILENCE

Courts must occasionally determine whether silence should be considered hearsay. The situation most often arises when, in defending against an allegation that plaintiff's injury was caused by a defect or unsafe condition in defendant's product or premises, defendant seeks to testify that no previous customers had complained about that product or premises. Such testimony is relevant if the fact-finder infers that because no previous customers complained, they must have perceived nothing about which to complain, and that therefore the product or premises were indeed safe. Because these inferences depend upon the perception of the previous customers and their perception cannot be tested at trial by cross-examination, prior to enactment of the Federal Rules of Evidence some courts categorized such testimony about an absence of complaints as hearsay.

Fed. R. Evid. 801 rejects this approach. Silence is usually ambiguous at best; and, as we have already seen, "ambiguous and doubtful cases will be resolved against [inferring an intent to assert.]"[9] Thus, testimony that prior to P's injury no one had complained about unsafe conditions on D's premises is not hearsay.[10]

---

[9] Fed. R. Evid. 801(a) (advisory committee's note).

[10] A trial judge nevertheless has discretion to exclude such evidence, because a lack of complaints may be so ambiguous that it is not very probative as to whether D's premises were safe.

Under Fed. R. Evid. 801, a person's silence cannot be considered hearsay unless we can conclude that by remaining silent, she intended to assert something. Suppose, for example, M asks F to join him that night for dinner. F responds, "Thank you, but I may have to ask for a rain check; I may have to go out of town this afternoon on business. If you don't hear from me by 4 p.m., you'll know I had to catch a flight for Cleveland." In this unusual situation, F has in effect told M that he should interpret her silence as communicating a particular fact.

§ 2.19 NON-HUMAN "DECLARANTS"

Fed. R. Evid. 801(b) defines "declarant" as "the person who made the statement." Thus, animals and inanimate objects (radar guns, thermometers, etc.) cannot be "declarants," and the things they "tell" us cannot be hearsay. Similarly, a computer is not a "declarant,"[11] and information produced by the internal operations of a computer program, such as long distance telephone records, is not hearsay. (But assertions written by human beings and stored in a computer are, of course, statements.)

PART D:
"OFFER[ED] IN EVIDENCE TO PROVE THE TRUTH OF THE MATTER ASSERTED IN THE STATEMENT"

1. Overview

§ 2.20 INTRODUCTION

The third element of the definition of hearsay, as defined in Fed. R. Evid. 801(c), is that the statement is one "that a party offers in evidence to prove the truth of the matter asserted in the statement." To determine whether an out-of-court statement fits within this element of the definition requires a two-step process.

> 1. Determine *what the declarant intended to assert*, and whether, if at all, we should apply the "implied assertion" doctrine beyond what the declarant explicitly intended to assert.

> 2. Determine *why the lawyer who is offering the evidence wants the judge or jury to hear it* — i.e., *why the statement is relevant* to the lawsuit being tried.

1. What the declarant intended to assert.

As we saw in § 2.10, sometimes it is necessary to look behind the words that DL spoke to discern what she really meant. Obviously there are limits: attorney Z cannot simply "rewrite" a declarant's words whenever it suits Z to do so. But in applying the term "the matter asserted by the declarant," we are not required to ignore the way

---

[11] This even includes "Watson," the IBM computer that went on *Jeopardy* in February of 2011 and thoroughly outplayed the two best human *Jeopardy* champions of all time.

people actually speak. If L says Leonardo DiCaprio is good looking and R responds, "You ain't just whistling Dixie," everyone understands that R isn't really commenting on L's taste in music; she is agreeing with L's assessment of Mr. DiCaprio's physiognomy.

Similarly, if a key issue at trial is whether a car driven by X was speeding, consider declarant's statement, "X just about broke the sound barrier." This statement is not being offered to prove that X was driving at roughly 770 miles per hour, the approximate speed of sound;[12] it is being offered as evidence that X was driving dangerously fast given traffic and road conditions. To categorize the statement as non-hearsay is absurd. It is perfectly consistent with the definition of hearsay to categorize the declarant's statement as such; we need only realize that the declarant was merely choosing a somewhat exaggerated and colorful way of saying "X was driving much too fast."

2. Why the statement is being offered.

If the out-of-court statement is relevant only if the trier of fact accepts that statement as both truthful and accurate, then it is hearsay. On the other hand, if the out-of-court statement is relevant regardless of whether the trier of fact believes that the out-of-court declarant spoke truthfully and accurately, then the out-of-court statement is *not* hearsay.

Another way of putting it, which has proven helpful to some students, is the following: an out-of-court statement is hearsay if it is offered in evidence to prove that *the words inside the quotation marks are true*. In the blizzard case (*see* § 2.2), an important issue is what time of year a man and woman first met. The woman is asked to describe when and how she first met the man. She testifies:

> It was in the middle of January. I had just gotten off a bus on my way home from work. It was a miserable day — snowing, windy. This man got off right behind me and said, "I enjoy these sunny summer days." I laughed and we struck up an acquaintance.

Is the man's statement, "I enjoy these sunny summer days," relevant only if the fact-finder believes that the man (the declarant) was telling the truth? In other words, is the attorney offering this evidence to prove that what's inside the quotation marks is true? Obviously not. Hence, the man's statement to the woman is not hearsay.[13]

Students sometimes interpret the phrase, "to prove the truth of the matter asserted in the statement," too expansively. Suppose Dervish is on trial for murdering Veginald, who was shot and killed on May 1. Dervish denies his guilt and claims that DL was the

---

[12] Sound travels at 1,126 feet per second, give or take a few feet depending upon atmospheric pressure, air temperature, and a few other variables. This translates to roughly 770 mph.

[13] But wait a minute, you might be thinking. When the man said to the woman, "I love these sunny summer days," wasn't he really asserting, "I hate this lousy weather"? Well, maybe. Or maybe he was asserting, "I am powerfully attracted to you and I hope this remark will impress you with what a clever, witty guy I am, so you'll say something back, and we'll introduce ourselves, and go have a cup of coffee and one thing will lead to another and who knows where it all might end?" But most likely he just felt like saying something he thought was mildly amusing, without any particular assertive intent in mind.

killer. Dervish calls W, who will testify that on April 27, he heard DL say, "I hate Veginald; I can't stand him!" The prosecutor objects: Hearsay! Ruling? Objection sustained: it is hearsay.

A student might respond, "But wait a minute! It's not hearsay, because it is not being offered "to prove the truth of the matter asserted in the stateent," i.e., it's not being offered to prove that DL *hated* Veginald; it is being offered to prove that DL *killed* Veginald!"

Well, yes, in a way: DL's hatred of Veginald is being offered as evidence of the ultimate fact of consequence — that DL, not Dervish, killed Veginald. But DL's statement is relevant to prove that ultimate fact, only *if what DL said was true*, i.e., only if DL in fact hated Veginald. Remember: if a statement is relevant only if the jury believes that the statement was true or accurate, then it *is* being "offer[ed] in evidence to prove the truth of the matter asserted in the statement," which means that it is hearsay.

§ 2.21 QUESTIONS

Question 1. In the bus-auto collision case, the key issue is which vehicle ran the light. Plaintiff has called Winston Smith as a witness, and Smith has testified that he was on the corner of Broadway and 48th Street at 1 p.m. on the day in question. Direct examination continues:

Q.   Did anything unusual occur at that time and place?

A.   Yes. I was looking at a movie poster when I heard a woman shout, "Oh my gosh, the bus is running the red light!"

Is the woman's statement relevant only if the fact-finder believes that she (the declarant) was telling the truth? Is plaintiffs' attorney offering this evidence to prove that what's inside the quotation marks is true?

Ans. Yes. Unless the judge or jury believes the woman's statement, what she said is irrelevant. Her statement is being offered to prove the truth of the matter asserted; hence, it is hearsay.

Question 2. A witness reported to police that two men robbed him at gunpoint. A few days later, police arrested D1 and charged him with being one of the perpetrators. Now D2 is on trial for being the other robber. At D2's trial, W will testify that a few days after D1 made bail, D1 came upon D2 and W and that D1 said to D2, "Don't worry, I didn't tell the police about you."

D2 objects that this is hearsay. The prosecutor responds that it's not hearsay because she is not offering it to prove "the truth of the matter asserted" in D1's statement, i.e., she is not offering it to prove that D1 did not tell the police about D2. Ruling?

Ans. To decide whether D1's statement is hearsay, apply the two-step analysis:

First, what did D1 mean when he told D2, "I didn't tell the police about you?"

D1 could have meant lots of things. He could have meant, "I didn't tell the police that you were the guy who hacked into the Defense Department's computer and inserted obscene cartoons on all their web sites." He could have meant, "I didn't tell the police you were the guy who put crazy glue on Mrs. McIntyre's chair in third grade." He could have meant, "I didn't tell the police that you were the other guy who pulled the robbery with me." He could have meant any number of things.

Second, why is the prosecutor offering D1's statement at D2's trial? Why is D1's statement relevant at D2's trial?

D1's statement is relevant to prove that D2 was the other robber only if D1 meant, "I didn't tell the police that you were the other guy who pulled the robbery with me." And the prosecutor is offering D1's statement to prove that D2 was the other robber. Therefore, D1's statement is hearsay. Objection sustained.

§ 2.22   "RECONSTRUCTING" THE TESTIMONY

Sometimes, of course, a witness will not be so considerate as to offset the declarant's out-of-court statement in formal quotation marks. In the bus-car collision case, for example, Smith might have testified: "Yes. I was looking at a movie poster when a woman shouted that a bus had just entered the intersection against the light." To analyze whether the out-of-court statement in this testimony is hearsay, we must mentally reconstruct the testimony and put quotation marks around what the woman said. That makes it is easier to determine why her statement is being offered. Having done so, we can determine whether it is hearsay.

2. Categories of Non-Hearsay

§ 2.23   IN GENERAL

Courts often overrule a hearsay objection by "explaining" that "the statement was not hearsay because it was not being offered to prove the truth of the matter asserted by the declarant, but merely to prove that the words were spoken." Unfortunately, this doesn't really explain why the mere *making* of the statement (regardless of its truth) is relevant. Each out-of-court statement must be analyzed in the context of the particular case being tried, to determine whether it is being offered to prove the truth of the matter asserted in the statement, or for some other purpose.

Some situations involving non-hearsay use of out-of-court statements recur often enough that it is comparatively easy to categorize the statement as non-hearsay. Widely recognized categories of non-hearsay include statements probative of a person's mental state; verbal acts; and verbal parts of acts.

§ 2.24   MENTAL STATE

The mental state with which a person acted is often a crucial issue in a lawsuit. The focus could be on the defendant's mental state; or the plaintiff's; or the victim's; or the complainant's. The issue can arise in either of two contexts: mental state as an element of a crime, claim or defense; or relevant facts inferable from someone's state of mind.

§ 2.25   MENTAL STATE AS ELEMENT OF CRIME, CLAIM, OR DEFENSE

Mental state (sometimes referred to in criminal cases as "mens rea" or "scienter") is an element of nearly all crimes, many civil claims, and some defenses. A prosecutor will have to prove, for example, that a defendant acted "willfully," "with malice aforethought," "knowingly," "intentionally," or the like. Some crimes require the prosecutor to prove something about the complainant's state of mind — that the alleged victim in a rape case did not consent to intercourse, that the alleged victim in a fraud case was in fact deceived by what the defendant said. Similarly, in many civil actions, in order to prevail, a litigant must show that a particular person acted "negligently" or "recklessly" or "with intent to defraud." Quite often a defendant will attempt to prove that she did *not* act with the mental state the prosecutor or plaintiff is attempting to prove; or she might assert an affirmative defense which has its own mental element, such as insanity, duress, or justification (see the questions in § 2.33).

A statement made by or to someone often provides important evidence from which the fact finder can infer the mental state of the person who made, or who heard, the statement. Such statements therefore often have evidentiary significance regardless of whether the statement was true.

Thus, applying the third element of the hearsay definition ("offer[ed] in evidence to prove the truth of the matter asserted in the statement") as evidence of someone's mental state requires several preliminary steps.

    1. Examine the court opinion, relevant statutes, or evidence problem, to determine:

        (a)   Whether mental state is a contested element of the crime, cause of action or defense, and if so,

        (b)   *Whose* mental state, and

        (c)   How (if at all) the law defines the particular mental state in question.

    2. An out-of-court statement made *by or to* that person ("X") must be examined to determine whether it casts light on X's mental state.

    3. Analyze whether the statement is relevant even if it was inaccurate or a lie.

If the answer to the final question is *yes*, then the statement is not hearsay. But if the answer to the final question is *no* (i.e., if the statement is relevant only if it is accurate), then the statement is being offered for a hearsay purpose, and cannot be admitted unless it fits within some provision of Rule 801(d), 803, 804, or 807, which set out the exceptions to the hearsay definition and hearsay rule.

§ 2.26　MENTAL STATE: RELEVANT FACTS INFERABLE FROM SOMEONE'S STATE OF MIND

Even when mental state is not a contested issue, important facts sometimes can be inferred from a person's state of mind. In this situation, too, words said by or to that person may be relevant even though the statement is not offered to prove the truth of the matter asserted. Assume, for example, that V is found dead — shot, poisoned *and* drowned. These circumstances leave no doubt that some killed V intentionally; the only question at trial is likely to be, who did it. The prosecutor charges that Farfel is the killer. Farfel, however, claims that DL killed V, and wants to call witness W, who will testify that, shortly before V's death, DL told W, "V is a no-good, lying, scurvy louse. He ruined my business, he convinced my fiancee to dump me, he seduced my daughter and he roots for the Yankees!" Whether or not any of this is true, it is highly relevant to suggest that (in DL's mind, at any rate) DL had several powerful motives to want to kill V, which makes it more probable than it would be without the evidence that DL (not Farfel) in fact is the killer. In other words, DL's statement is relevant, because it makes it more likely than it would be without DL's statement, that DL killed V — even if nothing DL said about V is accurate — even if V never told a lie in his life, did his best to help DL's business, had nothing to do with DL's fiancee's change of heart, never even met DL's daughter, and has been a life-long Red Sox fan. Therefore DL's statement is *not* hearsay, because it is relevant to show DL's attitude about V, even if what DL said about V was not accurate.

§ 2.27　MENTAL STATE: DECLARANT'S STATE OF MIND

The least complicated situation arises when we need to know the *declarant's* state of mind. Simply look at what DL (declarant) said. A direct statement by DL as to his or her state of mind is hearsay; it is relevant to prove DL's state of mind only if we accept that DL is communicating accurately and sincerely. Generally, such statements contain phrases such as "I like," "I'm bored by," "I understand," "I'm confused by," etc. If, on the other hand, the declarant's state of mind may be inferred indirectly, regardless of whether the statement is true and accurate, then the statement is not hearsay.

§ 2.28　QUESTIONS

Question 1. Assume that a key issue in a trial is the extent of F's emotional attachment toward M. W will, if permitted, testify that F said to her: "I'm in love with M." Is this hearsay?

Ans. Yes. It is a direct statement by F about her attitude toward M. It is relevant only if we assume that F was accurately and sincerely describing her feelings.

Question 2. Suppose instead W1 will testify that on one occasion, during a discussion among several women about the men they work with, F commented that M has "a great sense of humor." W2 will testify that on another occasion, while watching a video of *Titanic*, F commented, "There's a guy at work, M, who looks a little like Leonardo DiCaprio." W3 will testify that on a different occasion, when several friends were discussing their bosses, F described M as "very considerate and supportive." Is this hearsay, if offered to prove F's romantic interest in M?[14]

Ans. None of this testimony would be hearsay, because it would be offered, not to prove that M in fact had these admirable qualities, but to prove that F, correctly or not, *believed* that M had them — from which we can infer that she was very attracted to him. (Indeed, the evidence would be relevant even if, in fact, M could see the point of a joke only by appointment, was a dead ringer for the "human bug" in Men in Black, and was totally self-centered.)

And none of these statements would qualify as an "implied assertion" of F's romantic interest in M, because on each occasion, F apparently intended only a casual comment about a man she happened to know.

Question 3. But now comes W4, who will testify that on another occasion, F, with a dreamy look in her eyes, said, "There's this guy at work, M — he's my boss, actually. He's a dead ringer for Leonardo DiCaprio,[15] and he's got a great sense of humor, and he's so considerate and supportive. . . ." Is this hearsay, if offered to show her romantic interest in M?

Ans. If we apply the phrase "the matter asserted by the declarant" in the definition of hearsay literally, this statement still is not hearsay. But this result is silly, because presumably F knew, when she described M in these terms, that W4 would understand that F was really (or also) saying, "This is a guy who has real 'husband potential'!"

§ 2.29   MENTAL STATE: TO SHOW DECLARANT'S KNOWLEDGE

It is often important to prove, first, that a certain fact is true; and second, that a particular person ("X") had knowledge of that fact. In such a case, if a party can prove the existence of the fact independent of the statement in question, a statement by X demonstrating that X had knowledge of the fact is not hearsay.

§ 2.30   QUESTION

Question 1. D arranged for his mother to obtain a $25,000 loan, which D co-signed, to purchase a new car, but although bank officials asked about other indebtedness, D did not tell the bank that he and his mother owed $56,000 on a loan from another bank to purchase a motor home. Since D's mother was the primary obligor on the car loan, D was able to arrange an insurance policy on her life without a physical examination. Less than a month later, D's mother died of cancer; the insurance policy paid for the

---

[14] Of course, none of these statements "prove" that F has any romantic interest in M. Lots of people think highly of their bosses without having any romantic feelings toward them. But the fact that F perceives M to have these favorable traits has (to paraphrase Fed. R. Evid. 401's definition of relevance) at least *some* "tendency to make [it] more probable" that she feels that way toward him, than it would be without this evidence.

[15] Or Orlando Bloom, or Brad Pitt, or Tim McGraw, or Lawrence Fishburn, or Sean Connery, or Justin Bieber, depending on her age, interests, etc.

car, which D inherited free and clear from his mother's estate. D was subsequently indicted for misrepresenting his, and his mother's, indebtedness on the car loan with intent to defraud; the government's theory was that the loan was obtained to cash in on the fact that his mother was dying. As evidence of his knowledge of her condition, the government called the admitting nurse at the hospital to which D brought his mother only three days after applying for the auto loan. If permitted, the nurse will testify, "D said his mother was kept at home with the family, but apparently she had been doing worse and D felt that she was probably pre-terminal; that's why he brought her to the hospital." D objects that this is hearsay. Ruling?

Ans. Overruled. D's statements to the nurse were not offered to prove the truth of the matter asserted (i.e., were not admitted to prove that his mother *was* pre-terminal). That had already been proven by evidence that she died less than a month after she obtained the car loan. Rather, the statement was relevant to prove that defendant *knew* his mother would die long before she, or he as co-signer, would have to pay off the auto loan. (Moreover, even if she had *not* been pre-terminal, his statement would be relevant to show that he *believed* she was, which is all the government needs to show intent to defraud.)

§ 2.31   MENTAL STATE: TO SHOW THE EFFECT ON THE HEARER

Sometimes the focus is not on the declarant's mental state, but on someone else's ("X"). What DL said to X is not hearsay, if that statement is being offered to show what effect the statement had on X's mental state, regardless of its truth. (Before DL's out-of-court statement is admissible to show the effect it had on X, the offering party must offer sufficient evidence to establish that X actually heard or read the statement.)

§ 2.32   MENTAL STATE, EFFECT ON HEARER: STATEMENTS MADE TO THE DEFENDANT

In criminal cases, either the prosecutor or the defense attorney might offer evidence of something someone said to the defendant, to show the impact the statement had on the defendant's state of mind.

§ 2.33   QUESTIONS

Question 1. D is being tried on an indictment charging that he intentionally and unlawfully shot and killed V on March 1. In her opening statement, D's lawyer told the jury, "The evidence will show that D was legally justified in killing V, because D acted in the reasonable belief that if he didn't use deadly force to defend himself, V would have killed or badly injured D."

What must the prosecutor prove to obtain a conviction?

Ans. That D shot V; that he did so intentionally; and that he did so unlawfully.

Question 2. W1, a government witness, testifies that he, D and V all worked in a warehouse for XYZ Co. His testimony continues:

> On February 27, just as our shift was ending, V walked up to D and said, "Gimme $500." D said, "Why should I give you $500?" V said, "Cause if you don't, I'm gonna turn you in to the boss for stealin' stuff off the shelves." I walked away real quick, so I didn't hear any more.

Why is V's statement — "Cause if you don't [give me $500], I'm gonna turn you in to the boss for stealin' stuff off the shelves" — relevant?

Ans. It suggests that, once D heard V threaten him, D had a *motive* to kill V, to keep V from reporting him to their boss. Showing that D had a motive to kill V makes it more likely that D did so intentionally and without legal justification.

Question 3. Is V's statement hearsay?

Ans. No. The relevance of V's statement depends on the impact it had on D when D heard V say it. So long as D heard it and believed it, it is relevant *even if V never really intended* to report D to their boss. Therefore, V's statement to D is not being offered to prove the truth of what V said to D; the mere fact that it was said is relevant to show D had a motive to kill V.

Question 4. After the state rests, D takes the stand. First, he denies that the incident W1 testified about ever took place. He and V worked in different parts of the warehouse, on different shifts, and they hardly even knew each other — until late in February, when D attended a dance, met a very nice young woman, and danced several times with her:

Q.	And then what happened?
A.	W2 walked over to me and said, "Don't you know that she is V's girlfriend?" I said, "No, I didn't. What's the big deal?" W2 said, "It's a *very* big deal, because V is a guy it's a good idea to stay away from," and then W2 told me that once he parked his car in front of V's house, and V came running out and told W2 to move the car, that was "his" parking space. W2 said, "I don't see your name on it," and then V said "Yeah, well I got my name on this," and whacked W2 with a baseball bat and broke W2's collarbone.

What is the mental element in D's defense?

Ans. As you learned in criminal law, it is a defense to a charge of murder that the killer (D) acted in the *reasonable belief* that he had to use deadly force to protect himself from death or serious injury at V's hands.

Question 5. What is the relevance of D's testimony about what W2 said to him? What does D hope to prove by this testimony?

Ans. What W2 told D about V is relevant on two different theories.

1. If W2's story to D is true, it shows that V was a violent, assaultive person, which supports D's claim (about which he will soon testify) that V in fact would have injured or killed D if D hadn't shot V first.

2. Whether W2's story is true or not, the fact that W2 told it to D is relevant to show that, when D and V had their fatal encounter, D believed that V was violent, assaultive, irrational — and angry at D. (Remember, to assert a valid justification defense, all D has to prove is that D acted in the *reasonable belief* that he had to use deadly force to protect his life or health from V (*see* answer to Q. 4)).

Question 6. The prosecutor objects that what W2 told D is hearsay. Ruling?

Ans. What W2 told D (that V broke W2's collarbone because he didn't like where W2 parked his car) is certainly a statement, and the conversation between W2 and D occurred out of court. Whether it's hearsay depends on why the evidence is offered:

1. If it is offered to prove that V in fact broke W2's collarbone, W2's statement *is* hearsay, because it is offered to prove the truth of the matter asserted in W2's statement to D.

2. But if it is offered for the *limited* purpose of casting light on *D's state of mind* (his reasonable fear of V) when he and V encountered each other on March 1, W2's statement to D is *not* hearsay, because even if the collarbone incident never really happened (even if W2 lied to D when he told him the story), a person in D's position, having heard that story, might reasonably fear that V was out to "get" him.

Question 7. The evidence therefore has a valid non-hearsay purpose, and a tainted, hearsay purpose. How should the judge rule?

Ans. Overrule the objection and admit the evidence; but, if the prosecutor requests, the judge should deliver a limiting instruction (Fed. R. Evid. 105), telling the jury they may consider the evidence in assessing D's state of mind about V on March 1, but may not accept the collarbone story as true, or as evidence of what kind of person V really was.

§ 2.34   MENTAL STATE, EFFECT ON HEARER: WHY THE POLICE ACTED

AC ("anonymous citizen") walks up to Police Officer PO1 as he walks his beat or sits in his patrol car and reports, "There's a man over on 12th and Vine waving a gun in the air and threatening to shoot people!" He describes the man. PO1 goes to check it out, and sees a man (D) fitting the description, sitting on a stoop. PO1 searches D, seizes a revolver, and arrests him for unlawful possession. AC cannot be found, so the only charge against D is possession of the weapon. D pleads not guilty, denying that he possessed the gun. When the case comes to trial, the prosecutor seeks to have PO1 testify about what AC said to him.[16]

---

[16] Prior to trial, D's attorney would bring a motion to suppress the gun, arguing that PO1 searched D unlawfully. At the hearing on the motion, PO1 will be permitted to testify about what AC told him, because hearsay *is* admissible at a motion to suppress. But if the judge denies the motion to suppress the gun, the question becomes: may PO1 testify *at trial* about AC's statement to him?

Defense counsel objects: "Hearsay!" The prosecutor responds, "Your Honor, I'm not offering this to prove that D actually used the gun to threaten the anonymous citizen, but merely to explain why the officer took the action that he did! Therefore AC's statement to PO1 is not hearsay, because it is relevant to show why PO1 searched D, even if AC was lying." How should the judge rule?

The prosecutor has a valid point. If all PO1 is allowed to testify is, "I walked up to D, spoke to him, searched him and found the gun," the jury is likely to be dissatisfied; they will want to know *why* PO1 singled out D, and if they don't get an explanation, they will resent not hearing the whole story — and might disbelieve PO1's testimony. So the evidence is relevant for a non-hearsay purpose.

D's attorney should also object on Fed. R. Evid. 403 grounds: If PO1 is allowed to tell the entire story, the jury will hear that D supposedly engaged in conduct a lot more dangerous than merely possessing a loaded revolver. The risk of unfair prejudice is obvious. D's attorney might also argue that a limiting instruction per Rule 105 ("You can consider this testimony in assessing why PO1 did what he did, but not as evidence that D was in fact waving a gun around") would not suffice to protect against the unfair prejudice.

Perhaps the best solution is to allow PO1 to testify "Based on information I received from a passer-by, I went to 12th and Vine and approached the defendant . . ." This at least informs the jury that the officer had a reason to approach. (And perhaps the prosecutor or defense attorney or both, might ask the judge to instruct the jury not to speculate about what if anything the passer-by told him.)

§ 2.35　MENTAL STATE, EFFECT ON HEARER: CIVIL CASES

Evidence that a statement was made to X can be relevant in civil litigation, too, for the non-hearsay purpose of proving that X was aware of the statement. For example, if P sues D for negligence, alleging that D's store or building was unsafe and that P was injured as a result, P must prove, among other things, that D had *notice* of the unsafe condition sufficiently prior to P's injury to have taken corrective action. (Review your Torts notes.) To show this, P might offer evidence that other people complained to D about the situation before P was injured. This evidence is not admissible to prove the *existence* of the dangerous condition, but, once P has satisfied his burden of production to show that the condition existed, the prior complaints would be admissible to show that D had notice of the condition.

§ 2.36　VERBAL ACTS; "OPERATIVE LEGAL FACTS"

Certain acts have such legal significance in defining rights or liabilities that they are called "operative legal facts," because they become the facts around which a body of law "operates." Some operative legal acts can be performed only by uttering words. In such situations, even though the words might seem to fit the hearsay definition, the law considers the words to be "verbal acts," and therefore not hearsay. Thus, "verbal act" is a subcategory of "operative legal fact": it is an "operative legal fact" that is performed by the uttering of certain words in certain situations. Usually a court will use the term "verbal act" in this situation, but sometimes you will see the term "operative legal fact" instead. For purposes of the hearsay issue, they mean pretty much the same thing.

Forming a contract is a verbal act, because pretty much the *only* way two parties can form a contract is with words (i.e., by saying, orally or in writing, "We agree to the following terms . . ."). If a dispute later arises as to whether there was a contract, or as to its terms, the words spelling out the terms of the contract, and the words signifying that the parties agreed, comprise a verbal act, and are not hearsay.[17]

Other examples of verbal acts include:

1. *Defamation.* To establish a cause of action for defamation, a plaintiff must prove: (1) that the defendant uttered the words in question and communicated them to others; and (2) that defendant's defamatory words damaged plaintiff's reputation.[18]

Plaintiff therefore must offer evidence that defendant committed the verbal act of uttering the defamatory words, or suffer a directed verdict. Assume, for example, that P is suing D, alleging that D told X: "P is an ambulance chaser who suborns perjury in every case he tries." When P calls X as a witness to testify that D made that statement, D's statement is not hearsay; obviously, P is not offering D's statement to prove the truth of the matter asserted by D, but rather, to prove that D committed the verbal act of defaming him.

2. *Oath.* In a prosecution for perjury, the prosecutor must prove: (1) that on some prior occasion X testified under oath; (2) that X gave the testimony in question; (3) that X knew at the time that her testimony was untrue; and (4) that the testimony was "material" (i.e., had some relevance or significance) to the issues that were the subject of the proceeding. To prove the first element of the crime, the prosecutor will probably introduce a transcript of the prior proceeding, in which X was asked, "Do you solemnly swear that the testimony you are about to give is the truth," and answered, "I do." This looks like an assertion, but the law treats it differently: once a person takes the oath at a formal proceeding, she takes on a legal obligation to tell the truth, and subjects herself to legal penalties if she breaches that obligation, regardless of whether she "meant it" or not. We are not relying on X's accuracy or sincerity when she said "I do"; as long as she said those words, she performed the verbal act of being under oath.

---

[17] You may ask: When L and M sign a contract in which L says "I agree to undertake a particular project for M" and M says "If L performs as per this contract, I will pay L 'X' thousand dollars a year," aren't those both *assertions?* In a sense, they are; but the law treats them differently, because these words have legal significance regardless of whether they are "true." Suppose, for example, after L completes the project, M refuses to pay, saying, "We never really had a contract, because I never intended to pay him; I always intended to stiff L for his fee." Would the law recognize that defense? Of course not. When a person signs his name to a contract (or states his verbal agreement), this creates binding legal rights and obligations, regardless of whether the signer "intended" to agree. Thus, M is not permitted to object on hearsay grounds when L offers the contract in evidence.

[18] As a rule, defendant has the burden of pleading and proving the truth of the allegedly defamatory utterance as an affirmative defense.

3. *Fraud.* Where a prosecutor or plaintiff alleges that D committed fraud, uttering the fraudulent words may be considered to be a verbal act.

This does not exhaust the list of situations in which statements constitute verbal acts, but it should be enough to give you the idea.

§ 2.37 QUESTIONS

Question 1. B ("buyer") files a suit claiming that S ("seller") contracted to sell him 100,000 midget widgets at $1.00 each, that S failed to deliver, that B had to purchase them at the last minute from someone else at $1.50 each, and that S should therefore be required to compensate B for the $50,000 loss he suffered as a result of S's breach of contract. B takes the stand, testifies to these events, and then identifies a piece of paper as the contract that he and S had signed. His attorney offers it in evidence; S's attorney objects that the contract is hearsay. Ruling?

Ans. Objection overruled. The contract is a verbal act; therefore it is not hearsay.

Question 2. X, a motorist, was insured by the D Insurance Co. On October 1, X went to W, his insurance company's representative, and said, "I want to cancel the policy and receive a refund for the rest of the policy I've paid for." W secured X's signature on the appropriate form and promised X that the check would be in the mail shortly. On October 2, X, driving negligently, caused an accident in which he was killed and P was injured.

P sues X's estate; X's estate impleads D Company, alleging that as X's insurer, D Company is liable. At trial, D Company calls W, who will, if permitted, testify that on October 1, X came to him and said, "I want to cancel," and filled out the appropriate form. Is what X told W hearsay?

Ans. No. Forming a contract is a verbal act; so is canceling a contract. The words X and W uttered canceling the contract therefore are not hearsay.

§ 2.38 VERBAL PARTS OF ACTS

Litigation sometimes focuses on the legal significance of a physical act. In such cases, a statement made before or during the act, which was intended by the participants to define the act, is considered a verbal part of the act. Even though a statement that is the verbal part of an act may seem to fit the hearsay definition, a verbal part of an act is not considered hearsay because, technically, it is not being offered to prove the truth of the matter asserted; rather, it is offered to prove the legal significance of the act of which it was a verbal part.

§ 2.39 QUESTIONS

Question 1. Two well-dressed men, X and Y, are sitting in a hotel room. X opens an attache case, removes 50 bundles of currency, and places them on a desk. Each bundle contains twenty $50.00 bills, so the total amount of money is $50,000. After X finishes putting the money on the desk, Y just as methodically takes the money and puts it into his own attache case. Then Y leaves, taking the money with him.

A year or so later, X sues Y for $50,000 plus interest, claiming the money was a loan and that Y failed to repay it. X takes the stand at trial, and testifies:

> A few weeks earlier, Y had asked me to lend him $50,000. On the day in question, Y came into my hotel room. I put the money on the desk and said, "I am lending this money to you, as you requested."

Y objects that what X had said to Y is hearsay: X made the statement well prior to trial, and it is now being offered in evidence to prove the truth of what X asserted. Ruling?

Ans. Objection overruled. Handing over $50,000 is an act, but unless we know the words which accompanied or shortly preceded the act, we have no way of knowing the legal or factual significance of that act. Was X making a loan to Y, as X now claims; or was it a bribe; or was X paying a gambling debt; or . . . ? The point is, we don't know, unless we know the underlying circumstances including what was said before and during the act, because the words *define* the act.

What X and Y said to one another prior to or at the time of the act, therefore, are "verbal parts of the act." If the meaning or significance of the act becomes a fact of consequence in a lawsuit, the words which were a verbal part of the act are not hearsay.

Question 2. In the same lawsuit, X calls W1, his accountant, as a witness. W1 testifies: "On the afternoon in question, X called me on the phone and said, 'I just loaned $50,000 to Y.'" Objection: hearsay. Ruling?

Ans. Sustained. By the time X made *this* statement to W1, the act was over. Moreover, W1 was not a participant in the act. X's statement therefore was not "part" of the act; it fits the hearsay definition; hence, it is hearsay.

Question 3. Later in the trial Y takes the stand. He testifies:

> I remember exactly what happened. X invited me to his room and said to me, "I enjoyed your last novel so much that I am giving you this money as a gift, as a token of my esteem for you."

X objects that Y is testifying to an out-of-court statement which is now offered in evidence to prove the truth of what was asserted, and is therefore hearsay. Ruling?

Ans. Overruled. This statement was part of the act, and therefore is not hearsay. (X, of course, will deny ever having said this; but that's a factual issue for the jury to decide. Whichever version of X's statement the jury accepts — Y's version, given in this problem, or X's version, given in Q. 1 — the statement was a verbal part of the act of giving Y the money.)

§ 2.40 "RES GESTAE"

At common law, courts considered a statement non-hearsay if they were "part of the 'res gestae.'" That Latin phrase, which literally means "the thing itself," probably was first used to mean what we now call a "verbal act" or a "verbal part of an act." Courts also used it to describe a statement about an event as the event was taking place — a narrow version of what is now called an "excited utterance," discussed in §§ 8.2 et seq. Sometimes it is used to describe a sequence of events without any reference to statements at all. By now, it means pretty much whatever a court wants it to mean,[19] which means it comes close to not meaning anything in particular at all.

---

[19] Perhaps courts have taken their lead from the following:

"But 'glory' doesn't mean 'a nice knockdown argument,' " Alice objected.

"When *I* use a word," Humpty Dumpty said, in a rather scornful tone, "it means just what I want it to mean — neither more nor less."

"The question is," said Alice, "whether you *can* make a word mean so many different things."

"The question is," said Humpty Dumpty, "which is to be master — that's all."

Lewis Carroll, *Through the Looking Glass*, ch. 5.

Chapter 3

EXCEPTIONS TO THE HEARSAY DEFINITION, EXCEPTIONS TO THE HEARSAY RULE: AN INTRODUCTION

§ 3.1 INTRODUCTION

As explained in Chapter 1, the hearsay rule is simply one of several hurdles an attorney must overcome to secure the admissibility of an item of evidence. Whenever an offer of evidence consists of spoken or written words or arguably assertive conduct, you must analyze that evidence against the definition of hearsay set out in Fed. R. Evid. 801(c). If the evidence fits that definition, as spelled out in Chapter 2, it *is* hearsay, and if counsel for the adverse party interposes a hearsay objection, the evidence must be excluded — unless, of course, the evidence fits within any of the provisions of Fed. R. Evid. 801(d), 803, 804 or 807, in which case the hearsay objection must be overruled.

§ 3.2 EXCEPTIONS TO THE RULE; EXCEPTIONS TO THE DEFINITION

[1] Rules 803 and 804

Fed. R. Evid. 803 and 804 contain a total of 28 more-or-less specific separate *exceptions to the hearsay rule*, each with its own requirements, peculiarities, and procedural wrinkles. They have a common underlying theme: each describes a situation in which a statement fits the definition of hearsay set out in Fed. R. Evid. 801(c), but is nonetheless considered sufficiently *trustworthy* to overcome the hearsay hurdle.

[2] Rule 807

Fed. R. Evid. 807 is a catch-all (or "residual") exception, a central requirement of which is that the statement must be shown to be *trustworthy* enough to overcome the law's bias against hearsay.

[3] Rule 801(d)

In addition, Fed. R. Evid. 801(d) contains eight separate provisions that are classified as *exceptions to the hearsay definition*. A statement that fits within the 801(c) definition but also fits within a provision of Fed. R. Evid. 801(d) is categorized as *non*-hearsay. While the theoretical justifications for the Rule 801(d) provisions differ from those in Rules 803, 804 and 807, the practical effect is the same: a statement that satisfies the requirements of any provision of Rule 801(d), 803, 804 or 807 overcomes a hearsay objection.

In other words, to resolve the hearsay issue, first determine whether the evidence is hearsay, as defined in Fed. R. Evid. 801(c). If it is, determine whether it fits within any of the 37 provisions of Fed. R. Evid. 801(d), 803, 804 or 807. If it does, the hearsay objection must be overruled. The only practical difference between an "exception to the definition" and an "exception to the rule" is the label. Whether a statement satisfies an exception to the definition or an exception to the rule, the impact is the same: the hearsay objection is overruled.

§ 3.3 APPLYING THE 37 EXCEPTIONS: QUESTIONS

At this point, students often are troubled by several questions:

Question 1. "Do they really expect me to learn 37 more separate technical little rules, just to handle the hearsay issue?"

Ans. Yes. (That's why you bought this book, isn't it?)

Question 2. How will I know which of the 37 provisions to apply in any given situation?

Ans. Until you develop a feel for how these 37 provisions work, you *won't* know which of them to apply. The only safe way to assure that you don't overlook important issues, therefore, is to apply *each* of them, to determine which are worth detailed analysis. (That overstates it a bit, of course. If the statement consists of a person shouting, "Look out, look out, the bus is running the red light," for example, you can fairly quickly eliminate the exceptions dealing with ancient documents, records of religious organizations, dying declarations, learned treatises, and a few others besides.)

Question 3. Suppose a statement violates the requirements of one exception, but satisfies the requirements of a second exception. Which one "controls"?

Ans. The second one. To overcome a hearsay objection, it is only necessary to satisfy any *one* of the 37 exceptions in Fed. R. Evid. 801(d), 803, 804 or 807. The party offering the evidence gets to "choose" whichever exception (or exceptions) she thinks will provide the best chances for admissibility. Thus, "all exceptions are created equal."[1]

But she had better choose the right exception, and do so quickly. When a hearsay objection is made, a judge will expect a prompt and specific response. A lawyer can meet these expectations only if she is familiar with each of the hearsay exceptions.

---

[1] The only exceptions to *this* general rule relate to Fed. R. Evid. 803(8)(A)(ii) and 803(8)(A)(iii). *See* §§ 8.59, 8.60.

§ 3.4   BURDEN OF PROOF

When one party offers what appears to be hearsay evidence, to raise the issue of its admissibility, the adverse party must object. If the evidence falls within the definition of Fed. R. Evid. 801(c), the judge must exclude it unless the offering party persuades the judge by a preponderance of the evidence[2] that the statement satisfies the requirements of an exception to the hearsay definition (Fed. R. Evid. 801(d)) or of an exception to the hearsay rule (Fed. R. Evid. 803, 804 or 807).

§ 3.5   HEARSAY AND THE GRAND JURY

A witness testifies before a grand jury. Months or years later, a party (usually, the prosecutor; occasionally, the defendant; rarely, a litigant in a civil case) offers that grand jury testimony in evidence at a trial. The adverse party objects: hearsay. The offering party cites one or several hearsay exceptions.

To understand whether an exception will overcome the objection, it is important to understand what a grand jury is and the procedures it follows.

What it is. A grand jury consists of a group of civilians (usually 23 in number), empaneled by a court much in the same way a trial jury is empaneled. Generally a grand jury will sit for a specified term — one month, six months, or whatever.

During its term, a grand jury has two basic roles. The first is to screen the prosecutor's evidence in the cases presented to it. In the federal system and in some state systems, almost every felony charge must be presented to a grand jury if the prosecutor hopes to take the defendant to trial on that charge. The prosecutor's burden of proof is comparatively light: she need only establish "probable cause" to believe that X committed a particular crime. If the grand jury finds probable cause, it will vote an indictment (a formal accusation) of X for the crime or crimes. If the grand jury concludes that probable cause is lacking, the charges are dismissed.

The second role of a grand jury is to be the prosecutor's investigative partner. A grand jury can subpoena witnesses and physical evidence. It can force people to testify against their will, and can even overcome a witness's assertion of his Fifth Amendment privilege, by granting immunity from any use of his testimony against him. Grand jury investigations play a crucial role in investigating organized crime, white collar crime and political corruption.

Procedure. Picture what you know about the typical criminal *trial.* The judge presides. The defendant is always present, as is his attorney. Trials are open to the public, including the media. The defendant gets to see and hear every witness who testifies and to examine every shred of physical evidence that is offered. Defense counsel is entitled to make an opening statement to the jury, to object to alleged mistakes or misconduct by the prosecutor, to cross-examine every government witness, to call witnesses on behalf of his client, and to make a closing argument to the jury, urging it to acquit. Before the judge instructs the jury on relevant points of law,

---

[2] The Supreme Court established this as the burden of persuasion in United States v. Bourjaily, 483 U.S. 171, 176 (1987).

defense counsel has the right to suggest issues about which the judge should instruct, and to object if he believes that the judge has given an erroneous instruction.

Do you have that picture firmly in your mind? Good. Now take that picture and crumple it up. Tear it into pieces. Gather the pieces into a loose pile, and burn the pile. Because *none of the procedures I described in the previous paragraph apply to the grand jury.*

The grand jury meets, hears evidence, and deliberates in secret.[3]

The judge does not enter the grand jury room or participate any in way in its proceedings. Neither does the defendant or the defense attorney.[4] Because no defense attorney can enter the grand jury room, he or she cannot make an opening statement, cross-examine government witnesses, call defense witnesses, or make a closing argument.

The prosecutor decides what cases to bring, what witnesses to call, what questions to ask, what evidence to subpoena, and what charges to recommend to the jury against each potential defendant. (A grand jury has the power to do these things on its own or against the prosecutor's wishes, but this rarely happens.) The prosecutor, not the judge, is the grand jury's legal advisor. That means she, not the judge, instructs the grand jury on the law.[5]

Does this sound a little one-sided? Well, yes, it is; the system is designed that way. The Supreme Court has consistently refused to impose procedural safeguards on the grand jury that would interfere with its efficiency as an investigative body.

There are those of course who bemoan the one-sided nature of the grand jury system. "A grand jury," the famous complaint goes, "would indict a ham sandwich if the prosecutor asked it to." Personally, I believe this criticism is a broad exaggeration. In my eight years as a prosecutor, I only once asked a grand jury to indict a ham sandwich, and that was because it had claimed to be kosher.[6]

From time to time, a situation arises when a litigant offers grand jury testimony into evidence at a trial. Whether that testimony satisfies a hearsay exception will often depend, in part, on the nature of the grand jury. Thus, whenever you come upon

---

[3] Occasionally information about a grand jury investigation is leaked to the press. But such disgraces are happily the exception, not the rule.

[4] This is because, in a grand jury proceeding, technically there *is* no defendant unless and until the grand jury has voted to indict someone, at which point its job is done. Often, of course, the particular suspect or target has already been arrested and charged with the crime. Often it is a foregone conclusion that he or she will be indicted. Still, until the indictment, this suspect is not a "defendant," and therefore enjoys none of the constitutional rights granted to a criminal defendant.

[5] Also, the prosecutor is allowed to use illegally seized evidence in the grand jury, and to use evidence that if offered at trial would be inadmissible hearsay.

[6] The technical meaning of "Kosher" is, "in accordance with Jewish dietary laws." (The opposite of "kosher" is "trayf," the technical definition of which is . . . "not kosher.") Pork products (including ham) can never be kosher because . . . well, it has to do with how many stomachs an animal has, how it digests its food, and how its feet are shaped; for purposes of this book, just take my word for it. My point (yes, I had a point) is that a ham sandwich that claims to be kosher is guilty of fraud, and *deserves* to be indicted. Don't you agree? Of course you do. (This will not be on the exam.)

references to grand jury testimony in subsequent discussions or problems, reread this section.

§ 3.6   SIXTH AMENDMENT CONFRONTATION CLAUSE

When a prosecutor offers hearsay evidence against a defendant in a criminal trial, the evidence must not only satisfy a hearsay exception; if must also satisfy the Sixth Amendment Confrontation Clause. That subject is covered in Chapter 6 and, periodically, throughout the subsequent chapters.

Chapter 4

EXCEPTIONS TO THE HEARSAY DEFINITION: PRIOR STATEMENTS BY WITNESSES, RULE 801(d)(1)

PART A:
OVERVIEW

§ 4.1 IN GENERAL

In Chapter 2, we learned that a declarant's out-of-court statement is hearsay even if the declarant testifies at the trial (*see* § 2.4). Fed. R. Evid. 801(d)(1) creates three narrow exceptions to this rule, by defining three situations in which a prior statement by a declarant who is now a witness at the trial is *not* considered hearsay. Offering such statements poses issues relating to procedure and trial strategy, as well as evidentiary issues.

§ 4.2 "WITNESS; SUBJECT TO CROSS-EXAMINATION"

Fed. R. Evid. 801(d)(1)(A), 801(d)(1)(B), and 801(d)(1)(C) have a requirement in common: for a statement to be admissible under any of these provisions, it is necessary that "[t]he declarant testifies [at the current trial or hearing] and is subject to cross-examination about a prior statement." In other words, the declarant whose prior statement is being offered in evidence must now be a witness, in the courtroom, on the witness stand, in the ongoing trial, so that if the attorney for one party elicits testimony about a prior statement, the declarant can be cross-examined about the statement by any attorney in the case.

Don't be confused by the phrase, "is subject to cross-examination." The Rule 801(d)(1) provisions do *not* require that the declarant was subject to cross-examination when she made the *prior* statement. So far as cross-examination is concerned, Fed. R. Evid. 801(d)(1)(A), 801(d)(1)(B), and 801(d)(1)(c) require only that all the attorneys in the current trial have an opportunity *now*, during the present proceeding, to cross-examine the declarant about the statement.

§ 4.3   "MEANINGFUL CROSS-EXAMINATION"; *UNITED STATES v. OWENS*

Suppose the witness claims he cannot remember making the prior statement, or even worse, claims he cannot remember the events discussed in his statement. If the witness answers every question with "I don't remember," some state courts, and many professors, have argued that because he cannot really be cross-examined, the "subject to cross-examination about a prior statement" requirement of Fed. R. Evid. 801(d)(1) is not satisfied. In *United States v. Owens*, 484 U.S. 554, 559 (1988), however, the Supreme Court concluded otherwise. The Court held that the Rule 801(d)(1) "subject to cross-examination" requirement is satisfied even if a witness claims he can no longer remember anything about his prior statement or the underlying facts.

In dictum, the Court suggested that the result would be different if a declarant refused to testify at all by asserting the Fifth Amendment privilege against self-incrimination.

§ 4.4   PROVING THAT THE DECLARANT MADE THE STATEMENT

Before an attorney can introduce a prior statement by the witness, she must prove that the witness made the statement. This presents some interesting procedural and tactical wrinkles that are discussed in §§ 4.13, 4.23, and 4.27.

§ 4.5   SIXTH AMENDMENT CONFRONTATION CLAUSE

For reasons that will be made clear in Chapter 6, any hearsay statement that satisfies Fed. R. Evid. 801(d)(1)(A), 801(d)(1)(B), or 801(d)(1)(C), will automatically satisfy the Sixth Amendment Confrontation Clause. *See* § 6.14[1].

PART B:
PRIOR INCONSISTENT STATEMENTS — SWORN AND UNSWORN

§ 4.6   PRIOR INCONSISTENT *UNSWORN* STATEMENTS: RULE 613

This section is about Fed. R. Evid. 613. The first thing you need to know about Rule 613 is that it is *not an exception to the hearsay rule or to the hearsay definition.* I am discussing it here because it very closely resembles Fed. R. Evid. 801(d)(1)(A), which *is* an exception to the hearsay definition, and it is difficult to understand Rule 801(d)(1)(A) without understanding Rule 613.

P was injured when a bus collided with his car at the intersection of Broadway and 48th Street. At trial, the bus company calls W1 as a witness. Direct examination proceeds as follows:

Q.   Did you see what happened that day?

A.   Absolutely. I was standing right there. The light turned red for the eastbound traffic on 48th Street and green for the north-south traffic on Broadway. Suddenly this car on 48th went through the red light into the intersection and got hit by the bus heading south on Broadway.

Q.   The bus had the green light?

A.   The bus had the green light. Absolutely. I saw it all.

This may sound pretty convincing to the jury; but on cross examination by P's attorney, the following exchange occurs:

Q.   I believe you testified on direct that you saw the entire accident?

A.   Absolutely.

Q.   No question about that in your mind?

A.   Like I said, I saw it all.

Q.   Do you remember speaking to Police Officer Renko shortly after the collision?

A.   Yeah, there was cops there.

Q.   And you spoke to Officer Renko about the collision?

A.   Absolutely.

Q.   Did you tell Officer Renko, quote, "The bus went barreling through the red light and hit the car like a tank," unquote?

(D's lawyer):   Objection! Hearsay.

D has a valid objection, because if P offers W1's out-of-court statement to Officer Renko to prove that the bus ran the red light, the statement is hearsay. But W1's statement to Renko has another, more limited use. Even if the jury cannot consider it as evidence that the bus *ran the red light*, it is relevant in helping the jury assess how much weight or credibility it should give to W1's in-court testimony that the bus had the *green* light. The inconsistency between the two statements undermines (impeaches) the accuracy of W1's direct testimony.

The law has long permitted a party to use a witness' prior inconsistent statement to impeach that witness' testimony, even when, as here, the statement is inadmissible hearsay if offered as substantive evidence. Fed. R. Evid. 613 codifies this common law principle. Fed. R. Evid. 613 provides:

Rule 613. Witness's Prior Statement

(a) Showing or Disclosing the Statement During Examination. When examining a witness about the witness's prior statement, the party need not show it or disclose its contents to the witness. But the party must, on request, show it or disclose its contents to an adverse party's attorney.

(b) Extrinsic Evidence of a Prior Inconsistent Statement. Extrinsic evidence of a witness's prior inconsistent statement is admissible only if

the witness is given an opportunity to explain or deny the statement and an adverse party is given an opportunity to question the witness about it, or if justice so requires. This subdivision (b) does not apply to an opposing party's statement under Rule 801(d)(2).

[Prior to December 1, 2011, the rule read as follows:

Rule 613. Prior Statements of Witnesses

(a) Examining witness concerning prior statement. In examining a witness concerning a prior statement made by the witness, whether written or not, the statement need not be shown nor its contents disclosed to the witness at that time, but on request the same shall be shown or disclosed to opposing counsel.

(b) Extrinsic evidence of prior inconsistent statement of witness. Extrinsic evidence of a prior inconsistent statement by a witness is not admissible unless the witness is afforded an opportunity to explain or deny the same and the opposite party is afforded an opportunity to interrogate the witness thereon, or the interests of justice otherwise require. This provision does not apply to admissions of a party-opponent as defined in Rule 801(d)(2).

The Federal Rules of Evidence were rewritten solely to make them easier to understand, and no substantive change is meant by this amendment. The text of the old rule may remain useful in reading court decisions that precede the revision of the rules. Thus, this edition of the Student's Guide provides the text of both the new and the old version of each relevant provision of the Federal Rules of Evidence.]

An attorney can use a witness' prior inconsistent statement at two different stages of the trial. First, she can cross-examine the witness about the statement, as P's attorney did to W1 in the Q-and-A set forth above (*see* Fed. R. Evid. 613(a), *supra*). Second, under some circumstances, Fed. R. Evid. 613(b) permits the attorney to wait until it is her turn to call witnesses, then call a second witness to testify that the first witness made the prior inconsistent statement. Under this second option, instead of cross-examining W1 about his statement to Officer Renko, P could have waited until D rested, and then, in rebuttal, called Renko to testify that W1 told him that the bus ran the red light.

Sometimes an attorney can employ both options. For example, if P's attorney cross-examines W1 about the statement and W1 *denies* he said it, in rebuttal P could call Renko to testify that W1 in fact made the statement.

A statement is admissible under Fed. R. Evid. 613 if three conditions are satisfied:

1. The declarant is testifying (or has already testified) at the current trial or hearing about events that are relevant to the trial.

2. The prior statement is *inconsistent* with what declarant has testified to.

3. Except in unusual circumstances, at some point in the trial (usually, during cross-examination or redirect examination of the declarant), the declarant must be given an opportunity to deny or explain why he made the inconsistent

statement and each party's attorney must have an opportunity to question the declarant about the inconsistent statement.[1]

Thus, the cross-examination set forth above is likely to continue as follows:

(D's lawyer):   Objection! Hearsay!

(P's lawyer):   Prior inconsistent statement, your honor.

(Court):   Overruled.

Q.   Did you say that to Officer Renko?

A.   Uhhh . . .

Q.   Well, did you?

A.   Uh, I may have.

Q.   You "*may* have"? Did you say that, or not?

A.   I guess so.

Q.   You "guess so"?

A.   I gue — yeah. I did say that.

Q.   "Absolutely"?

A.   Yeah.

Q.   So now you're telling us that it was the *bus* that ran the light?

A.   No, no. It happened just like I said before: the bus had the *green* light.

Q.   Let me make sure I have this straight. Today you say the bus had the green light, even though back then, five minutes after the collision, you told Officer Renko that the bus ran the red light?

A.   Yeah.

§ 4.7   QUESTION

Question 1. What should D's attorney do at this point?

Ans. Request, per Fed. R. Evid. 105, that the judge instruct the jury that they can consider W1's statement to Renko ("red light") only in assessing how much weight to give to W1's testimony that the bus had the green light; they cannot consider W1's statement as substantive evidence that the bus ran the red light.

§ 4.8   PRIOR INCONSISTENT *SWORN* STATEMENTS: RULE 801(d)(1)(A)

Fed. R. Evid. 801(d)(1)(A) provides:

---

[1] Fed. R. Evid. 613 raises tactical and procedural issues that will not be covered in this book.

(d) Statements That Are Not Hearsay. A statement that meets the following conditions is not hearsay:

> **(1)** *A Declarant-Witness's Prior Statement.* **The declarant testifies and is subject to cross-examination about a prior statement, and the statement:**
>
> > **(A) is inconsistent with the declarant's testimony and was given under penalty of perjury at a trial, hearing, or other proceeding or in a deposition; ...**

[Prior to December 1, 2011, the rule read as follows:

Rule 801(d). A statement is not hearsay if —

> (1) The declarant testifies at the trial or hearing and is subject to cross-examination concerning the statement, and the statement is
>
> > (A) inconsistent with the declarant's testimony, and was given under oath subject to the penalty of perjury at a trial, hearing, or other proceeding, or in a deposition, . . .

The Federal Rules of Evidence were rewritten solely to make them easier to understand; the Advisory Committee did not intend to make any substantive change in the Rules. The text of the old rule may remain useful in reading court decisions that precede the revision of the rules. Thus, this edition of the Student's Guide provides the text of both the new and the old version of each relevant provision of the Federal Rules of Evidence.]

To satisfy Fed. R. Evid. 801(d)(1)(A), the party offering the statement has to persuade the judge that four conditions are satisfied:

> 1. The declarant is testifying (or has testified) at the current trial or hearing about events that are relevant to the trial.
>
> 2. The prior statement is inconsistent with what declarant has just testified to.
>
> 3. At some point in the trial, each party's attorney must have an opportunity to cross-examine the declarant concerning the prior statement.
>
> 4. The prior statement was made while the declarant was "under penalty of perjury [in other words, under oath] at a trial, hearing, or other proceeding or in a deposition."

Note that to satisfy Fed. R. Evid. 801(d)(1)(A), a statement must meet the requirements for Fed. R. Evid. 613, and must also satisfy a fourth requirement: it must have been made while the declarant was "under penalty of perjury [in other words, under oath] at a trial, hearing, or other proceeding or in a deposition." If the prior statement satisfies Rule 801(d)(1)(A), then, unlike a statement that satisfies only Rule 613, it is admissible over a hearsay objection as *substantive* evidence, to prove the truth of the matter asserted in the statement. If W1's statement in § 4.6, supra, had been made, for example, not to Officer Renko on the street, but at a pretrial deposition, then the statement would be admissible, not only to impeach W1's in-court testimony that the bus had the green light, but also as substantive evidence that the bus ran the red light.

Moreover, D's attorney would not be entitled to a limiting instruction. Instead, the judge might instruct the jury:

> W1 has told two conflicting versions of what happened. At a deposition a few months ago, he testified that the bus ran the red light. Today he testified the bus had the green light. You can believe whichever one you choose; or, if you think they cancel each other out, you can ignore W1's testimony on this point altogether.

Rationale. Congress excepted Fed. R. Evid. 801(d)(1)(A) statements from the hearsay definition for several reasons. First, that the prior statement was made under oath at a somewhat formal proceeding increases the likelihood that declarant spoke truthfully; a person is less likely to lie in such a setting. Second, because testimony at trials, hearings, depositions and other formal proceedings is recorded stenographically or electronically, the "proceeding" requirement makes it unlikely that a dispute will arise as to what the declarant actually said. Third, because declarant must testify at trial and be subject to cross-examination, the circumstances underlying the prior statement and the reasons for the inconsistencies between the trial testimony and the prior statement can be explored by all the attorneys in the case.

§ 4.9 "WITNESS"; "SUBJECT TO CROSS-EXAMINATION"

See the discussion in § 4.2.

§ 4.10 "INCONSISTENT"

The prior statement must be inconsistent with the testimony the declarant has just given at trial. Several decisions have pondered how the term "inconsistent" should be defined. If the two statements directly contradict each other, they are clearly inconsistent. But courts do not restrict application of Fed. R. Evid. 801(d)(1)(A) so narrowly. Judges have found sufficient inconsistency in evasive answers, silence, changes in memory as to some important details, and in claims of forgetfulness, particularly if the judge is convinced that the "forgetfulness" is really only a reluctance to testify.

§ 4.11 QUESTIONS

Question 1. In the trial of the bus-auto collision, D called W1, who testified on direct:

> . . . this car on 48th went through the red light and went into the intersection and got hit by the bus heading south on Broadway. . . . The bus had the green light. Absolutely. I saw it all.

During a deposition a few months earlier W1 had testified that "The bus ran the red light and smashed into the car."

On cross-examination, P's attorney brings out W1's deposition testimony. D objects: hearsay. Ruling?

Ans. Overruled. The "declarant testifies" and "under penalty of perjury" [i.e. under oath] requirements of Fed. R. Evid. 801(d)(1)(A) are satisfied. Moreover, W1's deposition testimony clearly contradicts, and therefore is inconsistent with, his trial testimony.

Question 2. Suppose, instead, W1's pretrial deposition testimony had been: "I wasn't paying that much attention at first. I think the bus had the green light, but it happened so fast I'm not sure." Is this "inconsistent" with his trial testimony?

Ans. Yes. Even though W1's conclusion was the same (both times, he said the bus had the green light), his lack of certainty at the deposition is inconsistent with his "absolute" insistence at trial that he "saw it all." Therefore the deposition statement is sufficiently inconsistent with his trial testimony to be admissible under Fed. R. Evid. 801(d)(1)(A).

The trickiest situation arises when, at trial, the witness claims to no longer remember the event in question.

Question 3. Police arrested X and Y on June 1 for a bank robbery committed on May 15, charging that Y went into the bank and took money from a teller at gunpoint while X drove the getaway car. (As you know from your criminal law course, if the charge is true, X was legally Y's accomplice, and therefore can be convicted of the robbery.)

The prosecutor worked out a deal with X and his lawyer: X would admit his guilt and testify against Y in the grand jury and at trial. In exchange, the prosecutor promised to recommend a lenient sentence for X. As agreed, X pleaded guilty. In the grand jury, X testified:

> Y told me it would be easy. He cased the bank, he stole the getaway car, all I had to do was drive. He picked me up that morning. I drove around for half an hour to get used to the car, then double-parked in front of the bank. Y went in, then came running out a few minutes later, jumped in, and said, "Let's get the hell out of here." When we got back to his place he gave me $400 and said I done real good.

At trial, though, when the prosecutor begins to question X about Y's plans to rob the bank, X responds, "I don't remember nothin' about Y and some bank." Moreover, he insists he doesn't remember driving the car, or getting arrested, or pleading guilty, or testifying in the grand jury, either.

The prosecutor therefore seeks to offer X's grand jury testimony into evidence. (We will talk about procedure in § 4.13, *infra*.) Y's attorney interposes a hearsay objection. The prosecutor responds by citing Fed. R. Evid. 801(d)(1)(A).[2] Ruling?

Ans. X's grand jury testimony is admissible under Fed. R. Evid. 801(d)(1)(A) only if, among other things, it is considered "inconsistent" with his trial testimony. There

---

[2] The defendant might object that he never had the opportunity to cross-examine X in the grand jury (*see* § 3.05). But Rule 801(d)(1)(A) does not require that the *prior sworn statement* was subject to cross-examination; it only requires that the declarant-witness can be cross-examined during the *current proceeding*. See § 4.2.

are two very different approaches to this issue.

One approach reasons that for all practical purposes, X *has not testified* at the trial. It is as if he wasn't called at all, because he has added not one iota of relevant evidence to the key issue, which is whether Y is the man who robbed the bank on May 15. Since X has said nothing, his prior statement is not "inconsistent" with his (non)testimony at trial. Moreover, how can Y's attorney "cross-examine" a witness who answers every question, "I don't remember"? Therefore the prosecutor should not be permitted to use Rule 801(d)(1)(A).

The second approach focuses on the likelihood that X's supposed forgetfulness is really an attempt to avoid testifying. (It is easy to guess why X is likely to be reluctant to testify. Perhaps Y threatened him, or maybe X simply knows how unpopular he'll be, in prison and on the street, if he testifies against Y at trial.) When a confessed criminal suddenly develops "amnesia" to avoid testifying against a co-defendant, advocates of the second approach argue, the judge should have discretion to declare such convenient memory loss "inconsistent" with the detailed factual testimony X gave in the grand jury just a few months earlier. Otherwise, we'd often be giving double-turncoat criminals like X the power to control the outcome of criminal prosecutions.

Most courts have taken the second approach, in essence ruling that if the trial judge is convinced that X's claim of forgetfulness at trial is feigned, the judge can classify such trial testimony as inconsistent with X's grand jury testimony, and admit the latter under Fed. R. Evid. 801(d)(1)(A).

§ 4.12 "PROCEEDING"

The prior inconsistent sworn statement must have been made "at a trial, hearing, or other proceeding or in a deposition." Courts have accepted testimony given at prior trials, depositions, preliminary hearings, motions to suppress, grand jury proceedings, and legislative hearings, as falling within Fed. R. Evid. 801(d)(1)(A). Somewhat less formal "proceedings" have also been accepted. In one case, an immigration officer at a Border Patrol Station gave *Miranda* warnings to two illegal immigrants, then placed them under oath and tape recorded his interrogation of them, during which they made statements incriminating D, the man who had brought them across the border from Mexico. At D's trial, however, the immigrants denied D had helped them enter the United States. Over D's hearsay objection, relying on Rule 801(d)(1)(A), the trial judge admitted their tape recorded statements as substantive evidence against D. On appeal, the Circuit Court affirmed. *United States v. Castro-Ayon*, 537 F.2d 1055, 1058 (9th Cir.), *cert. denied*, 429 U.S. 983 (1976).

But station house interrogations by the police are *not* 801(d)(1)(A) proceedings; neither are affidavits, except perhaps where special legislation so provides.

§ 4.13 PROCEDURE

The most direct way of proving that W1 made a prior inconsistent sworn statement is to ask him. Assume W1 testifies for D on direct. P's cross-examination would proceed as follows:

Q.   Do you recall testifying at a deposition in this case on September 17, 2011?

A.   Yes.

Q.   Do you recall being asked these questions and giving these answers?

P's attorney turns to her opponent, tells him where in the deposition transcript she'll be reading from, and then reads the relevant questions and answers that constitute the prior inconsistent statement. After reading the questions and answers, she again asks W1: "Do you recall being asked those questions and giving those answers?" If W1 answers "Yes," P's attorney has proved that W1 made the statements.

If W1 says "No, I don't remember saying that," then to prove that W1 made the statement the attorney must authenticate the transcript as accurate, per Article IX of the Federal Rules of Evidence. The most direct way is to call the stenographer to testify: "I took the transcript of that deposition, I took it accurately, I typed it accurately. W1 said precisely what I typed." Even if W1 denied having made those statements, the stenographer's testimony is sufficient "proof" of the transcript's accuracy (*see* Fed. R. Evid. 901(b)(1)) to get the issue to the jury. The difficulty with calling the stenographer is that it is inconvenient (the stenographer might be unavailable) and cumbersome. After all, W1 is D's witness. P won't be able to call witnesses on her own again until after D rests. Then, after the stenographer testifies, P or D may want to recall W1 to question him further about the prior statement.

There are two ways around this awkwardness. When the stenographer prepared the transcript, he included a paragraph at the end, attesting: "I hereby certify that the foregoing is a correct and accurate transcript of [the deposition, preliminary hearing, or whatever]." If the stenographer was an official court reporter, this certification will suffice to authenticate the transcript under Fed. R. Evid. 902(4). If the stenographer was a free-lancer or worked for a private company that provides stenographic services, this certification will suffice to authenticate the transcript under Fed. R. Evid. 902(11). And as a matter of practicality and professional courtesy, D's attorney will in all likelihood stipulate that if the stenographer were called as a witness, he would testify that the transcript accurately reflects W1's testimony. This, too, is sufficient proof of the transcript's accuracy to get the question to the jury.

PART C:
PRIOR CONSISTENT STATEMENTS TO REBUT CHARGES OF WITNESS MISCONDUCT

§ 4.14   PRIOR CONSISTENT STATEMENTS GENERALLY

The mere fact that W1, prior to trial, made a statement *consistent* with what W1 testifies to during the trial is no reason to admit the prior statement. The fact that W1 has told the same basic story for several months is not particularly relevant. Moreover, the prior statements usually are hearsay. There is no general exception to the hearsay definition or hearsay rule covering prior *consistent* statements. Thus, if a proper objection is made, such statements generally are excluded.

§ 4.15   QUESTIONS

Question 1. In the bus-automobile collision litigation, W2 told Officer Renko at the scene that the bus had the green light when it entered the intersection. That night he told his cousin about it. The next day he said the same thing to several colleagues at work. A month or so later, he told the same story to investigators for the lawyers in the case. Several months later, at a deposition, he said the same thing again.

At trial, W2 is asked:

Q.   Did you see what happened?

A.   Yes. The light changed, so traffic going north and south on Broadway had the green. The bus pulled into the intersection. Then this car sped eastbound into the intersection along 48th Street, right into the path of the bus.

Is there anything objectionable about this testimony?

Ans. No. W2 is testifying as to what he saw.

Question 2. Counsel for D Bus Co. asks, "Before testifying here today, did you ever tell anyone else that the bus had the green light?" P objects: hearsay. Ruling?

Ans. Sustained. There is no general "prior consistent statement" provision in Article VIII of the Federal Rules of Evidence. Nor (as you will know by the end of the book) are any of W2's prior statements in this case likely to qualify under other exceptions to the hearsay definition or rule.

§ 4.16   RULE 801(d)(1)(B): TEXT, RATIONALE, AND REQUIREMENTS

Fed. R. Evid. 801(d)(1)(B) provides:

> **(d) Statements That Are Not Hearsay. A statement that meets the following conditions is not hearsay:**
>
> > **(1) *A Declarant-Witness's Prior Statement.* The declarant testifies and is subject to cross-examination about the prior statement, and the statement: . . .**
> >
> > > **(B) is consistent with the declarant's testimony and is offered to rebut an express or implied charge that the declarant recently fabricated it or acted from a recent improper influence or motive in so testifying; ...**

[Prior to December 1, 2011, the rule read as follows:

> Rule 801(d). A statement is not hearsay if —

(1) The declarant testifies at the trial or hearing and is subject to cross-examination concerning the statement, and the statement is . . .

(B) consistent with the declarant's testimony and is offered to rebut an express or implied charge against the declarant of recent fabrication or improper influence or motive, . . .

The Federal Rules of Evidence were rewritten solely to make them easier to understand; the Advisory Committee did not intend to make any substantive change in the Rules. The text of the old rule may remain useful in reading court decisions that precede the revision of the rules. Thus, this edition of the Student's Guide provides the text of both the new and the old version of each relevant provision of the Federal Rules of Evidence.]

Rule 801(d)(1)(B) thus creates a special category of prior consistent statements — those that are relevant "to rebut an express or implied charge" that the declarant "recently fabricated" his testimony, or has shaped his testimony as a result of "improper influence or motive" — making those prior consistent statements admissible to prove the truth of the matter asserted.

Rationale. A prior consistent statement that rebuts an accusation of recent fabrication or improper motivation is relevant in helping the fact-finder decide whether, despite the accusation, to believe the testimony.

To utilize Fed. R. Evid. 801(d)(1)(B), the party offering the statement must persuade the judge that four conditions are satisfied:

1. "The declarant testifies [at the current proceeding] and is subject to cross-examination about the prior statement."

2. The prior statement is *consistent* with what the declarant has just testified to at trial.

3. At some point in the current trial or proceeding, an attorney has impeached the declarant by explicitly or implicitly accusing the declarant of having recently fabricated his testimony, or of allowing his testimony to be affected by a "recent" improper influence or motive.

4. The prior statement is relevant to rebut the accusation.

§ 4.17 "WITNESS"; "SUBJECT TO CROSS-EXAMINATION"

The declarant must testify at the trial or hearing being conducted, and the party against whom the prior statement is being offered must have an opportunity to cross-examine the declarant/witness about the prior statement (*see* § 4.2).

§ 4.18 "CONSISTENT"; PRIOR OATH NOT REQUIRED

The only requirement Fed. R. Evid. 801(d)(1)(B) imposes with regard to the prior statement itself is that it be consistent with what W has now testified to at trial.

Absolute consistency is not required; nobody tells a story exactly the same way twice, unless he or she is reciting from a memorized script. It suffices if the prior version is consistent enough with the current testimony to rebut the accusation of improper motive or recent fabrication.

Unlike Rule 801(d)(1)(A), an 801(d)(1)(B) statement need *not* have been made while under oath and need *not* have been made in a formal setting. A statement to a police officer, private investigator, attorney, bartender, barber, radio talk show host, or anyone else can qualify.

§ 4.19 "RECENTLY FABRICATED" OR PROMPTED BY "A RECENT IMPROPER INFLUENCE OR MOTIVE"

P sues D; D calls W2 as a witness. After W2 testifies on direct, P cross-examines, seeking to impeach W2's testimony. Later in the trial, P might also call W3 as a witness to further impeach W2's testimony. D, seeking to persuade the jury to believe W2 despite P's efforts at impeachment, wants to bring out the fact that W2 made one or more statements prior to trial consistent with what W2 testified to on direct.

D may do so under Fed. R. Evid. 801(d)(1)(B) only if, in addition to the other requirements discussed in §§ 4.16–4.18, supra, P's impeachment of W2 explicitly or implicitly accused W2 of recent fabrication, or accused W2 of allowing his testimony to be affected by "a recent improper influence or motive" such as friendship, a bribe, or bias or prejudice. If, instead, P's impeachment of W2 merely tries to show that W2's testimony is simply inaccurate, or that the jury shouldn't believe W2 because he is not a truthful person, D will *not* be able to use Rule 801(d)(1)(B) to introduce W2's prior statements.

The meaning of the term "recent" is discussed in § 4.21, infra.

§ 4.20 QUESTIONS

Question 1. In the bus-auto collision suit (see § 4.11, **Q. 1–2**, supra), after W2 testifies that the bus had the green light, P's attorney cross-examines W2 as follows.

Q.	How did you happen to be at that intersection at one o'clock when the collision occurred?
A.	I had just finished having lunch at a place up the block.
Q.	Do you remember the name of the restaurant?
A.	Uhhhh . . .
Q.	It was the "Bar None," wasn't it?
A.	Yeah.
Q.	And you'd been there that morning since they opened, hadn't you?
A.	Yeah.
Q.	You'd been drinking all morning and afternoon?

A.   I guess. Yes, I was.

Q.   So that by 1 p.m. you were quite intoxicated?

A.   I was feelin' pretty good, but I wasn't drunk or nothin'.

On redirect, D's attorney wants to bring out the fact that at about 1:20 that afternoon W2 told Officer Renko that the bus had the green light. P objects: hearsay. D responds: Rule 801(d)(1)(B). Ruling?

Ans. Objection sustained. P's cross-examination accused W2 of being drunk (and therefore, presumably, in no shape to accurately perceive how the collision occurred); but that is *not* an expressed or implied accusation of recent fabrication or improper influence or motive. ("Under the influence of alcohol" is not the kind of "improper influence" the Rule is concerned with.)

Question 2. Suppose instead P's cross-examination of W2 is as follows.

Q.   You just testified that you saw the car enter the intersection against the red light?

A.   That's right.

Q.   Do you recall being interviewed by PI, an investigator for my law firm, about a month after the collision?

A.   Yes.

Q.   Didn't you tell PI that you didn't really see what caused the collision?

Does this constitute accusing W2 of "recent fabrication"?

Ans. Perhaps. P's cross reveals that W2 made a prior inconsistent statement. Whether this implicitly accuses W2 of "recently fabricating" his current testimony is a judgment call. But as a general rule, merely bringing out a prior inconsistent statement does not constitute an accusation of recent fabrication or improper motive.

Question 3. Suppose instead P's cross-examination of W2 is as follows:

Q.   You testified on direct that the bus had the green light.

A.   That's right.

Q.   Why did you testify that way?

A.   'Cause that's the way it happened.

Q.   That's the only reason?

A.   Yes.

Q.   I see. — Oh, by the way, do you happen to be personally acquainted with the woman who was driving that bus?

A.   Yes —

Q.   And that acquaintanceship is more than just casual, I believe.

A.   We're engaged to be married.

Q.   The driver of the bus is your fiancee?

A.   That's right.

Q.   No further questions.

D later attempts to bring out the fact that approximately 20 minutes after the collision, W2 told Officer Renko that the bus had the green light. P objects: hearsay. D responds: Rule 801(d)(1)(B). Ruling?

Ans. P's cross-examination of W2 implicitly accused W2 of testifying the way he did to protect his fiancee. (Even love is an "improper influence or motive" if it prompts someone to lie under oath.) There is nothing improper with this cross-examination, but it does open the door to any prior consistent statements by W2 — but only if the prior consistent statement rebuts the implicit accusation.

Does this cross-examination open the door to W2's on-the-scene statement to Officer Renko? Not automatically; it depends on the circumstances (*see* § 4.21, *infra*).

§ 4.21   REBUTTING THE ACCUSATION: "RECENT"

A prior consistent statement qualifies as an exception to the hearsay definition only if it rebuts an accusation of "recent" fabrication or "recent" improper motive or influence. So, what does "recent" mean? The past ten minutes? Thirty days? Two years, four months, one week and three days?[3]

In *Tome v. United States*, 513 U.S. 150 (1995), the Supreme Court held that a prior consistent statement is admissible to rebut an accusation of "recent" fabrication, improper influence or motive only if the prior statement was made *before the improper influence or motive arose.*

§ 4.22   QUESTIONS

Question 1. In the bus-auto collision trial, on redirect, W2 testifies that he met the bus driver for the first time at a party several months after the collision. Then D's attorney calls Officer Renko as a witness:

Q.   On the day of the collision, did you interview a witness named W2?

A.   I did.

Q.   Did W2 tell you what he saw?

Q.   Yes. He said —

(P's attorney):   Objection! Hearsay!

(D's attorney):   801(1)(B), Your Honor.

If permitted, Renko will testify that W2 said, "The bus had the green light and the car zipped right into its path." How should the judge rule?

Ans. Objection overruled. The statement to Renko satisfies each of the Rule 801(d)(1)(B) requirements:

---

[3] That's how old my grandson Sam is, on the day I am writing this. — CSF

(1) W2 has testified at the trial and can be recalled for more cross-examination about the statement.

(2) W2's statement to Renko is consistent with his trial testimony.

(3) The cross-examination in § 4.20 **Q. 3** suggests that W2 testified as he did because he wants to protect his fiancee from possible loss of her job. W2's statement to Renko rebuts this implicit accusation, because W2 made the statement before he even met, let alone became engaged to, the bus driver.

Because the statement to Renko was made before W2 was interviewed by P's investigator (§ 4.20 **Q. 2**), that statement also rebuts the accusation in that question that W2's testimony is a "recent" fabrication.

Question 2. Suppose instead W2 had already been engaged to the bus driver at the time of the collision. Would his statement to Renko still have adequate "rebuttal value"?

Ans. According to Supreme Court's reading of Rule 801(d)(1)(A) in *Tome*, the answer is "no," because W2 would have had the same "improper motive" the day of the accident as he did at trial (unless, at the time he made the statement to Renko, he did not yet know that his fiancee was driving that particular bus).

The statement to Renko would, however, still rebut the "recent fabrication" accusation made in § 4.20 **Q. 2**.

§ 4.23   PROCEDURE AND TACTICS

The simplest way to prove that W2 made a prior consistent statement is to ask him: "Do you recall telling Officer Renko, about 20 minutes after the collision, that the bus had the green light?" But if the jury thinks W2's testimony is influenced by his desire to protect the bus driver, they may not believe his claim that he made the statement to Renko. Tactically, therefore, it might be better for D to wait until she can call Officer Renko and have Renko testify about W2's statement.

If testimony about the prior consistent statement is admissible under Fed. R. Evid. 801(d)(1)(B), D's attorney can choose either method of proving that W2 made the statement to Renko; however, the jury is much more likely to believe the testimony of a police officer with no stake in the case, than the fiancé of one of the motorists.

PART D:
STATEMENTS OF PRIOR IDENTIFICATION OF A PERSON

§ 4.24   RULE 801(d)(1)(C)

Fed. R. Evid. 801(d)(1)(C) provides:

(d) Statements That Are Not Hearsay. A statement that meets the following conditions is not hearsay:

(1) *A Declarant-Witness's Prior Statement.* **The declarant testifies and is subject to cross-examination about a prior statement, and the statement:**

. . .

(C) identifies a person as someone the declarant perceived earlier.

[Prior to December 1, 2011, the rule read as follows:

Rule 801(d). A statement is not hearsay if —

(1) The declarant testifies at the trial or hearing and is subject to cross-examination concerning the statement, and the statement is

(C) one of identification of a person made after perceiving the person. . . .

The Federal Rules of Evidence were rewritten solely to make them easier to understand; the Advisory Committee did not intend to make any substantive change in the Rules. The text of the old rule may remain useful in reading court decisions that precede the revision of the rules. Thus, this edition of the Student's Guide provides the text of both the new and the old version of each relevant provision of the Federal Rules of Evidence.]

The rationale underlying the Rule is demonstrated by the following example. On June 1, V was knocked down by two men, and his wallet was taken. A few minutes later he flagged down a passing police car and described the perpetrators. He got into the car, cruised the area with Sergeant Lucy Bates, and suddenly pointed and shouted: "That's one of them!" The sergeant hopped out of her car and arrested D1.

On June 2, V went to the police station and looked through several dozen pages of mugshots. Seeing D2's picture, he told Sergeant Bates: "This looks like the other one."

On June 3, Sergeant Bates phoned V: "Can you come back to the station house at four o'clock tomorrow? We've arranged for a lineup." At the lineup the next day, V selected D1 and D2 out of the ten men in the array. "They're the ones," he told Sergeant Bates.

V did not see D1 or D2 again until the following March, when the case comes to trial. On direct examination, the Assistant D.A. takes V through his carefully rehearsed recitation of what happened to him the prior June 1st. Then comes the dramatic moment when the A.D.A. asks:

Q.   And do you see the men who knocked you down and kicked you and stole your wallet — do you see those men in court today?

A.   Yes, I do.

Q.   Point them out for the judge and jury.

A.   (Pointing) That's them. The guy with the silver shirt and the one sitting next to him with the shaved head.

A.D.A.:   Your Honor, let the record reflect the witness has identified the defendants.

Judge: The record will so reflect.

This may be high drama, but as evidence of defendants' guilt, it is vulnerable to attack on at least two counts. First, it has been ten months between the crime and the trial; a jury might well question whether V can remember his attackers after so long a time. Second, the setting of the courtroom identification is far too suggestive to resolve such doubts: anyone familiar with the layout of an American courtroom could pick out the defendant even if he'd never before laid eyes on him.[4]

V's identification of D1 on the street shortly after the crime, his selection of D2's mug shot the next day, and his identification of both defendants at the June 3 lineup are all far more probative, and far more persuasive, evidence of the defendants' guilt than is the courtroom identification. Each occurred while the crime, and the perpetrators, were fresh in V's mind, and the circumstances of each were far less suggestive than the courtroom identification.[5]

Fed. R. Evid. 801(d)(1)(C) excepts such out-of-court identifications from the hearsay definition on grounds of reliability and necessity. First, they are usually much more reliable than in-court identifications, for the reasons just discussed. Second, admitting evidence of the out-of-court identifications is necessary to permit the jury to fairly evaluate a defendant's guilt or innocence, particularly if (as sometimes happens) the witness at trial cannot any longer identify the perpetrators, or may be too frightened to do so.

To invoke Rule 801(d)(1)(C), a prosecutor[6] must elicit testimony satisfying the following requirements:

1. Sometime prior to trial, declarant perceived a person, and made a statement to someone (usually, but not necessarily, a police officer or prosecutor) identifying that person.

2. The declarant testifies at the current trial and is subject to cross-examination about the statement.

---

[4] On the other hand, someone who is *not* familiar with an American courtroom can make life quite interesting for a prosecutor. When I was in the New York County District Attorney's Office, a colleague tried a robbery case in which the victim, a foreigner, identified the *foreman of the jury* as the perpetrator. What is truly astonishing is that the jury convicted the defendant anyway. Of course it helped that: (a) the foreman and the defendant looked somewhat alike; (b) the defendant had been arrested with the victim's wallet in his pocket; and (c) the foreman apparently had a good sense of humor and, presumably, a solid alibi as well.

[5] Many experts doubt the reliability of eye-witness identification as a general matter — it is very susceptible to inadvertent or intentional suggestion by the police or by the witness him-or-herself. But even given those doubts, V's identification of the robbers (on the street, from a book of mug shots, and at the lineup) are far less suggestive than the in-court identification.

[6] So far as I know, Rule 801(d)(1)(C) has been used only in criminal cases, and only by prosecutors. In appropriate circumstances, however, a defendant, or a civil litigant, could also use the Rule.

§ 4.25   "PERCEIVED" AND "IDENTIFIED"

The prosecutor must show that at some time after the crime, the declarant perceived the defendant. This may have happened in person, on the street or in the station house; or declarant may have picked out D's photograph. The "perceiving" might have been with a sense other than sight. Suppose, for example, D is accused of making extortionate phones calls to V. W1, V's receptionist, never met D, but answered some of the calls. The police thereafter arrange for W1 to hear D's voice (in person, over the phone or on a recording); if W1 is able to identify that voice as the one who made the threatening phone calls, evidence of W1's identification of the voice satisfies the 801(d)(1)(C) "perception" requirement.

It is worth noting that while Fed. R. Evid. 801(d)(1)(C) can resolve the *hearsay* objection to evidence of the prior identification, other objections might still require its exclusion. The Supreme Court has held that if the police employ an unnecessarily suggestive identification procedure, this may in some cases "taint" both the out-of-court identification and the in-court identification, too.

§ 4.26   DECLARANT TESTIFIES, IS SUBJECT TO CROSS-EXAMINATION

See §§ 4.2–4.3.

In *United States v. Owens*, 484 U.S. 554, 559 (1988), the Supreme Court held that so long as declarant testifies and can be cross-examined about his or her out-of-court identification of D, this requirement is satisfied, *even if, at trial, declarant can no longer identify D as the perpetrator*. All that is required is that declarant testify and can be cross-examined about the out-of-court identification.

§ 4.27   PROCEDURE

Evidence of an out-of-court identification will follow one of two sequences:

1. *If declarant is able to make an in-court identification:*

    a. Declarant testifies, describes what he saw or heard the perpetrator do or say, and makes an in-court identification of D as the perpetrator.

    b. Declarant also testifies that at some point after the crime but before the trial, he participated in an identification procedure of some kind (lineup, photograph or whatever) and made a statement to the police identifying D as the perpetrator.

    c. Declarant testifies, "The person I identified at the lineup (photo array, etc.) is the defendant, sitting over there in the gold and green pants."

    d. Declarant is cross-examined by D's attorney.

    e. (Optional:) The prosecutor calls the police officer, who testifies: "When Declarant attended the lineup, he identified D as the perpetrator."

  f. The officer is cross-examined (assuming the prosecutor has called her as a witness).

  g. D may recall declarant for further cross-examination.

 2. *If declarant cannot make an in-court identification:*

a. Declarant testifies, describes what he saw or heard the perpetrator do or say, and is asked:

Q.   Do you see that man in the courtroom today?

A.   I don't know. It's been so long, I really don't remember anymore.

b. Declarant also testifies that at some point after the crime but before the trial, he participated in an identification procedure of some kind (lineup, photograph or whatever) and made a statement (to a police officer, most likely) identifying the perpetrator.

Q.   Can you tell us now who you identified on that occasion?

A.   No, I can't. I'm sorry; like I said, I just don't remember anymore.

Q.   But at the time you attended the lineup, you made a statement to Sergeant Bates identifying the perpetrator?

A.   Yes, I did.

c. (Optional, if the prosecutor is confident of a helpful answer.)

Q.   When you identified the perpetrator at the lineup, were you sure you had the right man?

A.   Oh, yes. I was quite sure at the time. I'm sure I picked out the right man.

d. Declarant is cross-examined by D's attorney.

e. The prosecutor calls Sergeant Bates, who testifies: "When declarant attended the lineup, he identified D as the perpetrator."

f. Sergeant Bates is cross-examined.

g. Thereafter D may recall declarant for further cross-examination.

Chapter 5

EXCEPTIONS TO THE HEARSAY DEFINITION: OPPOSING PARTY'S STATEMENT, RULE 801(d)(2)

PART A:
"OPPOSING PARTY'S STATEMENT"

§ 5.1 OVERVIEW OF RULE 801(d)(2)

Fed. R. Evid. 801(d)(2) contains five exceptions to the hearsay definition. The common theme is that the declarant who made the statement must be a *party* to the lawsuit (or a spokesperson, agent, or co-conspirator of a party); and the litigant who is offering the statement must be the "opposing party" of the declarant.

Rationale. Most Article VIII provisions are based at least in part on the belief that statements made under certain circumstances are trustworthy enough to escape the hearsay ban. The Fed. R. Evid. 801(d)(2) provisions, by contrast, are based on two very different theories:

- First, there is the common-sense conviction that a party should not be permitted to exclude his own statement on hearsay grounds; to allow such an objection would amount to allowing a party to claim, "My own statement should not be admissible against me, because what I said was untrustworthy."

- Second, if a party is unhappy that his own statement is being offered against him, the antidote is simple: he can take the stand and attempt to explain what he said, what he meant, or why the jury should not hold what he said against him.

The Fed. R. Evid. 801(d)(2) provisions can be summarized as follows. In a lawsuit P v. D, P and D are "opposing parties," because they are on opposite sides of the "v". Therefore:

- Any statement D made or adopted is not hearsay, if it is offered in evidence by P. (Fed. R. Evid. 801(d)(2)(A), (B)).

- Any statement made by D's spokesperson, agent, servant, employee or co-conspirator, which satisfies the requirements of Fed. R. Evid. 801(d)(2)(C), (D) or (E) is not hearsay — if offered in evidence by P.

- Similarly, any statement P made or adopted, and any qualifying statement made by P's spokesperson, agent, servant, employee or co-conspirator, is not hearsay — if offered in evidence by D.

PART B:

RULE 801(d)(2)(A): "THE PARTY'S OWN STATEMENT"

§ 5.2   IN GENERAL

Fed. R. Evid. 801(d)(2)(A) provides:

> **(d) Statements That Are Not Hearsay. A statement that meets the following conditions is not hearsay:** . . .
>
> **(2)** *An Opposing Party's Statement.* **The statement is offered against an opposing party and:**
>
>> **(A) was made by the party in an individual or representative capacity;** . . .

[Prior to December 1, 2011, the rule read as follows:

> Rule 801(d). Statements which are not hearsay. A statement is not hearsay if —
>
>> (2) Admission by party-opponent. The statement is offered by the opponent of a party and is
>>
>>> (A) the party's own statement, in either an individual or a representative capacity . . .

The Federal Rules of Evidence were rewritten solely to make them easier to understand; the Advisory Committee did not intend to make any substantive change in the Rules. The text of the old rule may remain useful in reading court decisions that precede the revision of the rules. Thus, this edition of the Student's Guide provides the text of both the new and the old version of each relevant provision of the Federal Rules of Evidence.]

This is the simplest rule in the entire Federal Rules of Evidence — so simple that even law professors have a hard time complicating it. It can be summarized in a single sentence:

> Fed. R. Evid. 801(d)(2)(A) provides that in lawsuit R v. S, if R can prove that S made a statement, S's hearsay objection to the admission of that statement must be overruled.

So long as R and S are on opposite sides of the "v," anything S said that R offers into evidence will be admissible over a hearsay objection (and vice versa, of course).

It doesn't matter who S was speaking to at the time. If R can call a witness who heard S make the statement, S's hearsay objection will be overruled.

It doesn't matter who the witness is. W (the witness) can be R, he can be S's bartender, she can be a tinker, a tailor, a soldier, a sailor; if W heard S say it, and R, S's opposing party in the lawsuit, calls W as a witness to testify about it, S's hearsay objection will be overruled.

It doesn't matter *why* S said it. If W heard S say it, and R, S's opposing party in the lawsuit, calls W as a witness to testify about it, S's hearsay objection will be overruled.

It doesn't matter whether R is the plaintiff and S is the defendant, or the other way around.

It doesn't matter whether S was talking about past events, current conditions, or future expectations; in fact, it doesn't matter *what* S said!

So long as

- W heard S say it, and

- R, S's opposing party in the lawsuit, calls W as a witness to testify about it,

S's hearsay objection will be overruled.

And, of course, the rule applies in exactly the same way if the roles of R and S are reversed — if S calls W2 to testify about something R said, R's hearsay objection must be overruled.

The rationale underlying Fed. R. Evid. 801(d)(2)(A) is that a party should not be permitted to exclude his own statement on the ground that what he said was untrustworthy. The remedy is for the party to take the stand and deny he said it, or explain what he meant, or try to persuade the jury not to rely on it.

§ 5.3 QUESTIONS

Question 1. D contracted to supply P with left-handed gromleys, which P needed to manufacture midget widgets. D delivered, but subsequently P brought a breach of contract action against D, claiming the gromleys D delivered were defective and that, as a result, P had to scrap an entire production run of widgets. D answered that its gromleys complied with contract specifications, and that P's troubles must have been caused by mistakes in P's own production process.

At trial, after P presents his case, D calls W1, who will testify that he was present on March 1 when P inspected several ruined widgets.

Q.   And what, if anything, did P say?

A.   I heard P say, "I can't understand what went wrong. D's gromleys matched the contract specifications to a 'T'!"

P objects that W1's answer is hearsay. Would this be hearsay under Fed. R. Evid. 801(c)?

Ans. Yes. P's statement was made out-of-court; D is offering it in evidence, through W1's testimony, to prove the truth of what P asserted in his statement, i.e., to prove that D's gromleys fulfilled the specifications of D's contract with P.

Question 2. Is it hearsay under Fed. R. Evid. 801(d)(2)(A)?

Ans. No. W1 heard P say it, and D, P's opposing party in the lawsuit, has called W1 as a witness to testify about it. Therefore, P's hearsay objection will be overruled.

Question 3. Suppose P denies ever having said it. Does this change how the judge should rule on P's hearsay objection?

Ans. No. In ruling on admissibility, the judge must assume that W1's testimony is truthful. Later on, if P wants to take the stand to testify and deny he made the statement, he can do so; then it will be for the jury to decide whether P actually made the statement, as W1 claims, and if so, what use they should make of the statement.

Question 4. Suppose, instead, after D rests, P, in rebuttal, calls W2, who testifies:

Q.   Were you present on March 1 when P inspected the production run of midget widgets?

A.   Yes.

Q.   What, if anything, did you hear P say?

A.   I heard P say, "I was afraid it would come out all wrong. D's gromleys missed the contract specifications by a mile!"

Is this evidence admissible, if D objects that it is hearsay?

Ans. No; and yes.

(1)   It *is* hearsay, if P is offering it to prove that D's gromleys failed to comply with contract specifications. Fed. R. Evid. 801(d)(2)(A) does not overcome the hearsay objection, because this time P's statement is not being offered by D, P's opposing party in the lawsuit. Instead, P, the declarant, is offering his *own* statement; Fed. R. Evid. 801(d)(2)(A) never applies in that situation. Objection sustained.

(2)   But W2's testimony is also relevant on a second, subsidiary issue: did P in fact say on March 1 what *W1* claims P said? Because W1's testimony is potentially quite important, P is permitted to offer evidence contradicting that testimony. W2's testimony is relevant to help the jury assess whether W1 testified accurately. If offered for this limited purpose, D's hearsay objection should be overruled, and the evidence admitted.

Question 5. What should D do at this point?

Ans. Request a limiting instruction per Fed. R. Evid. 105. The judge should tell the jury, "You may not consider W2's testimony as proof that D's gromleys were defective. You may consider W2's testimony, however, in deciding whether to credit W1's testimony."

Question 6. Suppose, in **Q. 4**, P made his statement to W2 on March 3, not on March 1. When W2 seeks to testify about P's statement, D objects: "Hearsay!" Does P have a valid argument? How should the judge rule?

Ans. As we have seen in the answer to **Q. 4**, if P's statement to W2 on March 3 is offered to prove that the gromleys were defective, it is clearly hearsay. And, unlike the facts in **Q. 4**, here there is no legitimate non-hearsay purpose for W2's testimony. Objection sustained.

Question 7. Someone hit a golf ball through P's window, shattering it and causing P substantial injuries. An hour or so later, W1 told D, P's neighbor, what had happened. "It was probably my no-good son," D exclaimed. "If I told him once I told him a thousand times, not to hit golf balls in the back yard!" Because this occurred in a jurisdiction that makes parents liable for the torts of their minor children, P sued D, alleging that D's son hit the ball. At trial, P calls W1 to testify as to D's statement. D's attorney interposes a hearsay objection. Ruling?

Ans. Overruled: Fed. R. Evid. 801(d)(2)(A). D, the declarant, is the opposing party of P, who is offering the statement.

Question 8. D's attorney further objects that because D lacked first-hand knowledge whether his son hit the golf ball, the evidence should be excluded on that ground. Ruling?

Ans. Overruled! First-hand knowledge by the declarant is almost always a requirement for admissibility, but *not* if the statement fits one of the Fed. R. Evid. 801(d)(2) provisions.

§ 5.4   "OPPOSING PARTY" ("PARTY-OPPONENT")

As I've already mentioned, you can determine whether the declarant and the party offering the statement are "opposing parties" simply by looking at who is suing whom. If they are on opposite sides of the "v," they are opposing parties. Remember, though, that where plaintiff sues several defendants, each defendant is considered a separate party. Thus, in P v Apple, Berry, and Cantaloupe, if plaintiff offers a statement by Apple, it is admissible over a hearsay objection as to Apple per Rule 801(d)(2)(A), but that rule does not secure its admissibility against Berry and Cantaloupe.

In case law, law review articles, etc., you will often see the phrase "party-opponent." That's the term Fed. R. Evid. 801(d)(2) used until the rewrite of the Rules became effective on Dec. 1, 2011. And for the first semester or so after December 1, your professor may slip up from time to time and refer to an "admission by a party-opponent." He or she of course means to say "an opposing party's statement." Be forgiving if your prof uses the old vocabulary occasionally. After all, some evidence professors have been teaching this course since the Federal Rules first became effective in 1975,[1] and old habits die hard.

§ 5.5   QUESTIONS

Question 1. P purchased a Rockchecker electric saw at X's local Rockchecker hardware store. A year later, he brought it back for servicing. One week afterwards, the blade flew off the saw and badly injured P. P brought suit against Rockchecker, alleging negligent manufacture, and against X, alleging faulty and negligent servicing. Rockchecker and X filed a joint defense, asserting that the saw was well-manufactured and had been properly serviced, and that P must have abused the saw by using it in a reckless manner. The party line-up is:

---

[1] Not me, though; I'm much younger than that. I didn't start teaching evidence until 1978!

P v R & X

If permitted, W1 will testify that she heard X say, "I never should have let P's saw leave my store in that condition." If W1 so testifies on behalf of P, is X's statement hearsay?

Ans. No. X, the declarant, is an opposing party of P; hence, Fed. R. Evid. 801(d)(2)(A) overcomes the hearsay objection.

Question 2. Suppose Rockchecker, not P, called W1 as a witness. If W1 testifies about X's statement on behalf of Rockchecker, is X's statement hearsay?

Ans. Yes. Rockchecker and X are codefendants, not opposing parties. Therefore X has a valid hearsay objection if Rockchecker (rather than P) offers the statement.

Question 3. Suppose when P filed suit against Rockchecker and X, Rockchecker had filed an affirmative defense and cross claim against *X*, asserting that X's faulty servicing, not the saw itself, caused the malfunction. Would X's statement be hearsay if Rockchecker called W1?

Ans. Logically, you might think the answer should be no, because now the suit isn't just P v. Rockchecker and X, with Rockchecker and X on the same side of the "v"; rather, it is:

P v. Rockchecker;

P v. X;

Rockchecker v. X.

In a real sense, Rockchecker is an opposing party of X. Logically, therefore, X's hearsay objection should be overruled.

Unfortunately (*I* think it's unfortunate, anyhow), courts generally do not agree; even when each defendant blames the other, they do not consider X and Rockchecker to be "opposing parties." So in our lawsuit, Rockchecker is out of luck: it cannot call W1 to offer X's statement at this trial.

§ 5.6 DEFINING "OPPOSING PARTIES" IN CRIMINAL CASES

Suppose D is accused of assaulting L. If L sues D for damages, they are opposing parties, and if D offers a statement made by L into evidence, D can use Fed. R. Evid. 801(d)(2)(A) to overcome L's hearsay objection. But if D is prosecuted by the state or federal government, the case is no longer, L v. D; it is State v. D or United States v. D. L is no longer a *party* in the case (even though he's the alleged victim, complainant and key witness). In the criminal prosecution, therefore, D cannot use Fed. R. Evid. 801(d)(2)(A) to secure admissibility of statements by L.

If L's testimony at trial is inconsistent with any prior statements he made, however, D *will* be able to use those prior inconsistent statements pursuant to Fed. R. Evid 613 for the limited purpose of impeaching L's trial testimony. *See* § 4.6.

§ 5.7   PROVING THE PARTY MADE THE STATEMENT

The usual way to prove that a party made a statement is to call a witness who heard him or her say it, but that is not the only way. If D's statement was in writing, for example, P can call a witness who can authenticate the document as being in D's handwriting. A litigant can prove that her opposing party made a statement by playing a recording of it (assuming the conversation was recorded legally) and having a witness identify D's voice. And so on.

§ 5.8   "REPRESENTATIVE CAPACITY"

Occasionally one person legally "stands in" for another person or interest. The most frequent situation arises when an executor or administrator is appointed to handle the estate of someone who has died: he "represents" the estate. Suppose E is the executor of X's estate, and E sues M, or is sued by M, with regard to the estate. (For example, E may allege that M owed money to X, and sues on behalf of X's estate to recover it; or M may claim that X owed him money, and sues X's estate to recover it.) In that law suit, whatever E says that is relevant to the law suit is treated like statements "by the estate." Thus, if M offers evidence of such a statement and E objects on hearsay grounds, the objection is overruled per Rule 801(d)(2)(A).

The same situation may arise if someone is mentally incompetent, and a trustee or guardian is appointed to handle his affairs.

§ 5.9   SIXTH AMENDMENT CONFRONTATION CLAUSE

A defendant in a criminal case cannot assert a Confrontation Clause objection when a prosecutor offers the defendant's own statement against him. See § 6.14[2], infra.

§ 5.10   OTHER OBJECTIONS

Just a reminder: all Fed. R. Evid. 801(2)(A) does (all *any* Article VIII provision can do, for that matter) is overcome a hearsay objection. If additional objections are made to the evidence, the offering party will have to overcome those, as well, before the evidence is admissible.

§ 5.11   QUESTIONS

Question 1. D sold P some photography chemicals; when P used them, the chemicals ruined the film on a lengthy shoot P had done for her biggest client. P made an irate call to D, who promised to check into it. "You'd better," P said, "because it's going to cost me thousands of dollars to do the shoot again — if I don't lose the account altogether."

A few days later D called P back. "Look," he said, "the last thing I want is to get tied up in a lawsuit. You're right; the chemicals were defective. Let's see if we can work out an agreement on damages."

P's worst fears were realized: she lost the client, and suffered substantial harm to her professional reputation. She demanded $250,000 in damages, which D was unwilling to pay. P sued. At trial, P sought to testify to D's acknowledgment that the chemicals were defective. D objects that what he said to P was hearsay. Ruling?

Ans. Overruled. Fed. R. Evid. 801(d)(2)(A).

Question 2. What other objection should D assert? How should the judge rule?

Ans. If you've studied Fed. R. Evid. 408, you recognized (I hope) that, because D's remarks clearly were in the context of an attempt to compromise potential litigation ("the last thing I want is to get tied up in a lawsuit"), the entire statement should be excluded.

The point is that while Fed. R. Evid. 801(d)(2)(A) answers the hearsay objection, you still must analyze any other issues that exist, before you can determine admissibility.

Remember, too, that other issues (aside from evidence law) may have to be addressed. For example, in a criminal case, if a prosecutor offers a defendant's confession in evidence at trial, Fed. R. Evid. 801(d)(2)(A) overcomes the defendant's hearsay objection; but the prosecutor must still convince the judge that the police officers had given the defendant adequate *Miranda* warnings and that D made a knowing and intelligent waiver of her privilege against self-incrimination.

PART C:
RULE 801(d)(2)(B): ADOPTED STATEMENTS

§ 5.12   IN GENERAL

Fed. R. Evid. 801(d)(2)(B) provides:

(d) Statements That Are Not Hearsay. A statement that meets the following conditions is not hearsay:

> **(2)** *An Opposing Party's Statement.* **The statement is offered against an opposing party and: . . .**
>
> > **(B) is one the party manifested that it adopted or believed to be true; . . .**

[Prior to December 1, 2011, the rule read as follows:

> Rule 801(d). Statements which are not hearsay. A statement is not hearsay if
> —
>
> > (2) Admission by party-opponent. The statement is offered by the opponent of a party and is
> >
> > > (B) a statement of which the party has manifested an adoption or belief in its truth . . .

The Federal Rules of Evidence were rewritten solely to make them easier to understand; the Advisory Committee did not intend to make any substantive change in the Rules. The text of the old rule may remain useful in reading court decisions that precede the revision of the rules. Thus, this edition of the Student's Guide provides the text of both the new and the old version of each relevant provision of the Federal Rules of Evidence.]

Two cars collide. Twenty minutes later a police officer arrives on the scene. X, a bystander, walks up to the officer and says, "I saw the whole thing, officer. The red car ran the red light; that's what caused everything." D, the driver of the red car, nods and says "That's right, officer." At trial P seeks to offer evidence of this exchange, either through his own testimony, or the officer's, or through anyone else who heard what X and D said. D objects, arguing that X's statement is hearsay. Ruling?

By itself, X's out-of-court statement, offered by P to prove the truth of the matter asserted (that D ran the light), is hearsay. But D's adoption of X's statement ("That's right, officer") in essence makes it his (D's) own statement, which P can now offer against D, P's opposing party.

Fed. R. Evid. 801(d)(2)(B) covers two somewhat different situations: expressed or explicit adoptive admissions, and implicit or tacit admissions.

§ 5.13   EXPRESSED ADOPTIVE ADMISSIONS

In the example in the previous section, D expressly adopted the bystander's statement when he said, "That's right, officer." So long as D adopted or endorsed someone else's statement clearly and unambiguously, then P, who is D's opposing party in the case being tried, can offer the declarant's statement and D's adoption of it as an admission by D under Fed. R. Evid. 801(d)(2)(B), and D's hearsay objection will be overruled.

Fed. R. Evid. 801(d)(2)(B) applies to written as well as oral statements, so long as the party's adoption of it is clear and unambiguous. Signing a document prepared by someone else, for example, is often considered to be an adoption of what is stated in the document.

According to the Advisory Committee, Fed. R. Evid. 801(d)(2)(B) can apply even if the party does not know what the declarant actually said. Suppose W comes up to P and says, "I've been talking to X about your dispute with D." P responds, "X is a reliable person and knows what he is talking about." P thereby "adopts" whatever X said on the subject. If it turns out that what X said to W is helpful to D, D can call W to testify to what X said *and* to P's adoption of it.

§ 5.14   IMPLICIT OR TACIT ADMISSIONS

X says something in Y's presence. Y remains silent. In a subsequent lawsuit in which Y is a party, may Y's silence be offered as a tacit admission that what X said was true?

The answer depends on circumstances. To secure admissibility under this theory, the party offering X's statement as an admission by Y must show, at a minimum, the following:

1.   The party (Y) heard and understood the statement and its significance.

2.   Y had first-hand knowledge of the event, condition or situation X was speaking about.

3.   X's statement, and the circumstances in which X made the statement, were such that Y likely would have responded to or denied the statement if he did not mean to accept what X said. (Or, as the Advisory Committee Note to Fed. R. Evid. 801(d)(2)(B) puts it, "When silence is relied upon, the theory is that the person would, under the circumstances, protest the statement made in his presence, if untrue.")

The first requirement is self-explanatory. Concerning the second, note that, unlike all the other Fed. R. Evid. 801(d)(2) statements (including expressed adoptive admissions), there *is* a first-hand knowledge requirement for implicit adoptive admissions.

The third requirement is the most important, and the most difficult to resolve. As the Advisory Committee comments, "The decision . . . calls for an evaluation in terms of probable human behavior." Almost any fact can be relevant in making this determination:

• Who was X? If she was someone Y respected, Y's silence strongly suggests that he acquiesced in the truth of Y's statement. On the other hand, Y might have respected X too much to disagree publicly, even if Y was convinced that X was incorrect. If X was someone Y was likely to ignore, by contrast (an obviously intoxicated person, for example), Y's silence suggests nothing of the kind.

• Did some social, physical or psychological distraction prevent Y from responding? If X said something to Y about a business deal as Y's beloved grandmother was being lowered into her grave, Y's refusal to respond was probably prompted by grief or a sense of propriety, and therefore was not a tacit acknowledgment that what X said was true.

§ 5.15   CONVERSATIONS AMONG A GROUP

Eighteen months ago, L, M, N, and Q discussed whether or not to engage in certain conduct. Now L, M and N are being sued, and Q is called as a witness. Q can remember what the conversation was about — "we were discussing whether to do X, Y and Z" — and how it ended: ". . . and by the end of the conversation, everyone agreed to do X, Y and Z." But Q doesn't remember precisely who said what. In this situation, courts often hold that the conversation as a whole is non-hearsay (i.e., is admissible over a hearsay objection) against anyone who participated in it, on the theory that if any participant had *not* agreed to do X, Y and Z, he or she would have said so.

§ 5.16   CONSTITUTIONAL ISSUES IN CRIMINAL CASES

A defendant's refusal to respond to an accusation in a noncustodial setting should be analyzed on the same basis as in a civil case — so long as police officers are not involved in the situation. See § 5.18, **Q. 1**, infra. Applying the implicit or tacit admission rule in criminal cases becomes complicated, however, when the police are involved.

1. Once a defendant has been given *Miranda* warnings ("You have a right to remain silent; anything you say can be used against you in court . . ."), a prosecutor cannot use a defendant's refusal to answer questions as a tacit admission. To do so would violate the Fifth Amendment.

2. If a person has been arrested and a police offer questions her *without* giving the *Miranda* warnings, this also violates the Fifth Amendment.

3. Suppose, though, N is not in custody when the police question her. PO is investigating the theft of a valuable piece of equipment from an office building. "Excuse me, ma'am, from what others tell me, you were the last one in the building last night. Is that true?" N replies, "I'm not saying anything." Some courts hold that the state may have PO (or anyone else who was there) testify about this exchange, on the theory that N's refusal to answer was a tacit acknowledgment that she in fact was the last one in the building that night. Other courts hold that the Fifth Amendment precludes such use.

4. Suppose a police officer is with several other people in the room, and someone (not the police officer) says, "Why don't you ask N? She was the last person to leave the building!" N says nothing in response. Here again, the courts are divided: some courts hold that the state may have PO (or anyone else who was there) testify about this exchange, on the theory that N's refusal to answer was a tacit acknowledgment that she in fact was the last one in the building that night. Other courts hold that the Fifth Amendment precludes such use.

§ 5.17   SIXTH AMENDMENT CONFRONTATION CLAUSE

A defendant in a criminal case cannot assert a Confrontation Clause objection when a prosecutor offers in evidence a statement which the defendant has explicitly or tacitly adopted. See § 6.14[2], infra.

§ 5.18   QUESTIONS

Question 1. On January 2, two men rob a bank. A week later, S is arrested and charged with being one of the robbers. In May, D is arrested and charged with being the other robber. At D's trial, the prosecutor calls W.

Q.   Do you recall an incident involving D and S that took place in mid-January?

A.   Yeah. I was hangin' out with D when S walked up to us. D said "Hey, I heard you got busted for that bank robbery." S said, "That's right. But don't worry, I haven't told nobody about you, so you're still in the clear."

Q.   And what did D say?

A.   D didn't say nothing.

D objects that all of this is inadmissible hearsay. Ruling?

Ans. Overruled. The clear implication of S's remark ("I haven't told nobody about you, so you're in the clear") is that D was the other robber. We would expect an innocent man to vigorously deny this implication — "What d'you mean, you haven't told nobody about me — there's nothin' *to* tell!" or words to that effect. D's silence therefore may reasonably be interpreted as a tacit admission that he was the other robber.

Question 2. Police received a phone call about a late-night store break-in. They arrived as two men come running out. After a chase, the police arrested Dark and Stormy and charged them with being the burglars.[2] As they were being driven to the police station, Dark said to Stormy, "I can't believe we got caught. And there wasn't even anything much in the place worth taking!" Stormy remained silent.

At Dark and Stormy's trial, each defendant insists that he was never in the store; that the police arrested him merely because he happened to be in the vicinity. The prosecutor calls a police officer to testify to what Dark said, and Stormy's failure to respond. Both defendants object that the testimony will be inadmissible hearsay. Ruling?

Ans. As to Dark, overruled: Fed. R. Evid. 801(d)(2)(A). The prosecutor and Dark are "opposing parties," so Rule 801(d)(2)(A) allows the prosecutor to introduce Dark's statement againt him.

But Stormy did not make the statement, so the prosecutor cannot use Fed. R. Evid. 802(d)(2)(A) to introduce Dark's statement against Stormy. Instead, as to Stormy, the prosecutor's theory is that his silence is a tacit admission under Fed. R. Evid. 801(d)(2)(B), but this is a weak argument. First, if the defendants had been given *Miranda* warnings, the fact that Stormy exercised his right to remain silent cannot be used against him. Even if no warnings had been given, an innocent person in Stormy's situation might well decide that the smartest thing to do is keep his mouth shut. Stormy's objection should be sustained.

Question 3. Thus, the evidence is admissible against Dark but inadmissible against Stormy. Nevertheless the jury is likely to consider Dark's statement against Stormy even if the judge gives a limiting instruction (Fed. R. Evid. 105). How should the judge handle the resulting problem?

Ans. In essence, there are three options. (1) Try Dark and Stormy separately; the prosecutor can use the statement in Darks's trial, not in Stormy's. (2) Exclude the statement altogether in a joint trial of Dark and Stormy because a limiting instruction is inadequate to protect Stormy's right to a fair trial. (3) Redact (edit) Dark's statement, if possible, so the jury will not infer that it incriminates Stormy as well. In essence, the judge could instruct the officer: when you testify about this in front of the

---

[2] I guess it just wasn't Dark and Stormy's night, was it?

jury, say that Dark said "I can't believe *I* got caught" not ". . . *we* got caught." This gives the prosecutor what she is entitled to against Dark, while protecting Stormy somewhat from the risk that the jury will improperly use Dark's statement against Stormy as well.[3]

PART D:
RULE 801(d)(2)(C): STATEMENTS BY A PARTY'S AUTHORIZED SPOKESPERSON

§ 5.19   IN GENERAL

Fed. R. Evid. 801(d)(2)(C) provides as follows:

(d) Statements That Are Not Hearsay. A statement that meets the following conditions is not hearsay:

(2) *An Opposing Party's Statement.* The statement is offered against an opposing party and:

(C) was made by a person whom the party authorized to make a statement on the subject; . . .

The statement must be considered but does not by itself establish the declarant's authority under (C); . . . .

[Prior to December 1, 2011, the rule read as follows:

Rule 801(d). Statements which are not hearsay. A statement is not hearsay if —

(2) Admission by party-opponent. The statement is offered by the opponent of a party and is . . .

(c) a statement by a person authorized to make a statement concerning the subject, . . . The contents of the statement shall be considered but are not alone sufficient to establish the declarant's authority under subparagraph (C) . . .

The Federal Rules of Evidence were rewritten solely to make them easier to understand; the Advisory Committee did not intend to make any substantive change in the Rules. The text of the old rule may remain useful in reading court decisions that precede the revision of the rules. Thus, this edition of the Student's Guide provides the text of both the new and the old version of each relevant provision of the Federal Rules of Evidence.]

---

[3] Stormy's attorney may argue that the jury might use Dark's statement as evidence of Stormy's guilt even if it is redacted and the judge gives the limiting instruction. The judge's response is likely to be, "Counselor, I'm doing my best to give your client a *fair* trial; don't expect a *perfect* trial."

It is simple common sense that if X authorized S to speak for him on a subject, whatever S said on that subject while acting as X's spokesperson should be admissible against X. Fed. R. Evid. 801(d)(2)(C) provides that such statements, when offered at trial against X, are not hearsay. Under this provision, in a lawsuit (X v. Y or Y v. X), to overcome a hearsay objection by X, Y does *not* have to show that X authorized S to make the *specific* statement in question. It is enough for Y to show that X authorized S to speak for X on the subject.

When an attorney represents a client, for example, she is that client's authorized spokesperson on all matters relating to the subject of the representation. (It's not for nothing that lawyers are sometimes called "mouthpieces.") Thus, anything the attorney says on the client's behalf, whether in pleadings, in comments to the media, during interviews of potential witnesses, etc., if offered against the client, is excluded from the definition of hearsay by Fed. R. Evid. 801(d)(2)(C).[4] It is important to remember, once you are practicing law, that "anything you say may be used against your client."

Two issues sometimes arise regarding Fed. R. Evid. 801(d)(2)(C).

1. To use Fed. R. Evid. 801(d)(2)(C), Y must first show that S was in fact authorized by X to speak for X on the subject; S's statement, by itself, cannot satisfy this requirement.

2. The rule covers statements made "in-house" by one agent to another or by the agent to the principal, as well as statements made by an agent to someone unaffiliated with his principal.

The first issue is discussed in § 5.20. As to the second issue, because the same question arises with regard to Fed. R. Evid. 801(d)(2)(D), discussion is reserved to § 5.23.

§ 5.20   PROVING DECLARANT WAS AN AUTHORIZED SPOKESPERSON

The party seeking to admit the statement has the burden of convincing the judge by a preponderance of the evidence that the declarant was his opposing party's authorized spokesperson. The trick here is to realize that S's out-of-court statement, "I am authorized to speak for X," if offered to prove that S is authorized to speak for X, is hearsay. In assessing admissibility, the final sentence of Fed. R. Evid. 801(d)(2) directs that the judge should consider the statement but the statement "does not by itself establish the declarant's authority under (C); . . ."

---

[4] Remember, though, that Fed. R. Evid. 801(d)(2)(C) does not automatically assure that such statements are admissible against the client. Article VIII provisions don't guarantee admissibility; they only overcome a hearsay objection. Fed. R. Evid. 801(d)(2)(C) statements might be excluded on a variety of other grounds, such as Fed. R. Evid. 401–403, or 408–411.

§ 5.21 QUESTIONS

Question 1. On March 1, Y receives a letter from S:

Dear Ms Y:

I represent the Wingding Widget Company. I know that you utilize widgets in your factory, and Wingding wants to be your sole supplier.

To persuade you to purchase your widgets from us, we will sell you 1,000 widgets a month at the incredibly low price of $2 per widget, satisfaction guaranteed! Not only that; we'll deliver them to you at no extra charge!

Please call me at your earliest convenience.

Sincerely,
S
Sales Representative,
Wingding Widget Company, Inc.

Y, who is familiar with the excellent reputation of the Wingding Widget Company and is delighted with the low price, calls S and orders 1,000 widgets to be delivered to her factory on April 1. At the same time, she cancels her existing contract to purchase widgets from another supplier at $3 each.

April 1 comes, but the widgets don't. Y calls S back, only to learn that the number is disconnected. Next, she calls Wingding's main headquarters, and is connected with M, the company's sales manager. M tells her, "I'm sorry, ma'am, but S was never a representative of ours. We'll be happy to sell you widgets at $4.50 each, plus a delivery charge." Holding her temper with difficulty, Y says a cold "No thank you!" and hangs up. Eventually she finds another supplier at $4 per widget. Now she sues Wingding, alleging that the extra expense and production delays caused by its breach of contract cost her $35,000.

On the merits, should Y be able to recover damages from Wingding?

Ans. It depends. If S in fact had been a salesperson for Wingding on March 1, Wingding should be found liable, even if S was not supposed to go below $4 per widget, because, according to the law of agency, an employer is responsible for the acts, promises, etc. of its agent.[5] But if S had *falsely* represented himself to be an Wingding salesperson, then Wingding cannot be held liable, because neither Wingding nor any of its agents had anything to do with Y's dilemma.

Question 2. If Y seeks to testify about S's statements, are S's statements admissible over Wingding's hearsay objection?

Ans. The law of evidence takes the same basic approach to whether S's statements should be *admissible* against Wingding. *If* S was in fact a salesman for Wingding, Fed. R. Evid. 801(d)(2)(C) overcomes Wingding's hearsay objection, because a salesman is

---

[5] This is so, as a matter of agency law, even if Wingding had ordered S not to offer Widgets to anyone for less than $4.50 each.

(in the language of Fed. R. Evid. 801(d)(2)(C) "a person whom the party [Wingding] authorized to make a statement on the subject [of what the company sells and for how much]." But *before* Y can use the statement against Wingding, Y must show, by evidence independent of the statement as well as the statement itself, that S was Wingding's agent at the time S made the statement.

Question 3. How can Y attempt to show this?

Ans. In a variety of ways. Y can subpoena Wingding's personnel records to see if S was in fact a salesman for Wingding when he made the offer to Y. Y can subpoena other employees of Wingding, to elicit testimony that S was a salesman there; Y can subpoena S (if he can be found) and have him testify; and so on. But Y *cannot* establish that S was Wingding's agent simply by taking the stand herself and testifying, "S told me he was Wingding's agent."

If Y succeeds in offering offered evidence independent of S's statement showing that S, the declarant, was Wingding's agent, S's statement ("Wingding will sell you all the widgets you want at $2 each") will be admitted over Wingding's hearsay objection.

§ 5.22 SIXTH AMENDMENT CONFRONTATION CLAUSE

Applications of the Confrontation Clause to statements falling within Fed. R. Evid. 801(d)(2)(C) are discussed in § 6.14[4], infra.

PART E:
RULE 801(d)(2)(D): STATEMENTS BY A PARTY'S AGENT OR EMPLOYEE

§ 5.23 IN GENERAL

Fed. R. Evid. 801(d)(2)(D) provides as follows:

(d) Statements That Are Not Hearsay. A statement that meets the following conditions is not hearsay:

(2) *An Opposing Party's Statement*. The statement is offered against an opposing party and:

(D) was made by the party's agent or employee on a matter within the scope of that relationship and while it existed; . . .

The statement must be considered but does not by itself establish . . . the existence or scope of the relationship under (D); . . .

[Prior to December 1, 2011, the rule read as follows:

Rule 801(d). Statements which are not hearsay. A statement is not hearsay if
—

(2) Admission by party-opponent. The statement is offered by the opponent of a party and is . . .

> (D) a statement by the party's agent or servant concerning a matter within the scope of the agency or employment, made during the existence of the relationship. . . . The contents of the statement shall be considered but are not alone sufficient to establish . . . the agency or employment relationship and scope thereof under subparagraph (D), . . .

The Federal Rules of Evidence were rewritten solely to make them easier to understand; the Advisory Committee did not intend to make any substantive change in the Rules. The text of the old rule may remain useful in reading court decisions that precede the revision of the rules. Thus, this edition of the Student's Guide provides the text of both the new and the old version of each relevant provision of the Federal Rules of Evidence.]

At common law, a statement by an agent was admissible against his principal or employer as an "admission" only if the agent had been specifically authorized by the principal to make statements on that particular subject. (The common law rule is restated without significant change in Fed. R. Evid. 801(d)(2)(C). *See* §§ 5.19 and 5.20.)

Courts gradually became dissatisfied with this approach, however, because it often resulted in the loss of valuable, reliable evidence. In response to this dissatisfaction, Fed. R. Evid. 801(d)(2)(D) greatly expands the common law rule governing admissibility of agents' and employees' statements. The party offering the statement need only show the following:

1. The declarant was his opposing party's "agent or employee." *See* § 5.24.

2. The statement concerned "a matter within the scope" of the [declarant's] agency or employment.

3. The statement was made "while [that relationship] existed," i.e., while the declarant was working for the opposing party, not before she was hired or after she quit or was fired.

Two additional issues sometimes arise that are worth mentioning here:

4. The party offering the statement need *not* show that the declarant had first-hand knowledge of the particular event or situation that was the subject of her statement.

5. The rule covers statements made "in-house" by one agent of the party to another or by the agent to the party, as well as statements made by an agent to someone unaffiliated with that party.

The rationale underlying the rule is that an employee would not make a statement detrimental to his employer about a subject within the employee's responsibilities, unless the employee had good reason to believe the statement to be true.

§ 5.24   "AGENT OR EMPLOYEE . . ."

The rule uses the term "agent or employee." Clearly this covers any standard employer-employee relationship.

As to other relationships, however, the law is less clear. Suppose, for example, XYZ Corp. hires an R, an independent contractor or outside expert, to investigate or study a matter or audit certain records. In such a case, XYZ may well be relying on the fact that R is indeed independent, and not a part of XYZ. In such cases, many courts conclude that R is not an "agent or employee" of XYZ, and R's report to XYZ does not fall within Fed. R. Evid. 801(d)(2)(D).

On the other hand, suppose R's report reaches certain conclusions: "The manufacturing process has the following flaws . . . Therefore, I recommend the following changes in the process. . . ." If XYZ implements R's recommendations, someone suing XYZ might reasonably argue that by accepting R's recommendations, XYZ tacitly adopted R's conclusions.

In determining the nature of the relationship — was R an employee, or an independent contractor — we focus on the actual facts, not what XYZ called the relationship. If R has been working pretty much full time for XYZ for several years, has an office at XYZ, and has little or no outside income, a court should probably consider R an employee for purposes of Fed. R. Evid. 801(d)(2)(D) even if, technically, XYZ lists R as an "independent contractor."[6]

§ 5.25   BURDEN OF PROOF; EVIDENCE TO BE CONSIDERED

As a rule, the party offering the statement has the burden of satisfying the three requirements set forth in § 5.23 by a preponderance of the evidence. The rule explicitly directs that judge should consider the statement, but that the statement "does not by itself establish . . . the existence or scope of the relationship under (D); . . ."

---

[6] For an example of how complex and factually specific that issue can become, consider the government's perjury prosecution of former San Francisco Giant outfielder Barry Bonds. Greg Anderson was Bonds' personal trainer. On several occasions he brought blood samples to BALCO Laboratories, Inc. and told BALCO officials that the samples were Bonds' blood. If Anderson was acting as Bonds' agent when he brought those samples to BALCO, his statements (that they were Bonds' blood) would be admissible against Bonds; and since BALCO's analysis of the blood revealed the presence of steroids, that would be very useful evidence to help the government prove that Bonds lied when he told a grand jury that he did not knowingly take steroids. The trial judge concluded that Anderson had been acting as an independent contractor, not as Bonds' agent, and excluded those statements. The government appealed. The Ninth Circuit panel, by a 2-to-1 vote, concluded that the trial judge's decision was not an abuse of discretion. The majority and dissenting opinions devoted more than thirty pages to the agent-vs-independent contractor issue. U.S. v. Bonds, 608 F.3d 495 (9th Cir. 2010).

§ 5.26 QUESTIONS

Question 1. P, while driving in his brand new Decatur Daredevil, suffers serious injury in a collision. While P is recovering from his injuries, X comes to visit him. "Sorry to hear what happened," X tells P. "I'm an engineer for Decatur, and I worked on the brakes of the Daredevil. I tried to tell my boss they were designed badly, but he wouldn't listen. If the company knew I was telling you this, they'd fire me, but I think you have a right to know."

P sues the Decatur Auto Company, alleging that defective brakes caused the collision. At trial, P wants to testify about X's statement; Decatur objects that it is hearsay. Ruling?

Ans. Apply the checklist in § 5.23.

At this point, P has offered no evidence other than X's statement to show that X *was* in fact an employee of Decatur, or that he helped design the brakes of the Daredevil, or that he was still a Decatur employee at the time he made the statement. Unless he can do so, the statement cannot satisfy the Fed. R. Evid. 801(d)(2)(D) requirements.

In this respect, Fed. R. Evid. 801(d)(2)(D) is identical to Fed. R. Evid. 801(d)(2)(C) (*see* §§ 5.19-5.21).

Question 2. On March 1, Farmer orally contracted with Cropduster Co. for Cropduster to spray Farmer's fields. Subsequently insects infest Farmer's fields, and the crops are ruined. On September 1, Farmer files suit, claiming that Cropduster failed to spray his fields with insecticide as Cropduster had agreed to do. In his answering papers, Cropduster replies that the contract called for Cropduster to spray a weed killer, not insecticide, and that Cropduster's employee Pilot in fact sprayed weed killer over Farmer's fields. Consider the relevance, and the admissibility as an admission, of the following evidence.

In November at a pre-trial deposition of Ms Brooks, secretary for Mr. Duster, Cropduster's CEO, Farmer elicited the following testimony.

Q.   Did Mr. Duster and Pilot have a conversation on September 5, shortly after Farmer filed his lawsuit?

A.   Yes. Mr. Duster called Pilot into the office, and asked: "What did you spray on Farmer's fields?" Pilot responded: "I must have goofed. I think you told me insecticide, but I sprayed weed killer by mistake. Sorry about that! Incidentally, today's my last day on the job — I start my new job next month with the Environmental Protection Administration."

At trial, Farmer calls Ms Brooks as a witness, and asks her the same question. Cropduster Co. objects that Pilot's remarks to Duster constitute hearsay; Farmer responds by citing Fed. R. Evid. 801(d)(2)(D). How should the judge rule, and why?

Ans. Pilot's out-of-court statement to Mr. Duster, which was overheard by Ms Brooks, is admissible under Fed. R. Evid. 801(d)(2)(D) when offered by Farmer against Cropduster Co. Applying the checklist of requirements and issues, we see that the statement passes all the tests.

1. Pilot, the declarant, was Cropduster Co.'s agent or employee.

2. The statement concerned a "matter within the scope" of Pilot's job for Cropduster.

3. Pilot made this statement to Mr. Duster while Pilot was still an employee of Cropduster.

4. Pilot had first-hand knowledge of the subject-matter of the statement (what Pilot sprayed) (although this is not a requirement for admissibility).

5. Although this is an "in-house," employee-to-employer statement, the rule covers such statements; hence this is no reason to exclude it.

Question 3. A month after deposing Ms Brooks, Farmer's attorney deposed Pilot, as follows:

Q.   What did Mr. Duster tell you to spray on Farmer's fields?

A.   He told me to spray insecticide, but I sprayed weed killer by mistake.

At trial, instead of calling Pilot as a witness, Farmer offers a transcript of Pilot's deposition testimony in evidence. Cropduster objects that the testimony is hearsay. Farmer responds that Pilot's pretrial deposition testimony is admissible under Fed. R. Evid. 801(d)(2)(D). How should the judge rule, and why?

Ans. Objection sustained. Pilot's statement in his deposition fails to satisfy the first requirement of Fed. R. Evid. 801(d)(2)(D), because by the time Pilot was deposed, he was no longer an employee of Cropduster. (We know from Ms Brooks's testimony in **Q. 2** that Pilot left Cropduster Co. to take a position with EPA in September, shortly after Ms Brooks's overheard the conversation between Mr. Duster and Pilot; Pilot wasn't deposed by Farmer until November.)[7]

Question 4. How could Farmer introduce the equivalent evidence?

Ans. Call Pilot as a witness! If Pilot testifies at trial that he was told to spray insecticide but sprayed weed killer by mistake, Cropduster might object that Duster's instruction to Pilot, "Spray insecticide," is hearsay. Objection overruled: when Duster told Pilot, "Spray insecticide," that was not an assertion, it was an order or directive. See § 2.9. And Pilot's *trial* testimony as to what he sprayed does not constitute hearsay because we are not dealing with any "out-of-court" statements by Pilot; he is in court on the witness stand.

---

[7] If this paragraph confuses you, read the facts again, paying special attention to the dates: March 1, the contract; September 1, Farmer files suit; September 5, Ms Brooks overhears the conversation between Pilot and Mr. Duster, in which, among other things, Pilot tells Duster, "today's my last day on the job"; in November, Ms Brooks gives deposition testimony about this conversation; in December (a month after Ms Brooks' deposition), Pilot relates the conversation he had with Mr. Duster back in March. The point is that we know from what Pilot told Mr. Duster in September, that when Pilot made his statement in December, he was no longer an employee of Cropduster, so that statement cannot satisfy Fed. R. Evid. 801(d)(2)(D).

You may be thinking, "Fishman, that was sneaky, stacking the dates like that. Do you really expect us to pay attention to all those dates?" ... Well, yes, I do, and so does your evidence professor. If your prof includes a series of dates in an exam question, the odds are they are important. (By the way, it is generally a good idea to "pay attention to all those dates" when you are practicing law, too.)

Question 5. Farmer next calls Barber as a witness. Barber will, if permitted, testify that in December, while he was giving Z, Cropduster's warehouse foreman, a haircut, Z told Barber: "Poor Farmer! He hired us to spray insecticide on his fields, and we sprayed weed killer by mistake, and his crops were ruined." Cropduster objects that Z's remark is hearsay. If Farmer cites Fed. R. Evid. 801(d)(2)(D), how should the judge rule, and why?

Ans. It's unclear, but Farmer probably has not satisfied the rule. Again applying the issue-requirement checklist:

1. Z, the declarant, was an employee of Cropduster when he made the statement. (Note that *Barber*, to whom the statement was made, was not Cropduster's employee, but that doesn't matter. Barber is not the declarant; he is the in-court witness who will testify about declarant Z's statement. To satisfy the first Fed. R. Evid. 801(d)(2)(D) requirement, Farmer only has to show that the *declarant* was an employee of Cropduster.)

2. Did the statement concern "a matter within the scope of [Z's]" job responsibilities for Cropduster? Z isn't a pilot; perhaps his job for Cropduster has nothing to do with who sprayed what, and when. If this is the case, the statement does not satisfy Fed. R. Evid. 801(d)(2)(D), and the hearsay objection should be sustained.

    On the other hand, if Z's job as warehouse foreman included responsibility for making sure the proper chemicals are loaded into the appropriate airplanes, then the statement *did* concern "a matter within the scope" of Z's responsibilities for Cropduster.

    Because Farmer is offering the statement, he has the burden of persuading the judge that the statement satisfies this (and all other) requirements for admissibility. Unless he can do so, the judge should exclude the statement.

    Farmer can attempt to satisfy this requirement in a variety of ways, e.g., by calling Z or some other employee of Cropduster as a witness and asking him to describe Z's duties.

3. Z's statement to Barber satisfies the third requirement, because Z was still an employee of Cropduster when he made the statement.

    Cropduster may object that Z was "off-duty" when he made the statement: he was at the barber shop, not at the warehouse. But this is no reason to exclude the statement. Fed. R. Evid. 801(d)(2)(D) does not require that the declarant be "on duty" at the time he made the statement, but only that the declarant was an agent or employee at the time he made the statement, and that the statement concerned a matter "within the scope of" his job or duties for Cropduster.

Question 6. Subsequent to this lawsuit, the state brings a civil action against Mr. Duster for spraying weed killer without a permit. The state offers Cropduster's pleadings in the Farmer v. Cropduster suit, as evidence that Cropduster sprayed weed killer. Cropduster objects: hearsay. Admissible?

Ans. Yes. If Mr. Duster himself signed the pleadings, they are not hearsay because they satisfy Fed. R. Evid. 801(d)(2)(A): it was his own statement, offered by his opposing party (the state) in the current lawsuit; or else by signing the pleading he adopted it per Fed. R. Evid. 801(d)(2)(B). The fact that Mr. Duster originally made or adopted the statement in a different lawsuit against a different opposing party is irrelevant.

If Cropduster's pleading in the Farmer v. Cropduster lawsuit were signed by Cropduster's attorney, instead of by Mr. Duster, then the pleadings still are not hearsay in the new litigation because they satisfy Fed. R. Evid. 801(d)(2)(C) and 801(d)(2)(D): the attorney was Cropduster's spokesperson and agent with regard to that litigation. Even if that attorney no longer represents Cropduster, the pleading still qualifies under Fed. R. Evid. 801(d)(2)(C) and 801(d)(2)(D), because the attorney was Cropduster's "agent" or "spokesperson" when the attorney filed the pleading.

§ 5.27 STATEMENTS BY GOVERNMENT AGENTS

In *civil* litigation, courts generally hold that a statement by a government agent is admissible against the government per Fed. R. Evid. 801(d)(2)(D), so long as the requirements of the rule are satisfied. In *criminal* cases, however, where the stakes are higher, courts take a more nuanced approach. The majority, but by no means unanimous, approach is as follows:

1. Statements by a government attorney, in pleadings and other formal documents, come within Rule 801(d)(2)(D); likewise statements made on the record in open court. Statements made in less formal settings do not.

2. Statements by law enforcement officers in a formal document, such as an affidavit for a search or arrest warrant, are admissible against the government per Rule 801(d)(2)(D), but statements made in less formal documents or settings are not.

3. An informant is not considered a government "agent" for purposes of Rule 801(d)(2)(D). Suppose an informant reports certain information to a police officer. The officer is unable to confirm the information on her own, but thereafter includes that information in her investigative report or search warrant application.[8] This does *not* constitute an "admission" by an employee of the government per Rule 801(d)(2)(D).

---

[8] Standard language in a search warrant application might go like this: "I have been informed by CI-6, a confidential informant who has on several previous occasions provided information that proved reliable and led to the seizure of controlled substances, and whose identity and record of reliability have been made known to the judge to whom this application is being submitted, that during the week of March 22, CI-6 was present at 123 West 45th Street, and observed the following: . . . "

§ 5.28   QUESTION

Question 1. Aardvark is arrested and is brought to the prosecutor's office, where ADA, the prosecutor working with the police on the case, secretly records his conversation with Aardvark.[9] Trying to persuade Aardvark to inform against Bear and Cheeta, ADA tells Aardvark, "Look, I can cut you a pretty good break, because I know you're not as dirty as those other guys; they run the show, and you just do what you're told." Aardvark rejects the overture. When Aardvark goes to trial, ADA tells the jury in his opening statement, "The evidence will show that Aardvark, Bear and Cheeta were equal partners in overseeing this criminal conspiracy." After the state presents its evidence and rests, during the defense case, Aardvark's attorney seeks to play the portion of the ADA-Aardvark interview quoted supra.[10] The government objects: hearsay! Ruling?

Ans. The objection should be sustained. Even though ADA, as a prosecutor, clearly is an agent of the government, and his statement to Aardvark was well within the scope of his duties, courts understand that law enforcement officials, including prosecutors, have to be given leeway in situations like this. If courts held that a statement made by a prosecutor in this kind of setting was admissible against the government at trial, it would interfere significantly with the government's ability to investigate and prosecute crimes. Thus, on public policy grounds, courts limit the application of Rule 801(d)(2)(D) in such cases.

§ 5.29   SIXTH AMENDMENT CONFRONTATION CLAUSE

Applications of the Confrontation Clause to statements falling within Fed. R. Evid. 801(d)(2)(D) are discussed in § 6.14[4], infra.

PART F:
RULE 801(d)(2)(E): STATEMENT BY A PARTY'S CO-CONSPIRATOR

§ 5.30   IN GENERAL

Fed. R. Evid. 801(d)(2)(E) provides as follows:

(d) Statements That Are Not Hearsay. A statement that meets the following conditions is not hearsay:

(2) *An Opposing Party's Statement.* The statement is offered against an opposing party and: . . .

---

[9] This is entirely lawful under federal law, and the substantial majority of states also permit it.

[10] Rules governing pretrial discovery would require ADA to provide Aardvark's attorney with a copy of the recording.

(E) was made by the party's co-conspirator during and in further-ance of the conspiracy.

The statement must be considered but does not by itself establish ... the existence of the conspiracy or participation in it under (E).

[Prior to December 1, 2011, the rule read as follows:

Rule 801(d). Statements which are not hearsay. A statement is not hearsay if-

(2) Admission by party-opponent. The statement is offered by the opponent of a party and is . . .

(E) a statement by a coconspirator of a party during the course and in furtherance of the conspiracy. . . . The contents of the statement shall be considered but are not alone sufficient to establish . . . the existence of the conspiracy and the participation therein of the declarant and the party against whom the statement is offered under subdivision (E).

The Federal Rules of Evidence were rewritten solely to make them easier to understand; the Advisory Committee did not intend to make any substantive change in the Rules. The text of the old rule may remain useful in reading court decisions that precede the revision of the rules. Thus, this edition of the Student's Guide provides the text of both the new and the old version of each relevant provision of the Federal Rules of Evidence.]

A conspiracy is a combination of two or more people for the purpose of committing one or more unlawful acts. To convict a person of the crime of conspiracy, the prosecutor need show only that he *agreed* with at least one other person to commit a crime. (In some jurisdictions, the prosecutor must also show that at least one member of the conspiracy committed an overt act that was intended to bring the crime the conspirators agreed to commit closer to fruition. The overt act need not itself be unlawful, so long as it was performed by a member of the conspiracy with the requisite intent.)

The primary purpose of the law of conspiracy is to permit the authorities to apprehend, prosecute and convict would-be wrongdoers before they have had an opportunity to achieve their unlawful goal. Even where some defendants may be prosecuted for completed crimes, moreover, prosecutors frequently add a conspiracy count to those other charges. This permits the prosecution of individuals who might not be convictable for any of the completed crimes. Furthermore, the law of conspiracy affords the prosecution several additional tactical and procedural advantages.

Fed. R. Evid. 801(d)(2)(E) deals with the admissibility of out-of-court statements made by one member of the conspiracy that are offered in evidence against other conspirators.

It is worth noting that although the rule is most frequently invoked in criminal prosecutions when defendants are charged with the crime of conspiracy, if the rule's prerequisites are satisfied, statements by one conspirator are admissible against other conspirators in criminal and even in civil cases in which no specific conspiracy count has been alleged.

Finally, a word on the crucial issue: to hyphenate, or not to hyphenate? The version of Fed. R. Evid. 801(d)(2)(E) effective December 1, 2011 does not hyphenate "coconspirator." Nor did the older version of the rule. On the other hand, intermediate drafts of the restyled rules inserted the hyphen. Either form is acceptable, and you will find each version of the word in the case law, treatises, etc. My initial position was not to use the hyphen in this book. After all, who knows — it may be that each of us is allowed only so many hyphens in a lifetime, so why risk using them up when it's not completely necessary? But after a long and rancourous debate, my Committee on Context and Consistency[11] prevailed upon me to insert the hyphen (except where I am quoting a source that left it out).

§ 5.31   PREREQUISITES TO ADMISSIBILITY

Fed. R. Evid. 801(d)(2)(E) provides that a statement made by a co-conspirator of a party is not hearsay if it was made during and in furtherance of the conspiracy. To qualify for admissibility under the rule, the offering party must satisfy the judge that five conditions existed when the statement was made:

1.   A conspiracy in fact existed.

2.   The declarant was a member of the conspiracy.

3.   The non-declarant defendant, against whom the statement is being offered, was a member of the conspiracy.

4.   The statement was made "during" the conspiracy.

5.   The statement was made "in furtherance" of the conspiracy.

These issues are illustrated by the following example. X, Y and Z have been indicted for conspiring to distribute heroin. The indictment alleges that on three separate occasions, Y and Z sold heroin to an undercover agent, and that X supplied the heroin to Y and Z. A key issue at trial is the admissibility, against Z and X, of statements made by Y to the undercover agent.

At trial, the agent testifies that in January he met Y and negotiated a heroin purchase with him. After Y and the agent agreed as to price, quantity and quality, Y took the agent to Z, who accepted the money and gave him the heroin. Two weeks later the agent made a second purchase, which followed the same pattern. After the second purchase, the agent met with Y and complained that the purity of the heroin wasn't what Y and Z promised. Hoping to retain the agent as a customer, Y assured the agent, "Listen, Z and I work for X, and X insists that we keep our customers happy. X will make sure that the next package is pure."

Before the agent can testify about the third sale, X and Z each object that Y's statement is inadmissible hearsay. To determine admissibility against either X or Z, we have to assess whether the prosecutor has satisfied the five prerequisites outlined supra as to that particular defendant.

---

[11]   I.e., my wife Betty.

Admissibility against Z.

1. Because Y and Z acted together to sell drugs to the agent, it is obvious that the two of them agreed to do so; hence, a conspiracy existed.

2. It is equally obvious that Y, the declarant, was a member of the conspiracy: he negotiated the terms of each sale, and brought the agent to Z to complete the transactions.

3. Z, the non-declarant defendant, clearly was a member of the conspiracy: after all, Z actually delivered the heroin to the undercover agent.

4. Y's statement to the agent was made between the second and third sales; hence, "during" the conspiracy.

5. It is reasonable to conclude that Y's statement was made in the hope of retaining the agent as a customer; hence, his statement appears to have been "in furtherance" of the conspiracy. (Had Y made the same remark in an idle boast to his girlfriend, however, it would not have been "in furtherance.")

Thus, Y's statement is admissible against Z; and this is so even though Z was not present at the time it was made.

Admissibility against X.

Y's statement, if accepted as true, clearly establishes that X was a member of the conspiracy. X, of course, denies any involvement with Y and Z, and objects that Y's statement about him his hearsay.

The same evidence that satisfies requirements (1), (2), (4), and (5) with regard to admissibility against Z likewise satisfies those requirements with regard to admissibility against X: the government's evidence clearly establishes (1) that a conspiracy existed, (2) that the declarant, Y, was a member of it, and that the statement was made (4) during and (5) in furtherance of the conspiracy. The third requirement presents the crucial issue in this problem: was X, the non-declarant defendant against whom Y's statement is being offered, a member of the conspiracy? To resolve this question, we must address several procedural issues.

§ 5.32 PROCEDURAL ISSUES

To assess whether the prosecutor has adequately satisfied the five requirements (such as, in our example, that X, the non-declarant defendant, was a member of the conspiracy), we must first consider the following questions:

1. What evidence should the judge consider in deciding whether the prosecutor has satisfied the requirements? *See* § 5.33.

2. Against what evidentiary standard should the judge measure the prosecutor's showing (in our example, connecting X to the conspiracy)? *See* § 5.34.

3. What is the appropriate order of proof? Should the prosecutor be permitted to offer Y's statement against X *before* satisfying the requirements of Fed. R.

Evid. 801(d)(2)(E), or only after? *See* § 5.35.

In *United States v. Bourjaily*, 483 U.S. 171, 175 (1987), the Supreme Court resolved some of these issues; subsequently Fed. R. Evid. 801(d)(2) was amended to answer some of the remaining questions.

§ 5.33   EVIDENCE TO BE CONSIDERED; "BOOTSTRAPPING"; "INDEPENDENT EVIDENCE" REQUIREMENT

1. Evidence to be considered; "bootstrapping."

Prior to the enactment of the Federal Rules, courts had held that the prosecutor could not use Y's statement as evidence that X was a member of the conspiracy unless other evidence, *independent* of Y's otherwise inadmissible hearsay, connected X to the Y-Z heroin conspiracy. In other words, the contested statement could not "lift itself up by its own bootstraps"; in assessing admissibility, the judge was obliged to *ignore* the contested statement itself, and consider *only* other non-hearsay evidence.

In *Bourjaily* the Supreme Court, per Chief Justice Rehnquist, concluded that the Federal Rules of Evidence abrogated this approach. Fed. R. Evid. 104(a), the Court emphasized, provides that when deciding questions of admissibility of evidence, the trial judge "is not bound by the rules of evidence except those with respect to privileges." Thus, a court can and should consider the contested statement itself, *together with* any other relevant evidence, in deciding whether the requirements for admissibility have been satisfied.

2. The "independent evidence" requirement.

Bourjaily did *not* decide whether the trial judge could rely *solely* on the statement itself to determine whether the prosecutor had satisfied the rule's requirements. The subsequent amendment to Fed. R. Evid. 801(d)(2) provides the answer. It directs: "The statement must be considered but does not by itself establish . . . the existence of the conspiracy or participation in it under (E)." Thus, the prosecutor[12] must offer other evidence, besides the statement itself, to satisfy requirements listed in § 5.31.

§ 5.34   PROSECUTOR'S BURDEN OF PROOF

Against what evidentiary standard should the judge measure the prosecutor's attempt to satisfy the five requirements? Both before and after enactment of the Federal Rules, courts used a variety of verbal formulas, from "clear and convincing evidence" (a comparatively heavy burden) to "a preponderance of the evidence" (the same burden of proof as in civil cases) to merely "prima facie case" or "substantial independent evidence" (levels of proof somewhat less than a preponderance). In

---

[12] Remember, a civil litigant can also offer statements per Fed. R. Evid. 801(d)(2)(E). I use the word "prosecutor" when discussing this rule because that's who uses it the most, and "prosecutor" is less wordy than "the party who is offering the statement."

Bourjaily, the Court opted for the "preponderance of the evidence" test.

Thus, in our example, when the prosecutor offers a statement by hearsay declarant (Y) against a non-declarant defendant (X) and argues that Fed. R. Evid. 801(d)(2)(E) overcomes X's hearsay objection, the judge must decide whether all of the evidence (including Y's contested statement) establishes, by a preponderance of the evidence, the existence of the conspiracy, Y's participation in it, X's participation in it, and that the statement was made during the conspiracy and in furtherance of it. If so, then Y's statement is admissible, and the jury may consider it in determining whether X's participation in the conspiracy has been proven beyond a reasonable doubt.

§ 5.35 ORDER OF PROOF

A statement made by an alleged co-conspirator is not admissible against a non-declarant defendant unless the prosecutor has satisfied the Fed. R. Evid. 801(d)(2)(E) requirements. Suppose, though, the prosecutor wants a witness to testify about such a statement early in the trial, and the judge concludes that those requirements have not yet been met. Assuming the defendant interposes an objection, should the judge allow the jury to hear Y's statement about X before the prosecutor has offered enough evidence to satisfy the judge that the evidence is properly admissible against X?

The judge has three options. She can:

1. admit the statement as conditionally admissible, per Fed. R. Evid. 104(a), i.e., admit it based on the prosecutor's promise that he will satisfy the prerequisites to admissibility (see § 5.31) by the time he finishes presenting his evidence; or

2. reject the statement until the prosecutor has offered enough evidence (including the statement itself) to satisfy the rule; or

3. admit the statement when the prosecutor first offers it, subject to later satisfying the prerequisites to admissibility, but only if the prosecutor makes an offer of proof (out of the jury's hearing, of course) of the evidence he expects to offer later that will satisfy the requirements of admissibility.

Appellate courts have often expressed a preference for the second or third approach, while acknowledging that taking the first approach is within the trial judge's discretion.

§ 5.36 CONDITIONAL ADMISSIBILITY: PROCEDURE

By admitting the evidence conditionally, the judge in essence tells the prosecutor, "You haven't satisfied the rule yet, but I'll admit the evidence now on condition that you will satisfy the rule's requirements by the time you rest your case." When the government does rest, therefore, each non-declarant defendant against whom such statements were conditionally admitted should move to strike the statements. This motion requires the judge to determine whether, as to each defendant and as to each statement, the requirements for admissibility have been satisfied. If the judge concludes that, as to any particular statement and as to any particular defendant, the requirements have not been satisfied, the judge should instruct the jury to disregard the statement as to that defendant. If the statement is too prejudicial to be dealt with in that fashion, then any defendant adversely affected by the statement should move for and be granted a mistrial.

As in every criminal case, when the government rests, each defendant should also move for a judgment of acquittal on the ground that the government has failed to make out a prima facie case against her. The judge should grant the motion only if he concludes that, viewing all of the evidence (including any properly admitted co-conspirator statements) in the light most favorable to the prosecutor, no rational jury could find the defendant guilty beyond a reasonable doubt. If these motions are denied, the defendant presents her case; after both sides rest, each defendant again moves for a directed verdict.[13]

§ 5.37   SIXTH AMENDMENT CONFRONTATION CLAUSE

The Supreme Court has explicitly stated that a defendant does not have a viable Confrontation Clause objection with regards to statements that fall within the co-conspirator exception. See § 6.14[3].

§ 5.38   MISCELLANEOUS CO-CONSPIRATOR STATEMENT ISSUES

Co-conspirator statements are admissible even if no conspiracy has been charged, so long as the prosecutor offers sufficient evidence that a conspiracy in fact existed, and the other prerequisites for admissibility have been met.

The same is true in civil litigation. The issue arises with some frequency in antitrust actions, where plaintiff must allege and prove that defendants entered into a "contract, combination or conspiracy" in restraint of trade or commerce. The issue may also arise, however, where no conspiracy is alleged in the pleadings. In a suit by P against D1 and D2 for fraud, for example, if P can satisfy the five foundational requirements of Fed. R. Evid. 801(d)(2)(E) (see § 5.31), statements made by one of the defendants would be admissible over a hearsay objection against the other defendant as well.

---

[13] The procedures discussed in this section apply, incidentally, not just with regard to Fed. R. Evid. 801(d)(2)(E), but to all evidence a judge admits conditionally pursuant to Fed. R. Evid. 104(a) or Fed. R. Evid. 104(b), in civil as well as criminal litigation. If evidence has been admitted conditionally, when the party who offered that evidence rests, the other party should move to strike. Once such a motion is made, the judge must determine whether the requirements for admission have been satisfied. After the judge has ruled on the motion to strike, the appropriate litigant(s) should move for a directed verdict. (In a civil case, a judge should grant defendant's motion for a directed verdict only if no rational jury could find for plaintiff by a preponderance. Similarly, a judge should grant plaintiff's motion for a directed verdict only if no rational jury could find for defendant by a preponderance of the evidence.)

§ 5.39 QUESTIONS

Question 1. Borachio (D1) and Conrade (D2) are charged with assault and robbery. The indictment alleges that on March 1, 2011, they shot and seriously wounded Leonato and stole $5,000 from him.

As her first witness at trial, the prosecutor calls Don John, who will testify that before he was convicted in July 2011 on narcotics charges, he was a crack dealer. Don John testifies that in late February of 2011 (as best as he can remember, the 25th), Conrade told him, "Me and Borachio will be lookin' to score a quarter of a key soon. We been scopin' out a bad dude, and we're gonna take him off in just a couple of days."[14] What substantive and procedural issues are presented by this testimony?

Ans. First, Conrade and Borachio can both interpose a Fed. R. Evid. 404(b) objection, arguing that they are charged with assault and robbery, not a drug offense.[15] If you haven't covered Fed. R. Evid. 404(b) yet, don't worry about having missed this issue.

Next, both defendants will object that Conrade's statement is hearsay.

As to Conrade, the prosecutor is offering Conrade's own statement against him. The hearsay objection is overruled, per Fed. R. Evid. 801(d)(2)(A).

As to Borachio, the prosecutor will cite Fed. R. Evid. 801(d)(2)(E). Fed. R. Evid. 801(d)(2)(E) can apply even though no conspiracy is charged. The DA's theory is that the defendants conspired to rob Leonato to raise the money to purchase crack from Don John.

Because the prosecutor hasn't offered any other evidence yet, the state cannot possibly have satisfied the five prerequisites for admissibility (*see* § 5.31). Thus, the judge must decide the third procedural issue discussed in § 5.35:

a.   admit the evidence conditionally, per Fed. R. Evid. 104(a); or

b.   admit it now if the prosecutor can make an offer of proof out of the hearing of the jury, outlining how she expects to satisfy the prerequisites of Fed. R. Evid. 801(d)(2)(E); or

c.   sustain the objection until the prosecutor offers sufficient evidence at the trial to satisfy the prerequisites.

Question 2. Assume that the judge grants the prosecutor's request to allow Don John to testify, per Fed. R. Evid. 104(a). The following evidence is thereafter admitted

---

[14] Perhaps, to honor the author whose characters I am "borrowing" (William Shakespeare, Much Ado About Nothing, 1598–1600), I should rephrase Conrade's statement to Don John thus:

Don John, my friend Borachio and I
From you, a quarter kilo seek to buy.
For funds, we will hijack a fellow's purse
— A dude who thinks he's "bad," but we are worse.

[15] The prosecutor will respond to the Rule 404(b) objection that evidence about the drug purchase is admissible to prove Conrade and Borachio's motive for the robbery that they are being tried for. the judge would overrule the Rule 404(b) objection.

at trial.

    a. Don John also testifies that on March 2, Conrade purchased a quarter of a kilogram of crack cocaine from him for $8,800.

    b. The state next calls Claudia Benedict. She testifies that she was the bartender at the Aragon Bar on West 42nd Street on February 28, 2011 from 6 p.m. to midnight. She identifies Conrade and Borachio as customers. "I remember them. They kept asking me to go party with them after I got off duty. I tried to brush 'em off polite-like, but they just kept comin' on. I was afraid these guys were gonna follow me out the door when my shift ended, and I said to myself, this is no life for a nice girl from Brooklyn! So I tell my boss, 'Charlie, I'm quittin'! I can't take it no more, I'm gettin' outa here. You call me a cab, or I'm callin' me a cop!' Charlie called a cab for me, and I ain't been back there since. Anyhow, that's how come I remember them so good."

    c. The prosecutor calls Leonato. On direct examination, after Leonato is sworn and identifies himself as a "personal services broker," the following exchange takes place:

Q.   Where were you at about 2 a.m. on March 1?

A.   I had just come out of a client's apartment, 3rd floor, 12 West 34th Street, when I heard two guys on the stairs. I turned toward them, when, BOOM! BOOM! I heard these shots. I go down and two guys go through my pockets. I had $10,000 on me; they got it all. Then I passed out; next thing I knew I'm in the hospital.

Q.   Do you see those men here today?

A.   I recognize one of them — him, the one in the purple jacket and green tie (pointing at Conrade). He's one of the guys that held me up. I never got a good enough look at the other one.

    d. The prosecutor calls Detective Dogberry as her next witness. Dogberry testifies that on March 6, he executed a search warrant at Borachio's apartment, and seized 2 ounces of crack cocaine and a .22 caliber revolver.

    e. The government's final witness, Detective Verges, testifies that he is a ballistics expert, and that the two bullets that wounded Leonato were .22 caliber rounds.

The government rests. What are the substantive and procedural issues that should be addressed at this point?

Ans. Borachio should bring a motion to strike Don John's testimony about Conrade's statement (**Q. 1**). Issue: has the prosecutor satisfied the Fed. R. Evid. 801(d)(2)(E) requirements by a preponderance (including at least some "independent" evidence)?

    a. *Existence of conspiracy.* We know from Leonato's testimony that two men, acting together, committed the robbery. Their concerted action establishes that they acted pursuant to a prior agreement — i.e., a conspiracy to commit the robbery.

b. *Declarant's involvement in the conspiracy.* Leonato's in-court identification of Conrade establishes that Conrade (the declarant) was a member.

c. *Borachio's (the non-declarant defendant's) participation.* As "independent evidence" the prosecutor has offered Claudia Benedict's testimony and the crack and pistol Dogberry found in Borachio's home.

Ms. Benedict's testimony is significant because it puts Conrade (whom we know from Leonato's testimony was one of the robbers) together with Borachio only two hours before the crime was committed.

The quantity of crack seized from Borachio is roughly 1/4 what Borachio and Conrade allegedly bought from Don John a few days earlier. This amount is reasonably consistent with the government's theory: it's half of what Borachio's share would have been.

The revolver is also circumstantial corroboration, because it was a .22 and Leonato was shot with a .22.

In addition to Ms. Benedict, the cocaine and the pistol, the judge can consider Conrade's statement itself (*Bourjaily*). (*See* § 5.33.) Viewed in the context of that statement, Borachio's possession of crack is evidence of the conspiracy to rob Leonato to obtain the money needed to purchase the drugs.

It's a close call, but I think a judge could find this evidence (including Conrade's statement) sufficient to establish Borachio's participation by a preponderance of the evidence.

d. *During the conspiracy.* The statement (late February) was during the conspiracy (robbery: early March).

e. *In furtherance of the conspiracy.* The statement arguably furthers the conspiracy (to buy drugs) by encouraging Don John to have crack available for Borachio and Conrade after they robbed Leonato.

In sum, if I were the judge, I'd deny Borachio's motion to strike.

Question 3. After the judge rules on Borachio's motion, what should defense counsel do next? What is the proper outcome?

Ans. Each attorney should move for a directed verdict (or for a judgment of acquittal, which is the same thing). *See* § 5.36. This requires the judge to assess whether a rational juror, viewing the evidence in the light most favorable to the prosecution, could find each defendant guilty beyond a reasonable doubt.

Clearly, Conrade's motion should be denied. Leonato's testimony alone is enough to convict, if the jury finds it truthful and accurate.

If the judge denied Borachio's motion to strike in the prior question, he should also deny Borachio's motion for a directed verdict. Conrade's statement to Don John, together with the circumstantial corroboration discussed in the previous question, makes out a strong enough case to allow a jury to decide whether Borachio was one of the robbers. On the other hand, if the judge granted Borachio's motion to strike in **Q.2**, he must also grant Borachio's directed verdict motion, because without that statement, there is not enough evidence against Borachio to allow a rational juror to find him guilty.

Chapter 6

HEARSAY AND THE SIXTH AMENDMENT CONFRONTATION CLAUSE

§ 6.1 INTRODUCTION

The Sixth Amendment Confrontation Clause reads:

In all criminal prosecutions, the accused shall enjoy the right . . . to be confronted with the witnesses against him.

Whenever a *prosecutor* seeks to use an out-of-court statement as evidence in a *criminal case*, defense counsel should respond, in Pavlovian fashion,[1] "Objection, hearsay! Objection, Confrontation Clause!"[2] Once defense counsel does so, the prosecutor must overcome both objections, or the evidence is excluded.

To be "confronted with" a witness means the witness must come to court, testify in the presence of the defendant, and be available for cross-examination by defense counsel. The primary purpose of the Confrontation Clause, the Supreme Court has said, is to assure that a criminal conviction is based on evidence the reliability of which has been tested by the traditional safeguards: oath, demeanor, and cross-examination.

If the Clause was applied literally, it would require, on objection, the exclusion of any out-of-court statement offered by a prosecutor unless the declarant who had made the statement testifies at the trial. This result, however, the Supreme Court has "long

---

[1] Ivan Petrovich Pavlov, 1849–1936, was a Russian physiologist and experimental psychologist. In his most famous experiment, he observed how dogs salivated when food was brought to them. He began ringing a bell just before bringing the food. Pretty quickly dogs started salivating when they heard the bell, even if no food was brought: they had been conditioned to associate the bell with food, and their bodies responded in a "conditioned reflex" to its sound. Please understand that I am *not* comparing defense attorneys to salivating dogs! My point is that defense counsel — and for that matter, law students — should train themselves to respond, "Objection, hearsay! Objection, Confrontation Clause!" whenever a prosecutor offers an out-of-court statement. If counsel makes only a hearsay objection, this waives the Confrontation Clause issue. If a student discusses only hearsay on an exam question that fits this pattern, he or she will forfeit the points the professor has allocated to a discussion of the Confrontation Clause. Remember to discuss *both* issues.

[2] Actually, an experienced defense attorney sometimes won't bother objecting, because (a) he or she knows the judge would properly overrule the objections, or (b) he or she thinks the evidence might wind up being helpful to the defense, or (c) for some other strategic reason. But if the prosecutor presents such evidence in an exam question, a *law student* should discuss both hearsay and Confrontation Clause, because a law school exam is not the real world; it is an opportunity for you, the student, to demonstrate that your professor is a brilliant teacher who has taught you how to recognize and handle hearsay and Confrontation Clause issues.

rejected as unintended and too extreme." *Ohio v. Roberts*, 448 U.S. 56, 63 (1980).[3] Thus, some otherwise admissible hearsay *will* survive a Confrontation Clause objection even if the declarant does not testify. The law has struggled to define when this should be permitted, and when it should not.

This chapter outlines the principles governing the Confrontation Clause that have emerged from the Supreme Court's decisions, and also tells you how the Confrontation Clause interacts with Fed. R. Evid. 801(d)(1)(A)–(C), which were covered in Chapter 4, and Fed. R. Evid. 801(d)(2)(A)–(E), which were covered in Chapter 5. Coverage of each exception to the hearsay rule found in Fed. R. Evid. 803 (Chapters 8–10), 804 (Chapter 11) and 807 (Chapter 12) will include a discussion of the application of the Confrontation Clause to that exception.

§ 6.2   DON'T BLAME ME!

You did not buy a book because you wanted a list of challenging questions without answers. You bought this book because you want *answers*. And in most of this book that's what I provide. But I can't do that with regard to the Confrontation Clause. Why?

Because in 2004, the Supreme Court threw out the previous quarter-century of law on the subject, but gave us only a vague outline of what it was putting in its place. Since then, the Court has decided six more cases involving the Confrontation Clause (with more on the way), and . . . well, let's just say that mostly what we have are questions, not answers. Accordingly, the main goal of this chapter is to tell you the right questions to ask and, where I can, to suggest what some of the answers *might* be.

§ 6.3   AUTHOR'S WEB SITE

Catholic University of America Law School has set up a web site on which I will post updates to this chapter and on any other major developments in hearsay law. The address is: http://law.cua.edu/Fac_Staff/FishmanC/studentguidetohearsay.cfm.

§ 6.4   STATEMENTS OFFERED FOR NON-HEARSAY PURPOSES

In *Tennessee v. Street*, 471 U.S. 409, 414 (1985), the Supreme Court unanimously held that no Confrontation Clause violation occurs when a declarant's out-of-court statement is admitted for a non-hearsay purpose. Street, Peele, and others were charged with murder. At Street's trial, after his own confession was admitted in evidence, Street testified that the confession had been coerced: that the officers interrogating him had forced him to repeat the statements contained in a confession made earlier by Peele. In rebuttal, the prosecutor was permitted to offer Peele's confession in evidence, not to prove the truth of what Peele said in his own confession

---

[3] As you will see, other aspects of *Roberts* have since been rejected by the Court, but this holding is still good law.

(i.e., not to prove, directly, that Peele and Street committed the murder), but to show that there were factual inconsistencies between the two confessions — inconsistencies that contradicted Street's claim that he had been forced to repeat what Peele had told the police. The Court held that the trial judge's instructions to the jury, to consider Peele's confession only for rebuttal purposes and not to consider the truthfulness of the statement itself, was consistent with, and satisfied, Street's Confrontation Clause rights.

In *Crawford v. Washington*, 541 U.S. 36 (2004), the Supreme Court reaffirmed that the Confrontation Clause does not apply to a statement offered for a non-hearsay purpose.

§ 6.5   THE *OHIO v. ROBERTS* APPROACH TO THE CONFRONTATION CLAUSE

In 1980, in *Ohio v. Roberts, supra,* the Supreme Court held, in essence, that because the purpose underlying the Confrontation Clause was to guarantee that convictions must be based on trustworthy evidence, if hearsay evidence was sufficiently trustworthy, it could be admitted even if the declarant did not testify and defendant had no opportunity to confront and cross-examine him. *Roberts* and subsequent decisions developed an elaborate set of tests to determine whether a statement was sufficiently trustworthy. The result was substantial confusion and inconsistency.

§ 6.6   *CRAWFORD v. WASHINGTON*

In 2004, in *Crawford v. Washington,* supra, the Supreme Court rejected the *Roberts* "trustworthiness" approach. The Court, per Justice Scalia, insisted that the men[4] who drafted and ratified the Sixth Amendment were not merely seeking to impose a general assurance of trustworthiness; rather, they specified a particular *procedural* right — confrontation — as the means of assuring trustworthiness. After an extensive review of the historical record, Justice Scalia for the Court concluded that the Confrontation Clause was intended to restrict a prosecutor's ability to offer "testimonial" hearsay statements as evidence. (A prosecutor can introduce testimonial hearsay in only three circumstances. See § 6.11.)

§ 6.7   DEFINING "TESTIMONIAL": "SOLEMN DECLARATION"; THREE FORMULATIONS

All this makes it rather important, of course, to have a clear definition of "testimonial." But the facts of *Crawford* did not require the Court to develop an elaborate definition. No doubt you have read the case thoroughly and are intimately familiar with the facts; but in case they've slipped your mind for the moment, in essence: Crawford stabbed a man, and was charged with attempted murder, despite his claim that he acted in self-defense because he thought the man was reaching for a

---

[4] Back in the 18th century, remember, only men could hold public office. It's amazing, isn't it, how well the Founding Fathers did, considering that they wouldn't let any women help them?

weapon. Police officers interrogated Mrs. Crawford about what happened; her answers to the police officers' questions did not support her husband's version of events, and at trial, over defense counsel's hearsay and Confrontation Clause objections, the prosecutor played a recording of Mrs. Crawford's statements. The Supreme Court held that Mrs. Crawford's statements to the police were testimonial by any definition, and that, because Mrs. Crawford did not testify at trial,[5] admitting her statements violated Crawford's rights under the Confrontation Clause.

Although the Court provided no clear definition of "testimonial," it did offer the following:

> The text of the Confrontation Clause . . . applies to "witnesses" against the accused — in other words, those who "bear testimony." "Testimony," in turn, is typically *"[a] solemn declaration or affirmation made for the purpose of establishing or proving some fact."* An accuser who makes a formal statement to government officers bears testimony in a sense that a person who makes a casual remark to an acquaintance does not. . . .[6]

Okay, well, that helps a little: a "solemn declaration for the purpose of proving a fact," like Mrs. Crawford's "formal statement to government officers," is testimonial; a "casual remark to an acquaintance" is not. But that leaves a fairly big "gray area" in between.

In attempt to be helpful, the Court offered three "formulations" or definitions of testimonial, without endorsing any of them (and without foreclosing the Court's right to come up with a completely different one later on):

> 1. *"ex parte* in-court testimony or its functional equivalent — that is, material such as affidavits, custodial examinations, prior testimony that the defendant was unable to cross-examine, or similar pretrial statements that declarants would reasonably expect to be used prosecutorially";
>
> 2. "extrajudicial statements . . . contained in formalized testimonial materials, such as affidavits, depositions, prior testimony, or confessions";
>
> 3. "statements that were made under circumstances which would lead an objective witness reasonably to believe that the statement would be available for use at a later trial . . ."[7]

From this, we can conclude without difficulty that the following are clearly testimonial: formal testimony, depositions, affidavits (i.e., sworn written statements), and confessions and other statements made during formal police questioning.

Crawford also gave examples of two kinds of statements which are *not* testimonial: coconspirator statements (see § 6.14[3]) and business records (see § 9:36. infra). Nor,

---

[5] Mrs. Crawford did not testify because Crawford invoked a state privilege which allows a defendant to preclude his or her spouse from testifying against him or her.

[6] Crawford at 51, quoting an early 19th century American dictionary.

[7] Id. at 51–52.

as we have already seen, is a "casual remark to an acquaintance."[8]

The potential wild cards consist of the last part of the first "formulation" — "similar pretrial statements that declarants would reasonably expect to be used prosecutorially"; and the entire third "formulation." Crawford offered no real clue as to which is the "right" formulation; nor how broadly or narrowly the courts should read them.

§ 6.8 SUBSEQUENT SUPREME COURT CONFRONTATION CLAUSE DECISIONS

As this Fourth Edition is being written, the Supreme Court has issued 5 more decisions involving six cases applying its post-*Crawford* approach to the Confrontation Clause.

1. In *Davis v. Washington*, 547 U.S. 813 (2006), the Court decided two cases — the *Davis* case, and *Indiana v. Hammond*. The Court held that a person's statements to police questioning during an "emergency" are not testimonial, but that statements in response to formal police questioning after the emergency is over, are testimonial.

2. In *Wharton v. Bockting*, 549 U.S. 406 (2007), the Court held that *Crawford* applies only prospectively, not retroactively. In other words, if a defendant was convicted and had exhausted his direct appeals before the *Crawford* decision, he cannot cite *Crawford* in an attempt to set aside his conviction.

3. In *Giles v. California*, 554 U.S. 353 (2008), the Court spelled out what a prosecutor had to show in order to use the "forfeiture" exception to the Confrontation Clause. For a full discussion, see §§ 11.51-11.54, but here's a sneak preview: it will often be a lot more difficult for a prosecutor to use the forfeiture exception than many people hoped or expected. *Giles* also cast some doubts on the "emergency-non-emergency" distinction the Court made in *Davis*. See § 8.11.

4. In *Melendez-Diaz v. Massachusetts*, 129 S.Ct. 2527 (2009), the Court held that reports prepared by a police forensic lab technician are testimonial — at least, if those reports are in the form of sworn affidavits. See §§ 9.50–9.52.

5. In *Bryant v. Michigan*, 131 S.Ct. 1143 (2011), the Court discussed when an "emergency" exists for purposes of the rule announced in *Davis*, that responses to police questioning in an "emergency" are not testimonial. See §§ 8.12–8.14. (Unfortunately, that decision is likely to cause more confusion than clarity on several aspects of the Confrontation Clause.)

6. In 2011, in *Bullcoming v. New Mexico*, 131 S.Ct. 2705 (2011), the Court again considered the application of the Confrontation Clause to forensic lab reports, and by a 5–to-4 vote followed the precedent set in *Melendez-Diaz*. See § 9.53, infra.

---

[8] Of course, many (perhaps most) "casual remarks to an acquaintance" will not satisfy any hearsay exception, and will be inadmissible on that ground regardless of whether they are "testimonial."

§ 6.9   A WHOLE LOT OF DICTA

In *Crawford* and in each of its Confrontation Clause decisions since, the Supreme Court has gone out of its way to include dictum pronouncements about what kinds of statements are or are not testimonial, and about situations in which the Clause will or will not apply. Dictum is better than nothing; if I'm arguing a case I'd rather have Supreme Court dictum on my side, than against me. But as you know, dictum is not the same as a holding, and in *Giles* and *Melendez-Diaz* the Court handed down decisions holding that the Confrontation Clause applies in situations that previous dicta hinted the Clause would not apply.

Where the Court has issued a dictum about the Clause, or about the testimoniality of certain statements, I've labeled it as such, and discussed situations in which the Court's dictum might not apply. If an exam question raises an issue in which the Court has made a dictum pronouncement, make sure your answer mentions that dictum — and make sure that you specify that it is only dictum, not holding.

§ 6.10   STATEMENTS TO NON-GOVERNMENT OFFICIALS

In 2008, in *Giles v. California*, dictum in Justice Scalia's opinion for the Court can be read as suggesting that only certain *statements to government officials* will be classified as testimonial, but that statements to non-government officials are inherently non-testimonial. In 2011, *Bryant*, the Court alluded to that issue again, without resolving it. See § 8.15.

§ 6.11   TESTIMONIAL STATEMENTS: SATISFYING THE CONFRONTATION CLAUSE

If a statement is testimonial and is offered "to prove the truth of the matter asserted in the statement,"[9] the Court said in *Crawford*, there are three ways to get it admitted over a Confrontation Clause objection.

(1)   Call the declarant as a witness so the defendant can confront and cross-examine him or her. Or:

(2)   Demonstrate that the declarant is unavailable, and that the defendant had a prior adequate opportunity to confront the declarant and cross-examine him or her about the statement. (See § 11.19, infra.) Or:

(3)   Demonstrate that the defendant's wrongdoing is responsible for the declarant's unavailability in a way which satisfies the "forfeiture doctrine" exception to the Confrontation Clause. This is discussed more fully in § 11.51-11.54.

Per *Crawford*, if a hearsay statement is testimonial and the prosecutor cannot do any of these three things, it is not admissible.

---

[9]   The quoted phrase is from the definition of hearsay in Fed. R. Evid. 801(c).

§ 6.12   NONTESTIMONIAL HEARSAY: *DAVIS v. WASHINGTON; WHARTON v. BOCKTING*

In *Crawford*, the Court strongly hinted that nontestimonial hearsay might not be subject to the Confrontation Clause at all. Two years later, in *Davis v. Washington*, 547 U.S. 813, 126 S.Ct. 2266 (2006), the Court unanimously said so more explicitly, and said so again in *Wharton v. Bockting*, 549 U.S. 406 (2007). In other words, if a statement is not "testimonial," a defendant's Confrontation Clause objection is automatically overruled.

Technically, those passages in *Davis* and *Bockting* are dictum; but unlike some of the other dicta in *Crawford* and its potency, this is dictum you can bank on: when the Supreme Court goes out of its way to say something twice by a 9–0 vote, as far as I'm concerned, dictum or not, it's good enough for me. On the other hand, your professor may not agree. If so, then he or she is of course absolutely right — at least until after the final exam.

§ 6.13   SUMMARY SO FAR: YOUR CONFRONTATION CLAUSE CHECK LIST

If a hearsay statement is "testimonial," a prosecutor cannot offer it into evidence against a defendant in a criminal trial unless (a) the declarant testifies at trial and defense counsel has the opportunity to cross-examine the declarant about the statement, or (b) the declarant is unavailable, but the defendant had a prior opportunity to confront and cross-examine the declarant about the statement, or (c) the defendant caused the declarant's unavailability and thereby forfeited his rights under the Confrontation Clause, as set out in §§ 11:51–11:54.

Here is the summary in greater detail, as a checklist you can use.

A.   The Confrontation Clause issue need be addressed *only in a criminal case*, and only when the *prosecutor* offers an out-of-court statement in evidence. If the case on trial is civil, or if the statement is offered by a defendant, there is no Confrontation Clause issue, and the rest of this outline can be ignored.

B.   If the hearsay objection is sustained, the evidence is excluded as inadmissible hearsay, and the constitutional issue need not be considered. (In the real world, that would mean that you could ignore the rest of this outline. But law school is not the real world.[10] Your professor may want you to discuss the Confrontation Clause anyway. Besides, suppose you are wrong about whether the evidence survives hearsay objection; if you ignore the Confrontation Clause issue, you are giving away a chance at getting at least partial credit on the question.)

C.   If the hearsay objection is overruled because the statement was offered for a non-hearsay purpose, its admission does not violate the Confrontation Clause, and the rest of this outline can be ignored.

---

[10]   I assume you've noticed this already.

D. If the *declarant testifies at trial and is cross-examined*, the Clause has been satisfied, and the rest of this outline can be ignored. Thus, statements falling within Fed. R. Evid. 801(d)(1)(A)–(C) *automatically satisfy the Confrontation Clause.*[11] And if the prosecutor calls the declarant to testify, statements falling within Fed. R. Evid. 801(d)(2)(C)–(E), any of the Rule 803 exceptions, or Rule 807, also survive a Confrontation Clause challenge without further analysis.

E. If the *declarant is unavailable and the defendant had a prior opportunity to confront and cross-examine the declarant about his statement*, the Clause has been satisfied and the rest of this outline can be ignored.

F. *If the statement falls within either Fed. R. Evid. 801(d)(2)(A) or (B)*, it automatically satisfies the Confrontation Clause, because in each case the declarant is the defendant himself. If the defendant wants to deny that he made or adopted the statement, or wants to explain why it should not be used against him the way the prosecutor claims it should, the defendant can do so by taking the witness stand.

G. If you haven't been able to "solve" the Confrontation Clause objection in ¶¶ A–F, however, it is necessary to analyze the issue further.

H. The next step is to determine whether the hearsay statement is "testimonial." As of the spring of 2011, we know this much for sure:

(1) The following *are* testimonial: formal testimony, whether at a trial, preliminary hearing, grand jury presentation, etc.; depositions; statements made by a defendant while pleading guilty in court; affidavits (i.e., sworn written statements); confessions made during custodial interrogations; and statements made during other formal police questioning (unless perhaps this takes place during an "emergency"[12]).

(2) The following are *not* testimonial:

(a) A "casual remark to an acquaintance." (Dictum, in *Crawford*, *Giles*, and *Bryant*.)

(b) Coconspirator statements. (Dictum in *Crawford* and *Bryant*.)

(c) Most business records and public records. (*Melendez-Diaz*.) Some, however, certainly *are* testimonial, and the law is uncertain about others. See § 9.36 (business records) and §§ 9.45 & 9.50-9.53 (public records), *infra*.

(d) Statements made for purposes of medical diagnosis or treatment, per Fed. R. Evid. 803(4). (Dictum in *Bryant*.) See § 8.42.

(e) Statements falling into the following miscellaneous Rule 803 exceptions: 803(9) (Records of Vital Statistics); 803(11) (Records of Religious

---

[11] Stop here for a moment: *why* do statements falling within Fed. R. Evid. 801(d)(1)(A)–(C) automatically satisfy the Confrontation Clause? Re-read those Rules until you understand the answer.

[12] Concerning the "emergency" issue, see § 8.14, *infra*.

Organizations); 803(12) (Marriage, Baptismal, and Similar Certificates); 803(13) (Family Records). (Dictum in *Bryant.*) These provisions are covered in Chapter 10.

(f) Statements against interest per Fed. R. Evid. 804(b)(3). (Dictum in *Bryant.*)

I.   Follow your professor's lead (of course) if he or she wants you to apply a particular definition of "testimonial." Otherwise, if you are answering an essay question, after identifying the Confrontation Clause as an issue, discuss the italicized "solemn declaration" phrase at the beginning of § 6.7, and refer to the "three formulations" listed later in that section, and do your best to apply *each* of those four definitions to the facts.

J.   Check the table of contents of this book[13] to see if it discusses how to apply the Confrontation Clause in a fact situation like the one in the question you are addressing. You will find such discussions regarding calls to 911; on-scene questioning by the police; statements by someone who was later murdered, expressing fear of the defendant (or of someone else); children's statements to parents about sex abuse; complainants' statements to doctors or counselors about sex abuse or sexual assault; forensic lab reports; dying declarations; and other situations.

K.   If the statement is "testimonial" hearsay and the prosecutor has not satisfied ¶¶ C, D, E or F *supra*, the statement is not admissible as substantive evidence (i.e., is not admissible to prove the truth of the matter asserted). Remember, though, something might happen *during* the trial that might make it admissible for some limited non-hearsay purpose, subject to Fed. R. Evid. 403 and a limiting instruction per Fed. R. Evid. 105.

L.   If the statement is *not* testimonial, then the Confrontation Clause does not apply at all — see § 6.12.

§ 6.14   THE PROVISIONS COVERED THUS FAR

[1]   Rules 801(d)(1)(A), 801(d)(1)(B), 801(d)(1)(C)

A statement that satisfies any of these provisions automatically satisfies the Confrontation Clause as well, because to satisfy any of the Fed. R. Evid. 801(d)(1) provisions, the declarant must testify at the current trial and be subject to cross-examination about the statement. This guarantees the defendant the right to confront and cross-examine.

---

[13] Do this on the final *only* if it is an open book exam.

[2]   Rules 801(d)(2)(A), 801(d)(2)(B)

Statements satisfying Fed. R. Evid. 801(d)(2)(A) or (B) are exempt from the Confrontation Clause because these provisions cover statements that the defendant himself has made or adopted. A defendant cannot complain that he is being denied the right to "confront" himself.

[3]   Rule 801(d)(2)(E)

In *Crawford* and again in *Bryant*, the Supreme Court stated that statements that fall within the coconspirator exception, Fed. R. Evid. 801(d)(2)(E), are not "testimonial." True, this is dicta; but it is about as reliable as dicta can be. Take it to the bank.

[4]   Rules 801(d)(2)(C), 801(d)(2)(D)

A statement that falls within either of these exceptions will have to be analyzed to determine whether it is testimonial. In other words, apply the outline in § 6.13.

Chapter 7

EXCEPTIONS TO THE HEARSAY RULE: PRELIMINARY MATTERS; MULTIPLE HEARSAY; CREDIBILITY AND IMPEACHMENT

§ 7.1 INTRODUCTION

As we saw in Chapter 1, hearsay is considered unreliable for three basic reasons. The typical out-of-court statement is not made under oath. The fact-finder had no opportunity to observe the declarant's demeanor when the statement was made. Most important, the adversely affected party is unable to test the declarant's accuracy and credibility by cross-examination. Despite this distrust of hearsay, however, the law recognizes numerous exceptions to the hearsay rule, based on the assumption that utterances made in certain more-or-less specific situations are trustworthy enough to overcome the absence of an oath and the inability to observe demeanor or to cross-examine. The Federal Rules of Evidence codify 28 specific exceptions: Rules 803(1)–803(23) and Rules 804(b)(1)–804(b)(5). Most of these exceptions were recognized at common law, although several of the Federal Rules of Evidence exceptions are broader than their common law antecedents. In addition, Rule 807 permits a judge, under certain circumstances, to admit hearsay that does not fall within any of the specific exceptions. Chapters 8–12 analyze when these provisions apply, when they do not, and the factual and legal issues that have arisen in the application of each.

First, however, it is worthwhile to note certain requirements and issues that are common to almost all of the exceptions.

§ 7.2 THE REQUIREMENT OF FIRST-HAND KNOWLEDGE

In general, a witness is not permitted to testify unless he or she has first-hand knowledge of the facts to which he will testify (*see* Fed. R. Evid. 602). In a hearsay situation, this usually imposes a dual requirement. First, the *witness* who is to testify to the declarant's statement must have first-hand knowledge of the statement (i.e., *must have heard the declarant make the statement*); it would not suffice for the witness to have heard about the declarant's statement from someone else.[1] Second, as the Advisory Committee's Note to Fed. R. Evid. 803 specifies, before hearsay can qualify under most exceptions to the rule, it must appear that the *declarant must have seen,*

---

[1] If the statement was written rather than oral, the witness must have personally read the statement; if the statement was in the form of assertive conduct, the witness must have seen the declarant engage in the conduct.

heard or experienced the event or condition that he or she was speaking about or describing in the statement.[2]

The fact that declarant had first-hand knowledge may be proved, the Advisory Committee's Note to Rule 803 observes, by direct evidence, or "[i]t may appear from [the declarant's] statement or be inferable from the circumstances." The following examples illustrate each of the possible methods.

1. Direct evidence that declarant had first-hand knowledge.

Assume it is important to prove the temperature of the water in a hotel swimming pool. W testifies, "I saw declarant dive into the pool. As soon as he surfaced he exclaimed, 'Good grief, this is cold!' " W's testimony is direct evidence that he heard DL make the statement, and also is direct evidence that DL had first-hand knowledge of the water temperature.

2. Declarant's first-hand knowledge inferable from declarant's statement.

Recall the bus and auto collision case discussed in Chapter 1. Winston Smith takes the stand and testifies:

Q.   Did anything unusual occur?

A.   Yes, I was looking at a movie poster when I heard a woman shout, "Look out, the bus is running the red light!" A second later I heard a crash.

The woman's very words — "Look out!" — provide convincing evidence that she had first-hand knowledge of what was happening at the intersection (i.e., that she saw the bus run the red light).

3. Declarant's first-hand knowledge inferable from circumstances.

In the same lawsuit, a police officer testifies:

Q.   What happened?

A.   I heard a crash; then, a few seconds later, a man rushed up to me and said, "Come quickly! A bus just ran the light and collided with a car!"

Here we are less sure that the declarant actually saw (had first-hand knowledge of) the fact he asserted. He didn't say he saw the collision. Perhaps he was only repeating what someone else had said, or was assuming the bus driver was at fault because of some previous experience with (or bias against) bus drivers. On the other hand, a judge probably has discretion to *infer* first-hand knowledge from the brief time between the crash and the statement, and the declarant's apparent lack of doubt as to the cause of the collision, etc.

---

[2] The only significant exceptions to this requirement arise when a party offers "diagnoses or opinions" under Fed. R. Evid. 803(6) or "factual findings" under Fed. R. Evid. 803(8)(A)(iii). Several rarely used exceptions also relax the first-hand knowledge requirement: Rules 803(9), (11)–(13), (19)–(23), and 804(b)(4).

Question

Q. 1. Who makes the preliminary determination as to whether the declarant had first-hand knowledge? What rule provides the answer?

Ans. Fed. R. Evid. 104(a) provides, in pertinent part: "Preliminary questions concerning . . . the admissibility of evidence shall be determined by the court. . . ."

§ 7.3   HEARSAY WITHIN HEARSAY: FED. R. EVID. 805

When a declarant's statement quotes or paraphrases another statement, both statements must be analyzed to determine if they constitute hearsay. Fed. R. Evid. 805 addresses this situation:

Rule 805. Hearsay within hearsay.

Hearsay within hearsay is not excluded by the rule against hearsay if each part of the combined statements conforms with an exception to the rule.

[Prior to December 1, 2011, the rule read as follows:

Rule 805. Hearsay within hearsay.

Hearsay included within hearsay is not excluded under the hearsay rule if each part of the combined statements conforms with an exception to the hearsay rule provided in these rules.

The Federal Rules of Evidence were rewritten solely to make them easier to understand; the Advisory Committee did not intend to make any substantive change in the Rules. The text of the old rule may remain useful in reading court decisions that precede the revision of the rules. Thus, this edition of the Student's Guide provides the text of both the new and the old version of each relevant provision of the Federal Rules of Evidence.]

For example, in lawsuit Plaintiff v. Defendant, where Plaintiff is suing her employer to recover for a job-related injury, if Defendant calls Z to testify, "Y told me that Plaintiff said she hurt her back last week cleaning her basement," we have two separate out-of-court statements within Z's testimony:

1. Plaintiff to Y

2. Y to Z

To overcome a hearsay objection, Defendant must find an exception to the hearsay definition or an exception to the hearsay rule as to each level of potential hearsay.

In this hypothetical, we can easily solve the hearsay issue as to the first statement: Plaintiff's statement to Y, if offered by Defendant, fits within Rule 801(d)(2)(A). If Y takes the stand and testifies, "Plaintiff said to me, . . ." then we only have one level of hearsay to deal with (Plaintiff to Y). Y's credibility can be tested by the oath, by cross-examination, and by the fact-finder observing Y's demeanor. But if Y is unavailable, then the only way for Defendant to prove that Plaintiff made the statement is by putting Z on the stand; in that case, the second level of hearsay (Y to Z) must be overcome or Z will not be permitted to testify.[3]

Defendant can attempt to overcome the hearsay objection as to the second level (Y to Z) in a variety of ways. Defendant might show that the Y-to-Z statement is not hearsay for any of the reasons discussed in Chapter 2, or that the statement falls within one of the exceptions to the hearsay definition (Rule 801(d)(1) or 801(d)(2)), or that it satisfies one of the exceptions to the hearsay rule (Rule 803, 804 or 807). If Defendant is unable to overcome the hearsay objection, however, the objection must be sustained.

Let me make one more point about multiple hearsay. Look again at how I diagramed our fact pattern:

1. Plaintiff to Y

2. Y to Z

This is really a short-hand way of saying:

1. Plaintiff to Y (or: Plaintiff overheard by Y)

2. Y to Z (or: Y overheard by Z)

It generally does not matter, for purposes of the hearsay rule, whether Plaintiff was speaking to Y, or was speaking to someone else and was overheard by Y. (Suppose, for example, Plaintiff and Q were having lunch at the local pizza place, unaware that Y, coincidentally, was sitting at the next table and was able to overhear their conversation.) The important fact is that Y heard what Plaintiff said; as a result, Y's testimony is a valid way of proving what Plaintiff said. Thus, whether Plaintiff was speaking to Y, or was overheard by Y while speaking to Q, if Y is available as a witness, Defendant could call Y, who could then testify, "I heard Plaintiff say that she hurt her back that week cleaning her basement." Regardless of whether Defendant calls Q or Y to testify about Plaintiff's statement, if Plaintiff objects on hearsay grounds, D can easily overcome that objection, because Plaintiff is the declarant, and his statement (whether testified to by Q or Y) is being offered by Defendant, his opposing party. See § 5.2.

For simplicity sake, when I diagram hearsay, I will diagram it as "Declarant to witness," whether the declarant was actually speaking *to* the witness, or was overheard *by* the witness.

Multiple hearsay issues are discussed from time to time in Chapters 8-10.

§ 7.4 ASSESSING CREDIBILITY

Hearsay evidence usually involves the credibility of two people: the declarant who made the statement and the witness who is to testify to it at trial. "Credibility" as used here has two different meanings. The first meaning covers all of the testimonial

---

[3] Defendant can of course call Plaintiff and ask him whether he made the statement; but if Plaintiff denies that he said it, then, unless Y's statement to Z satisfies a hearsay exception, Defendant is out of luck.

inferences. Perception: did DL, the declarant, in fact see the event in question; did W, the witness called to testify about DL's statement, hear it correctly? Memory: did DL accurately remember the event at the time he made the statement; did W accurately remember what DL said? Narration: are the words that DL used to describe the event mean more or less the same to him, as they did to W; and the words W used on the witness stand to relate what DL said, mean the same to W they mean to the jury. Sincerity: Did DL have a reason to spin or slant what he said to W; did W have a reason to spin or slant what he or she says on the witness stand?

The second meaning of "credibility" relates to a person's character for truthfulness. Is there anything in his or her background that suggests he or she cannot, as a general matter, be trusted to tell the truth? This aspect of credibility relates mainly to the kind of impeachment that is regulated by Fed. R. Evid. 608 and 609.

As a rule, of course, the issue of *witness* credibility is exclusively within the province of the jury; a judge may not normally exclude a witness' testimony simply because she does not believe that the witness is telling the truth, or fears that the witness would testify inaccurately. The same is generally true with regard to *declarant* credibility; a judge is not permitted to exclude a statement which appears to satisfy a hearsay exception, simply because she has doubts as to the declarant's truthfulness or accuracy.

There are, however, exceptions to these general rules. As will be seen *infra*, under *some* circumstances the judge may be permitted or required to assess the *declarant's* credibility before ruling on the admissibility of hearsay statements offered under Fed. R. Evid. 803(6), 803(8), 804(b)(3) and 807. Further, some courts have concluded that, at least in *some* circumstances, the judge is also obliged to assess the *witness'* credibility before ruling on the admissibility of hearsay statements offered under Fed. R. Evid. 804(b)(3) and 807.

§ 7.5   IMPEACHING AND DEFENDING THE HEARSAY DECLARANT: FED. R. EVID. 806

We're trying the bus-auto collision case. P calls Warble as a witness.

Q.   Where were you at about 1 p.m. that day?

A.   I was at the intersection of Broadway and 48th in Manhattan.

Q.   And what, if anything, did you see?

A.   I happened to be looking at the intersection, and I saw the bus run the red light and crash into the car.

On cross-examination, counsel for the bus company may attempt to impeach Warble's testimony in a variety of ways:[4] (1) by suggesting, for example, that Warble was several dozen yards away from the intersection, and therefore could not really see what happened; (2) by asking whether Warble had consumed any alcoholic beverages earlier

---

[4] Depending on what the lawyer asks and how she asks it, she may need a good faith basis before she can ask certain questions.

day, and therefore was in no condition to accurately see or remember what happened; (3) by asking Warble whether, at various times prior to trial, he made statements about the collision that were inconsistent with what he just said on direct examination (see §§ 4.6–4.7); (4) by suggesting that Warble had some bias in favor of the driver of the car, or against the bus company.

Moreover, after the plaintiff rests, the bus company's lawyer can call other witnesses to impeach Warble's testimony. She might call Croon, for example, to testify that she saw Warble consume several rye-and-gingers at lunch that day between noon and 1 p.m, and that when the collision occurred, Warble was several dozen yards away from the intersection. And she might call Drone to testify that a few days after the collision, Warble told her, "I was right there when the collision occurred, but I wasn't really paying attention to traffic, so I'm not sure what happened."

Now suppose instead that Warble does not testify. Instead, Plaintiff calls Echo:

Q.   Where were you at about 1 p.m. that day?

A.   I was at the intersection of Broadway and 48th in Manhattan.

Q.   Did anything unusual happen at that time?

A.   Yes. I was looking at a movie poster when I heard this guy I know, named Warble, shout out: "Look out, the bus is running the light!" Then I heard a crash. I ran to the intersection and saw that a bus had smashed into a car.

The judge overrules the bus company's hearsay objection, concluding that Warble's statement is an excited utterance (see § 8.2 et seq.). The bus company's lawyer can cross-examine Echo, of course, but if Warble does not testify, she cannot cross-examine Warble.

Nevertheless, the bus company's lawyer is permitted to impeach Warble as well as Echo, because Warble, the hearsay declarant, is the original source of the evidence that Echo has provided.

Fed. R. Evid. 806 provides:

Rule 806. Attacking and Supporting the Declarant's Credibility

When a hearsay statement — or a statement described in Rule 801(d)(2)(C), (D), or (E) — has been admitted in evidence, the declarant's credibility may be attacked, and then supported, by any evidence that would be admissible for those purposes if the declarant had testified as a witness. The court may admit evidence of the declarant's inconsistent statement or conduct, regardless of when it occurred or whether the declarant had an opportunity to explain or deny it. If the party against whom the statement was admitted calls the declarant as a witness, the party may examine the declarant on the statement as if on cross-examination.

[Prior to December 1, 2011, the rule read as follows:

Rule 806. Attacking and Supporting the Declarant's Credibility

> When a hearsay statement, or a statement defined in Rule 801(d)(2)(C), (D), or (E), has been admitted in evidence, the credibility of the declarant may be attacked, and if attacked may be supported, by any evidence which would be admissible for those purposes if declarant had testified as a witness. Evidence of a statement or conduct by the declarant at any time, inconsistent with the declarant's hearsay statement, is not subject to any requirement that the declarant may have been afforded an opportunity to deny or explain. If the party against whom a hearsay statement has been admitted calls the declarant as a witness, the party is entitled to examine the declarant on the statement as if under cross-examination

The Federal Rules of Evidence were rewritten solely to make them easier to understand; the Advisory Committee did not intend to make any substantive change in the Rules. The text of the old rule may remain useful in reading court decisions that precede the revision of the rules. Thus, this edition of the Student's Guide provides the text of both the new and the old version of each relevant provision of the Federal Rules of Evidence.]

This rule permits the bus company's lawyer to call Drone and Croon to impeach Warble's hearsay statement, just as she could if Warble had testified.

§ 7.6 ADMISSIBILITY DETERMINED BY OTHER RULES

Keep in mind that merely because a statement fits within an exception to the hearsay rule does not automatically mean that it is admissible. The Advisory Committee's Note to Rule 803 reminds us that "[t]he exceptions are phrased in terms of nonapplication of the hearsay rule, rather than in positive terms of admissibility, in order to repel any implication that other possible grounds for exclusion are eliminated from consideration." A statement that fits within a hearsay exception must also be analyzed to determine whether any other provision of the Federal Rules of Evidence requires its exclusion.

Chapter 8

RULE 803: THE "REGARDLESS OF WHETHER THE DECLARANT IS AVAILABLE AS A WITNESS" EXCEPTIONS: COMMON ORAL STATEMENTS, RULES 803(1)–803(4)

PART A:
"REGARDLESS OF WHETHER THE DECLARANT IS AVAILABLE AS A WITNESS"

§ 8.1 IN GENERAL

Fed. R. Evid. 803 contains 23 exceptions to the hearsay rule, each of which applies to a more or less precisely defined situation. The rule begins by instructing that a statement fitting into any of the provisions of Fed. R. Evid. 803 is "not excluded by the rule against hearsay, regardless of whether the declarant is available as a witness." This means that in assessing admissibility over a hearsay objection, we don't care whether the declarant could be or has been called as a witness or not; we simply look at the statement and the circumstances in which it was made. If the statement fits within a Fed. R. Evid. 803 exception, the hearsay objection is overruled.

Recall the collision between a bus and an automobile discussed in Chapter 2. A second or two before the collision, a man named Winston Smith heard a woman shout, "Look out, the bus is running the red light!" P's lawyer subsequently learns that her name was Julia Albion.

At trial, P wants the jury to hear what Julia Albion shouted just before the crash. To do so, P subpoenas Smith to testify. Ms. Albion's statement is hearsay, but (as you will see in a few more pages) fits within Fed. R. Evid. 803(2), the "excited utterance" exception. D's hearsay objection, therefore, is overruled; Smith can repeat Ms. Albion's hearsay statement while testifying.

As it turns out, Julia Albion lives only three blocks from the courthouse. She is perfectly willing to testify, but for some reason, P would rather have the jury hear about her statement through Smith, than call Albion to testify about what she saw or what she said. P has the right to do so: if a statement fits within a Fed. R. Evid. 803 exception, there is no obligation to call the declarant as a witness, even if the declarant is available.[1]

Suppose instead P does subpoena Ms. Albion. She testifies, "I saw the bus go right through the red light; it never even attempted to stop." This isn't hearsay, because she is relating from the witness stand what she saw. Next, P's attorney asks:

Q.   Did you say anything at the time?

A.   Yes. Just before the bus collided with the car I shouted out, "Look out, the bus is running the red light!"

D's hearsay objection will still be overruled, because (as you will learn in § 8.2) Ms. Albion's statement fits within the excited utterance provision of Fed. R. Evid. 803(2). She (the declarant) is not only available, she's actually testifying, but that doesn't affect the applicability of a Fed. R. Evid. 803 provision, because as to Fed. R. Evid. 803 exceptions, the availability of the declarant is immaterial.

After Ms. Albion completes her testimony, P calls Winston Smith. Direct examination proceeds:

Q.   . . . Where were you at one o'clock in the afternoon on April 4?

A.   I was on the corner of Broadway and 48th Street in Manhattan.

Q.   Did anything unusual occur?

A.   Yes. I heard a woman shout, "Look out, the bus is running the red light!" A second later I heard a crash.

D's hearsay objection is still (or again) overruled: because declarant's statement fits within a Fed. R. Evid. 803 provision, it is immaterial whether declarant was available to testify or has already testified.[2]

PART B:
SPONTANEOUS STATEMENTS: RULES 803(1)–803(2)

§ 8.2   IN GENERAL

Fed. R. Evid. 803(1) and 803(2) provide as follows:

Rule 803. Exceptions to the Rule Against Hearsay — Regardless of Whether the Declarant Is Available as a Witness

The following are not excluded by the rule against hearsay, regardless of whether the declarant is available as a witness:

---

[1] This is always true insofar as the hearsay rule is concerned. Remember, though, that in criminal cases, whenever a prosecutor offers hearsay evidence against a defendant, you must also consider whether the statement is "testimonial" and therefore is subject to the Sixth Amendment Confrontation Clause. *See* Chapter 6.

[2] If Ms. Albion has already testified as to what she saw and what she said, D may succeed in excluding Smith's testimony on Fed. R. Evid. 403 grounds (needless presentation of cumulative evidence), but not on hearsay grounds.

(1) *Present Sense Impression.* **A statement describing or explaining an event or condition, made while or immediately after the declarant perceived it.**

(2) *Excited Utterance.* **A statement relating to a startling event or condition, made while the declarant was under the stress or excitement that it caused.**

[Prior to December 1, 2011, these provisions read as follows:

Rule 803. The following are not excluded by the hearsay rule, even though the declarant is available as a witness:

(1) Present sense impression. A statement describing or explaining an event or condition made while the declarant was perceiving the event or condition, or immediately thereafter.

(2) Excited utterance. A statement relating to a startling event or condition, made while the declarant was under the stress of excitement caused by the event or condition.

The Federal Rules of Evidence were rewritten solely to make them easier to understand; the Advisory Committee did not intend to make any substantive change in the Rules. The text of the old rule may remain useful in reading court decisions that precede the revision of the rules. Thus, this edition of the Student's Guide provides the text of both the new and the old version of each relevant provision of the Federal Rules of Evidence.]

These provisions are closely related. The common theme is lack of time to forget or fabricate. Fed. R. Evid. 803(1) statements are assumed to be reliable on the theory that if a statement is made during or immediately after the declarant perceives something, there is no appreciable risk of misremembering, and he is unlikely to have time to fabricate a false statement about it. Fed. R. Evid. 803(2) statements are considered reliable because (as the Advisory Committee puts it) "circumstances may produce a condition of excitement that temporarily stills the capacity of reflection and produces utterances free of conscious fabrication."[3]

Thus, both provisions rely upon spontaneity to reduce the risks of lapses of memory and fabrication. That makes sense with regard to memory. The idea that people need time to come up with a lie, however, underestimates one of the less flattering qualities of human nature: we all know people who can invent a self-serving fabrication within nanoseconds of an event. In fact, the tendency to do so is probably instinctual;[4] as we

---

[3] Of course, if the event is exciting enough to "still the capacity of reflection," it also may interfere with declarant's ability to perceive or communicate accurately; nevertheless, the common law recognized an excited utterance exception, and Fed. R. Evid. 803(2) codifies it.

[4] A colleague at another school says a friend ("F") told him this story. (That makes it double-hearsay, but who's counting?) F's two sons, Tommy (age 8) and Brian (age 6), went away for a week to visit grandparents; meanwhile, F removed the carpet and wallpaper from the family room, and began to prepare the walls to put up paneling. (The room, in other words, was a mess.) When the boys returned from their week away, F said, "C'mon downstairs, I want you guys to see this." The two boys entered the room and, instantaneously, Tommy said, "Brian did it!"

grow older and more mature, we (hopefully) learn *not* to do so, (a) because doing so is wrong, and (b) because more often than not, we wouldn't get away with it anyhow.

Because Rules 803(1) and 803(2) are so closely related, many statements will satisfy both. Still, there are differences, and to overcome a hearsay objection, an attorney must persuade the judge that a statement satisfies *all* of the requirements of at least one of these provisions; it would not suffice to satisfy some of the requirements of 803(1) and some of 803(2).

In older cases, statements that fall within these exceptions were sometimes described as coming within the *"res gestae."* See § 2.40.

The requirements for these two provisions, and the issues likely to arise, are as follows:

Rule 803(1): present sense impression	**Rule 803(2): excited utterance**
1. Declarant must have had *first-hand knowledge* of the facts asserted in the statement.	1. Declarant must have had *first-hand knowledge* of the facts asserted in the statement.
2. *Nature of the event or condition and its effect on declarant.* Any event or condition will suffice; there is no need to show that it had any particular effect on the declarant.	2. *Nature of the event or condition and its effect on declarant.* The rule requires that the event or condition be "startling" and caused the declarant "stress or excitement."
3. *Subject-matter of the statement.* The statement must "describe or explain" the event or condition.	3. *Subject-matter of the statement.* The statement need only "relate to" the event or condition.
4. *Spontaneity; lapse of time between the event or condition and the statement.* The statement must have been made "while or immediately after the declarant perceived it."	4. *Spontaneity; lapse of time between the event or condition and the statement.* The statement need not have been made during or immediately after the event; it suffices that declarant made the statement "while the declarant was under the stress or excitement that it caused."
5. *Sixth Amendment Confrontation Clause.* See §§ 8.9 et seq.	5. *Sixth Amendment Confrontation Clause.* See § 8.9 et seq.

The party offering the statement must persuade the judge by a preponderance of the evidence that the exception's requirement has been satisfied.[5]

---

[5] In United States v. Bourjaily, 483 U.S. 171, 176 (1987), the Supreme Court, citing Fed. R. Evid. 104(a), held that the offering party must persuade the judge by a preponderance of the evidence that the requirements of any hearsay exception have been satisfied.

§ 8.3   FIRST-HAND KNOWLEDGE REQUIREMENT

To satisfy either rule, the offering party must persuade the judge that the declarant perceived the event or condition that is the subject matter of the statement. (There is no requirement that the declarant *participate* in the event; perception is enough.)

Proof that the declarant perceived the event or condition can be made in a variety of ways. Assume, for example, that P needs to establish that X was driving a Volkswagen Passat on a certain morning. DL, who lived across the street from X at the time, commented to his wife that morning, "X is driving the VW again today; I wonder if something is wrong with the Mercedes." This will qualify under Fed. R. Evid. 803(1) if it is clear that DL in fact saw X driving the VW.

If DL is a witness at trial, he can simply testify, "I saw X pull out of the driveway, and I remember commenting to my wife, 'X is driving the VW today; I wonder if something is wrong with the Mercedes.'" If declarant is not a witness, someone else can testify to facts establishing declarant's perception. DL's wife could testify, for example, "DL was standing at the window and said to me, 'X is driving the VW today; I wonder if something is wrong with the Mercedes.'" Because we know from DL's wife's testimony that DL was looking out of the window at the time he made the statement, we can comfortably conclude that DL in fact saw X in the VW.

Suppose DL's wife is blind, or had her back turned to DL when he made the statement. In that case, it is less clear that DL actually saw X in the VW. (It is also less clear that the statement was made "at or near the time" that he saw whatever it is he saw.) Still, it would be well within judicial discretion to conclude that the statement fits within Fed. R. Evid. 803(1). In other words, the statement itself, together with surrounding circumstances, can suffice to establish DL's first-hand knowledge of the event.

Thus, federal courts generally do not require the offering party to introduce corroborative evidence that the event in fact occurred; the statement itself generally will suffice.

When the declarant is an unidentified bystander, on the other hand, the Advisory Committee Note to Fed. R. Evid. 803(1) and 803(2) observes that pre-Federal Rules of Evidence cases "indicate hesitancy in upholding the statement alone as sufficient" to establish that declarant perceived the event first-hand. Such hesitancy, according to the Advisory Committee, "would under appropriate circumstances be consistent with" these rules. In other words, a judge has discretion to reject a statement attributed to an unidentified bystander even if the statement itself indicates the bystander saw the event. A judge is most likely to do so if she thinks the witness who claims to have heard such a statement is lying. In a traffic accident case, for example, P, a pedestrian, claims D, who was driving a Lincoln Continental, ran the light and knocked him down, causing permanent soft-tissue back injuries; D denies it ever happened. P and D are the only eyewitnesses available at trial, but P wants to testify that, just before being struck, he heard an unidentified man shout out, "O my gosh, the Lincoln is running the light!" The judge may be sorely tempted to exclude this testimony as too pat and too convenient to be believable. Although a judge should not consider witness credibility in determining admissibility, such a result (as the Advisory Committee delicately put it) "would under appropriate circumstances be consistent with the rule."

Even when no one questions that the declarant existed, a court should exclude the statement if it is doubtful the declarant actually saw the event. In one case, a court excluded a tape of a call to 911 in which the caller purported to describe a shooting incident outside a bar. The problem was that the caller's description of events did not include certain important facts that all of the witnesses who testified, for the prosecution or the defense, agreed upon. These omissions, the court concluded, raised so much doubt as to whether the caller actually saw the incident, that his statements to the 911 operator could not qualify as excited utterances or present sense impressions. *Brown v. Keane*, 355 F.3d 82 (2d Cir. 2004).

§ 8.4   TRUSTWORTHINESS OR RELIABILITY OF THE STATEMENT; SELF-SERVING STATEMENTS

Fed. R. Evid. 803(1) and 803(2) are based on the theory that a statement made under circumstances that fit the exceptions is inherently trustworthy and reliable. Logically, therefore, a court should not require any additional evidence of trustworthiness or reliability. Still, courts occasionally exclude such statements because specific facts suggest lack of trustworthiness. For example, if other evidence makes it clear that it was impossible for the declarant to have seen what she claims occurred, the statement should be excluded. If strong doubts exist as to whether the declarant is competent — e.g., it is fairly clear that the declarant was extremely intoxicated, or was suffering from delusions, when he saw the event and made the statement — it should be excluded.

Courts sometimes discuss whether it is appropriate to exclude an excited utterance or present sense impression because it is so self-serving. For example, police come upon D assaulting V, and D immediately exclaims: "V started it!" Occasionally a court will exclude such a statement.[6] Most courts, however, conclude that if the statement satisfies the exception, the judge should allow it, and that its self-serving nature is something the jury should consider in deciding whether to believe it.

§ 8.5   NATURE OF EVENT OR CONDITION; EFFECT ON DECLARANT

Any event or condition may suffice to be the subject matter of a statement of present sense impression (Fed. R. Evid. 803(1)): "I see X is driving her VW today." "I smell ammonia." "This feels very smooth." "It tastes salty."

To qualify as an excited utterance, by contrast, Fed. R. Evid. 803(2) requires a showing that the event or condition was "startling" and caused the declarant "stress"

---

[6] You might wonder: "So what if the statement is excluded? D can simply take the stand and tell his version to the jury." True. But D's attorney may prefer not to put D on the stand. Perhaps D has several felony convictions that the prosecutor could bring out on cross-examination; or perhaps D's attorney simply doesn't think D would make a very good witness. Moreover whether or not D testifies, some jurors might be impressed by the fact that D "spontaneously" attested to his innocence the instant he saw the police.

or "excitement." Certain events are pretty much guaranteed to qualify: being assaulted, abducted, shot at, or robbed, for example, or witnessing a perpetrator commit such a crime against someone else. More generally, a colleague of mine tells his students, "If it begins with 'Oh my gosh' and ends with an exclamation point, it's an excited utterance." That should give you a pretty good idea.

The offering party can prove that a startling event occurred, and that it had the necessary effect on the declarant, in a variety of ways. W1 could testify, for example, "I heard a crash, came running around the corner, and saw DL. He was very upset, actually shaking. He pointed to the intersection and said, 'A bus just ran the red light and broadsided that car!'" The wreckage of the two vehicles proves the event occurred; W1's testimony about DL's shaken state is persuasive evidence that DL saw the collision and was upset by it.

§ 8.6 SUBJECT MATTER OF THE STATEMENT

To fit within Fed. R. Evid. 803(1) (present sense impression), the statement must be closely tied to the event or condition that prompted it, i.e., must "describe or explain" the event or condition.

A Fed. R. Evid. 803(2) statement (excited utterance) need not be so narrowly connected to the event or condition; it suffices that the statement "relat[es] to" whatever prompted the statement. *Murphy Auto Parts Co. v. Ball*, 249 F.2d 508, 511 (1957), *cert. denied*, 355 U.S. 932, a pre-Rules case that is still in some evidence casebooks, provides a useful example. Two cars collided. The Balls were injured, and sued James Murphy, the owner-operator of the other vehicle, and his employer, Murphy Auto Parts, which was owned by his stepfather. Murphy Auto Parts carried more insurance than the individual defendant, and therefore, in legal parlance, was the "deep pockets defendant" in the case; but to show that the company was liable, the Balls had to show that James Murphy was on an errand for the company at the time of the collision. To do so, Mrs. Ball testified that, just after the collision, James jumped out of his car and said, "I'm sorry, I hope your son isn't hurt, I had to call on a customer and I was in a bit of a hurry to get home." The D.C. Circuit Court, per Circuit Judge (later Chief Justice) Burger, overruled Murphy Auto Parts' hearsay objection because the statement "related to" the exciting event (the collision), and therefore came within the excited utterance exception.

§ 8.7 SPONTANEITY; PASSAGE OF TIME BETWEEN THE "EVENT OR CONDITION" AND DECLARANT'S STATEMENT

Spontaneity is the underlying justification for both of these provisions. Evidence that suggests the declarant thought about what to say or considered the long-range implications of her statement detracts from its spontaneity and weighs against admissibility. For example, the fact that a statement is in response to a question may, under appropriate circumstances, suggest reflection rather than spontaneity.

The passage of time between the event or condition and the statement is a key factor in each rule, as well as a significant distinguishing feature between them. Fed. R. Evid. 803(1) (present sense impression) requires that the statement be made "while or immediately after the declarant perceived it." The Advisory Committee Note observes that often "precise contemporaneity is not possible, and hence a slight lapse is allowable." A lapse of a few seconds generally will not prevent a statement from qualifying under Fed. R. Evid. 803(1), but if the span between perception and statement is measured in minutes, courts often (but by no means always) conclude that 803(1) no longer applies.

Fed. R. Evid. 803(2) (excited utterance) requires that the statement be made "while the declarant was under the stress or excitement that [the startling event or condition] caused." But don't take that literally! A starting event can leave a person "stressed out" for hours or even days, but that does *not* mean that something he says relating to the event, hours or days later, the will be admissible as an excited utterance. The Advisory Committee Note comments that "the standard of measurement is the duration of the state of excitement," so long as the "condition of excitement . . . *temporarily stills the capacity of reflection and produces utterances free of conscious fabrication.*"[7] In other words, the time frame for an excited utterance is fairly short: it lasts only so long as the declarant is so excited and stressed that he can't really *think* ("reflect") about what just happened, and therefore cannot "spin" what he will say about it; all he can do is respond to it, almost as a reflex reaction.

. . . At least, that's how the Advisory Committee intended the excited utterance exception to be read and applied. Some courts give the exception a much broader scope. Even when the declarant has not suffered any physical injury or loss of consciousness, courts have admitted, as excited utterances, statements made many minutes, and even several hours, after the "startling event or condition," so long as there is sufficient evidence that the declarant is still under the influence of the startling event. A variety of factors are relevant: the nature of the event, its physical impact (if any) on the declarant, the declarant's age and health, etc.

Courts are particularly willing to overlook or discount lengthy delays in cases involving young children; delays of several hours and even days are sometimes excused.

When declarant was unconscious or in shock for much of the period between the event and the statement, courts generally hold that the declarant was still "under the stress or excitement" caused by the event or condition when he or she regained consciousness.

§ 8.8 QUESTIONS

Question 1. P brings a wrongful death action against EC, the electric company, alleging that its negligence caused the electrocution of her husband, Lineman, an employee of EC. EC, by contrast, asserts that Lineman's own negligence caused his

---

[7] Advisory Committee Note to Fed. R. Evid. 803(2) (emphasis added).

death, because Lineman failed to ascertain whether the power was turned off before he began working on a damaged line.

At trial P calls Co-worker, also an employee of EC. Co-worker will, if permitted, testify that he and Lineman were sent to inspect a section of power line; that he (Co-worker) climbed the pole, made a preliminary inspection, then went back to their truck, and radioed EC's plant, was connected to the appropriate supervisor, and was told, "The power has been shut off at that pole." Co-worker testifies that he relayed this information to Lineman. Lineman then climbed the pole, began working on the line, and was electrocuted.

EC objects that Co-worker's testimony about what he was told, when he radioed the plant, is hearsay. How should P respond?

Ans. There are two responses. The most direct is that P is not offering the supervisor's statement — "We've turned off the power at that pole" — to prove the truth of the matter asserted, because P's whole case is based on the fact that although the supervisor *said* the power was off, in fact EC had *not* turned off the power; that's how and why Lineman was electrocuted.

A second, equally acceptable response is: Rule 801(d)(2)(D). Applying the check list from § 5:23: (1) P is suing EC. The declarant, the supervisor, was an employee or agent of EC at the time he stated that the power was turned off at the pole. (2) The supervisor's statement was "on a matter within the scope" of his duties. (3) The supervisor was an employee of EC when he made the statement. (4) P need not show that the supervisor had first-hand knowledge of whether the power was on or off. (5) The rule includes "in-house" statements.

Objection overruled.

Question 2a. Let's make a significant change in the facts. Suppose Co-worker will, if permitted, testify that Lineman (not Co-worker) went into the truck; when Lineman emerged from the truck a minute or two later, he told Co-worker, "I radioed the plant, and they told me the power is shut off"; Lineman climbed the pole, began working on the line, and was then electrocuted. EC interposes a hearsay objection to Co-worker's testimony. How should P respond? How should the judge rule?

Ans. We now have potential double hearsay, because there are two "layers" or levels of statement:

    1. Supervisor to Lineman

    2. Lineman to Co-worker

The first level, supervisor to Lineman, raises no real problems, for the reasons set out in the answer to Q1: what the supervisor said to Lineman is not hearsay, and in any event would fall within Fed. R. Evid. 801(d)(2)(D). — That is, if P can find an acceptable way of proving that the supervisor in fact made that statement. That brings us to the second level of potential hearsay: Lineman to Co-worker. Unless P can overcome EC's hearsay objection to *this* statement, the jury will never get to hear what the supervisor supposedly said to Lineman.

Note, first, that if Co-worker had been able to hear what the supervisor said to Lineman, we would only have one level of hearsay: "Supervisor to Lineman and Co-worker." This is true whether the supervisor was aware that Co-worker was within listening range or not, because if Co-worker himself heard what the supervisor said to Lineman, we would not be relying on Lineman's statement to prove what the supervisor said; Co-worker would have first-hand knowledge of that.

Under the facts, though, Co-worker did not himself hear what the supervisor said; he can only testify as to what Lineman said the supervisor said. That is why this problem presents the second level or layer of potential hearsay.

Lineman's statement to Co-worker ("I radioed . . . they told me the power is off"), *is* hearsay, because P is offering it to prove the truth of the matter asserted by declarant Lineman, i.e., to prove that "they" *told* Lineman the power was off.[8] But it should be admitted, because Lineman's statement to Co-worker satisfies all of the requirements of Fed. R. Evid. 803(1). Apply the check list in § 8.2 of this chapter:

1) Lineman, the declarant, had first-hand knowledge of the "event" in question (his conversation with the supervisor at the power plant).

2) While there is nothing "startling" about Lineman's conversation with the supervisor, Fed. R. Evid. 803(1) doesn't require that the event be "startling."

3) Lineman's statement to Co-worker "described" his conversation with the supervisor.

4) Lineman's statement to Co-worker was made "immediately after" his conversation with the supervisor.

Question 2b. The company also objects on Confrontation Clause grounds. Ruling?

Ans. Apply the § 6.13 check list.

Actually, we don't get very far on the checklist; in fact we stop at ¶ A. This is a civil case. The Confrontation Clause applies only when a prosecutor offers hearsay in a criminal case. The Confrontation Clause objection is overruled.

Question 3. Suppose five minutes had elapsed between Lineman's conversation with the supervisor and his statement to Co-worker, instead of just a few seconds. Would this make his statement to Co-worker inadmissible hearsay?

Ans. Not necessarily. Issue # 4, spontaneity - lapse of time, now is a problem for P. But while a longer time period increases the hearsay risks of impaired memory and opportunity to fabricate, Lineman would have had no conceivable motive to lie to Co-worker about his conversation with power plant personnel, and it is unlikely that he would misremember such an important piece of information. And Lineman's own conduct — working on the wire — tends to corroborate that, as he told Co-worker, he had been assured that the power had been turned off.

---

[8] Obviously P did not offer the statement to prove that the power was in fact off; P's whole case depends on proving that power company officials *told* Lineman that the power was off, even though it had *not* been turned off.

Trial judges have substantial discretion in deciding whether the requirements for a hearsay exception have been satisfied. When the plaintiff is a widow, perhaps with young children, suing a multimillion dollar company, it is not unknown for judges to apply hearsay exceptions rather expansively.[9]

§ 8.9   SIXTH AMENDMENT CONFRONTATION CLAUSE: *CRAWFORD*

In *Crawford v. Washington*, the Supreme Court's 2004 Confrontation Clause decision, the Supreme Court, in a footnote, commented that the excited utterance exception was based on the common law "res gestae" concept, and that "to the extent the hearsay exception for spontaneous declarations existed at all, it required that the statements be made 'immediat[ely] upon the hurt received, and before [the declarant] had time to devise or contrive any thing for her own advantage.' "[10] A few courts have accordingly narrowed the time frame for the excited utterance exception.

§ 8.10   CONFRONTATION CLAUSE: *DAVIS v. WASHINGTON:* CALLS TO 911; CRIME-SCENE QUESTIONING BY THE POLICE

After *Crawford*, prosecutors sometimes argued (and some courts agreed) that all excited utterances are *not* testimonial, because the declarant was too excited to think about the possible courtroom uses of the statement. Defense attorneys argued with roughly equal plausibility that all calls to 911, and all statements that victims or witnesses make to the police at the scene of a crime, *are* "testimonial," because the declarant expected or hoped that the police would take official action as a result of his or her statement. In *Davis v Washington*, the Supreme Court rejected both of these extremes. Instead, it insisted that a trial court must carefully examine the facts and circumstances in which each statement was made:

> Without attempting to produce an exhaustive classification of all conceivable statements — or even all conceivable statements in response to police interrogation — as either testimonial or nontestimonial, it suffices to decide the present cases to hold as follows: Statements are nontestimonial when made in the course of police interrogation under circumstances objectively indicating that the *primary purpose of the interrogation* is to enable police assistance to meet an ongoing emergency. They are testimonial when the circumstances objectively indicate that there is no such ongoing emergency, and that the *primary purpose of the interrogation* is to establish or prove past events potentially relevant to later criminal prosecution.[11]

Thus, in deciding whether someone's responses to police interrogation were non-testimonial, the key issue is whether "the primary purpose of the interrogation

---

[9] This is known informally as the "poor widow rule."

[10] Crawford v Washington, 541 U.S. 38, 58 n 8 (2004).

[11] Davis v Washington, 547 U.S. 813, 822 (2006) (emphasis added).

was to enable police assistance to meet an ongoing emergency." The Court applied four factors:

1. Whether the primary purpose of the questioning was to determine past fact, or to ascertain ongoing events.

2. Whether the current situation could be described as an "emergency."

3. Whether the nature of the questions asked or answers given focused on the present situation, or past events.

4. The "level of formality" involved in the questioning.[12]

Facts: Davis's ex-girlfriend called 911[13] to report that the Davis was beating her. The operator elicited facts essential to get the police on the way and to alert them to what to expect: Was the man still in the house? Was he using a weapon? Was he drunk? What was his name? The victim answered these questions, and then reported that Davis, her assailant, was "running now," i.e., was leaving her home. The operator continued to question the caller about Davis, their relationship, etc. By the time the police arrived, Davis was gone. As all too often happens in domestic violence cases, the victim refused to testify; thus the only real evidence against Davis consisted of the victim's 911 call, and police testimony about her injuries.

Applying the definition of "testimonial" quoted *supra*, the Court held that what the victim told the 911 operator while Davis was still in her house was *not* testimonial, because she said those things during an "ongoing emergency." The state court had held that once Davis left her house, the emergency was over, and the rest of what the victim told the operator *were* testimonial statements. The Supreme Court accepted this conclusion without ruling on it, adding that questioning which began as non-testimonial will sometimes "evolve" into testimonial questioning as events develop.[14]

In a companion case *(State v. Hammon)* decided together with *Davis*, by contrast, police arrived at the scene of an apparent domestic assault after the violence was over. The Court held that the victim's statements to the police were testimonial — even though her husband was still in the house. They were in separate rooms; police officers were on the scene; thus, Mrs. Hammon was in no immediate danger when she answered the officers' questions.

Incidentally, the Court went out of its way to comment that there is nothing improper about the police interrogating Mrs. Hammon, or the 911 operator continuing to question the victim in *Davis* after Davis left her home. A finding that statements were testimonial in no way depends on a finding that anyone acted incorrectly.

---

[12] Id. at 827.

[13] The Court said that under the facts, it regarded the 911 operator's questions as the equivalent of police questioning.

[14] Id. at 828. The Court held that even if only the portion of the 911 call before Davis left the house should have been admitted, admitting the remaining, "testimonial" statements, was harmless error.

§ 8.11 CONFRONTATION CLAUSE—QUESTIONING BY THE POLICE: *GILES v. CALIFORNIA*

Caution: confusion lies ahead! Students are invited to skip this section unless your professor discusses the impact that Giles v. California might have on the definition of "testimonial."

In *Giles v. California*, 554 U.S. 353 (2008), the Court decided its fourth post-*Crawford* Confrontation Clause case. Unlike *Crawford* and *Davis-Hammon*, the *Giles* case did not require the Court to decide whether certain statements were testimonial. The issue in *Giles* focused on the "forfeiture" doctrine. That is the issue on which the Court granted certiorari, and that is the issue the Court decided (sort of, anyway; see §§ 11.51 et seq). In deciding that issue, the Court fractured: the nine Justices wrote a total of 5 opinions. But even though the definition of what "testimonial" means was not before the Court, the 5 opinions in *Giles* cast doubts on what we thought the *Davis-Hammon* decisions told us regarding when answers to police questioning were "testimonial."

It may be that whatever confusion *Giles* introduced into the definition of "testimonial" law has been subsumed by the Court's subsequent decision, *Michigan v Bryant*, discussed extensively in the following sections. My suggestion: read *this* section *only* if your professor discusses whether *Giles* signals a shift in the Court's basic definition of "testimonial."

Police, responding to a domestic violence complaint, went to the home Giles shared with his then-girlfriend, Brenda Avie. She described how, a few minutes earlier, he had assaulted her, choked her and threatened her with a knife. By the time the police arrived, however, the incident was over and, although Giles was still in the house, he was no longer assaulting or threatening her. Thus, the facts in *Giles*, for Confrontation Clause purposes, seem indistinguishable from those in *Hammon*.[15] Presumably for this reason, the prosecutor in *Giles* conceded that Ms Avie's statements to the police were testimonial,[16] and argued that her statements fell within the forfeiture doctrine. Along the way, however, one Justice (Thomas) stated flatly that he did not consider the statements to be testimonial, a second (Alito) strongly suggested that he agreed with Thomas's view, and three Justices (Breyer, joined by Stevens and Kennedy) at least hinted that they would be willing to reconsider whether such statements should be classified as testimonial.

1 (Thomas) + 1 (Alito) + 3 (Breyer-Stevens-Kennedy) = 5, which means that — maybe! — a majority of the Court *might* be ready to reverse what it said in *Hammon*. I would not bet on that, exactly; but if I were a prosecutor in a case involving a witness-victim's statements in a *Hammon-Giles* situation, I would refuse to stipulate or concede that the statements were testimonial, on the wild off-chance that, if the Justices are in fact looking for a chance to revisit the issue, my case might be the one they choose.

---

[15] The facts in *Giles* differed from *Hammon* dramatically and tragically in other respects, however. See § 11.51.

[16] I am not criticizing the prosecutor; I probably would have done the same thing.

"Well, OK, great," you may be thinking, "when I become a prosecutor I'll keep that in mind, but right now I'm a law student, trying to learn this stuff well enough to handle it on the exam. What advice do you have for *me*, O Great Seer of Hearsay?"[17]

Fair question. I tell my students, if I give you a fact pattern like the one in *Hammon*, your answer should include something like:

> These facts closely parallel those in *Hammon*, where the Court ruled the statements were testimonial, although in *Giles*, a majority hinted they might consider revisiting the issue. Assuming they are testimonial, however, they are excluded by the Confrontation Clause unless the prosecutor can fit them into some exception to the Clause.

Then discuss any exceptions to the Clause that the prosecutor might urge with at least superficial plausibility.

Unless and until the Court tells us more, this accurately describes the state of the law, so I cannot reasonably ask my students to do more than that.

Once more, though, remember what I said at the beginning of this section. Your goal this semester is not, "to boldly go where no evidence student has gone before";[18] it is to learn evidence and do well on the exam. If your prof ignores this aspect of *Giles*, you should, too, at least until after the final exam.

§ 8.12 CONFRONTATION CLAUSE — POLICE INTERROGATION: *MICHIGAN v. BRYANT* — FACTS

In February, 2011, in *Michigan v. Bryant*,[19] the Supreme Court, for the fourth time in the *Crawford* era, addressed whether answers to police interrogation were testimonial.[20] Around 3:25 a.m. on an April morning in 2001, Detroit police responded to a radio dispatch that a man had been shot and was in a gas station parking lot. They found the victim, Anthony Covington, lying in great pain on the ground next to his car with a gunshot wound in the abdomen. Over the next few minutes, until the ambulance arrived, five different officers asked Covington who shot him and where it had happened. He answered that "Rick" shot him through the back door of Rick's house, about six blocks away and some twenty or so minutes earlier. (Covington had driven himself to the gas station.) Then an ambulance arrived to take him to a hospital, where, a few hours later, he died.

The officers identified "Rick" as Richard Bryant. Bryant was arrested a year later in California, and charged with murder. At his trial, which was held before *Crawford* was decided, Covington's statements to the police were admitted as excited utterances. On appeal the Michigan Supreme Court held that those statements were testimonial

---

[17] I don't actually consider myself a Great Seer of anything, but you may think of me in such terms if you like.

[18] Cf the introductory narrative for each *Star Trek* episode. (I split the infinitive on purpose.)

[19] 131 S.Ct. 1143 (2011).

[20] The other three are *Crawford*, *Davis* and *Hammon*.

and their admission violated the Confrontation Clause. The State appealed, and in February 2011, the Supreme Court, by a 6-2 majority,[21] reversed, concluding that the statements were *not* testimonial.

§ 8.13   BRYANT — "PRIMARY PURPOSE"; "OBJECTIVE" TEST

The Court, per Justice Sotomayor, focused on the rule, set forth in *Davis*, that statements made in response to police questioning are not testimonial if the "primary purpose" of the interrogation was to respond to an ongoing emergency; but that the statements are testimonial if the primary purpose of the interrogation was to "establish or prove past events potentially relevant to later criminal prosecution."[22]

The Court in *Bryant* emphasized that the "primary purpose" test is *objective*, not *subjective*. This means that the "primary purpose" of the conversation must be judged, *not* on what the *actual* participants in the conversation believed or intended, but "on the purpose that *reasonable* participants would have had," based on all the circumstances. In other words:

(a) If the actual participants *thought* they faced an emergency, but a reasonable person in their situation, knowing only what the actual participants knew at the time, would *not* have considered it an emergency, then the declarant's statements made in response to police questioning *are* testimonial.

(b) But if the actual participants did *not* think they faced an emergency, but a reasonable person in their situation, knowing only what the actual participants knew at the time, *would* have considered it an emergency, then the declarant's statements made in response to police questioning probably are *not* testimonial.

§ 8.14   BRYANT — "EMERGENCY"

Bryant contains an elaborate discussion on how should a judge decide whether, viewed objectively, an emergency existed.

1. The judge should view the case from what the participants in the conversation knew about the situation at the time, not what they learned later.

2. Whether (viewed "objectively") an emergency still existed at the time the police questioned the declarant depends on several factors.

(a) The "zone of potential victims." In a domestic violence case, like those in *Davis* and *Hammon* (the companion case decided with *Davis*), that "zone" is usually a single victim. In contrast, if the situation (viewed objectively) might involve a broader threat to public safety, the emergency may last a lot longer,

---

[21] Justice Sotomayor wrote the majority opinion, which was signed by Chief Justice Roberts and Justices Breyer, Kennedy and Alito. Justice Thomas concurred in the result. Justices Scalia and Ginsberg dissented. Justice Kagan recused herself from the case.

[22] Davis, 547 U.S. 813, 822, quoted in Bryant.

which means that statements in response to police questioning over a longer period of time are more likely to be considered non-testimonial.

(b) The weapon the suspect used. If the suspect used his fists, once he and the victim have been physically separated, the emergency is over. On the other hand, if the suspect used a gun, then (viewed objectively), even if the suspect is no longer within a few feet of victim, the danger to the victim — and the police, and ambulance attendants, and the general public — may continue for a much longer time period. This, too, increases the likelihood that the victim's statements will be considered non-testimonial.

(c) The medical condition of the victim. In essence, the more serious the victim's injuries, the more likely it is that (viewed objectively) the police and victim would both consider the situation an emergency, which makes it less likely that the questions or answers would be testimonial in purpose.

(d) The "formality" or "informality" of the interrogation. Statements made during a formal interrogation (such as the one in *Crawford*, see § 6.7) will almost always be testimonial, because formal questioning strongly suggests that no emergency exists. Quick, hurried, informal questioning, on the other hand, may lend support to the argument that an emergency exists (although the Court emphasized that police cannot avoid the Confrontation Clause merely by "informalizing" their questioning).[23]

(e) In deciding whether the victim's statements were testimonial, a court should consider the primary purpose the police had in questioning the victim, as well as the primary purpose the victim had in answering the questions. (The Court recognized that both police and victim might have "mixed motives" — i.e., both emergency-response and evidence-gathering.)

(f) The Court reiterated the statement in *Davis* that an interrogation might "evolve," and what begins as a non-testimonial, emergency context might evolve into an evidence-gathering, testimonial one. Such might be the case, for example, once the suspect was arrested, thus ending the emergency. (Other than that, the Court did not give any general guidance on how long such an emergency might last.)

The Court then examined the facts in *Bryant.* The Court emphasized that the suspect had used a gun, not fists; his whereabouts were unknown; Covington was not merely bruised, he'd been shot and was seriously — and, as it turned out, mortally — wounded; and that, based on the circumstances, including the questions they asked and the answers Covington gave, the police did not know whether the shooting was merely a private vendetta against Covington, or whether the shooter might be hunting down additional victims. The majority concluded that, viewed objectively, the primary purpose of the officers' questions, and of Covington's answers, was to respond to an ongoing emergency, and that Covington's statements therefore were not testimonial;

---

[23] The word "informalizing" is mine, not Justice Sotomayor's, so I get the credit (or blame), not her.

and since they were not testimonial, they were admissible over a Confrontation Clause objection.[24]

§ 8.15 CONFRONTATION CLAUSE: STATEMENTS TO NON-GOVERNMENT OFFICIALS

In 2008, in *Giles v. California*, dictum in Justice Scalia's opinion for the Court can be read as suggesting that only certain *statements to government officials* will be classified as testimonial, but that statements to non-government officials are inherently non-testimonial. See §§ 8.37.1; 11:11.3. But in *Bryant*, the majority noted that because the statements there were made to police officers, the Court had no occasion to address the "statements to non-government actors" issue, and Justice Scalia, dissenting, declared himself "agnostic" on the issue. So the short and simple answer is: we still do not know whether statements to a private person (i.e., to someone who is not a government official) will ever be categorized as testimonial for purposes of the Confrontation Clause.

§ 8.16 CONFRONTATION CLAUSE: STATEMENTS TO "FRIENDS AND NEIGHBORS"

Davis, Hammon and *Giles* all involved domestic violence, and in each of those opinions, the Court was very conscious of the impact its decisions would have on domestic violence prosecutions. Addressing these concerns, in *Giles*, Justice Scalia wrote that the Confrontation Clause barred "only *testimonial* statements,"[25] and added, in dictum, "Statements to friends and neighbors about abuse and intimidation, and statements to physicians in the course of receiving treatment would be excluded, if at all, only by hearsay rules, . . ."[26] In other words, such statements would not be testimonial.

Putting aside the reference to physicians (I discuss that in § 8:42, infra), this dictum is certainly true for most "statements to friends and neighbors."[27] But is it true for all such statements? If the Confrontation Clause applies *only* to statements made to government officials, and *never* applies to statements made to civilians, then Justice Scalia's dictum in *Giles* would always be true. But see § 8:17 **Q3**.

---

[24] This conclusion sounds plausible enough, until you consider that the police who responded apparently did *not* consider the situation an ongoing general public safety emergency. (For details, see Justice Scalia's dissent, or the Michigan Supreme Court decision, *People v. Bryant*, 483 Mich. 132, 768 N.W.2d 65 (2009).) Justice Scalia, in a scathing dissent, described the majority's reading of the facts as "transparently false." Justice Scalia also insisted that in assessing whether statements made during police interrogation were testimonial, only the declarant's purpose in answering the questions, not that of the officers in asking them, should be considered. (Justice Scalia and the majority also disagreed vigorously as to what Covington's "primary purpose" was in answering the officers' questions.)

[25] 554 U.S. 353, 376 (emphasis in original).

[26] Id.

[27] It's safe to assume that this would also include statements to relatives, co-workers, and even casual acquaintances.

§ 8.17 QUESTIONS

Question 1. D is charged with shooting and killing V, his former girlfriend, some time between 4 p.m. and 6 p.m. on April 2.

The prosecutor seeks to elicit testimony from W, a friend of V, who will testify that V approached her about one o'clock that afternoon, trembling and pale, literally shaking, more upset than W had ever seen her. Asked what was the matter, V replied that D had picked her up to take her to school, stopped along the way, threatened to kill her and himself if she didn't take him back, and fired a shot in the air as she broke away. (The only corroboration of V's statement is that she had missed an 8 a.m. class that morning, and that she appeared extremely nervous and upset at 1 p.m. that afternoon.) Then V seemed to calm down a little, and insisted that W promise not to tell anyone for fear of getting D in trouble.

Is W's testimony about V's statement admissible over a hearsay objection?

Ans. The prosecutor should cite Fed. R. Evid. 803(2). Applying the § 8.2 checklist:

1. Declarant (V) had first-hand knowledge of her encounter with D.

2. Being threatened and shot at certainly qualifies as a startling, stressful event! On the other hand, aside from the statement itself, the only corroboration that the event ever occurred is that V missed a class that morning and was extremely upset at 1 p.m.

3. V's statement to W certainly "relates to" the event; in fact, it describes it.

4. The lapse of time is the main potential barrier here to admissibility. Still, in the trial on which this problem is based, the trial judge admitted W's testimony, and the appellate court affirmed. Even though the event had occurred an indefinite number of hours before declarant made the statement, "[t]he lapse of time between [the] event and the statement relating to it did not significantly erode the stress of excitement resulting to [declarant] from the event. Personal observations by [declarant's] best friend and her choral music teacher vouch for the physical and emotional manifestations . . . of the continued existence of that stress or excitement at the time of the utterance . . ." *State v. Robinson*, 94 N.M. 693, 616 P.2d 406 (1980). On the other hand, some courts are now less "liberal" with regard to the passage of time than they were before *Crawford v. Washington*.

Question 2. D's attorney of course also objects that admitting V's statement violates the Confrontation Clause. Ruling?

Ans. Apply the check list in § 6.13.

¶ A. The prosecutor is offering the statement in a criminal case.

¶ B. Let's assume that the court holds that V's statement is an excited utterance.

¶ C. V's statement is being offered for a hearsay purpose.

¶ D. V, the declarant, is dead, and obviously cannot testify.

¶ E. D never had an opportunity to confront and cross-examine V about her statement to her friend.

¶ F. None of the provisions listed in ¶ F apply.

¶ G. Therefore we have to apply the rest of the check list.

¶ H. V's statement does not fall within any of the "obviously testimonial" situations, but it certainly cannot be described as a "casual remark," either. And for that matter, neither *Davis* nor *Bryant* gives any clear indication as to how we should categorize V's statements.

¶ I. Applying the various definitions of "testimonial" offered by the Court (see § 6.7), does it appear that V's statement to her friend was *"[a] solemn declaration or affirmation made for the purpose of establishing or proving some fact"*? Was it a statement that V "would reasonably expect to be used prosecutorially" (the open-ended aspect of "formulation 1")? Did V make her statement "under circumstances which would lead an objective witness reasonably to believe that the statement would be available for use at a later trial" (the third formulation)?

There is no absolutely right-or-wrong answer, but I'd categorize V's statement as non-testimonial, because, as I read the situation,[28] V's primary purpose in telling her friend W what happened was to share a frightening experience as a way of helping herself deal with what happened; her purpose probably was not to "create evidence" or "establish[] or prov[e] some fact." After all, she made W promise not to tell anyone!

¶ J. This case does not fall into any of the "¶ J" scenarios.

¶ K. Not applicable.

¶ L. Because the statement was non-testimonial, the Confrontation Clause objection is overruled.

Question 3. Suppose, after V told W the story related in **Q1**, instead of making W promise not to tell anyone, V added, "If anything happens to me, make sure the police know about this!" D objects: hearsay; Confrontation Clause. Ruling?

a, As to the hearsay objection, let's assume the court rules that the statement was an excited utterance, per **Q1**.

b. As to the Confrontation Clause, apply the § 6.13 checklist.

¶¶ A–H. The answers to **Q3** are the same as they were in **Q2**.

¶ I. Here's the hard part: even though there was no police involvement here and W did not "interrogate" V in any formal way, when V told W "If anything happens to me, tell the police," doesn't that make her whole narrative *"[a] solemn declaration or affirmation made for the purpose of establishing or proving some fact"*? V "would reasonably expect [her

---

[28] Maybe I should say, "As I *wrote* the situation"?

statement to W] to be used prosecutorially" if V should be killed. And D's attorney also has a pretty good argument that V made that statement "under circumstances which would lead an objective witness reasonably to believe that the statement would be available for use at a later trial." Unless the Clause applies *only* to statements to government officials, I think a judge (perhaps very reluctantly) would have to categorize V's statement as testimonial.

¶ J. This case does not fall into any of the "¶ J" scenarios.

¶ K. There is no legitimate non-hearsay purpose for which the state can offer this statement.

¶ L. The statement *is* testimonial. See ¶ I.

¶ M. Thus, it must be excluded. . . .

¶ N. . . . unless the prosecutor can persuade the judge that the situation comes within the "forfeiture" doctrine — which does not seem likely. See § 11.47 et seq.

§ 8.18   YOUNG CHILDREN AS DECLARANTS

Courts frequently must address whether statements by young children are admissible over hearsay and Confrontation Clause objections. In most of these cases, the child has allegedly been sexually abused. Often, for a variety of reasons, the child is unable to testify at trial; accordingly, if the prosecutor cannot introduce the child's hearsay statements about what happened, the state may not be able to survive a defendant's motion for a directed verdict.

As discussed in § 8.7, courts applying the excited utterance exception tend to be particularly expansive when considering how soon after an event the statement must be made. Lower court decisions after *Crawford* and *Davis* have classified, as non-testimonial, statements the child made to a parent or other family member, even if the parent had to question the child to find out what was wrong. The reasoning behind such rulings is simple enough: the parent's primary goal is to find out what is bothering the child, and the child's primary reason for answering is, simply, to obey the parent.

Once a police officer or some other official agent or agency enters the picture, however, courts after *Crawford* and *Davis* generally categorize the child's statements as testimonial: whether or not the child understands why he is being asked these questions, an objective observer would clearly understand that the questions are being asked with the goal of helping to establish whether a crime was committed, and if so, who committed it.

We will address this situation further in § 8.38, discussing Fed. R. Evid. 803(4).

Note, by the way, that the child's statements are not being suppressed to deter official wrongdoing; indeed, it is entirely proper for the authorities to ask such questions. After all, it is their job to determine whether a crime was committed and, if so, to gather and preserve evidence of it, and to help the child, and the parents, deal with the situation. Unlike, say, the Fourth Amendment exclusionary rule, which suppresses evidence only if the police engaged in an unlawful search or seizure, the right to exclude hearsay pursuant to the Confrontation Clause exists independent of whether the authorities have behaved properly or not.

PART C:
THE "STATE OF MIND" EXCEPTION: RULE 803(3)

§ 8.19 IN GENERAL

Rule 803(3) provides as follows:

> **The following are not excluded by the rule against hearsay, regardless of whether the declarant is available as a witness: . . .**
>
> > **(3) *Then-Existing Mental, Emotional, or Physical Condition.* A statement of the declarant's then-existing state of mind (such as motive, intent, or plan) or emotional, sensory, or physical condition (such as mental feeling, pain, or bodily health), but not including a statement of memory or belief to prove the fact remembered or believed unless it relates to the validity or terms of the declarant's will.**

[Prior to December 1, 2011, the rule read as follows:

> Rule 803. The following are not excluded by the hearsay rule, even though the declarant is available as a witness:
>
> > (3) Then existing mental, emotional, or physical condition. A statement of the declarant's then existing state of mind, emotion, sensation, or physical condition (such as intent, plan, motive, design, mental feeling, pain, and bodily health), but not including a statement of memory or belief to prove the fact remembered or believed unless it relates to the execution, revocation, identification, or terms of declarant's will.

The Federal Rules of Evidence were rewritten solely to make them easier to understand; the Advisory Committee did not intend to make any substantive change in the Rules. The text of the old rule may remain useful in reading court decisions that precede the revision of the rules. Thus, this edition of the Student's Guide provides the text of both the new and the old version of each relevant provision of the Federal Rules of Evidence.]

In § 2.24-2:35 we saw that when declarant's state of mind is a fact in issue, a statement about something else, from which we must *infer* declarant's state of mind, is *not* hearsay, but that a direct statement by the declarant as to her state of mind *is* hearsay. Fed. R. Evid. 803(3) provides that many (but not all!) hearsay statements directly stating declarant's state of mind come within the "state of mind" hearsay exception and therefore are admissible over a hearsay objection.

The last clause of Rule 803(3) ("unless it relates . . .") tacks on a rather different concept, relating to the declarant's will.

Application of Fed. R. Evid. 803(3) raises the following issues:

1. *Declarant's first-hand knowledge.* The rule admits only statements by a declarant concerning his or her *own* state of mind, so first-hand knowledge is not really an issue. Regardless of whatever psychologists may tell us, Fed. R. Evid. 803(3) accepts that, for hearsay purposes at any rate, a person knows what he thinks, feels, wants, intends, fears, etc.

2. *Relevance of declarant's state of mind.* To understand the application of Fed. R. Evid. 803(3), it is important to pinpoint how evidence of the declarant's state of mind can be relevant to a lawsuit. State of mind can be relevant in a wide range of circumstances. The following are among the most common:

    (a) State of mind is often an element of a crime, cause of action or defense. *See* § 8.20.

    (b) A statement by the declarant as to pain, mental feeling or bodily health is often relevant in personal injury and similar actions. *See* § 8.22.

    (c) A statement by the declarant as to his then-existing *intent* is a basis from which we can infer the declarant's subsequent conduct. This is sometimes referred to as the "*Hillmon* doctrine." *See* § 8.23.

    (d) A statement by the declarant as to his then-existing intent to do something with another person is a basis from which we can infer that other person's subsequent conduct. I call this situation, "second party *Hillmon*." *See* § 8.25.

3. *"Then-existing" state of mind v. "backward-looking" statements.* The rule covers only statements by the declarant about her state of mind at the time she is speaking, not statements about what she felt, thought, etc. at some time in the past. *See* § 8.27.

4. *Victim's fear of defendant.* In homicide cases, prosecutors often offer, and judges sometimes admit, testimony that a few days before V was killed, V told a friend that he or she was afraid that the defendant was going to kill him or her. Do such statements truly fall within Fed. R. Evid. 803(3)? *See* § 8.29. (I discussed the Confrontation Clause implications of such statements in § 8.17.)

5. *Will cases.* The rule recognizes an important exception to the "then-existing" restriction in litigation concerning declarant's will: in such cases, "backward-looking" statements are admissible. *See* § 8.31.

6. *Sixth Amendment Confrontation Clause. See* § 8.33.

§ 8.20 STATE OF MIND AS AN ELEMENT OF A CRIME, CAUSE OF ACTION, OR DEFENSE

In many civil lawsuits and in almost all criminal cases, a litigant is required to prove what a person's state of mind was. Failure to offer such proof will result in a directed verdict. To determine the mental element of a given crime, cause of action or defense, we look at the substantive law that defines that crime, cause of action or defense. Examples:

1. In a murder prosecution, the prosecutor must prove that the defendant killed the victim *intentionally* or with *malice aforethought;* while the defense might be that the defendant acted in the *reasonable belief* that he had to use deadly force in self-defense.

2. In an extortion trial, the prosecutor must prove that D placed the victim in *fear of death or bodily harm.*

3. In a libel action brought by a "public figure," P must establish that D's defamatory remarks were uttered *knowingly, or with reckless disregard* of whether, they were false.

4. In a fraud suit, P must prove that D did what she did with the *intent to defraud.* Often this involves showing that D *knew* that certain representations she made were untrue. D, on the other hand, might want to show that these representations were not "material" because P *did not rely* on D's representations.

In each instance, statements that shed light on the key person's state of mind (D in example 1; the extortion victim in example 2; D in example 3; both D and P in example 4) are highly relevant. Fed. R. Evid. 803(3) allows many such statements to be admitted even if they are hearsay.

§ 8.21 QUESTIONS

Question 1. An indictment charges JH with first degree murder, alleging that, acting intentionally and with premeditation, she shot and killed Dr. T at four o'clock in the afternoon on June 1. (Dr. T had been JH's long-time lover, but had jilted her for another woman a month before he died.) JH, however, insists it was all a tragic accident. Her breakup with Dr. T had been quite amicable; she had gone to his home that day to return some items he had loaned her, including a .38 caliber pistol; that as she was handing it to him it slipped from her hand, fell to the ground, and discharged one bullet, which struck him in the chest and killed him.

What is the "mental element" of the crime JH is charged with?

Ans. The indictment spells it out: JH is accused of killing Dr. T "intentionally and with premeditation." Thus, any evidence that either side can offer concerning how JH felt toward Dr. T on or near June 1 is highly relevant in assessing her guilt or innocence.

Question 2. At trial, the prosecutor calls W1, a friend of JH's, who will (reluctantly) testify that when JH found out on May 10 that Dr. T was seeing another, younger woman, JH exclaimed, "That louse! He's nothing but a two-timing gutter rat! He doesn't deserve to live!" If JH objects that this is hearsay, how should the prosecutor respond? How should the judge rule?

Ans. Fed. R. Evid. 801(d)(2)(A). JH said it; the prosecutor, her opposing party in the case, is offering it. Objection overruled. If a statement satisfies Fed. R. Evid. 801(d)(2)(A), there is no reason to cite any other provision of Article VIII.

Question 3. On cross-examination, JH has W1 testify that on May 30, JH told W1, "I hope I can persuade Dr. T to come back to me, but if not — well, I'll always be grateful to him anyway, and I wish him every happiness." If the prosecutor interposes a hearsay objection, can JH's attorney cite Fed. R. Evid. 801(d)(2)(A), like the prosecutor did in the previous question?

Ans. No. Here, JH is calling a witness to offer her (JH's) own statement. A party cannot use Rule 801(d)(2)(A) to offer her own statement. See § 5.4.

Question 4. How should JH respond to P's hearsay objection?

Ans. Fed. R. Evid. 803(3). JH's statement was of her "then-existing state of mind" toward Dr. T. This is relevant because (if the jury believes that she said it and that she meant it at the time), if she felt no animosity toward him on May 30 about the breakup, this makes it less likely that (as the prosecutor charges) she visited him on June 1 with a premeditated plan to kill him. Objection overruled.

Note that W's testimony may be manufactured — she may be lying to help JH beat a murder charge; or JH may have already decided to kill T, and may have made the statement to W1 as part of a plan to manufacture a defense. Fed. R. Evid. 803(3) does not, however, authorize the judge to exclude a statement merely because the judge thinks the witness is lying or doubts that the declarant was sincere when she made the statement. If the statement satisfies the rule's requirements, it comes in; it is up to the jury to decide (1) whether in fact she said it, and if so, (2) whether she meant it, and if so, (3) whether that grateful and benevolent attitude toward Dr. T existed at the time he was killed by shot fired from the gun JH "happened" to have brought with her.

§ 8.22   MENTAL FEELING, PAIN, BODILY HEALTH

In litigation where someone's mental or physical condition is an issue, statements by that person describing mental feeling, pain, or bodily health may be admissible over a hearsay objection under Fed. R. Evid. 803(3). In a personal injury action, for example, P and D both may seek to offer out-of-court statements by P, such as "My back hurts"; "Thank you, I'm feeling much better, the pain is almost gone"; "I still can't concentrate; I feel so lethargic all the time." So long as such statements describe declarant's then-existing mental or physical feeling, they fit within the scope of Fed. R. Evid. 803(3).

§ 8.23   INTENT AS A BASIS TO INFER DECLARANT'S SUBSEQUENT CONDUCT: *"HILLMON* DOCTRINE"

If on March 4, X told Y, "I plan to leave tomorrow for Colorado," or "This time tomorrow I'll be on my way to Colorado," that statement is relevant as tending to prove that X in fact left for Colorado on March 5. In *Mutual Life Ins. Co. v. Hillmon*, 145 U.S. 285, 295–297 (1892), the Supreme Court held that such a statement of intent, if offered as proof that the declarant subsequently did what he'd said he intended to do, is within the "state of mind" exception to the hearsay rule. The Advisory Committee Note to Fed. R. Evid. 803(3) makes it clear that the *Hillmon* rule, "allowing evidence of intention as tending to prove the doing of the act intended, is . . . left undisturbed."

Now suppose that on March 4, X had said to T, "Last week Z offered me a job in Colorado, so tomorrow I'm leaving for Colorado." If this statement is offered to prove that X left for Colorado on March 5, the statement clearly fits within the *Hillmon* doctrine: if offered for that purpose, it is no different, really, than the statement in the first paragraph of this section. On the other hand, if this statement is offered as proof that *Z had offered X a job* in Colorado, it falls outside the scope of 803(3), because X's statement that Z had offered him a job looks backward to something that (according to X) has already happened. See § 8.27, infra.

§ 8.24   QUESTIONS

Question 1. Suppose both facts (whether Z offered X a job, and whether X left for Colorado on March 5) are relevant to the lawsuit. We've just seen that X's statement to T in the previous paragraph is admissible over a hearsay objection if offered to prove that X left for Colorado on March 5, but is inadmissible hearsay if offered to prove that Z had offered him a job there. How can we resolve the conflict?

Ans. There are several potential solutions.

(a) The judge could redact the statement,[29] instructing T to testify only that X said "I'm leaving for Colorado tomorrow."

(b) If T testifies to the entire statement, the judge could issue a limiting instruction, per Fed. R. Evid. 105: the jury should consider the statement only regarding whether X left for Colorado on the 5th, but not as evidence that Z had offered X a job.

(c) If the risk of unfair prejudice on the job offer issue substantially outweighs the statement's legitimate probative value on whether X left for Colorado on the 5th, the judge should exclude the statement per Fed. R. Evid. 403.

In the problem as given, clearly the most appropriate answer is (a).

---

[29] In a civil case, after T testified in a pretrial deposition, either litigant could bring a motion in limine, per Fed. R. Evid. 103, and ask the judge to rule on how much of this exchange T would be allowed to testify to at trial.

§ 8.25 "SECOND-PARTY *HILLMON*": DECLARANT'S STATEMENT OF INTENT TO DO SOMETHING WITH Z, AS PROOF OF Z'S SUBSEQUENT CONDUCT

Z is charged with killing X, whose body was found behind a barn. The last person known to have seen X alive is W, who will, if permitted, testify that "X told me, 'Z and I are meeting tonight in back of the barn, to settle our dispute once and for all.' " The prosecutor offers this evidence, not (or not just) to prove that X went behind the barn that night, but to prove that *Z met with X* behind the barn that night. This differs from straightforward application of the *Hillmon* doctrine because declarant X's statement of intent is being offered to prove, not only what *X* subsequently did, but also what a second party (Z) subsequently did.

For years prior to the enactment of the Federal Rules of Evidence, "second-party *Hillmon*" was a matter of considerable debate among judges and scholars. The House Judiciary Committee Report on the Federal Rules rejected second-party *Hillmon*: "the Committee intends that [Fed. R. Evid. 803(3)] be construed to limit the [*Hillmon* doctrine], so as to render statements of intent by a declarant admissible only to prove his future conduct, not the future conduct of another person." But the Reports of the Senate Judiciary Committee and the House-Senate Conference Committee were silent on the subject.

Various courts currently take three different approaches to the issue:

1. Despite the House Judiciary Committee's Report, some courts admit second-party *Hillmon* statements so long as the statement appears to fall within the language of the rule.

2. Some courts, following the House Judiciary Committee lead, apparently have rejected second-party *Hillmon* outright.

3. Some courts admit such statements only when independent evidence strongly corroborates that the second party in fact engaged in the conduct predicted in declarant's statement.

Which approach should you take? Whichever one your professor tells you is the correct one, of course! — unless your professor expects you to know that courts take different approaches, and to apply each approach to a particular problem.[30] In that case, of course, that's what you should do.

Suppose your professor doesn't mention the different approaches, what should you do then? You have two choices: pretend the problem doesn't exist, and hope he or she doesn't ask a question about it on the exam; or ask the professor, during or after class, how you should handle such a question.[31]

---

[30] That's how I handle it in my evidence courses. A professor, after all, is supposed to teach students the law. If the *law* is confused, it's my job to see to it that my *students* are confused! — No, wait, that didn't come out quite right . . . Let me try it again: it's my job to teach my students to *understand* where and how the law is confused, and to be able to explain the confusion and argue in the alternative.

[31] I don't mind when a student asks me a challenging question in class; in fact, I enjoy it. If I know the answer, I give it. If I'm not sure or haven't a clue, I say so, and ask the student to send me a follow-up e-mail

§ 8.26 QUESTIONS

Question 1. Borachio (D1) and Conrade (D2) are charged with assault and robbery. The indictment alleges that on March 1, 2011, they shot and seriously wounded Leonato and stole $5,000 from him.

As her first witness at trial, the prosecutor calls Don John, who will testify that before his conviction on narcotics charges in the summer of 2011, he was a crack dealer. Don John testifies that in late February (as best as he can remember, the 25th), Conrade told him, "Me and Borachio will be lookin' to score an eighth of a key soon. We been scopin' out a bad dude, and we're gonna take him off in just a couple of days."

Why is this relevant?

Ans. Conrade's statement, "Me and Borachio . . . we're gonna take [a bad dude] off in just a couple of days," tends to prove that Conrade (the declarant) and Borachio (the "second party") were planning to rob someone soon so they could purchase an eighth of a kilo cocaine from Don John. Thus, the statement tends to prove that Conrade and Borachio subsequently did precisely that.

Question 2. Both defendants object: hearsay. Ruling?

Ans. Conrade's objection is easily overruled, per Fed. R. Evid. 801(d)(2)(A) or 803(3). As to the latter, Conrade's statement of intent is admissible to prove that he later did what he said he intended to do.

The prosecutor cites 803(3) to Borachio's objection as well. But Borachio is not the declarant here. Hence, 803(3) admits Conrade's statement against Borachio only if we accept "second-party *Hillmon*." At this point in the trial, the prosecutor has offered no corroboration of Borachio's alleged involvement in any robbery; hence, the statement should not be admitted, unless the judge admits it conditionally, per Fed. R. Evid. 104(a). See the discussion of conditional admissibility in § 5.36.

Incidentally, if this question sounds familiar, it should: In Chapter 5, I used the same facts to illustrate the requirements of Fed. R. Evid. 801(d)(2)(E). *See* § 5.39, Q. 1. Recall from §§ 5.31–5.36 that Rule 801(d)(2)(E) does not admit a statement against a nondeclarant defendant unless the prosecutor can satisfy that rule's requirements (which in essence go to the propriety of the statement's use against the nondeclarant defendant) by a preponderance of the evidence, including at least some evidence independent of the statement itself which tends to satisfy the requirements of Rule 801(d)(2)(E). Imposing a similar "independent evidence" requirement on second-party *Hillmon* use of Fed. R. Evid. 803(3) is a logical middle ground between automatic exclusion of evidence which may be both needed and reliable, and admission of unreliable evidence.

Question 3. Both defendants also object: Confrontation Clause. Ruling?

---

to remind me to look for an answer. But if you sense your professor might not welcome such an approach in class, it might be wiser to ask after class. (And don't be disappointed if the professor says, "Don't worry about it — it won't be on the exam." I sometimes say that to my students when I *do* know the answer, because if the issue is both complex and relatively unimportant, it is not worth class time to discuss it.)

Ans. Conrade's objection is easily overruled, because it is his own statement. Borachio's statement requires us to apply the Confrontation Clause check list from § 6.13.

¶ A. This is a criminal case.

¶ B–H. If the judge overrules the hearsay objection per Fed. R. Evid. 801(d)(2(E), the co-conspirator exception, we can safely skip down to ¶ H, because in *Crawford* and again in *Bryant*, the Court plainly said that statements that fit within the co-conspirator exception are not testimonial. Which allows us to skip down to . . .

¶ L: if a statement is not testimonial, the Confrontation Clause does not apply to it, and the Confrontation Clause objection is therefore overruled.

Suppose, though, the judge concludes that the statement does not satisfy Fed. R. Evid. 801(d)(2)(E), but rules that the statement does satisfy Fed. R. Evid. 803(3). Applying the check list:

¶ B. Fed. R. Evid. 803(3).

¶ C. The statement is being offered for a hearsay purpose, i.e., to prove that Conrade and Borachio were in fact planning to "take off" [i.e., rob] a "bad dude" [i.e., Leonato] — and in fact did so.

¶ D. The prosecutor cannot call Conrade, the declarant, as a witness, because Conrade is a defendant who has the privilege, guaranteed by the Fifth Amendment, not to testify at his own trial.

¶ E. N/A

¶ F. N/A

¶ G. Therefore we must continue to apply the checklist, to determine whether Conrade's statement to Don John was testimonial.

¶ H. None of these possibilities apply here.

¶ I. Apply the four potential definitions of testimonial discussed in § 6:7. There was nothing "solemn" about what Conrade told Don John, no suggestion that Conrade was attempting to create or establish evidence; Conrade's purpose was to alert Don John that he and Borachio would soon be able to purchase an eighth of a kilogram of crack cocaine. Thus, his statement to Don John was not testimonial.

¶ J., K. N/A

¶ L. Because Conrade's statement to Don John was not testimonial, the Confrontation Clause objection is overruled.

§ 8.27 "THEN-EXISTING" vs. "BACKWARD-LOOKING" STATEMENTS; "STATEMENT OF MEMORY OR BELIEF"

Fed. R. Evid. 803(3) admits, over a hearsay objection, statements by the declarant as to his "*then-existing* state of mind." By "then-existing" the rule means, existing at the time the declarant made the statement. "I am happy," "I feel depressed," "I'm hungry," "I don't trust her," "I plan to fly to Cleveland tomorrow" are all statements of the declarant's "then-existing" state of mind, because in each, the declarant is telling the listener what he is thinking or feeling or planning to do as he is speaking. By contrast, statements such as "I didn't like her back then," "Boy, was I hungry," "at the time I intended to take the job," etc. are *not* statements of the declarant's "then-existing" state of mind, because declarant is not telling us what she *is* thinking, feeling, or planning; rather, she's telling us what she thought, planned or felt *at some time in the past*.

Another example of the ban on "backward-looking" statements is illustrated by the following example. Varitek and Hayrod got into a fight, and Varitek sued Hayrod for assault. Hayrod pleads self-defense, claiming Varitek was the initial aggressor. At trial, Hayrod calls W, who will testify:

Q.   . . . After you heard about the fight, did you have a conversation with DL about what happened?

A.   Yes. DL told me, "I was there, I saw it all, and I remember that Varitek hit Hayrod first."

Varitek objects that DL's statement to W is hearsay. Hayrod responds: "Fed. R. Evid. 803(3), Your Honor. 'Remembering' is a state of mind, and DL was telling W what he remembered about the fight."

Hayrod's response is clever, but Varitek's objection must be sustained. DL's statement to W is not be admissible under Fed. R. Evid. 803(3) as evidence that Varitek hit Hayrod first because, as Fed. R. Evid. 803(3) mandates, the rule does not "includ[e] a statement of memory or belief to prove the fact remembered or believed . . ." In other words, a declarant cannot avoid the rule's ban on backward-looking statements merely by including in his statement, "I now remember" or "I now believe . . ."[32]

§ 8.28 QUESTIONS

Question 1. Pedestrian brings a personal injury action, alleging that while he was out jogging, he was run over by Drayman's horse, and suffered serious injury and considerable pain as a result. Consider the applicability of Fed. R. Evid. 803(1)-803(3) to each of the following:

(a) W1 will testify that as she passed Pedestrian lying on the path, Pedestrian shouted "Oh, my knee, my leg! It feels like it's broken! Oh, I can't stand it!"

[32] DL could, of course, testify at the assault trial and relate what he remembers seeing; that would not involve hearsay, because he'd be on the stand, under oath, and subject to cross-examination.

Ans. This statement is admissible under each of these provisions.

(b) W2 will testify that as they were standing by the water cooler at work, Pedestrian said, "I was knocked down by a horse last week, and I've felt dizzy and weak ever since."

Ans. "I feel dizzy and weak" would be admissible Fed. R. Evid. 803(1) or 803(3), but "I was knocked down by a horse last week" probably would not be. It is not spontaneous enough for 803(1) or (2) and is backward-looking, so cannot fit within 803(3). (Nor, probably, will it satisfy Fed. R. Evid. 803(4). See §§ 8.35, 8.39, infra.

Question 2. JH is charged with murdering Dr. T. The indictment alleges that she shot and killed him at 4 p.m. on June 1. At trial the government introduces evidence that JH and Dr. T had been lovers for many years, until Dr. T dumped JH for a younger woman. JH's defense is that she was merely returning several things to Dr. T, including a revolver he had loaned her; that it fell and went off accidentally, with tragic results. JH wishes to have W2, a homicide detective, testify that when he arrested her at 6 p.m. on June 1, she cried, "I loved Dr. T! I could never do anything to hurt him!" The prosecutor objects: hearsay. JH responds: Fed. R. Evid. 803(3). How should the judge rule?

Ans. A judge might understandably be tempted to reject this statement simply because it is so self-serving: JH's protestations of a lack of criminal intent are precisely what we'd expect from someone who has just been arrested for murder. On the other hand, a judge does not have the authority to exclude a statement that satisfies Fed. R. Evid. 803(3), merely because the judge doesn't believe the statement is true.

The better basis to exclude the statement is that it isn't really about her state of mind toward Dr. T at 6 p.m., when she made the statement; rather, the statement looks backward in time to 4 p.m., when Dr. T was shot. Under a proper application of Fed. R. Evid. 803(3), the evidence should be excluded. (You might come across a decision or two that admits such a statement in a case like this — a judge occasionally bend the rules a bit to help a defendant who he or she feels should be acquitted — but that would be breaking the rule, not applying it.)

Question 3. JH responds: 803(2), excited utterance. How should the judge rule?

Ans. Sustained. Two hours is a long time. Even assuming JH was still stressed and excited about Dr. T getting shot, two hours is more than enough time to realize she that she would be facing a murder charge, and to start thinking about creating a defense for herself. (Besides, the very self-serving nature of her statement may prompt a judge to conclude that it was the product of reflection and fabrication. Concerning self-serving statements and Fed. R. Evid. 803(1) or 803(2), see § 8.4.)

§ 8.29   HOMICIDE CASES: VICTIM'S FEAR OF DEFENDANT

V is found murdered, and D is charged. At trial, the prosecutor wants to call W1 who will, if permitted, testify that a few days before V was killed, V told W1, "I'm afraid D is going to kill me." Similarly, W2 will testify that V told W2, "I believe D is planning to kill me." D objects: "Hearsay." The prosecutor responds: "Fed. R. Evid. 803(3): V's state of mind." Ruling?

In essence, the prosecutor is arguing that "belief" and "fear" are states of mind, and V was telling a friend what she[33] believed at the time, i.e., her "then-existing state of mind." Ah, but how is V's state of mind relevant? In each case, the statement is one of *belief*: V told W2 that she *"believes"* D is planning to kill her, and told W1 that she is afraid D will kill her; and fear, in this context, is another way of expressing a *belief* that something will happen.

Flip back for a moment to § 8.19, and re-read the text of Fed. R. Evid. 803(3).

V's statements are relevant only if we accept V's "statement of belief . . . to prove the fact . . . believed." Fed. R. Evid. 803(3) explicitly provides that the exception does not include a declarant's "statement of . . . belief to prove the fact . . . believed . . ." The judge should sustain the defendant's hearsay objection.

Besides, such statements are often simply too speculative to have much legitimate probative value, while the risk of unfair prejudice from such an uncross-examinable accusation "from the grave" is likely to be substantial. The statement should also be excluded on Fed. R. Evid. 403 grounds.

Do not be surprised, though, to find cases in which courts cite Fed. R. Evid. 803(3) to admit such statements. Sometimes judges rely on labels ("statement of the victim's state of mind") without thinking things through.[34] And sometimes a judge will interpret a rule in a way that helps a prosecutor convict someone who (in the judge's opinion) deserves to be convicted.

§ 8.30 QUESTIONS

Question 1. D is accused of killing V, whose raped and strangled body was found in a motel room. The state presents evidence that D and V had lived together for several months; that V moved out; that D kept trying to get V to "take him back"; that he constantly called her, came to the school where she taught, and followed her frequently. Evidence is introduced that the semen found in and on the victim matches D's DNA; his fingerprints were found in the hotel room. In addition, W1 will testify that, a few days before V was killed, she told W1, "D is going to kill me soon. I just know it!" Objection, hearsay; objection, Confrontation Clause. Ruling?

Ans. Hearsay objection sustained.

The prosecutor cannot successfully cite Fed. R. Evid. 803(3),because V's belief that D would kill her is not admissible under Fed. R. Evid. 803(3) to "prove the fact believed."

---

[33] This scenario occurs with distressing frequency where a defendant is accused of killing his wife, ex-wife, girlfriend or ex-girlfriend. It also occurs in cases where one alleged criminal is accused of killing another, for example in a dispute over who will control drug selling on a particular block or when a higher-up in a criminal organization suspects an underling of keeping more than his allotted share of the merchandise or profits.

[34] That's why they are only judges, rather than (ahem) law professors.

Nor can the prosecutor successfully cite Fed. R. Evid. 803(2), because, unlike § 8.17 **Q. 1**, which this case somewhat resembles, V's statement does not apparently relate to any particular "startling event" — at least not one whose time we can pinpoint.

As to the Confrontation Clause objection, consider whether this question more closely resembles § 8.17 **Q. 1–2**, or § 8.17 **Q. 3**.

Question 2. After the state rests, D takes the stand and admits that he took V to the motel on the evening in question, but insists that she went willingly, and they made passionate and consensual love. Then they fell asleep. A few hours later, D testifies, he woke up, got dressed and drove off, looking for food; when he returned to the hotel, V was dead. Someone must have broken in and done it while he was away.

In rebuttal, the state recalls W1 and proffers her testimony anew. Defendant renews the hearsay and Confrontation Clause objections. Ruling? Is there an argument the state can make now that was not available in **Q. 1**?

Ans. Now the prosecutor has a plausible non-hearsay use for the evidence: V's belief that D would kill her is relevant to rebut the defendant's testimony that V went with him willingly and consented to have sex. The evidence carries an obvious Fed. R. Evid. 403 risk, but a judge could legitimately admit the evidence and give a limiting instruction: "You may consider V's statement, that she believed the defendant would kill her soon, in deciding whether she went with D willingly and consented to have sex with him. You should not consider it, however, as evidence that D killed her." Granted, the likelihood that a jury could, or would, follow that instruction is, shall we say, not too great. But it would still be within a judge's discretion to allow the prosecutor to introduce V's statement.

Because the statement is now legitimately admissible for a non-hearsay purpose, the Confrontation Clause objection is also overruled. See § 6.13 ¶ C.

§ 8.31 WILL CASES

We have seen that Fed. R. Evid. 803(3) does not admit a backward-looking "statement of memory or belief to prove the fact remembered or believed . . ." *See* § 8.27. Rule 803(3) *does* admit a backward looking statement, however, if it "relates to the validity or terms of the declarant's will."[35]

Whether such statements are inherently reliable is open to question. But litigation about a declarant's will occurs only after declarant is deceased, so the need for such evidence is obvious, particularly in cases where the will has been lost or where doubts have been cast upon the document's authenticity. This is an exception in which need for the evidence trumps doubts about its reliability.

---

[35] It would make more sense simply to codify a separate exception for statements by a declarant about the existence or contents of his or her will, rather than tacking it onto the end of the "state of mind" exception. But the two were linked together at common law, and the Federal Rules of Evidence retained this approach.

§ 8.32 QUESTIONS

Question 1. Testator dies; Segunda, the executor of her estate, files a document dated July 2, 2011, purporting to be Testator's will. Guy, Testator's son, challenges the document (in which Guy was left only $100 and the rest of Testator's assets are to go to Segunda, a second cousin) as a forgery. After Guy presents his case, Segunda calls W1, who will testify that on July 1, 2011, Testator told W1: "I'm signing my new will tomorrow. I warned my son that if he didn't stop drinking and gambling I'd disinherit him, and tomorrow I'm going to do just that." Guy objects: irrelevant, and hearsay. Ruling?

Ans. Overruled. This is straightforward *Hillmon* doctrine: Testator's statement to W1 about her intent to sign such a will is offered as evidence that she subsequently did what she said she intended to do. (W1's testimony is relevant because it tends to support the authenticity of the contested will.)

Question 2. Segunda also calls W2, who will testify that on July 9, 2011, Testator told W2: "Well, I've gone and done it. I signed a new will last week leaving my son Guy only $100." Objection, hearsay. Response, 803(3). Ruling?

Ans. Overruled. This is backward-looking, so normally Fed. R. Evid. 803(3) would be inapplicable; but in a will case, backward-looking statements *are* admissible where the statement "relates to the validity or terms of the declarant's will."

§ 8.33 SIXTH AMENDMENT CONFRONTATION CLAUSE

Statements that satisfy Fed. R. Evid. 803(3) do not fall into any easy classification, as far as the Confrontation Clause is concerned. We know that a "casual remark to a friend or relative" is not testimonial, but a "solemn declaration" to a friend or relative would be, assuming the Confrontation Clause applies at all to statements to someone other than a government official. See, e.g., § 8.21, **Q2-Q3**.

The same is true regarding a declarant's statement about his will: it could easily be a "casual remark to a friend," and therefore not testimonial; or could be a "solemn declaration" seeking to establish a fact, and therefore testimonial. But since I do not recall a single *criminal* case in which a court admitted a declarant's statement about his will, the issue is unlikely to arise.

§ 8.34 QUESTIONS

Early in January, cars driven by Plaintiff and Yert collided. Yert was killed and Plaintiff was badly injured. It is clear that the collision was Yert's fault. Plaintiff sues XYZ Co., alleging that Yert was acting as XYZ's employee at the time of the collision. XYZ defends on the ground that although Yert had been their employee until December 31, he was no longer their employee as of January 1. Rather, XYZ claims, starting January 1, Yert was employed by a man named Boss. Consider the admissibility over a hearsay objection of each of the following:

Question 1. XYZ calls W1, who will testify that on December 29, Boss told W1, "I'm going to offer Yert a job at $2,000 per week for the coming year."

Ans. Admissible, Fed. R. Evid. 803(3), per the *Hillmon* doctrine, to prove that Boss subsequently made the offer. *See* § 8.23. (The Sixth Amendment Confrontation Clause need not be considered, since this is a civil, not a criminal, case.)

Question 2. XYZ calls W2, who will testify that on December 28, Boss said, "Yert and I are going to sign a contract on the 31st: he'll work for me for a year at $2,000 a week." D objects: "Hearsay!" Ruling?

Ans. This is "second-party *Hillmon*": declarant Boss's statement of intent to do something with Yert is offered, not only to prove what Boss subsequently did, but also as proof of what Yert (the "second party") subsequently did. *See* § 8.25. At least absent corroboration, it should be excluded.

Question 3. XYZ calls W3, who will testify that on January 4, Yert said, "Boy, am I glad my money troubles are over! I just started a new job with Boss on the first of the year — at two thou a week!"

Ans. This might look admissible under Fed. R. Evid. 803(3): it is Yert's statement about his then-existing "gladness," which is certainly a state of mind. But this law suit isn't about whether Yert was "glad" or not, it is about whether Boss offered and Yert accepted an oral employment contract at $2,000 per week.

Thus, on the issue on which the statement is relevant, the statement looks backward: it is relevant only if we accept Yert's assertion that he had started working for Boss. (If Yert had simply said, "I work for Boss," that statement, if offered to prove that Yert worked for Boss at the time, would fall outside Fed. R. Evid. 803(3); so would a statement such as "I'm glad I work for Boss.")

Question 4. Diabella shot and killed Valleygirl after they argued, and Diabella is accused of murder. Diabella claims she acted in self-defense, which, as you know from your criminal law course, depends on whether she acted in the reasonable belief that she had to use deadly force to protect herself from death or serious injury. At trial, Diabella calls W1, who will testify that a few days before Diabella and Valleygirl had the fatal encounter, Diabella said, "I'm afraid Valleygirl is out to get me, because she thinks I've been messing around with her husband." Admissible, over a hearsay objection?

Ans. It depends on why Diabella is offering it. If Diabella is trying to prove that Valleygirl really *was* "out to get" her, it is not admissible. But if it is offered to support Diabella's defense that she had a *reasonable belief* that she would have to defend herself against possible violence from Valleygirl, it is admissible evidence of Diabella's then-existing state of mind per Fed. R. Evid. 803(3). (That Diabella was afraid of violence from Valleygirl a few days before the fatal encounter supports the inference that Diabella was still afraid of Valleygirl on the day Valleygirl was killed, which supports the inference that her fear was reasonable, which supports her self-defense claim.)

The Sixth Amendment Confrontation Clause need not be considered, because here it is the defendant, not the prosecutor, who is offering the hearsay.

Question 5. In a different homicide trial, Loosecannon is accused of killing Viddler; Loosecannon's defense is a straightforward denial of all involvement. At trial the prosecutor calls W1, who will, if permitted, testify that a few days before Viddler was shot, Viddler told W1, "I'm afraid Loosecannon is out to get me, because he thinks I've been messing around with his wife." Admissible, over a hearsay objection? If so, should the evidence be excluded on any other ground?

Ans. The prosecutor may argue that Fed. R. Evid. 803(3) overcomes the hearsay objection, at least as to the first portion of Viddler's statement ("I'm afraid Loosecannon is out to get me").

But the evidence should be excluded. Fed. R. Evid. 803(3) does not admit a declarant's "statement of belief [i.e., Viddler's fear that Loosecannon was 'out to get' him] . . . to prove the fact . . . believed [i.e., that Loosecannon was in fact 'out to get' Viddler]." *See* § 8.29.

Superficially, this question looks a lot like **Q4**, in which we admitted Diabella's pre-homicide statement that she was afraid of Valleygirl. But there is a fundamental difference between the two questions. In *this* question, evidence relates, not to the *defendant's fear of the victim*, but the *victim's fear of the defendant*. Unlike the previous question, where the *defendant's* state of mind (fear of the victim) *was* an element of the defense, here, the *victim's* fear is *not* an element of the crime or defense. Viddler's statement is relevant, therefore, only if we assume he could accurately gauge the state of *someone else's* mind ("Loosecannon thinks . . .") and could accurately predict what Loosecannon would do ("Loosecannon's out to get me"). The law should not admit such speculative evidence.

Question 6. Assuming Diabella in question 4 and Loosecannon in question 5 are married to each other, can this marriage be saved? If so, is it worth it?

PART D:
STATEMENTS FOR MEDICAL DIAGNOSIS OR TREATMENT: RULE 803(4)

§ 8.35 IN GENERAL

Fed. R. Evid. 803(4) provides as follows:

> **The following are not excluded by the rule against hearsay, regardless of whether the declarant is available as a witness:**
>
> **(4) *Statement Made for Medical Diagnosis or Treatment.* A statement that:**
>
> **(A) is made for — and is reasonably pertinent to — medical diagnosis or treatment; and**
>
> **(B) describes medical history; past or present symptoms or sensations; their inception; or their general cause.**

[Prior to December 1, 2011, the rule read as follows:

Rule 803. The following are not excluded by the hearsay rule, even though the declarant is available as a witness:

> (4) Statements for purposes of medical diagnosis or treatment. Statements made for purposes of medical diagnosis or treatment and describing medical history, or past or present symptoms, pain, or sensations, or the inception or general character of the cause or external source thereof insofar as reasonably pertinent to diagnosis or treatment.

The Federal Rules of Evidence were rewritten solely to make them easier to understand; the Advisory Committee did not intend to make any substantive change in the Rules. The text of the old rule may remain useful in reading court decisions that precede the revision of the rules. Thus, this edition of the Student's Guide provides the text of both the new and the old version of each relevant provision of the Federal Rules of Evidence.]

Statements that fall within this provision are considered trustworthy because the declarant has a strong motive to be truthful and accurate when providing information on which health care providers will be diagnosing a condition or devising a treatment scheme. Moreover, because the declarant is (usually) describing her own symptoms, the risk of misperception or misremembering are also thought to be comparatively minor.

Application of Fed. R. Evid. 803(4) involves the following issues:

1. *First-hand knowledge and second-party statements.* Although first-and knowledge is generally required, under unusual circumstances, statements may be admissible even if the declarant is speaking about a second party, not herself. *See* § 8.36.

2. *Purpose.* A statement falls within Fed. R. Evid. 803(4) only if it was "made for — and is reasonably pertinent to — medical diagnosis or treatment." *See* §§ 8.37–8.38.

3. *Person to whom the statement was made.* The Advisory Committee Note points out that "the statement need not have been made to a physician. Statements to hospital attendants, ambulance drivers, or even members of the family might be included" so long as they were made for medical diagnosis or treatment. See §§ 8.36; 8.38; 8.41 **Q.1.**

4. *"Pertinent"; cause; fault.* Statements are admissible only to the extent that they are "pertinent" to diagnosis or treatment. While this often includes information concerning the cause of the patient's condition, statements attributing fault or blame are not included within the rule. *See* § 8.39.

5. *Interplay with other rules. See* § 8.40.

6. *Sixth Amendment Confrontation Clause. See* § 8.42.

§ 8.36 FIRST-HAND KNOWLEDGE; SECOND-PARTY STATEMENTS

When a patient describes her own condition and symptoms ("Doctor, my back has been hurting ever since I —"), she is relating facts of which she has first-hand knowledge; such statements pose no particular difficulties.

Suppose, though, the patient is an infant, or an adult who is unable to communicate with health care personnel. For example, at four in the afternoon a baby's mother tells a doctor, "He started acting cranky and fussy this morning, right after he had a jar of Beechbaby's strained applesauce. He wouldn't eat his lunch, didn't even want to nurse. At around one-thirty I noticed he was feeling feverish, and even after I gave him baby aspirin, he felt warm." In subsequent litigation (against, perhaps, the Beechbaby Food Company), the doctor should be permitted to testify as to the mother's statements, because her statements fit within 803(4): she made those statements to help the doctor diagnose and treat her baby, and she has first-hand knowledge of what happened, even though she is describing someone else's condition, not her own.

Suppose instead the statement is: "Doctor, my husband came home this evening complaining of heartburn. He said he had some very spicy pastrami for lunch and it's been bothering him all afternoon. He took a bicarb and lay down and now he's hot all over and he's drooling and I can't wake him up!" (Let us assume she and her husband are suing the restaurant at which he purchased the sandwich.) This situation differs a bit from the two previous ones, because here the declarant lacks first-hand knowledge of some important information (the nature of the ailment at its onset, when the symptoms started, and their probable cause). But should it be excluded as unreliable for this reason? She obtained the information from her husband. *He* had first-hand knowledge of these facts; it's unlikely he misperceived or misremembered them. Unless specific reasons exist to doubt the trustworthiness of what the husband told his wife, there is no logical reason to exclude those aspects of what she said to the doctor.

On the other hand, in this situation we are dealing with multiple hearsay: (1) husband to wife; (2) wife to doctor. The second level clearly comes within Fed. R. Evid. 804(4): she said what she said to the doctor to help the doctor diagnose and treat her husband. Level one, husband to wife poses the difficulties.

a. That the husband complained of heartburn that afternoon comes within Fed. R. Evid. 803(3), the "state of mind" exception, but the part of the statement that is most important for litigation purposes, that his trouble started with the pastrami sandwich, does not, because that part of the statement is backward looking.

b. Husband to wife might come within Fed. R. Evid. 803(4), but only if the judge concludes that he told her about the sandwich and the heartburn while seeking "diagnosis or treatment." A sympathetic judge might agree. A skeptical judge might reason that a passably intelligent adult male would not need his wife's advice before taking a bicarb or antacid for heartburn.

c. If the judge concludes that the husband's statement to the wife does not come within Fed. R. Evid. 803(4), plaintiffs might argue that Fed. R. Evid. 807, the "residual" exception, applies. Fed. R. Evid. 807 is covered in Chapter 12.

§ 8.37 "FOR MEDICAL DIAGNOSIS *OR* TREATMENT"

Fed. R. Evid. 803(4) is used most often in physical injury or similar suits. P is injured; he tells Dr. PW1 what hurts, how long it has hurt, and why. Dr. PW1 forms an opinion of the nature and extent of the injury or ailment and decides on a regime of treatment. Months or years later, P files suit against D, alleging D's negligence caused his injury.

Prior to trial, P's attorney arranges for him to be examined by Dr. PW2. Dr. PW2 will not participate in any way in the treatment of P's condition; he is being consulted solely so he can give expert testimony about the nature, cause, severity and duration of P's ailment. As part of his examination of P, PW2 asks P a detailed series of questions about P's condition and medical history.

At trial, P calls Dr. PW1, to have her testify as to her diagnosis and the treatment she prescribed. In explaining her conclusions, prognosis, and treatment, Dr. PW1 will naturally want to include what P told her during that first visit and during subsequent examinations and treatment.

Similarly, P calls Dr. PW2, to have him testify as to his diagnosis of P's condition and its probable cause. In explaining his conclusions, Dr. PW2 will naturally want to include what P told him during his examination of P.

Prior to the enactment of the Federal Rules, the law recognized a hearsay exception only for statements made with the ultimate goal of seeking *medical treatment*. P's statements to PW1 were admissible to prove the truth of the matter asserted by P, because P made those statements so PW1 could diagnose, and thus prescribe a treatment for, P's condition. P's statements to Dr. PW2, by contrast, fell outside the pre-Federal Rules hearsay exception, because P's appointment with Dr. PW2 wasn't so Dr. PW2 would *treat* P, but only to help PW2 form a *diagnosis* so he could give expert testimony at trial.

This may seem like a logical enough distinction, but there is a complicating factor. Rules governing expert testimony permit an expert to testify to some extent as to the information on which the expert based his opinion. See Fed. R. Evid. 703. Such information might include statements P had made to PW2. When this occurred, the judge would have to instruct the jury that P's statements to PW2 were not admissible to prove the truth of what P told PW2, but only to inform the jury of the basis upon which PW2 formed his opinion. If this arcane distinction doesn't make much sense to you, you can imagine how much sense it would make to the typical jury.

Fed. R. Evid. 803(4) solves this dilemma by providing that statements made for diagnosis *or* treatment fall within the scope of the hearsay exception. Thus, PW2, like PW1, can repeat statements made to him by P without the need of a limiting instruction.

§ 8.38 CHILD AS DECLARANT IN A CHILD ABUSE PROSECUTION

Fed. R. Evid. 803(4) admits over a hearsay objection, "statements made *for* — and . . . reasonably pertinent to — medical diagnosis or treatment . . ." When the declarant is an adult, determining why he or she made the statement rarely presents difficulty: the declarant's purpose in providing the information is generally fairly clear. When the declarant is a young child who allegedly was sexually assaulted or otherwise physically abused, on the other hand, determining why the child made the statement raises both definitional and factual problems. A young child may have no particular purpose for relating what happened, other than to satisfy an adult who asked a question. A number of courts have ruled, or at least indicated, that the hearsay exception is inapplicable, when the child lacks the traditional motive (to help someone diagnose and treat the injury) that underlies the exception. Other courts have criticized this focus on the child's purpose in making the statement as "not contemplated by the rule and [not] necessary to ensure that the rule's purpose is carried out."

Confrontation Clause issues are discussed in § 8.43.

§ 8.39 "PERTINENT"; CAUSE; FAULT

Fed. R. Evid. 803(4)(A) includes only statements that are "reasonably pertinent" to treatment or diagnosis. This often includes an explanation of (as Rule 803(4)(B) puts it) the "inception . . . or general cause" of the patient's "symptoms or sensations." As the Advisory Committee Note to the exception makes clear, however, "Statements as to fault would not ordinarily qualify" under the exception. If the patient tells the doctor, "As I was crossing the street I was struck by a car *that ran a red light*," the first part of the statement would be admissible but the italicized portion would not be.

Courts sometimes encounter difficulties applying this requirement with statements made to a psychiatrist or psychologist, because arguably almost anything could be "pertinent" in that setting, including attributions of fault.

§ 8.40 INTERPLAY WITH OTHER RULES

If a statement about a physical sensation doesn't satisfy Fed. R. Evid. 803(4) because it was not made for diagnosis or treatment, it still may be admissible under Fed. R. Evid. 803(1)–(3).

Fed. R. Evid. 803(4) is often used together with Fed. R. Evid. 803(6) or 803(8), the business and public record exceptions. *See* § 9.37. Fed. R. Evid. 803(4) is often used together with rules regulating expert testimony. This is discussed briefly in § 8.37.

The law recognizes a privilege for statements made by a patient to a doctor. (*See* Article V of the Federal Rules of Evidence.) The privilege entitles the patient to prevent a litigant from forcing the doctor to repeat such statements. Fed. R. Evid. 803(4) in no way defeats this privilege. On the other hand, if P is suing for personal injuries, P has every right to waive the privilege and elicit such testimony from doctors P calls as witnesses. Once P does so, D can also elicit such testimony from doctors who examined P. As a practical matter, therefore, the privilege does not very often interfere with the admissibility of such statements.

§ 8.41 QUESTIONS

Question 1. P sues for compensation for on-the-job injuries she claims she suffered on June 1, 2011. During a pretrial deposition, W1, P's husband, testified that when P came home from work that evening, she said, "My back is killing me! My supervisor ordered me to lift some heavy boxes and now I can hardly stand up!" P's attorney intends to elicit the same testimony from W1 at trial. If D makes a hearsay objection, what are P's best arguments for admission? How should the judge rule?

Ans. (a) Fed. R. Evid. 803(4).

Because the statement was not made to a health care professional, the first question is whether it falls within Fed. R. Evid. 803(4) at all. The Advisory Committee Note observed that statements to non-doctors, including family members, can come within the rule. To satisfy 803(4), though, P must persuade the judge that what she said was pertinent to, and for, "diagnosis and treatment." The facts don't give much indication of this, and unless P can make that showing, 803(4) is not likely to apply.

If P made the statement to her husband for "diagnosis or treatment" — because, even though he is not a health care professional, she respects her husband's judgment about how to treat aches and pains — then most of it should be admitted under Fed. R. Evid. 803(4), but not all. W1 should be permitted to testify that his wife said "I hurt my back lifting heavy boxes and now it's so bad I can hardly stand up," but not that the injury occurred at work or that her supervisor ordered her to lift them. Why? Because those parts of the statement are not really relevant to diagnosis or treatment; they are only relevant to assign blame or fault for the injury.

(b) We would arrive at the same result under Fed. R. Evid. 803(3). P's husband can repeat the portions of the statement in which she told him about her then-existing sensations: "My back is killing me! . . . I can hardly stand up!" The middle portion of her statement ("supervisor . . . boxes") looks backward in time, though, and for that reason is not admissible under 803(3).

(c) P can also argue that a sharp jab of pain was a "startling event"; that her statement therefore was an excited utterance, Fed. R. Evid. 803(2); and that her explanation ("supervisor . . . boxes") "related to" the event and is therefore admissible. A sympathetic judge might accept this argument and admit, but to do so would require a considerable stretch. After all, P presumably has had plenty of time to think about having to lift the boxes, and the resultant discomfort, long before she made her statement to her husband.

Keep in mind that even if the judge excludes the middle portion of the statement, *P* can still *testify* about how she hurt her back; P's *testimony* doesn't involve hearsay. All that would be excluded is W1's testimony about part of what P said when she arrived home that night.

Question 2. Later in the trial, P calls W2, a chiropractor who treated P's back injury. W2 will, if permitted, testify that on June 7, when she first visited his office, P told him, "I hurt my back on June 1 at work when my supervisor told me to move some heavy boxes." Admissible, over D's hearsay objection?

Ans. P's best argument is Fed. R. Evid. 803(4). A strict application of the rule, however, would admit only "I hurt my back on June 1 moving some heavy boxes," and the judge would likely tell the jury to consider only that much of the statement. Reason: while the chiropractor needs to know how P injured herself ("lifting some heavy boxes"), it is not pertinent to treatment for him to know that P did so on orders of her supervisor.

§ 8.42 SIXTH AMENDMENT CONFRONTATION CLAUSE

In dicta, the Supreme Court, in *Giles* and again in *Bryant*, pronounced that statements that fall within Fed. R. Evid. 803(4) are not testimonial. No doubt these dicta are accurate — most of the time. But exceptions could arise.

Suppose, for example, an assault victim says to an examining doctor: "I am going to tell you, blow by blow, what X did to me, and I want you to make a careful notation of each bruise and contusion and fracture, so there is a clear record of what he did!" All of these details (except the fact that X was the declarant's assailant) are, presumably, "reasonably pertinent" to diagnosis and treatment. Yet, wouldn't the declarant's very insistence on making a "clear record" of the details of the assault make the entire conversation testimonial (at least, if statements to non-government personnel come within the Confrontation Clause)?

A statement made to an expert witness primarily to assist the expert in preparing to give expert testimony, moreover, must certainly be considered testimonial. After all, the very reason the declarant is speaking to the expert witness is to help the expert testify.

§ 8.43 STATEMENTS TO CHILD ABUSE, DOMESTIC VIOLENCE AND SEXUAL ASSAULT COUNSELORS

Many jurisdictions now have special protocols in place when an allegation is made concerning child abuse or sexual assault. Medical personnel routinely take rape kits in such cases, and ask questions relevant both to treatment and possible prosecution. A child complainant may be referred to a child protection worker. An adult complainant may be referred to a rape crisis intervention center. Such protocols and agencies have a dual purpose: to help the victim deal with what has happened, and to assist law enforcement in identifying and prosecuting the perpetrator. In such cases, the assumption should be that the declarant's statements to such personnel are testimonial, unless circumstances strongly indicate to the contrary. As a body of case law develops, perhaps a more detailed picture will emerge.

§ 8.44   QUESTIONS

Question 1. D is accused of sexually assaulting V, a six-year-old boy. M (V's mother) learned of the assault when V came crying to her and said, "D made me do bad things and it hurts!" When M asked "What bad things?" V described them. May M testify as to what V said, if D interposes hearsay and Confrontation Clause objections?

Ans.

(a) As to the hearsay objection, the prosecutor will cite two exceptions: excited utterance, Fed. R. Evid. 803(2); statement for medical treatment, Fed. R. Evid. 803(4). A judge could legitimately admit the statement under either. For example, that V came crying to M strongly suggests he was still "under the stress" of the startling event. But some courts are very skeptical about admitting the portion of the statement in which the child names the alleged perpetrator.

(b) As to the Confrontation Clause: if V testifies, this automatically satisfies the Confrontation Clause. § 6.13, checklist ¶ D.

Otherwise, we will reach ¶ H: were V's statements to his mother testimonial? Clearly, the answer is: no. It seems obvious that M's main concern at this point is V's welfare, and V's main concern is to obtain comfort from M.

From ¶ H we move to ¶ L: since these statements are not testimonial, the Confrontation Clause objection is overruled.

Question 2. The next day, M took V to MD, a doctor. V told MD, "D made me [etc.]." Is MD's testimony about the what V's statements admissible, over hearsay and Confrontation Clause objections?

Ans.

(a) Fed. R. Evid. 803(2) probably will not apply here, because many hours, perhaps a full day, has elapsed between the event and these statements.

(b) As to whether Fed. R. Evid. 803(4) overcomes the hearsay objection, there are several uncertainties.

First, some courts refuse to apply the exception to such statements unless it is clear that V, the child, understood that telling MD what happened will be useful for diagnosis and treatment. Other courts hold that such statements come within the exception so long as the *doctor* believed the information was useful for diagnosis and treatment. See § 8.38. (It would be particularly helpful to the prosecutor if, at a hearing to determine admissibility of V's statements to MD, MD testified: "I told V, 'I need you to tell me what happened, so I can make it stop hurting and help you get better.'" Such testimony not only establishes MD's purpose, but also helps establish that V was aware of why it was important to answer the questions.)

Second, let's assume that V's statement to MD as to *what* was done to him comes within Fed. R. Evid. 803(4). We then must address whether V's statement that D was the perpetrator comes within the exception. Many courts hold that the hearsay exception does not include the part of the child's statement in which the child identifies *who* did those things to him. After all, Fed. R. Evid. 803(4) does not admit statements relating to fault or blame. Unless the prosecutor can come up with a counterargument that brings the identity of the perpetrator within the scope of information pertinent for diagnosis and treatment, D should succeed in excluding the fact that V identified him to MD as the perpetrator.

The prosecutor can argue that the identity of the perpetrator is important in helping diagnose and treat V for at least two reasons. (1) The information could be vital in assessing the risk that V may have contracted a sexually transmitted disease. (2) A doctor would need to know the perpetrator's identity in diagnosing and treating the emotional impact of the assault. Courts are sharply divided about the admissibility of the part of a child's statement identifying the perpetrator.

Confrontation Clause. If the part of the statement identifying the perpetrator survives a hearsay objection i.e., if MD can persuade the judge that she needed the perpetrator's name to help her diagnose and treat V, it will probably also survive a Confrontation Clause challenge.

Chapter 9

RULE 803: THE "REGARDLESS OF WHETHER THE DECLARANT IS AVAILABLE AS A WITNESS" EXCEPTIONS: COMMON WRITTEN STATEMENTS RULES 612 & 803(5)–803(10)

PART A:
INTRODUCTION

§ 9.1 OVERVIEW

§ 8.1 introduced the "Declarant Unavailable Immaterial" hearsay exceptions collected in Fed. R. Evid. 803. The discussion in that section applies equally to the exceptions discussed in this chapter.

Chapter 8 examined the Rule 803 hearsay exceptions for common oral statements. This chapter examines the Rule 803 exceptions covered by Fed. R. Evid. 803(5)–803(10), the most commonly used Rule 803 exceptions for written statements (i.e., documents), and another rule, Fed. R. Evid. 612, which is closely associated with Fed. R. Evid. 803(5).

PART B:
"REFRESHING RECOLLECTION," RULE 612;
"RECORDED RECOLLECTION," RULE 803(5)

1. Refreshing Recollection: Fed. R. Evid. Rule 612

§ 9.2 IN GENERAL

When a witness takes the stand at trial, the preferred form of testimony comes from the witness's unaided memory. Every trial lawyer quickly learns, however, that given the pressures and tensions of the courtroom, a witness's unaided memory can be remarkably unreliable. Whenever possible, therefore, an attorney should employ a variety of techniques to enhance a witness's recollection. The most frequently used methods are preparation and repetition. Prior to trial, a lawyer should rehearse the direct and probable cross-examination with a willing witness as often as circumstances seem to require and time permits. When documents or written memoranda exist concerning the subject matter of the witness's testimony, the lawyer should urge the witness to study them prior to trial to further enhance his memory.

Nevertheless, a cooperative witness may suffer a lapse of memory on the witness stand. When this occurs, the attorney need not forgo eliciting the information; instead, the law provides a variety of options. The first step is attempting to refresh the witness's recollection. The most direct is simply to supply the missing information to the witness in the guise of a question:

Q.   Ms. White, tell us, please, who attended the meeting.

A.   Let's see, quite a few people were there — um, there was Bashful, and Dopey, and Grumpy, and Happy, and Sleepy, and Sneezy.

Q.   Anyone else?

A.   Not that I recall.

Q.   What about Doc. Was he there?

A.   Oh, yes, that's right, he was there, too.

This may not be quite as impressive to the jury as if Ms. White could rattle off all seven names without prompting, but it gets the information out, and that's the important thing.

Suppose, though, that the important details are too complex to be put into a simple question; or suppose the witness gets very confused and flustered. When this happens, the attorney can attempt to refresh the witness's recollection by showing her a document or memorandum (or anything else, for that matter).

Q.   Ms. White, tell us who was there.

A.   Um, let me see. There was Greasey and Weepy and Sleazy and — no, wait, that's not right — Uh, . . . I'm sorry, I, uh —

Q.   Your Honor, may I show the witness a document to refresh her recollection?

(Judge):   Yes. Have it marked first as an exhibit for identification.

              (The clerk marks the document.)

Q.   Ms. White, examine Defense exhibit 12 for identification. Does that refresh your recollection?

A.   Yes. Thank you.

Once Ms. White has refreshed her recollection, the attorney can resume direct examination.

This technique of using a writing to refresh a witness's recollection during testimony can also be used on an uncooperative witness who professes a lack of memory to avoid testifying to certain facts. The attorney may confront the witness with a writing under the guise of refreshing his recollection in an effort to browbeat the witness into saying what the witness would prefer to keep unsaid.

The use of a document to refresh memory is governed by Fed. R. Evid. 612,[1] which provides:

Rule 612. Writing Used to Refresh a Witness's Memory

(a) Scope. This rule gives an adverse party certain options when a witness uses a writing to refresh memory:

(1) while testifying; or

(2) before testifying, if the court decides that justice requires a party to have those options.

(b) Adverse Party's Options; Deleting Unrelated Matter. Unless 18 U.S.C. § 3500 provides otherwise in a criminal case, an adverse party is entitled to have the writing produced at the hearing, to inspect it, to cross-examine the witness about it, and to introduce in evidence any portion that relates to the witness's testimony. If the producing party claims that the writing includes unrelated matter, the court must examine the writing in camera, delete any unrelated portion, and order that the rest be delivered to the adverse party. Any portion deleted over objection must be preserved for the record.

(c) Failure to Produce or Deliver. If a writing is not produced or is not delivered as ordered, the court may issue any appropriate order. But if the prosecution does not comply in a criminal case, the court must strike the witness's testimony or — if justice so requires — declare a mistrial.

[Prior to December 1, 2011, the rule read as follows:

Rule 612. Writing Used to Refresh Memory

[I]f a witness uses a writing to refresh memory for the purposes of testifying, either —

(1) while testifying, or

(2) before testifying, if the court in its discretion determines it is necessary in the interests of justice,

an adverse party is entitled to have the writing produced at the hearing, to inspect it, to cross-examine the witness thereon, and to introduce in evidence those portions which relate to the testimony of the witness. . . .

The Federal Rules of Evidence were rewritten solely to make them easier to understand; the Advisory Committee did not intend to make any substantive change in the Rules. The text of the old rule may remain useful in reading court decisions that precede the revision of the rules. Thus, this edition of the Student's Guide provides the text of both the new and the old version of each relevant provision of the Federal Rules of Evidence.]

---

[1] I will not cover certain procedural aspects of Fed. R. Evid. 612.

Note that Fed. R. Evid. 612 is *not* a hearsay exception, and does not permit the party using a writing to refresh a witness's memory to introduce the writing into evidence, or ask the witness to read it aloud, or in any other way get its contents directly before the jury. Rather, the rule assures that the *adverse* party has the right to examine and use the document while cross-examining the witness, and to offer the document in evidence — if it chooses to do so.

Thus, if, while W1 is testifying, D's attorney shows W1 a document to refresh W1's memory, D's attorney must then also show the document to P's attorney. P's attorney can cross-examine W1 about the document and, if she thinks it will help her case, can introduce the relevant portions of the document into evidence.

What happens, though, when a witness — cooperative, neutral, or hostile — asserts, sincerely or not, that she cannot remember the event (or the important details) in question, even after the attorney has attempted to use a writing to refresh her memory? Depending upon circumstances, an attorney may have a number of alternate ways to get the information into evidence — or may have none at all. One such alternative is Fed. R. Evid. 803(5), which is covered later in this chapter.

§ 9.3   *ANY* WRITING MAY BE USED

An attorney may use *any* writing to refresh a witness's recollection. It might be a note or memorandum written by the witness herself; it could be a note or memorandum written by someone else; it could be a newspaper article that was written about the event; it could be a photograph or a cartoon. There is no need to authenticate the writing; there is no need to show that it is accurate. Thus, in the second Q & A sequence in § 9.2, supra, even if the writing ("Defense exhibit 12 for identification") consisted of a sheet of paper with what looks like 7 scribbles on it, it is entirely permissible for the attorney to show it to the witness to refresh her memory. (Of course, the adverse party may score some points with the document on cross-examination.)

§ 9.4   "WHILE TESTIFYING"; "BEFORE TESTIFYING"; PRIVILEGED WRITINGS

If a witness uses a writing to refresh her recollection *while* she is testifying, the adverse party has a clear right to see the writing, and use it on cross-examination.

If W uses a privileged writing to refresh her recollection while she is on the stand, courts generally agree that W thereby waives the privilege.

But if the witness refreshed her memory with the writing *before* testifying, it is up to the judge whether to allow the adverse party to examine the writing. You might wonder: if W1 used the writing before testifying — say, the night before she took the witness stand — how would the adverse party's attorney even know about it? Simple: he would ask on cross-examination.

Q.   Tell me, Ms W, did you read anything, or use anything, to refresh your memory about these events, before coming to court today to testify?

A.   Yes, I keep a personal diary. Last night I went back and read over what I wrote the day this all happened.

At this point, the cross-examining attorney will ask the judge to require W to turn over her diary. The judge has discretion to deny this request or grant it. If the judge grants it, she would first examine it *in camera* and decide whether, and if so how much of it, should be turned over.

§ 9.5   THE JENCKS ACT: 18 U.S.C. § 3500

Fed. R. Evid 612(b) begins by referring to 18 U.S.C. § 3500, also known as the Jencks Act. 18 U.S.C. § 3500 regulates a defense attorney's access to any "statement or report which is in the possession of the United States which was made by a Government witness or potential witness." Suppose GW1 witnessed certain events. (a) That night he wrote a description of the events in his diary. (b) Later that week he wrote letters to friends, discussing the events, and kept copies of the letters on his computer hard drive. (c) Months later, when FBI agents interviewed him about what happened, he gave the agents a signed statement describing what he saw. (d) Several weeks after that, he testified about the events before a grand jury.

18 U.S.C. § 3500(a) provides that defense attorneys are not entitled to invoke the Federal Rules of Criminal Procedure to obtain discovery of any of these documents unless and until GW1 testifies at trial. 18 U.S.C. § 3500(b) provides that if GW1 testifies as a government witness, the prosecutor must turn over to the defense copies of all statements or reports made by GW1 that are *in the government's possession* that relate to what GW1 testified about on direct examination, whether or not GW1 used them to refresh his memory before or while testifying. This means that once the prosecutor finishes questioning GW1 on direct, she must turn over GW1's signed statement to the FBI agent, and his grand jury testimony, to the defense attorney. But unless the government also has possession of the diary and the letters, the Jencks Act does not entitle the defense attorney to them; defense counsel's only avenue to obtain those is per Fed. R. Evid. 612, as described in § 9.4, supra.

2. Recorded Recollection: Fed. R. Evid. 803(5)

§ 9.6   RULE 803(5): "RECORDED RECOLLECTION"

Fed. R. Evid. 803(5) provides as follows:

> **The following are not excluded by the rule against hearsay, regardless of whether the declarant is available as a witness:**
>
> 5) *Recorded Recollection.* **A record that:**
>
> > **(A) is on a matter the witness once knew about but now cannot recall well enough to testify fully and accurately;**
> >
> > **(B) was made or adopted by the witness when the matter was fresh in the witness's memory; and**

(C) accurately reflects the witness's knowledge.

If admitted, the record may be read into evidence but may be received as an exhibit only if offered by an adverse party.

[Prior to December 1, 2011, the rule read as follows:

> Rule 803. The following are not excluded by the hearsay rule, even though the declarant is available as a witness:
>
>> (5) Recorded recollection. A memorandum or record concerning a matter about which a witness once had knowledge but now has insufficient recollection to enable the witness to testify fully and accurately, shown to have been made or adopted by the witness when the matter was fresh in the witness's memory and to reflect that knowledge correctly. If admitted, the memorandum or record may be read into evidence but may not itself be received as an exhibit unless offered by an adverse party.

The Federal Rules of Evidence were rewritten solely to make them easier to understand; the Advisory Committee did not intend to make any substantive change in the Rules. The text of the old rule may remain useful in reading court decisions that precede the revision of the rules. Thus, this edition of the Student's Guide provides the text of both the new and the old version of each relevant provision of the Federal Rules of Evidence.]

In essence, the law establishes a sequence of preferences. The first preference is testimony by unaided memory; next comes testimony by refreshed memory (the Fed. R. Evid. 612 procedure). If the witness simply cannot recall the important details, even after attempting to refresh his memory by looking at a Fed. R. Evid. 612 writing, a "record" that satisfies Fed. R. Evid. 803(5) is an accepted substitute: instead of testifying from memory, the witness reads the document aloud to the jury.

§ 9.7   RULE 803(5): REQUIREMENTS AND ISSUES

Application of Fed. R. Evid. 803(5) imposes the following requirements and raises the following issues:

1. *Declarant must testify*: The person whose memorandum is to be offered under Fed. R. Evid. 803(5) must be on the witness stand when it is offered. *See* § 9.9. (To emphasize this point, a Fed. R. Evid. 803(5) declarant is hereinafter referred to as "DL/W" — i.e., declarant-witness.) DL/W's testimony must suffice to establish the remaining requirements listed infra.

2. *First-hand knowledge.* DL/W must testify that at one time he had first-hand knowledge of the facts at issue.

3. *Lacks sufficient recollection.* DL/W must testify that he now "now cannot recall well enough to testify fully and accurately" about the matter. Fed. R. Evid. 803(5)(A). *See* § 9.14. To satisfy this requirement, the party who will offer evidence via Fed. R. Evid. 803(5) should first attempt to refresh the witness's recollection (Fed. R. Evid. 612).

4. *Record.* DL/W must identify (authenticate) the document, electronic recording or file, or whatever that is being offered as a substitute for his "live" testimony. *See* § 9.10.

5. *"Made or adopted"; time.* DL/W must testify that he "made or adopted" the record "when the matter was fresh in the witness's memory." Fed. R. Evid. 803(5)(B). *See* § 9.15.

6. *Accuracy.* DL/W must testify that the record "accurately reflects the witness's knowledge" (Fed. R. Evid. 803(5)(C) — that is, it accurately reflects the knowledge he once had about the matter, before his memory faded. *See* § 9.17.

7. *Read but not received.* When Fed. R. Evid. 803(5) has been satisfied, the memorandum or record is read aloud to the judge and jury, but cannot be physically moved into evidence by the offering party. *See* § 9.9.

8. *Sixth Amendment Confrontation Clause. See* § 9.18.

§ 9.8   DECLARANT/WITNESS

Before a "record" can be read to the jury per Fed. R. Evid. 803(5), the offering party must call a witness who (a) had first-hand knowledge of the facts in question, and who (b) made or adopted the record. This is so because only the declarant (who made or adopted the writing) can give the testimony necessary to demonstrate that the record satisfies the rule's requirements. Moreover, this assures that the adverse party has an opportunity to cross-examine the person who made or adopted the writing. Even if the declarant/witness doesn't remember very much about the facts in question, cross-examination can help the jury assess his credibility as a person and the reliability of the record.

To require the declarant to be a witness, as Fed. R. Evid. 803(5) does, may seem inconsistent with Fed. R. Evid. 803 generally, which is, after all, entitled, "Exceptions to the Rule Against Hearsay — Regardless of Whether the Declarant Is Available as a Witness." The Advisory Committee conceded that, conceptually, this rule does not fit very comfortably into Fed. R. Evid. 803, but decided to put it there anyway.

§ 9.9   READ, BUT NOT RECEIVED

Because a "record" admitted under Fed. R. Evid. 803(5) is considered a less-preferred substitute for testimony, it is treated the same way testimony would be: the witness reads it aloud to the jury, just as if the witness would speak aloud to the jury if testifying from memory. The party using Fed. R. Evid. 803(5) cannot offer the document as an exhibit for the jury to examine in the courtroom or (once jury deliberations begin) in the jury room; if this were allowed, the jury might give the memorandum greater emphasis than it gives to "live" testimony, the preferred form of evidence.

The other party in the suit may, however, offer the document into evidence if, for example, she thinks it may help her impeach the witness.

§ 9.10 "RECORD"

The rule does not require that the "record" take any particular form, so long as the information is recorded in some way; on paper (handwritten or typed), on a hard drive or flash drive, dictated onto a cassette tape, etc.

§ 9.11 A STRAIGHTFORWARD EXAMPLE

W1 was the manager of the XYZ store. On September 10, 2010, she conducted an inventory of its merchandise. That night a fire broke out and everything in the store was destroyed. (Fortuitously, W1 brought the inventory form with her when she left the store.) Subsequently, XYZ sues INSCO, its insurance company, to collect on the policy. The case goes to trial in June 2012.

To prove how much merchandise was on hand, XYZ calls W1 to the stand. Direct examination proceeds as follows.

Q. 1.   Describe how you conducted the inventory.

A.   After the store closed for the night, I counted how many pieces we had of each item of merchandise, and wrote the number down on our monthly inventory sheet.

Q. 2.   You personally counted each item before recording it on the list?

A.   That's right.

Q. 3.   Do you recall, today, how many pieces of each item of merchandise you had in stock that night?

A.   Oh, no. The store carried dozens of items; I couldn't even remember all that then, let alone two years later!

Q. 4.   Your Honor, may I have this document marked as Plaintiff's exhibit 17? [It is so marked.] Ms. W1, please examine Plaintiff's 17. Do you recognize it?

A.   Yes, that's the inventory I filled out on September 10, 2010.

Q. 5.   How do you know?

A.   I recognize the form as the kind we used; I see where I wrote the date down on it; and it's got my signature on the bottom.

Q. 6.   And when did you write each entry?

A.   Right after I finished counting that particular item.

Q. 7.   Read it over, please. [W1 does so.] Could you now testify from memory as to how many of each item were on stock on September 10, 2010?

A.   Sorry, no, I can't.

Q. 8.   Are you satisfied now that this inventory correctly recorded the merchandise on hand on September 10, 2010?

A.   Oh, yes. I was always very careful when I took inventory.

XYZ: Your Honor, I now offer Plaintiff's exhibit 17 in evidence.

[INSCO's attorney:] Objection! Hearsay!

XYZ: Rule 803(5), Your Honor.

[Judge:] Objection sustained. Plaintiff's 17 is not admissible as an exhibit. Counselor, you may have the witness read her inventory aloud to the jury.

[Whereupon, it is read into the record.]

This sequence of questions methodically takes W1 through each of the requirements of Fed. R. Evid. 803(5). Q1 and Q2, and W1's answers, establish that W1, the declarant/witness, once had first-hand knowledge of the information on the form: she personally counted each piece of merchandise. W1's answer to Q3 establishes that W1 cannot testify fully and accurately without refreshing her recollection; her answer to Q7 establishes that she cannot do so even after examining the form. Her answers to Q4 and Q5 identify and authenticate the document as the document in question, and establish that it was made while the facts recorded on it were still fresh in W1's memory. Her answer to Q6 establishes that the inventory list accurately reflects the information of which W1 had first-hand knowledge at the time she was counting each item of merchandise.

Note: where a document qualifies for the "business record" exception, Fed. R. Evid 803(6), it can be introduced much more easily than under R. 803(5)— and the document itself is available to the jury. See § 9.31 **Q.4.**

§ 9.12 MULTIPLE-PERSON DOCUMENTS

Often a record or memorandum is a collaborative effort; more than one person participates in its creation. This is no automatic bar to using the document under Fed. R. Evid. 803(5); the Advisory Committee Note states that "[m]ultiple person involvement in the process of observing and recording is entirely consistent with the exception." The Senate Judiciary Committee gives, as examples, "employer dictating to secretary, secretary making memorandum at direction of employer, or information being passed along a chain of persons . . ." Again, the key requirement is that someone who had first-hand knowledge of the facts in question testifies to the accuracy of the memorandum.

The typical multiple-person document presents no difficulties. Suppose E, an employer, attends a meeting; when she returns to her office, she dictates a memorandum about the meeting to her secretary, S. S types up the memo and puts it in E's in-box. A day or two later, E reads the typed memo, initials and dates it, and gives it back to S for filing. If, sometime later, E is unable to recall the details of the meeting, a litigant can have her read it to the jury per Rule 803(5) without any need to call S as a witness, because E can testify to all of the facts necessary to satisfy that rule: she had first-hand knowledge of what happened to the meeting, and she read and initialed the memo that S typed up while the meeting was still fresh in her memory and confirmed that what S typed accurately reflected what E dictated to S about the meeting.

Sometimes, though, multiple person documents can present greater difficulties.

§ 9.13 QUESTIONS

Question 1. In the inventory discussed in § 9.11, suppose two employees worked together to take inventory. DL/W testifies that he and Counter spent several hours doing the inventory; that Counter examined each shelf or storage bin and told DL/W what it contained, and DL/W kept a tally on a company form. DL/W testifies that he recalls what kinds of merchandise were in the warehouse, but cannot remember how many of each had been there at the time. He is shown a document (which P's attorney first had marked as Plaintiff's exh. 1 for identification) and is asked, "do you recognize it?"

"Yes, that's the form I wrote the inventory down on, based on what Counter told me. It's in my handwriting and I put the date on it, here."

Plaintiff's lawyer seeks to have the contents of exhibit one read into evidence. INSCO's lawyer objects: hearsay. In response, P cites Fed. R. Evid. 803(5). Ruling?

Ans. Objection sustained. Fed. R. Evid. 803(5) requires that a showing that, at one time, the witness/declarant (DL/W) had first-hand knowledge of the information recorded in the document. DL/W did not have such knowledge, because he didn't do the actual counting; Counter did.

Question 2. Is the inventory admissible if DL/W further testifies that after all of the merchandise was inventoried in this fashion, Counter read DL/W's list over, said "Yup, that's right," and signed it?

Ans. No. Fed. R. Evid. 803(5) requires that the person who had first-hand knowledge (in this case, Counter) testify, to authenticate and vouch for the accuracy of the list. It is not enough that DL/W assert that Counter vouched for it.

Question 3. Counter now takes the stand and testifies that he is sure that he counted accurately the number of each items and reported accurately to DL/W. Does DL/W's list now qualify under Fed. R. Evid. 803(5)?

Ans. Yes. The Advisory Committee and Senate Judiciary Committee cite approvingly to cases upholding admissibility in this kind of situation. The key, again, is that Counter, the person who once had first-hand knowledge, testifies that he in fact perceived the facts in question and communicated them accurately to DL/W.

Question 4. If Counter is unavailable, how can P get the list into evidence, using only rules we have covered thus far?

Ans. The difficulty is that the information on DL/W's list represents two statements, not one:

(1) Counter's verbal statement to DL/W ("There are 27 midget widgets"); and

(2) DL/W's written statement (putting the number "27" on the inventory form next to the listing, "midget widgets").

Fed. R. Evid. 803(5) is not by itself enough to overcome INSCO's hearsay objection, because (in the absence of Counter's testimony) 803(5) only provides a hearsay exception for the second statement; it doesn't cover the first. But, as Fed. R. Evid. 805, the multiple hearsay rule, provides (*see* § 7.3), "Hearsay included within hearsay is not excluded by the rule against hearsay if each part of the combined statements conforms with an exception to the rule." Applied to this case, because we have already found a hearsay provision to cover the second statement, we can overcome the hearsay objection if we can find a provision to cover the first statement (Counter's verbal report to DL/W).

> (1) Suppose at trial DL/W could testify, "I clearly recall Counter calling out, 'There are 27 midget widgets.' " If INSCO objected that this is hearsay, how should P respond?
>
> Counter's statement to DL/W is hearsay, but it should nonetheless be admissible, because it satisfies Fed. R. Evid. 803(1). It is Counter's "statement describing a . . . condition [the number of midget widgets], made while or immediately after [Counter] perceiv[ed] the [number of widgets]." See § 8.7.
>
> (2) DL/W cannot now recall how many midget widgets Counter told him there were on the shelves that day. But that is no barrier to admissibility, because instead of his memory, DL/W can rely on his list.
>
> In other words, each listing on the inventory is DL/W's 803(5) record of Counter's 803(1) oral statement. That's how multiple hearsay works: no matter how many different levels of hearsay are included within an item of evidence, the hearsay objection is overcome if an Article VIII provision can be found for each level of hearsay.
>
> As we will see later on, many of the complexities we encounter using the "recorded recollection" exception in this sort of situation disappear where (as in this hypothetical) the document would also qualify under Fed. R. Evid. 803(6), the "business record" exception.

§ 9.14 "NOW CANNOT RECALL WELL ENOUGH"

The party seeking to use Fed. R. Evid. 803(5) need not show that the witness lacks *all* recollection of the event or condition described in the memorandum (which some courts, prior to the Federal Rules, foolishly insisted upon). It is enough that the witness "now cannot recall well enough to testify fully and accurately."

Occasionally a witness will feign insufficient memory, in the hopes that he can evade the scrutiny of cross-examination (by answering "I'm sorry, I can't remember" to all questions) while getting his story across to the jury through a memorandum that qualifies under Fed. R. Evid. 803(5). The judge has at least some discretion in deciding whether a witness's protestations of lack of memory are true.

The reverse situation also sometimes arises, particularly in criminal trials: a witness will claim lack of memory because she doesn't want to testify at all. Assume, for example, that Dark and Stormy were charged with a burglary. Prior to trial, the prosecutor agreed to allow Stormy to plead guilty to a lesser charge in exchange for his testimony against Dark. Stormy took the plea, but when Dark goes to trial, Stormy is suddenly "unable to remember" anything whatsoever about the burglary he pleaded guilty to only a few weeks before. In such a case, the prosecutor may attempt to qualify a document (such as a signed confession) as Stormy's "recorded recollection" under Fed. R. Evid. 803(5). If it appears that Stormy is deliberately trying to avoid testifying, many judges will give the prosecutor the benefit of the doubt in deciding whether the 803(5) requirements have been satisfied.

§ 9.15 "MADE OR ADOPTED"; "FRESH IN MEMORY"

We saw in § 9.3 that under Fed. R. Evid. 612, an attorney may use *any* writing, photograph, etc. to *refresh* a witness's recollection. Fed. R. Evid. 803(5), by contrast, is much more demanding as to the kind of record that can be used as a *substitute* for the witness's memory. To satisfy Rule 803(5), the offering party must elicit testimony from DL/W that establishes either: (a) that DL/W herself made (e.g., wrote or dictated) the memorandum or record while the events in question were still fresh in her memory; or (b) that DL/W "adopted" someone else's memorandum or record while the events in question were still fresh in her memory.

§ 9.16 QUESTIONS

Question 1. At a board meeting of ABC Corporation, MCP, an ABC officer, boasted that he had used a variety of tactics to avoid hiring women for managerial positions. Worthy and Justin attended that meeting. Incensed at what MCP said, Justin that night wrote a memo detailing MCP's remarks. The next day Justin showed his memo to Worthy, who agreed that Justin had accurately related what MCP had said.

Plaintiff, a woman who had been turned down for a managerial position, subsequently filed a Title VII sex discrimination suit against ABC. The corporation defends by asserting that Plaintiff was denied the job solely because the man it hired instead of Plaintiff was better qualified.

Learning of Plaintiff's suit, Justin sent Plaintiff a copy of his memo; it is so detailed that if Plaintiff can get it into evidence, it will make her case substantially stronger. Unfortunately, Justin is not available to testify at trial, and although Worthy is willing to testify, he can no longer remember precisely what it was that MCP said.

If Plaintiff calls Worthy as a witness and attempts to use Justin's memo to prove what MCP said at the meeting, how many different levels of hearsay are involved?

Ans. Two. First, there is MCP's verbal statement ("MCP to the board"). Second, there is Justin's written memorandum ("Justin to paper" or "Justin to hard drive"). Thus, we have another "multiple hearsay" issue.

Question 2. Is Justin's memo admissible, over a hearsay objection?

Ans. Yes.

(1) If Worthy could remember MCP's statements, he could repeat them, over a hearsay objection, per Fed. R. Evid. 801(d)(2)(D). MCP, an officer of ABC Corp., is its "agent or employee," and the subject of his statements — the company's hiring practices — are "a matter within the scope" of his responsibilities.

(2) Because Worthy's memory of what MCP said has faded with time, Worthy cannot testify fully and accurately about what MCP said. Thus, we encounter multiple hearsay. The two layers of statements are:

a. MCP to Justin and Worthy (and everyone else who attended the meeting). As noted in (1), supra, we can overcome this level of hearsay with Rule 801(d)(2)(D).

b. Justin to paper or hard drive. We can overcome this level of hearsay if we can qualify Justin's memorandum as Worthy's "recorded recollection" per Rule 803(5).

(3) To qualify Justin's memo as Worthy's Fed. R. Evid. 803(5), Plaintiff must show that Worthy "adopted" Justin's memo in accordance with the rule.

To do so, Plaintiff calls Worthy as a witness. Worthy testifies that he and Justin attended the meeting and heard what MCP said; that it was about gender discrimination; but that he can no longer recall the important details.

While Worthy is still on the stand, Plaintiff has Justin's memorandum marked as an exhibit for identification.

Q.   Do you recognize this document?

A.   Yes. This is a memo Justin showed me the day after the board meeting, detailing what MCP said.

Q.   Did you read it when he showed it to you?

A.   Yes.

Q.   When you read it, were you satisfied that it was accurate?

A.   Yes. I remember commenting to Justin that he wrote it exactly as I remembered it.

Q.   Read it to yourself, please. [Worthy does so.]

Q.   Having read it, do you now recall what it was that MCP said?

A.   The general thrust, yes, not the details. Sorry!

Q.   But are you satisfied now that this memorandum accurately reflected what MCP said?

A.   Yes.

The document is now admissible as a memorandum of Worthy's recorded recollection. Even though Worthy did not write it, he "adopted" it (satisfied himself that it was accurate) while the events in question were still fresh in his memory.

Question 3. If the trial judge permits Plaintiff to employ this procedure, may she now offer the memo into evidence as an exhibit?

Ans. No. The last sentence of Fed. R. Evid. 803(5) states, in pertinent part, "If admitted, the record may be read into evidence but may be received as an exhibit only if offered by an adverse party." *See* § 9.9.

Question 4. Can ABC offer the exhibit into evidence? Why might ABC want to do so?

Ans. ABC may do so. The final clause of the last sentence of Fed. R. Evid. 803(5) specifically permits it. ABC might want to offer it as an exhibit if its lawyer thinks that to do so will help impeach Worthy's testimony. Perhaps, for example, the memo "sounds" more impressive than it looks — perhaps it is written on the back of a third grade homework assignment, in a semi-legible scrawl with crossouts and circles and arrows, adorned with coffee stains and doodles in the margins. Whether to offer it in evidence is a tactical decision for ABC's attorney.

§ 9.17   TIME; ACCURACY; FOUNDATIONAL TESTIMONY

To qualify a writing under Fed. R. Evid. 803(5), the declarant/witness must testify that she made or adopted it "when the matter was fresh in the [declarant/witness's] memory; and accurately reflects the witness's knowledge." This poses two questions: (1) how much time may elapse between the event and writing the memorandum; and (2) what kind of testimony will satisfy the "accuracy" requirement.

Time. There is no rigid cut-off; minutes, days, weeks and perhaps even longer periods should in appropriate cases create no insurmountable barriers. Once the witness testifies that she made or adopted the memorandum while the events were fresh in her mind, the judge has discretion whether to accept this testimony. Relevant factors, besides the passage of time, include the nature of the event or fact in question, its importance to the witness/declarant when it occurred, and the degree of detail in the writing.

Foundation testimony. Testimony such as "I remember being very careful to get it down on paper correctly" or "I remember thinking, when I read X's memorandum, that X described it accurately" suffices. So would "I'm sure I wouldn't have filed it until I was satisfied it was accurate," or "I always check reports like these for accuracy before I file them." A bit weaker, but still probably sufficient, would be testimony such as "I really don't remember anything about the incident, but I'm sure I wouldn't have signed this memo if I had any doubts about its accuracy at the time."

Keep in mind that foundational testimony of some kind is a *prerequisite* to using Fed. R. Evid. 803(5). A stubborn witness probably can frustrate an attorney, simply by refusing to acknowledge that he considered the memorandum accurate at the time he wrote, signed or verbally adopted it.

§ 9.18   SIXTH AMENDMENT CONFRONTATION CLAUSE

Fed. R. Evid. 803(5) requires the declarant to testify as a witness. This assures a defendant the opportunity to cross-examine him; hence, to satisfy the requirements for 803(5) automatically satisfies the Confrontation Clause, as well.

Some scholars argue that if the witness professes complete lack of memory on the subject, the Confrontation Clause is left unsatisfied because the defendant is denied an opportunity to conduct "meaningful" cross-examination. The Supreme Court rejected this argument with regard to Fed. R. Evid. 801(d)(1)(C) (*see* § 4.3), and courts generally reject this argument with regard to Fed. R. Evid. 803(5), as well. During cross-examination, it is up to the defense attorney may attempt to make the witness look foolish and perhaps untruthful by asking the witness a series of questions which the witness answers, "I don't remember."

§ 9.19   QUESTIONS

Question 1. D, an investment advisor, is indicted for mail fraud. The indictment alleges that on February 1, 2009, as part of a scheme to defraud, she mailed investment advice to X (a client) concerning the DEF Company, containing factual assertions that she knew were not true.

During the preindictment investigation in November of 2009, an FBI Agent interviewed W2, D's research director. W2 told Agent W1:

> D showed me the letter she was planning to send to X. I told her, "Am I missing something? You know that DEF hasn't shown a profit in the last three years!"

> D just smiled and said, "You know it and I know it, but X doesn't know it." Then she put the letter in the envelope and licked it shut.

A few days later Agent W1 showed W2 her typed memo about what W2 told Agent W1. W2 signed the bottom of the form, just below the words, "I affirm under penalty of perjury that the statements contained in this memorandum are accurate to the best of my knowledge."

At trial, in April of 2012, the prosecutor calls W2 as a witness, expecting him to testify to the same facts as he had told Agent W1. Instead, W2 says he can no longer remember anything relating to X, although he acknowledges that he probably knew a good deal about the X account at the time. The prosecutor has Agent W1's typed memo marked as Government exhibit 6 for identification, shows it to W2, asks him to read it silently to himself, and then asks,

Q.   Does this refresh your memory?

A.   Sorry, it doesn't.

Q.   Well, do you recognize this piece of paper?

A.   'Fraid not.

Q.   Is that your signature at the bottom of the page?

A.   Yes.

Q.   To the best of your knowledge, today, are the statements in that memorandum accurate?

A.   I told you, I don't remember anything about the X account, I don't remember meeting with D about it, and I don't remember this piece of paper!

Q.   Do you see where it says, just above where you signed, "I affirm under penalty of perjury that the statements contained in this memorandum are accurate to the best of my knowledge"?

A.   Yes.

Q.   I ask you again: To the best of your knowledge, today, are the statements in that memorandum accurate?

A.   I guess they are, yes, or I wouldn't have signed them.

The prosecutor asks W2 to read the memorandum aloud. D's attorney objects: "Hearsay! Sixth Amendment Confrontation Clause!" How should the judge rule?

Ans. Once again, we have a multiple hearsay issue to deal with: D's statement to W2, and W2's adoption of Agent W1's memorandum.

The first level, D's statement to W2, poses no problem. D, the declarant, is a party; it is offered in evidence by the Government, D's opposing party. Fed. R. Evid. 801(d)(2)(A). If W2 could (or would) remember what D said, the hearsay and Confrontation Clause objections could be overruled without a second thought.

But because W2 can't (or won't) remember what D said, the prosecutor has to use Agent W1's memorandum as a substitute for W2's testimony, to prove that D made the crucial statement to W2. It's close, but the judge could properly overrule the objection, because W2's direct examination satisfies all of the Fed. R. Evid. 803(5) requirements.

D's best arguments against admissibility relate to the "fresh in memory" and accuracy requirements.

"Fresh in memory." W2 didn't adopt Agent W1's memorandum until nine months after the event in question occurred. (If you read the fact pattern carefully, you'll recall that in February, D told W1 that she was going to lie to client X; W1 told Agent W2 about that conversation in November.) That's a rather long time. Still, is nine months an excessive period, under the circumstances? If your boss (in essence) told you, "I am about to knowingly defraud a client," do you think you would have trouble remembering it nine months later?

Vouching for accuracy. W2's endorsement of the memorandum at trial was reluctant and lukewarm at best; but (particularly if the judge concludes that W2 is simply trying to avoid testifying against D), the judge can legitimately rule that the "vouching" requirement has been satisfied.

Regarding the Confrontation Clause, *see* § 9.18, supra.

Question 2. Suppose instead that when the prosecutor asked, "To the best of your knowledge today, are the statements in that memorandum accurate?" W2 had answered:

> "No, I don't see how they can be. I'm sure that D never said those things to me. She's not that kind of person. And besides, if she said anything like that, I'm sure I'd remember it! I guess I must have signed this form without reading it."

Can the prosecutor use Fed. R. Evid. 803(5) to get the facts in the memorandum before the jury?

Ans. I don't think so. If W2 stonewalls and insists that the memorandum is not accurate, the prosecutor is probably stymied.[2]

Question 3. Suppose, in the previous problem, the prosecutor calls Agent W1, who testifies, "When I showed my memorandum to W2, I asked him to read it out loud to me. He did so. I asked him, 'Is that accurate?' He said it was, and I asked him to sign it and he did." Would this suffice to qualify the memorandum under Fed. R. Evid. 803(5)?

Ans. Probably not. The traditional view is that the witness who had first-hand knowledge (W2) of the key events (D's conversation with W2) is the one who must vouch for the accuracy of the memo while testifying at trial; here, instead, the prosecutor is trying to use Agent W1 to prove that W2 endorsed its accuracy. So if W2 wants to frustrate the prosecutor and words his answers with the precisely right kind of evasiveness, he could succeed. Fortunately, people in W2's situation usually are not sharp enough verbally to outmatch an attorney who knows how to word questions on cross-examination.

PART C:
RECORDS OF REGULARLY CONDUCTED ACTIVITY (THE "BUSINESS RECORDS" EXCEPTION): RULES 803(6)–803(7)

§ 9.20 IN GENERAL

Fed. R. Evid. 803(6) provides as follows:

> **Rule 803. Exceptions to the Rule Against Hearsay — Regardless of Whether the Declarant Is Available as a Witness**
>
> **The following are not excluded by the rule against hearsay, regardless of whether the declarant is available as a witness: . . .**

---

[2] Stonewalling a prosecutor like this is not without its risks: depending on circumstances, W2 might find himself indicted for perjury.

(6) *Records of a Regularly Conducted Activity.* A record of an act, event, condition, opinion, or diagnosis if:

> **(A) the record was made at or near the time by — or from information transmitted by — someone with knowledge;**
>
> **(B) the record was kept in the course of a regularly conducted activity of a business, organization, occupation, or calling, whether or not for profit;**
>
> **(C) making the record was a regular practice of that activity;**
>
> **(D) all these conditions are shown by the testimony of the custodian or another qualified witness, or by a certification that complies with Rule 902(11) or (12) or with a statute permitting certification; and**
>
> **(E) neither the source of information nor the method or circumstances of preparation indicate a lack of trustworthiness.**

[Prior to December 1, 2011, the rule read as follows:

> Rule 803. The following are not excluded by the hearsay rule, even though the declarant is available as a witness: . . .
>
> > (6) Records of Regularly Conducted Activity. — A memorandum, report, record, or data compilation, in any form, of acts, events, conditions, opinions, or diagnoses, made at or near the time by, or from information transmitted by, a person with knowledge, if kept in the course of a regularly conducted business activity, and if it was the regular practice of that business activity to make the memorandum, report, record or data compilation, all as shown by the testimony of the custodian or other qualified witness, or by certification that complies with Rule 902(11), Rule 902(12), or a statute permitting certification, unless the source of information or the method or circumstances of preparation indicate lack of trustworthiness. The term "business" as used in this paragraph includes business, institution, association, profession, occupation, and calling of every kind, whether or not conducted for profit.

The Federal Rules of Evidence were rewritten solely to make them easier to understand; the Advisory Committee did not intend to make any substantive change in the Rules. The text of the old rule may remain useful in reading court decisions that precede the revision of the rules. Thus, this edition of the Student's Guide provides the text of both the new and the old version of each relevant provision of the Federal Rules of Evidence.]

This provision, like so many others in Article VIII, is based on the twin considerations of reliability and necessity.

The necessity for such a rule is obvious. It is often impractical and inconvenient, and sometimes impossible, to identify, let alone call as a witness, every person who participated in making a typical business record. Picture, for example, a salesman who jots down on a company form the particular items he sold to each customer on whom he called during a business trip. At the end of each day, he calls, faxes or e-mails the home office to inform sales department personnel how much of which items he sold to each customer. That employee in turn enters the information into the appropriate company computer file.[3] Once in the computer, the information is automatically available to the shipping, accounting and salespersons' compensation departments.

To identify, let alone call as a witness, everyone who participated in the creation of the record would pose absurd difficulties. Under Fed. R. Evid. 803(6)(D), a party need only call one witness, "the custodian or another qualified witness," who need not have participated in any way in the creation of the record, to secure its admissibility over a hearsay objection. Indeed, the offering party can authenticate and qualify the record without calling a witness at all.

The reliability of business records is based on three considerations: (1) reliance, (2) routine practice, and (3) duty. The typical business enterprise relies upon the accuracy of its records in deciding what to ship, whom to bill, what bills to pay, how to plan for the future, and so on. Thus, the enterprise has a very powerful motive to assure that its records are accurately made and kept. To qualify, moreover, the rule requires that each participant in creating and keeping the record must act in accord with established procedures, and must have done so pursuant to a duty or responsibility to the enterprise.

The legislative history of Fed. R. Evid. 803(6) is worth a mention. The common law antecedent of Fed. R. Evid. 803(6) covered only "business records," and generally adhered to a fairly narrow, traditional, commercial definition of "business." The Advisory Committee sought to broaden its scope, and therefore chose not to use the word "business"; instead, its title and its language referred only to "regularly conducted activity." The House Judiciary Committee thought this was too broad; it amended the text of the rule (but not its title!) to restrict it to records of "regularly conducted *business* activity," and provided a fairly traditional definition of "business." The Senate Judiciary Committee preferred the broader, Advisory Committee approach, and deleted the House-added references to "business" from the Senate version of the bill. The Conference Committee restored the narrower House version, but broadened the definition of "business" somewhat.

Fed. R. Evid. 803(6) imposes the following requirements and raises the following issues:

1. *Original source of information.* The person who provides the information that is recorded in the "business record" must

    (a) have first-hand knowledge of the information 803(6)(A), and

    (b) must have a regular "business duty" to acquire and report the information. *See* § 9.23.

2. *"Record."* The evidence must be in some physical (or physically reproducible) form: on paper, on tape, on computer disk or data base. "Mental business

---

[3] In some companies, the salesman might go on line and enter the information himself; in companies that are less sophisticated electronically, the information might be handled by an additional employee or two before it is finally entered.

records" don't qualify.

3. *"Business [etc.]."* To qualify, the record must have been created in connection with a "business, organization, occupation or calling" per Fed. R. Evid. 803(6)(B). *See* § 9.21.

4. *Making the record: time, duty, "regularity."* Making the record must have been a "regular practice" of the entity, occupation or calling, Fed. R. Evid. 803(6)(C), and the record must have been made "at or near the time" of the event or information included in the record, Fed. R. Evid. 803(6)(A). *See* § 9.26.

5. *Keeping the record.* The record must also be "kept" as part of the "regularly conducted activity" of the entity, occupation, or calling. Fed. R. Evid. 803(6)(B). *See* § 9.28.

6. *Subject matter and contents.* The subject of the record may be an "act, event, condition, opinion, or diagnosis." *See* § 9.29.

7. *Multiple hearsay.* One particularly noteworthy feature of this exception is that it *sometimes* (not always!) "compresses" what might otherwise be several levels of hearsay into one; this simplifies securing admissibility, but adds confusion in assessing whether a record consists of multiple hearsay. *See* §§ 9.25, 9.30.

8. *Procedure for admission.* The rule establishes two different streamlined procedures for admitting such records. (1) The offering party can call the record custodian to identify the record and give pro forma foundation testimony. (2) In the alternative, Fed. R. Evid. 803(6)(D). the offering party can authenticate and qualify the record by certification. *See* § 9.32.

9. *Trustworthiness clause.* A record that appears to qualify for admission is nevertheless excluded "if the source of information [or] the method or circumstances of preparation indicate a lack of trustworthiness." Fed R. Evid. 803(6)(E). This clause requires the judge to assess declarant credibility to a greater extent than normal. *See* § 9.35.

10. *Sixth Amendment Confrontation Clause. See* § 9.36.

11. *Interplay with other rules. See* § 9.37.

Note, by the way, that a record that qualifies under Fed. R. Evid. 803(6) is admissible in a law suit whether or not the "business, organization, occupation or calling" which created the record is a litigant in the law suit. In a law suit brought by Smith against Jones, either Smith or Jones could introduce a relevant business record created by the XYZ Manufacturing Corporation, even if neither Smith nor Jones ever worked for or did business with XYZ.

§ 9.21 "BUSINESS, ORGANIZATION, OCCUPATION, OR CALLING . . ."

Fed. R. Evid. 803(6)(B) provides that to fit within the exception, the record must have been made and kept "in the course of a regularly conducted activity of a business, organization, occupation, or calling, whether or not for profit . . ." The legislative history makes it clear that "the records of institutions and associations like schools, churches and hospitals are admissible under this provision."[4] An individual's business records are likewise admissible. Thus, for example, a lawyer's appointment book comes within Fed. R. Evid. 803(6); so do a doctor's medical records of his patients. But purely private records (e.g., an individual's personal check book or diary) probably do not, no matter how meticulously and regularly kept.

I will often use the word "business" or the phrase "business record" in quotes discussing this hearsay exception. Keep in mind that when I do, "business" is shorthand for a commercial business, an organization such as a labor union, civic association, political party, private school, investment club, and so on; and "business record" includes an individual's records, so long as those records involve an "occupation or calling." But the rule does not include a person's private financial records, nor records made and kept as part of a hobby.

§ 9.22 RECORDS OF CRIMINAL ACTIVITY

Records of illegal activities (e.g., a ledger of bribes paid to public building inspectors) and illicit organizations (e.g., a narcotics network's records of drugs bought and sold) may also come within Rule 803(6), if the records meet the requirements of the rule.

To establish that such records were made and kept in a way that satisfies the technical requirements of Fed. R. Evid. 803(6), it is usually necessary for the prosecutor to call as a witness the person who made and kept the records. (Criminal organizations rarely have "record custodians" or someone qualified to make the required certification.) Thus, the only way the prosecutor can rely on Fed. R. Evid. 803(6) to introduce such records is to persuade the person who made the records to testify, usually by offering a reduced plea or sentence in exchange.

Sometimes this is impossible — that person is dead, or missing, or refuses. Sometimes the prosecutor is unwilling to offer such a deal: the record-keeper might be "Mr. Big" in the organization. In such situations, the prosecutor has other options. If she can prove (say, by circumstantial evidence) that D1 made and kept the records, then the records would be admissible against D1 as statements by a party-opponent, Fed. R. Evid. 801(d)(2)(A). And it may be possible to show, by testimony or circumstantial evidence, that the records were made during and for the purpose of furthering a conspiracy among several defendants, in which case they would be admissible against other conspirators as well per Fed. R. Evid. 801(d)(2)(E).

---

[4] Conference Committee Report.

§ 9.23   ORIGINAL SOURCE OF INFORMATION

Fed. R. Evid. 803(6) directs that "[a] record of an act, event, condition, opinion, or diagnosis" comes within the exception if "**(A)** the record was made . . . by — or from information transmitted by — someone with knowledge;" "**(B)** the record was kept in the course of a regularly conducted activity . . . ;" and "**(C)** making the record was a regular practice of that activity; . . ." This language, as interpreted and explained by the legislative history of the rule, requires that a person who provides the information that is recorded in the "business record" have:

(1)   first-hand knowledge of the information, and

(2)   a regular "business duty" to acquire and record the information.

If these requirements are not met, the record fails to comply with the mandates of Fed. R. Evid 803(6)(E) that "neither the source of information nor the method or circumstances of preparation indicate a lack of trustworthiness," and the record will not satisfy the exception.

In the typical business record situation, this causes no difficulties. A salesman who sells merchandise to a customer, for example, has first-hand knowledge of what he sold, thereby satisfying subparagraph (1). He also has a regular, routine business duty to report this back to the home office, thereby satisfying subparagraph (2). (The company, after all, needs the information so it knows whom to bill and for how much, how much commission to pay the salesman, etc.) Similarly, a research chemist in a corporation's research and development department has first-hand knowledge of the experiments she conducts, and, like any good scientist, makes it part of the regular conduct of her "business" as a research scientist to record each step in the experiment and the information she acquires as a result.

Problems sometimes arise, however, with regard to each subpart of Fed. R. Evid. 803(6)'s "original source of information" requirement.

Johnson v. Lutz, 253 N.Y. 124, 170 N.E. 517, 518 (1930) is the classic example of information that fails to satisfy the first-hand knowledge requirement (subparagraph (1), supra). A motorcycle and a truck collided, and the motorcyclist was killed. His heir (Johnson) brought a wrongful death action against the truck driver (Lutz). A police officer, investigating the collision, interviewed bystanders, who told him that the collision was the motorcyclist's fault. The officer included that information in his report. At trial, Lutz offered the report into evidence as a business record of the police department.[5]

The officer (and his report) satisfied subparagraph (2): it was part of his regular duties to acquire and report the information that the bystanders told him. But while this satisfied subparagraph (2), it did not satisfy subparagraph (1), because the officer was not the original source of the information about how the collision occurred. (The

---

[5] If the same situation arose today, we would probably look to Fed. R. Evid. 803(8), the official records exception, rather than Fed. R. Evid. 803(6), the business record exception; but if Lutz attempted to introduce the bystanders' statements through the officers's report, the analysis and result would be precisely the same under either rule.

bystanders, assuming they saw the accident, had first-hand knowledge; but because *they* owed no "business duty" to the police department to provide the information,[6] they cannot satisfy paragraph (2).)

Another way of looking at *Johnson v. Lutz* is to analyze it in terms of multiple hearsay. The officer's report involved two different levels of hearsay. First, the bystanders made statements to the officer ("bystanders to officer"). Second, the officer included what they said in his report ("officer to paper"). Fed. R. Evid. 803(6) covers the second level of hearsay, but because the bystanders had no business duty to provide the officers with information, Fed. R. Evid. 803(6) cannot cover the first level.

The fact that the bystanders' statements do not come within Fed. R. Evid. 803(6) does not necessarily mean they are inadmissible. Consider the questions in the next section.

§ 9.24   QUESTIONS

Question 1. Suppose, in *Johnson v. Lutz*, Lutz called the officer as a witness at trial. Direct examination proceeds:

Q.   Officer, what happened that day?

A.   I heard a squeal of brakes, the sound of an impact, and several people screaming; it came from around the corner. I ran to where the sound came from, and saw a motorcycle crushed under the wheels of a truck. As I got there, several bystanders called to me, —

(By Johnson's attorney):   Objection, your honor! Hearsay!

(Judge):   Sustained.

Q.   Officer, how much time elapsed from when you heard the squeal of brakes and so on, to when you arrived at the accident and the bystanders started telling you something?

A.   It could not have been more than 30 seconds.

Q.   These bystanders you mentioned: describe their demeanor.

A.   They were pretty upset. One man was crying, and I remember a woman's hand was shaking while she pointed toward the intersection.

Q.   How many bystanders gave you statements?

A.   Several. Two gave me their names and addresses.

Q.   Tell us, officer, what the bystanders said to you?

(By Johnson's attorney):   Objection, your honor! Hearsay!

How should the judge rule?

---

[6] A citizen has a moral duty to cooperate with law enforcement officials, but there is no *legal* duty to do so (unless he or she is served with a subpoena).

Ans. First of all, if your answer even mentions Fed. R. Evid. 803(6), you weren't paying attention to the question. In this question, the officer is on the witness stand, testifying from memory. Therefore 803(6) has no role in the problem at all.

The judge should overrule the objection. Following Johnson's initial objection, Lutz's attorney elicited testimony from the officer that clearly qualifies the bystanders' statements to him as excited utterances. (If you don't see why, review Fed. R. Evid. 803(2), §§ 8.2–8.7.)

Question 2. The officer's report contains the following:

> I heard a squeal of brakes, the sound of an impact, and several people screaming; it came from around the corner. I went to where the sound came from, and saw a motorcycle crushed under the wheels of a truck. I arrived at the scene no more than 30 seconds after hearing the crash. As I got there, several bystanders called to me that the motorcycle ran the stop sign at the intersection and got hit by the truck. They were terribly upset, shaken, pale. When I looked, I could see why. The cyclist was obviously dead [etc.]

Lutz's attorney calls the officer as a witness.

Q.	Officer, did you investigate this accident?
A.	Yes, I did.
Q.	Tell us, please, what you saw, what you heard, and what you did after you arrived there.
A.	I'm sorry, counselor. This accident was more than five years ago and I've investigated hundreds of traffic accidents since then. I'm afraid the details tend to run together in my memory.

What options are available to Lutz's attorney?

Ans. First, he should have the officer's report marked as an exhibit for identification; then he should ask the officer to read the report to himself, to see if it refreshes his recollection (Fed. R. Evid. 612).

If that doesn't work, Lutz's attorney has a two-level hearsay problem: "bystanders to officer" and "officer to paper." But it is clear from the report itself that the bystanders' statements qualify as excited utterances (just as in the previous problem). Therefore, Lutz's only remaining problem is how to prove that the bystanders made their statements. In the previous problem, Lutz accomplished this through the officer's testimony. Since in this problem the officer does not remember the events well enough to testify, Lutz must use the report to prove what the bystanders said and under what circumstances. To do so, Lutz must find an Article VIII provision to overcome the objection that the report is hearsay.

Lutz has two options: (1) ask the officer the questions necessary to qualify his report under Fed. R. Evid. 803(5); or (2) ask the officer the questions necessary to qualify his report under Fed. R. Evid. 803(6).[7] Because we can find a hearsay provision to

---

[7] As noted earlier, a police officer's report is more likely to be offered per Fed. R. Evid. 803(8), the public

overcome each level of hearsay, the objection should be overruled, and the entire report, including the bystanders' statements, should be admissible, either under Fed. R. Evid. 803(2) and 803(5) or Fed. R. Evid. 803(2) and 803(6).

Question 3. Suppose the officer is not available as a witness. What are Lutz's options?

Ans. Lutz can, of course, try to locate the bystanders and subpoena them. But if that doesn't work (or even if it does), Lutz will want to get the officer's report into evidence.

The officer's report still involves two levels of hearsay: "bystanders to officer" and "officer to paper." If, as in **Q.2**, the report describes the impact the accident had on the bystanders, their statements to the officer will still come within Fed. R. Evid. 803(2), but Fed. R. Evid. 803(5) is no longer available as a means of proving that they made the statements contained within the report, because 803(5) requires putting the person who made or adopted the report (the officer) on the stand.

As you will see more fully in § 9.32, however, under Fed. R. Evid. 803(6), the officer's report *is* admissible — even if the officer is unavailable.

§ 9.25   MULTIPLE HEARSAY (1)

Note that in the previous two problems, we had to resort to multiple hearsay analysis to attempt to overcome a hearsay objection, because the key statements in the report did not satisfy the Fed. R. Evid. 803(6) "original source of information" requirement.

Suppose the person who was the original source of information, and the person who made the record, both had a "duty" to the business or organization to do what they did (i.e., to gather, report and record the information)? Is the report still treated as multiple hearsay? See § 9.30.

§ 9.26   MAKING THE RECORD: TIME, DUTY, "REGULARITY"

The record must be made "at or near the time" the events occurred, Fed. R. Evid. 803(6)(A), close enough in time to minimize the risk that the person providing the information might misremember. The record must be of a kind that is made as part of the "regular practice" of the "business," Fed. R. Evid. 803(6)(C), and kept in the regular course of the "business" Fed. R. Evid. 803(6)(B). In essence, therefore, the information gatherer, maker and keeper must have acted as part of their regular responsibilities to the "business." (This could involve only one person, or several, so long as everyone who participated in making and keeping the record did so as part of his or her regular responsibilities to the "business.")

The "regularity" and "duty" requirements need not be formal obligations imposed by the entity in its official manual. Suppose Professor C has a routine practice:

---

record exception. I'm using this scenario in discussing Fed. R. Evid. 803(6) because it is a convenient way to illustrate certain aspects of both 803(6) and 803(8).

whenever a student comes to see him in his office, Professor C makes a brief entry about the meeting in a daily log he keeps, naming the student, the time, and what the meeting was about: "Ms M — reviewed her second quiz"; "Mr. L — discussed what courses he should take next year"; "Mr. K — personal matter — family difficulties [etc.]." Although the school has never issued a directive requiring or suggesting that professors keep such a log, Professor C does so because it helps him do his job better by helping him keep track of what's going on with his students. This "business" purpose suffices to make Professor C's log a "record of [a] regularly conducted activity" that satisfies the requirements of Fed. R. Evid. 803(6).

Remember that the "regularity" with which such records are made and kept is an important aspect of their presumed reliability. A special record of an unusual event would *not* qualify as a Fed. R. Evid. 803(6) record. Suppose, for example, that Professor Z, unlike Professor C, does not keep a regular log of his meetings with students, but on one occasion a meeting with a student was so unusual and disturbing that he wrote himself a detailed memo about it. Professor Z's memo would not qualify under Fed. R. Evid. 803(6). If Professor Z is available, he can testify about that meeting, of course, and his memo could be used per Fed. R. Evid. 612 to refresh his memory, or read to the jury per Fed. R. Evid. or 803(5) if Professor Z could no longer remember the meeting well enough. But a litigant could not introduce Professor Z's memo into evidence per Fed. R. Evid. 803(6), which means (among other things) that if Professor Z is not available to testify, there may be no way introduce into evidence the information contained in Professor Z's memo.

§ 9.27 QUESTIONS

Question 1. X supervises several employees at Warehouse, Inc. Her duties include submitting weekly reports on how well each worker does his or her job, how well each gets along with others, etc.

X happens to be something of a nutrition faddist. She makes a point of noticing what each worker brings for lunch from home, and includes this information in her weekly reports. X's superiors don't complain about these unorthodox additions to her reports (she may be a bit nutty, but she's a good supervisor), which provide them with a bit of comic relief as they lunch on tofu in peanut sauce or watercress salad and sun-dried tomato bagels and veggie-spread lite cream cheese.

One evening after returning home from work, Z, a Warehouse employee, falls sick. Eventually doctors diagnose the ailment: food poisoning. Z sues a neighborhood supermarket, alleging that it sold him spoiled lunchmeat.

To corroborate his own testimony that he ate the supermarket's lunch meat earlier on the day he took ill, Z wants to introduce the weekly employee evaluation form that X filled out for the week in question. D (the food store) objects: hearsay. Does Fed. R. Evid. 803(6) overcome the objection?

Ans. No. X's report of what Z had to eat that day satisfies the first element of the "original source of information" — she saw what Z ate, so she had first-hand knowledge; but it fails to satisfy the second element, since it was not part of her responsibility to Warehouse, Inc., to acquire or record that information, and Warehouse did not need it or rely on it in the regular course of its business.

Question 2. How else might Z attempt to offer the same evidence?

Ans. Z can call X as a witness. If X remembers that Z ate lunchmeat that day, X can testify from memory. If not, Z can use X's report for the week to refresh X's memory (Fed. R. Evid. 612). If that doesn't work, Z can attempt to qualify the relevant portion of X's report as X's "recorded recollection" under Fed. R. Evid. 803(5).

§ 9.28   KEEPING THE RECORD

Fed. R. Evid. 803(6)(B) requires that the party offering the document must also show that the "record was kept in the course" of the "business." It would not suffice, for example, if a witness testified, "We generally don't hang on to this kind of record, but I happened to find these in a shoe box in the back of the closet."

§ 9.29   SUBJECT MATTER AND CONTENTS OF THE RECORD

A record that qualifies as a Fed. R. Evid. 803(6) record can be used to prove "an act, event, condition, opinion, or diagnosis" — in other words, to prove pretty much anything that a "business" might regularly make and keep "business records" about. Courts applying Fed. R. Evid. 803(6) have admitted records of: hotel telephone logs; written prescriptions issued by a clinic and filled by a pharmacy; an elevator maintenance logbook; an office lease (to prove who the lessee was); a charitable organization's checking account records; a company's employee evaluation forms; computerized benefit and payroll records; corporate officials' diaries describing business meetings; appraisals of the value of a major league baseball team; hospital emergency room records of symptoms, diagnosis and treatment; and so on, and so on. Note that this list includes examples of objectively verifiable data (hotel logs, payroll forms, checks paid, elevator maintenance) and matters of judgment open to disagreement and dispute (employee evaluations, financial appraisals, medical diagnoses).

As to the latter category ("diagnoses and opinions"), the only significant restriction as to subject matter is the "trustworthiness" clause in Fed. R. Evid. 803(6)(E). An opinion or diagnosis recorded in a business record should be admitted only to the extent that the opinion would be admissible if offered by a witness while testifying. If the topic is one that only an expert witness could testify about (medical diagnoses, financial appraisals, and so on), then an opinion recorded in a business record will be admitted only if the person expressing the opinion is qualified as an expert on that subject. A doctor's diagnosis or opinion as to the cause, extent and duration of someone's injury, included in a hospital record, would be admissible as proof of the cause, extent or duration of the injury; a janitor's opinion on the same subject, even if "regularly" recorded in the hospital record (!), would not be admissible.

§ 9.30   MULTIPLE HEARSAY (2); "COMPRESSION"

Business records can quite often pose multiple hearsay problems. *See*, for example, the questions in § 9.24. But sometimes what looks like multiple hearsay is not. Even though there may be several declarants who participate in the process of acquiring, communicating and recording the information, if everyone in the chain of communication has a "business" duty to acquire, pass on or record the information, they are treated as "one" declarant; or to put it differently, what would otherwise be several layers of hearsay are "compressed" into one.

§ 9.31   QUESTIONS

Question 1. P was injured on June 1 when a shelf fell on him, and he is suing his former employer, claiming permanent disability. (At issue: the extent and permanency of injuries, and P's claim for punitive damages because D Co. allegedly knowingly maintained an unsafe workplace.) P was rushed to the hospital immediately after the mishap. The hospital emergency room's admitting form contains the following:

> *Patient suffered back injury when poorly-built temporary shelving fell on him. He complains of intense pain and lack of sensation in lower body. Legs show a lack of reflexive response. He has a large bruise in his mid-to-lower back, with a deep laceration just above the waist.*

P offers this record into evidence. Assuming he satisfies the procedural requirements (*see* § 9.32), is it admissible, over a hearsay objection?

Ans. Most of it is; some of it is not.

The entire record is, of course, a business record of the hospital. It was made by a hospital employee who is a health care professional, who had a "business" duty to acquire the information (by asking questions and by conducting a physical examination). The record was (let us assume) made and kept in accord with the rule. Still, it is incorrect to treat the record as if it was one statement; it consists, really, of four separate statements (one in each sentence). Each has to be analyzed separately.

> *(1) "Patient suffered back injury when poorly-built temporary shelving fell on him."*

This statement cannot be admitted pursuant to Fed. R. Evid. 803(6) alone, because the admitting nurse who wrote the report did not have first-hand knowledge of how the injury occurred. (She, after all, was not with P when the shelf fell.) Thus, this part of the report is multiple hearsay: someone (presumably P) told the nurse how P was injured ("P to nurse"); the nurse entered the information into the hospital admitting record ("nurse to paper"). This statement is admissible over a hearsay objection, therefore, only if some other Article VIII provision can be found for the first level of hearsay.

The provision that comes most readily to mind is Fed. R. Evid. 803(4). The declarant (presumably P) made this statement to the nurse "for purposes of diagnosis." But 803(4) covers at most only part of the statement: "Patient suffered back injury when . . . shelving fell on him." It does not cover aspects of the statement that attribute fault ("poorly built"). See § 8.39, supra. Thus, Fed. R. Evid. 803(4) and 803(6), taken together, may overcome the hearsay objection as to most of the first sentence in the report; but the trial judge would have to redact the inadmissible words before allowing the report to be circulated to the jury.

(2) "He complains of intense pain and lack of sensation in lower body."

The analysis is basically the same. This is double hearsay, but it is admissible: P to nurse, Fed. R. Evid. 803(3) or 803(4); nurse to paper, Fed. R. Evid. 803(6).

(3) "Legs show a lack of reflexive response."

This is only one level of hearsay: the nurse examined P, and wrote what she observed into the admitting record. Objection overruled, Fed. R. Evid. 803(6).

(4) "He has a large bruise in his mid-to-lower back, with a deep laceration just above the waist."

This, similarly, is only one level of hearsay: the nurse examined P, and wrote what she observed into the admitting record. Objection overruled, Fed. R. Evid. 803(6).

Question 2. ABC Realty maintains a large apartment complex. As part of its regular maintenance, public areas (walkways, stairways, etc.) in each building are inspected every three months by employees, who submit regular reports of the results of their inspections.

In litigation P v. D (assume for these problems that ABC Realty is not a party), a fact at issue is the condition on September 14, 2011, of the north and south staircases of building 1224 Tara Drive. ABC's maintenance records for September–December 2011 are subpoenaed. They contain the following notation:

On Thurs. aft. 9/4/11, the undersigned and R. Butler conducted an inspection of 1224 Tara. Most of building is in good repair. The undersigned noticed [etc.]

Several paragraphs later:]

On Mon. 9/8/11 R. Butler reported that the staircase on the north side of the building is in good repair but that the tread on the south side staircase is becoming worn on several steps between the 2nd and 3rd floor & again between 4 and 5.

The report is dated September 10, 2011, and is signed, "S. O'Hara."

P establishes the required foundation (*see* § 9.32) and offers the report; D objects: hearsay.

How many levels of hearsay are there in O'Hara's report?

Ans. Even though there are *two* statements involved in this record ("Butler to O'Hara"; "O'Hara to paper"), *they are treated for Fed. R. Evid. 803(6) purposes as if they were only one statement.* Why? Because both declarants, Butler and O'Hara, had a duty to ABC Realty to acquire and report the information. When one employee, acting pursuant to a "business" duty, acquires and then passes first-hand information to another, who then, acting pursuant to a "business" duty, records what the first has said into a "business record," multiple statements are "compressed" into one so long as the record itself qualifies under Fed. R. Evid. 803(6).

In other words, instead of treating it as two layers of hearsay — Butler to O'Hara, O'Hara to paper — we treat it as one layer: ABC to paper.

Question 3. Is the report admissible over a hearsay objection?

Ans. Yes, assuming the proper foundation for admissibility is established (*see* § 9.32). The only real issue is whether the record was made "at or near the time" the conditions described in the report were perceived. O'Hara and Butler inspected the staircases on September 4; Butler reported to O'Hara what he saw on September 8. We don't know whether Butler's report to O'Hara was a formal typed memo, an e-mail, a handwritten note or a casual comment in the elevator. O'Hara completed her report on the 10th; again, we don't know what kind of notes she took to assure she would not forget important details between the 4th and the 10th. But assuming the proper foundation was established, we do know that O'Hara's report was prepared in accordance with an established procedure and that such reports were relied upon by ABC Realty for business purposes. Delays of four to six days between observation and the final report should not cast sufficient doubts on trustworthiness to raise a serious question.

Question 4. Reconsider the inventory situation in § 9.13. Would Fed. R. Evid. 803(6) make it easier to introduce the inventory into evidence?

Ans. Absolutely. First, the two levels of hearsay (Counter to DL/W; DL/W writing the information on the inventory form) are compressed into one level, because each participant in inventory had a regular responsibility to XYZ, their employer, to acquire, communicate, and record the information. Second, it would not be necessary to call either DL/W or Counter as a witness, because any employee who can testify that XYZ routinely takes inventory and keeps records of them could qualify the inventory under Rule 803(6); or XYZ could avoid calling any witnesses at all, and submit the inventory per Fed. R. Evid. 902(11) (*see* § 9.32).

§ 9.32 PROCEDURES FOR ADMISSION

Fed. R. Evid. 803(6)(D) provides two ways that a party can establish that a record qualifies as a Fed. R. Evid. 803(6) business record. First, this can be shown "by the testimony of the custodian or other qualified witness." "Qualified witness" means pretty much anyone who qualifies as the company's "record custodian" — someone who works in a company's file room, for example — who can (a) identify and authenticate the record in a way that satisfies Article IX of the Federal Rules, and (b) testify about the company's record-making and record-keeping process. The witness need not have any first-hand knowledge whatsoever about the particular document in question; he need not have participated in its creation; he need not even have been an employee when that record was created. It is probably enough that the witness can be trained to answer "yes" to the following questions on direct examination:

Q.   Are records of this type made, kept and used in the ordinary course of the company's business?

A.   Yes.

Q.   And is it a regular part of the company's business to make, keep and use these records?

A.   Yes.

On the other hand, if an attorney suspects that his opponent may try to make him and his authentication witness look bad, it would be a good idea to choose the witness carefully — i.e., choose someone who actually knows something about the business and its records; don't settle for the most junior clerk in the file room. And it would also be a good idea to prepare the witness to testify in general terms about the following:

• how records of the kind about to be offered into evidence are made;

• that it is (or was) part of the company's regular practice to make such records;

• that the original source of the information in this type of record has first-hand knowledge of and a business duty to report that information;

• that this type of record is made from information that is reported and recorded at or near the time of the event, condition, opinion or diagnosis recorded in the record;

• how the company uses that kind of record;

• that it is part of the regular practice of the company to keep such records, and how it does so; and

• how the witness retrieved this particular record from the company's files.

Such testimony establishes that the document in question satisfies the Fed. R. Evid. 803(6) requirements.

The second alternative in Fed. R. Evid. 803(6)(D) is for the offering party to authenticate the record by a certification that satisfies Fed. R. Evid. 902(11) (for domestic "businesses") or 902(12) (for foreign "businesses"),[8] or satisfies some other special statute permitting the authentication of such records by certification. The certification must explicitly state that the records were made and kept in a way that would satisfy Fed. R. Evid. 803(6).

§ 9.33 COMPUTERIZED RECORDS; DATA COMPILATIONS

Computerized records differ from paper records in that the computer can reorganize, sort and categorize data if directed to do so by specific commands or by special programs. This presents no barriers to admissibility so long as a qualifying witness can explain in general terms that such data is collected, recorded and stored in the routine course of the "business."

---

[8] Those provisions require that the certification be made by "the custodian or another qualified person" — in other words, the same category of people who would qualify to give in-court authentication testimony.

§ 9.34   RECORDS CREATED BY MULTIPLE ENTITIES

Sometimes a record made by one company is incorporated into the records of a second company. Consider, for example, a nation-wide company with thousands of local outlets or franchises. The national company routinely delivers supplies to each of the local stores, and prepares a shipping manifest or packing slip detailing the quantity of each item that is to be delivered to each individual franchise. There is no reason why a local franchise could not routinely adapt its copy of the regional office's shipping manifest or packing slip as its own business record of what it received. That document would be admissible as a business record of the local franchise, so long as the offering party can establish that the local franchise regularly incorporates such records as its own, and relies on them in the routine course of its business.

There are several variations on this theme. Company A may hire Company B to make and keep certain records for it. This would impose on employees of Company B a business duty to Company A to acquire, transmit and record such information. Another common situation arises where Company X and Company Y regularly do business together, and even though there is no formal arrangement between them relating to records of those transactions, Company Y has come to routinely accept and rely on the records which Company X generates about their transactions. Courts generally conclude that if Company Y considers X's records to be accurate enough for Company Y to rely on (e.g., in deciding how much it should pay Company X, in predicting its personnel needs for the coming year, or the like), then they are reliable enough to be admitted as Company Y's business records.

§ 9.35   THE "TRUSTWORTHINESS" CLAUSE

A record which apparently satisfies the requirements of Fed. R. Evid. 803(6)(A)-(D) is admissible so long as, per Fed. R. Evid. 803(6)(E), "neither the source of information nor the method or circumstances of preparation indicate a lack of trustworthiness."

Prior to the restyling of the rules, federal courts applied the trustworthiness clause as follows. To secure admission of a document under Fed. R. Evid. 803(6), the party offering the document had to call a "qualified witness" to give testimony, or offer a certification, that establishes the foundation outlined in § 9.32. Once the offering party did so, the burdens of production and persuasion shifted: the document was admissible over a hearsay objection unless the other party persuaded the judge by a preponderance of the evidence that the document is insufficiently trustworthy.

Given the restyling committee's insistence that the restyling was not intended to make any substantive changes in the law, the courts will probably continue to apply the rule the same way. Still, as the rule is now worded and formatted, it could be read differently. I can picture an attorney arguing, "Your Honor, 803(6)(A)-(D) each state a requirement that the offering party must satisfy; it stands to reason that the same is true of 803(6)(E)." (My advice to students: if your professor discusses who has the burdens with regard to trustworthiness, follow her lead. If she doesn't, it is probably safe to ignore this paragraph.)

The leading case on trustworthiness, cited in the Rule's legislative history, is *Palmer v. Hoffman*, 318 U.S. 109 (1943). Following a railroad grade crossing accident in which someone was killed, the engineer gave a lengthy, extremely self-serving statement to company and state investigators, denying that he or the company had done anything wrong. Thereafter the engineer became unavailable. In a subsequent wrongful death action brought by decedent's plaintiff against the railroad, the company sought to offer the engineer's statement into evidence. The Supreme Court quite reasonably concluded that the lower courts were correct in excluding the statement, but did a poor job explaining its reasons.

First, the Court said, the engineer's statement was not a record made in the "regular course" of the railroad's business, because the business of the railroad is running a railroad, not investigating accidents. This rationale ignored the fact that it was a regular part of the railroad's operating procedures to investigate all accidents and take statements from all employees who had knowledge of what had happened. (To do so was certainly "good business" on the railroad's part. Very few of us would willingly ride a railroad that did not bother to investigate all accidents.) Despite the flawed reasoning, some courts, citing *Palmer*, for many years held that accident reports can never be accepted as business records, even if prepared by a neutral party.

Second, the Court rejected the engineer's statement as untrustworthy because it had been prepared in anticipation of potential litigation. This is an appropriate basis for the holding, so long as it is not applied too broadly. Consider: an experienced attorney does *everything*, e.g., negotiates a contract, drafts a will or separation agreement, etc., in anticipation of potential litigation. (Your clients will want you to help them arrange their affairs to *avoid* litigation if possible, while increasing the chances of winning if a matter does go to litigation. Thus, you must "anticipate potential litigation" even when you have no reason to expect the matter will wind up as part of a potential law suit.)

Thus, both of the articulated bases for *Palmer* were over-stated. Accident reports often can be admissible as business records; so can documents, of whatever nature, that were prepared in anticipation of possible litigation. The trustworthiness issue focuses, not on whether the record in question fits into a broad general category ("accident report, "contemplation of litigation"), but on the specific facts surrounding the document that is being offered in evidence. Are there specific circumstances surrounding this *particular* document, or the procedure by which it was produced, or the quality of the foundational testimony, that create serious and unanswered questions about the document's trustworthiness? If so, it should be excluded; if not, Fed. R. Evid. 803(6) overcomes the hearsay objection.

In *Melendez-Diaz v. Massachusetts*, 129 S.Ct. 2527 (2009), the Supreme Court endorsed the consensus reading of *Palmer v. Hoffman:*

> Documents kept in the regular course of business may ordinarily be admitted at trial despite their hearsay status. See Fed. Rule Evid. 803(6). But that is not the case if the regularly conducted business activity is the production of evidence for use at trial.

Id. at 2538, citing the engineer's statement in *Palmer* as an example of a record that would not qualify under Fed. R. Evid. 803(6). (*Melendez-Diaz* held that a forensic lab report, that a substance obtained from the defendant contained cocaine, was testimonial. That case is discussed in § 9.50, infra.)

It is not possible to compile an exhaustive list of circumstances that might cast doubt on the trustworthiness of business records. The fact that the person or entity that prepared the document *expected* it to be used as evidence in court is certainly a significant factor, and this is particularly the case if the person or entity who prepared the report is one of the litigants in that case, or is closely associated with a litigant (like the railroad engineer in *Palmer v. Hoffman*). If a record includes opinion on a subject requiring expertise, it would be untrustworthy if those whose opinions are reported are not qualified to give expert opinions. A report could be deemed untrustworthy if it purports to have been prepared by employee X, but X denies having done so. And so on.

The hearsay exception for public (i.e., governmental) records, Fed. R. Evid. 803(8), also contains a trustworthiness clause, discussed in §§ 9.41 & 9.47, infra. Issues that arise applying the trustworthiness clause in Rule 803(8) may also arise regarding business records, so when reviewing trustworthiness issues regarding Fed. R. Evid. 803(6), you should review those sections, as well.

§ 9.36 THE SIXTH AMENDMENT CONFRONTATION CLAUSE

In *Crawford v. Washington*, the Supreme Court, albeit in dictum, said: "Most of the hearsay exceptions covered statements that by their nature were not testimonial — for example, business records . . ."[9] No doubt this is true of most business records — payroll records, accounts receivable, accounts payable, inventories, personnel records, etc.

But some records are created with litigation clearly in mind; by definition, such records should fit within the definition of "testimonial." Many of the reports that fit into this category are produced by government agencies: forensic lab reports, autopsies, etc. In *Melendez-Diaz v. Massachusetts*, 129 S.Ct. 2527, 2540 (2009), the Supreme Court stated that business records that are prepared for use as evidence in court are "testimonial."

Melendez-Diaz, and *Bullcoming v. New Mexico*, another lab report case that was argued before the Supreme Court on March 2, 2011, are discussed in §§ 9.50-9.53, infra.

§ 9.37 INTERPLAY WITH OTHER RULES

As discussed in previous sections, Fed. R. Evid. 803(6) often involves multiple hearsay. Hospital records, for example, frequently include statements that may fall within Fed. R. Evid. 803(1)–803(4). Accident reports may require application of Fed. R. Evid. 801(d)(2)(A), 801(d)(2)(D) or 803(2).

---

[9] 451 U.S. at 56.

Keep in mind that other rules may also be used to secure admission of a document over a hearsay objection. If the person who wrote the record testifies at the trial, it may be admissible under Fed. R. Evid. 801(d)(1)(A)–(C), or its contents may be read into the record per 803(5). If the person who wrote the record is unavailable as a witness, provisions of Fed. R. Evid. 804(b) may apply (*see* Chapter 11).

If a party in a lawsuit is offering a document that was written by the opposing party, Fed. R. Evid. 801(d)(2)(A) answers the hearsay objection; there is no need to satisfy the more demanding requirements of 803(6). Similarly, if the document was written by the agent or coconspirator of the opposing party, the offering party can overcome the objection by satisfying either Fed. R. Evid. 801(d)(2)(C), 801(d)(2)(D), or 801(d)(2)(E) instead of 803(6).

The two preceding paragraphs simply belabor the basic point that when a party offers an out-of-court statement in evidence, she can overcome a hearsay objection by satisfying the requirements of *any* Article VIII provision. The fact that a document was prepared as part of a "business" does not restrict the offering party to using only Fed. R. Evid. 803(6).

§ 9.38   FED. R. EVID. 803(7): ABSENCE OF ENTRY IN BUSINESS RECORD

Fed. R. Evid. 803(7) provides as follows:

The following are not excluded by the rule against hearsay, regardless of whether the declarant is available as a witness:

7) *Absence of a Record of a Regularly Conducted Activity.* Evidence that a matter is not included in a record described in paragraph (6) if:

(A) the evidence is admitted to prove that the matter did not occur or exist;

(B) a record was regularly kept for a matter of that kind; and

(C) neither the possible source of the information nor other circumstances indicate a lack of trustworthiness.

[Prior to December 1, 2011, the rule read as follows:

Rule 803. The following are not excluded by the hearsay rule, even though the declarant is available as a witness:

(7) Absence of entry in records kept in accordance with the provisions of paragraph 6. Evidence that a matter is not included in the memoranda, reports, records, or data compilations, in any form, kept in accordance with the provisions of paragraph (6), to prove the nonoccurrence or nonexistence of the matter, if the matter was of a kind of which a memorandum, report, record, or data compilation was regularly made and preserved, unless the sources of information or other circumstances indicate lack of trustworthiness.

The Federal Rules of Evidence were rewritten solely to make them easier to understand; the Advisory Committee did not intend to make any substantive change in the Rules. The text of the old rule may remain useful in reading court decisions that precede the revision of the rules. Thus, this edition of the Student's Guide provides the text of both the new and the old version of each relevant provision of the Federal Rules of Evidence.]

The Advisory Committee Note says pretty much all there is to say about this provision:

> Failure of a record to mention a matter which would ordinarily be mentioned is satisfactory evidence of its nonexistence. . . . While probably not hearsay as defined in Fed. R. Evid. 801, [pre-Federal Rules of Evidence] decisions may be found which class the evidence not only as hearsay but also as not within any exception. [Fed. R. Evid. 803(7) has been drafted] in order to set the question at rest in favor of admissibility. . . .

In other words, such evidence is not hearsay, but in case the judge doesn't get the message and insists that it *is* hearsay, it is admissible over a hearsay objection per this exception to the hearsay rule.

To satisfy the rule, a party presumably could prove the non-existence of a particular record the same way he or she could prove that such a record *does* exist. The first method would be to call a "qualified witness" who can testify that the company has a regular procedure for making records of the kind of event or condition in question; that such records are made and kept in the regular course of business, and so on; that he or she conducted a diligent search of the relevant records; and that this search produced no evidence of the event or condition in question. The other method would be to establish the same facts by certification. See § 9.32.

Confrontation Clause. If a prosecutor wants to invoke this rule, then, unless the defendant waives her Confrontation Clause objection, the prosecutor will have to call a "qualified witness" to testify about the record's non-existence. A certification of its non-existence — i.e., a document prepared specifically to be used in evidence at a trial — would clearly be testimonial. In *Melendez-Diaz v. Massachusetts*, 129 S.Ct. 2527, 2540 (2009), the Supreme Court, in dictum, said as much. See § 9:56.

PART D:
PUBLIC RECORDS AND REPORTS: RULES 803(8), 803(9) & 803(10)

§ 9.39   FED. R. EVID. 803(8)

Fed. R. Evid. 803(8) provides as follows:

The following are not excluded by the rule against hearsay, regardless of whether the declarant is available as a witness:

(8) *Public Records.* A record or statement of a public office if:

(A) it sets out:

   (i) the office's activities;

   (ii) a matter observed while under a legal duty to report, but not including, in a criminal case, a matter observed by law-enforcement personnel; or

   (iii) in a civil case or against the government in a criminal case, factual findings from a legally authorized investigation; and

(B) neither the source of information nor other circumstances indicate a lack of trustworthiness.

[Prior to December 1, 2011, the rule read as follows:

   Rule 803. The following are not excluded by the hearsay rule, even though the declarant is available as a witness:

   (8) Public records and reports. Records, reports, or data compilations, in any form, of public offices or agencies, setting forth (A) the activities of the office or agency, or (B) matters observed pursuant to duty imposed by law as to which matters there was a duty to report, excluding, however, in criminal cases matters observed by police officers and other law enforcement personnel, or (C) in civil actions and proceedings and against the Government in criminal cases, factual findings resulting from an investigation made pursuant to authority granted by law, unless the sources of information or other circumstances indicate lack of trustworthiness.

The Federal Rules of Evidence were rewritten solely to make them easier to understand; the Advisory Committee did not intend to make any substantive change in the Rules. The text of the old rule may remain useful in reading court decisions that precede the revision of the rules. Thus, this edition of the Student's Guide provides the text of both the new and the old version of each relevant provision of the Federal Rules of Evidence.]

   This provision closely parallels Fed. R. Evid. 803(6): what the latter does for the records of a non-government "business, organization, occupation or calling," Fed. R. Evid. 803(8) does for records of government offices and agencies. Like Fed. R. Evid. 803(6), it is based on the twin considerations of reliability and necessity; the comments made in § 9.20 relating to necessity and reliability with regard to 803(6) apply equally to Fed. R. Evid. 803(8). Moreover, the law recognizes a presumption that public servants are honest and impartial and carry out their official duties carefully and efficiently. Additionally, just as Fed. R. Evid. 803(6) covers the records of a wide range of businesses, organizations, occupations and callings, from the multinational corporation to the individual potter or seamstress, Fed. R. Evid. 803(8) applies to the records of any government office or agency, from the United States Department of Defense to a village Board of Selectmen or a local school board. It also covers foreign countries' records, subject to a trustworthiness challenge if reasons exist for such a challenge.

A record (or portion of a record) that satisfies any of the subdivisions of Fed. R. Evid. 803(8) is admissible over a hearsay objection regardless of who the parties are in the law suit. Examples:

- If the Federal Environmental Protection Agency (EPA) brings a law suit against XYZ Manufacturing Co., EPA can introduce an appropriate portion of its own record into evidence; or XYZ could introduce the EPA report against EPA.

- If instead the Department of Labor was suing XYZ, either the Department of Labor or XYZ could introduce appropriate portions the EPA report in that law suit.

- If the town of Bagel Bend sues XYZ, the town, or the company, could introduce appropriate portions of the EPA report in that litigation.

- If Ms Sesame Pumpernickel of Bagel Bend sues XYZ, she, or XYZ, could introduce appropriate portions of the EPA report in that litigation.

Nevertheless, while the parallels between Fed. R. Evid. 803(6) and 803(8) are many and obvious, there are significant differences, too. These are discussed in the succeeding sections.

§ 9.40   PROCEDURE FOR ADMISSION

Before a public record may be introduced into evidence, it must be authenticated. This can be done through the same procedure set out for business records, by calling a record "custodian or other qualified witness" (*see* § 9.32). Alternatively, a public record can be authenticated pursuant to Fed. R. Evid. 902. The document might be self-authenticating (Fed. R. Evid. 902(1)), or it can be accompanied by an affidavit of authenticity by an official who is authorized to certify the authenticity of such documents (Fed. R. Evid. 902(2), 902(4)).

§ 9.41   TRUSTWORTHINESS (1)

The rule's trustworthiness clause, contained in Fed. R. Evid. 803(8)(B)(ii) applies to each of Fed. R. Evid. 803(8)(A)'s three subdivisions. If a record can be shown to be untrustworthy, it simply should not be allowed as proof of the matter asserted within it.

Courts applying Fed. R. Evid. 803(8) prior to the restyling have held that the party *offering* the report does not have to offer affirmative evidence of the report's trustworthiness; he, she or it need only establish that the report fits into what are now 803(8)(A)(i), or 803(8)(A)(ii), or 803(8)(A)(iii). Once the offering party had done so, the report was admissible, unless the *adverse party* convinced the judge, by a preponderance of the evidence, that, as the prior version of the rule put it, "the source of information or other circumstances indicate a lack of trustworthiness," This is probably how courts will continue to read the rule.

Most of the litigation about trustworthiness focuses on reports offered under what used to be numbered Fed. R. Evid. 803(8)(c) and is now numbered Fed. R. Evid. 803(8)(A)(iii). See § 9.47, infra. But trustworthiness issues could also arise with regard to reports offered under the other two subdivisions. Assume, for example, an indictment charges Clerk with selling heroin to an undercover agent of the federal Drug Enforcement Agency on the corner of 14th and Girard Streets, at 10:45 a.m. on Monday, February 4. Clerk denies he did so, and as part of his alibi defense, he offers the time sheet record at the city Department of Motor Vehicles office, located at 23rd and Peppercorn Streets. The time sheet shows that he clocked in for his clerical job at 8:50 that morning and remained at the DMV office until 5 p.m. that evening. That record is presumptively admissible as evidence that Clerk was at work many blocks away from 14th and Girard when the sale took place.

If the prosecutor opposes admission of the record, it is not enough to show that it was theoretically possible for an employee at that DMV office to slip away from his desk for an hour or two without someone noticing.[10]

Suppose, though, the prosecutor could demonstrate to the judge[11] that the supervisor of that DMV office was fired in April for allowing employees to leave work for lengthy periods on a regular basis without clocking out. Such evidence creates significant doubt about the general trustworthiness of employee time sheets at that DMV office, and would justify the judge in concluding that "the source of information or other circumstances indicate a lack of trustworthiness" with regard to Clerk's time sheet for that day.

§ 9.42   THE THREE SUBSECTIONS OF FED. R. EVID. 803(8)(A)

Fed. R. Evid. 803(8)(A) divides public records into three categories, and promulgates a somewhat different rule for each. Thus, the first step in applying Fed. R. Evid. 803(8)(A) is to determine within which of its subsections the record most logically falls. Although this not always a simple matter (some records can fall within more than one of the categories, for example), the basic distinctions are fairly clear. In essence: Rule 803(8)(A)(i) covers what public offices and officers *did*. Rule 803(8)(A)(ii) cover what public officers *"observed"* — i.e., what they saw or heard — and reported. Rule 803(8)(A)(iii) covers what public offices and officers *concluded* — their factual findings, evaluations, assessments, etc. — after an investigation.

Regardless of the relevant subsection, the rule does not require admitting an entire public report. (Such reports, particularly with regard to Fed. R. Evid. 803(8)(A)(ii) and 803(8)(A)(iii), may run dozens, or even hundreds, of pages, and contain substantial material that is not admissible.) Rather, the rule admits only those portions of the report which: (1) are relevant, and (2) satisfy one of the subdivisions of Rule 803(8)(A),

---

[10] The prosecutor could call witnesses during the government's rebuttal case to testify about this possibility, but the mere possibility that defendant could have slipped away for a while would not be enough to exclude the time sheet.

[11] The admissibility of the record would be litigated at a motion *in limine* out of the hearing of the jury.

and (3) survive any other objections that the adverse party might make.

§ 9.43   RULE 803(8)(A)(i): ACTIVITIES OF THE OFFICE OR AGENCY

Fed. R. Evid. 803(8)(A)(i) provides as follows:

The following are not excluded by the rule against hearsay, regardless of whether the declarant is available as a witness:

(8) *Public Records.* **A record or statement of a public office if:**

(A) it sets out:

(i) the offices's activities; ...

This provision includes records that reflect what the office and its employees did, but not what the office or its employees saw or heard or concluded. It covers records of the internal functioning the office (e.g., individual employee pay and time records; inventories of equipment on hand; etc.) and the routine, non-judgmental actions of the office or its employees. Thus, for example, Fed. R. Evid. 803(8)(A)(i) permits a litigant to use a record from the Department of the Treasury to prove that a particular social security check was issued and mailed to a specified individual. In a divorce action, W v H, W could introduce payroll records to show how much H, a sergeant in the state police force, earned in the previous year. Records of the Federal Deposit Insurance Corporation are admissible to prove that a particular bank was federally insured. Similarly, Fed. R. Evid. 803(8)(A)(i) would permit records from the Occupational Safety and Health Administration to be used to prove that an OSHA inspector visited a particular job site. (Fed. R. Evid. 803(8)(A)(i) would not, however, suffice to secure admission of records of what the OSHA inspector saw when she visited the workplace, or the conclusions she arrived at after her inspection; to admit those records would involve Fed. R. Evid. 803(8)(A)(ii) and 803(8)(A)(iii), respectively.)

To demonstrate the similarities and differences between Fed. R. Evid. 803(8)(A)(i) and Fed. R. Evid. 803(6), the Fed. R. Evid. 803(6) outline is used here, adapted to make it appropriate to Rule 803(8)(A)(i). Rule 803(8)(A)(i) imposes the following requirements and raises the following issues:

1. *Original source of information.* Implicit within the rule is the requirement that the record is based upon information provided by a public office's employee with first-hand knowledge. But the offering party does not have to offer evidence that a public employee had first-hand knowledge of the information. If the document is properly authenticated, it is presumed to satisfy this requirement unless the adverse party can show otherwise.

2. *"Record."* The evidence must be in some physical (or physically reproducible) form: on paper, tape, computer disk, hard drive, data base, etc. "Mental public records" don't qualify.

3. *"Public office."* This requirement is basically self-explanatory. It is unclear whether it would include an audit of a government agency commissioned by the

agency but conducted by a private firm.

4. *Making the record: time, duty, "regularity."* Unlike Fed. R. Evid. 803(6), Fed. R. Evid. 803(8)(A) does *not* require that the agency made the record as part of the "regular course of business." An extraordinary record of an extraordinary event therefore might well satisfy Fed. R. Evid. 803(8)(A)(i), assuming the adverse party was unable to raise a successful trustworthiness challenge.

   Moreover, Fed. R. Evid. 803(8)(A)(i) does not explicitly require that the record be made "at or near the time" the events recorded in the record occurred; nor does it require that the record be made by someone who had an "official duty" to make it. On the other hand, if the adverse party could show that a long delay occurred between the event and the recording of it, or that the person who made it was without a duty to do so, this might cast strong doubts on the report's trustworthiness.

5. *Keeping the record.* Similarly, Fed. R. Evid. 803(8)(A)(i) does not explicitly require that it be part of the "regular course of business" to keep the record.

6. *Permissible contents: activities of the office.* This provision includes records that reflect what the office and its employees did, but not what the office or its employees saw or heard or concluded. It covers records of the internal functioning of the office (e.g., individual employee pay and time records, inventories of equipment on hand, etc.) and the routine, non-judgmental actions of the office or its employees.

7. *Multiple hearsay.* Fed. R. Evid. 803(8)(A)(i) often "compresses" what might otherwise be several levels of hearsay into one. *See* § 9.30.

8. *Procedure for admission. See* § 9.40.

9. *Trustworthiness clause. See* § 9.41.

10. *Sixth Amendment Confrontation Clause.* Public records that fall within Rule 803(8)(A)(i) will almost assuredly be categorized as non-testimonial. In *Melendez-Diaz v. Massachusetts*, 129 S.Ct. 2527, 2532 n 1 (2009), discussed in detail in § 9.52, the dissent speculated that as a result of the majority's decision, the person who regularly checked laboratory equipment to make sure it was operating correctly would have to testify before a prosecutor could offer evidence that a quantity of powder purchased or seized from a defendant contained a controlled substance. In response, the majority, in dictum, stated: "documents prepared in the regular course of equipment maintenance may well qualify as nontestimonial records."

§ 9.44   RULE 803(8)(A)(ii): MATTERS OBSERVED AND REPORTED PURSUANT TO DUTY

Fed. R. Evid. 803(8)(A)(ii) provides as follows:

The following are not excluded by the rules against hearsay, regardless of whether the declarant is available as a witness;

(8) *Public Records.* **A record or statement of a public office if:**

(A) it sets out:

(ii) a matter observed while under a legal duty to report, but not including, in a criminal case, a matter observed by law-enforcement personnel; . . .

To qualify under this provision, (1) the report must be based upon information obtained first-hand by a government agent or employee; (2) the agent or employee must have had an official duty to observe and report on the event or condition in question; and (3) the office or agency must have an official duty or purpose to observe and report on such matters.

The "matters observed" are generally restricted to objectively verifiable facts. Examples include an OSHA inspector's description of conditions she observed at a workplace; a U.S. Customs Service record that a particular car (make, model, year, license number) crossed the border from Mexico into the United States on a particular date; weather bureau records of the weather conditions at a particular location; and an accident investigation report, filed by a police officer, describing the collision scene and extent of damages. But 803(8)(A)(ii) does *not* include the office's or officer's conclusions, or evaluations, or diagnoses or opinions. For example, in the traffic accident case, the officer's conclusions as to what caused the collision or who was at fault could not be admitted via Fed. R. Evid. 803(8)(A)(ii); that part of his report would have to be offered under Rule 803(8)(A)(iii).

Fed. R. Evid. 803(8)(A)(ii) is subject to a significant restriction that 803(8)(A)(i) is not: a prosecutor cannot use Fed. R. Evid. 803(8)(A)(ii) to offer records of "matters observed" by "law-enforcement personnel." *See* § 9.45.

Again, the same basic outline is used to set out the requirements and issues.

1. *Original source of information.* For a report to qualify under Fed. R. Evid. 803(8)(A)(ii), an employee of the public office must have observed first-hand the condition or event described in the report.

2. *"Record."* The evidence must be in some physical (or physically reproducible) form: paper, tape, computer disk, hard drive, data base, etc. "Mental public records" don't qualify.

3. *"Public office."* This requirement is basically self-explanatory. It is unclear whether it would include matters observed by a private investigator commissioned by a public agency to conduct an investigation. It may include at least some kinds of reports from private individuals or companies who are under a legal duty to report such matters to a public agency.

4. *Making the record: time, duty, "regularity."* For a report to qualify under Fed. R. Evid. 803(8)(A)(ii), it must be shown that the office or agent an official duty to observe and to report the event or condition in question.

    The "duty" requirement should not be read too literally. The offering party need not show that the public office is explicitly required by statute to observe and report on the kind of events or conditions in question; it is enough that observing and reporting that particular kind of event or condition helps the public office fulfill its responsibilities.

Fed. R. Evid. 803(8)(A)(ii) does not explicitly require that the record be made "at or near the time" the events described in the record occurred. On the other hand, if the adverse party could show that a long delay occurred between the event and the recording of it, this might cast strong doubts on the report's trustworthiness.

5. *Keeping the record.* Fed. R. Evid. 803(8)(A)(ii) requires that the record be *made* pursuant to a legal duty (*see* points 4, supra, and 6, infra), but does not explicitly require that it be *kept* pursuant to duty.

6. *Permissible contents: "a matter observed while under a legal duty to report."* To qualify,

    a. the report must be based upon information obtained first-hand by a government employee;

    b. the employee must have an official duty to observe and report on the event or condition in question; and

    c. the office must have an official duty or purpose to observe and report on such matters.

Fed. R. Evid. 803(8)(A)(ii) "matter[s] observed" are generally restricted to objectively verifiable facts, not value judgments and opinions, and generally cannot include statements made or information provided by private citizens (unless those statements also come within some provision of Article VIII).

7. *Multiple hearsay.* Fed. R. Evid. 803(8)(A)(ii) often "compresses" what might otherwise be several levels of hearsay into one. *See* § 9.30.

8. *Procedure for admission. See* § 9.40.

9. *Trustworthiness clause. See* § 9.41.

10. *Sixth Amendment Confrontation Clause.* See § 9.45.

11. *Law enforcement exclusionary clause. See* § 9.45.

§ 9.45 RULE 803(8)(A)(ii): LAW ENFORCEMENT EXCLUSIONARY CLAUSE; CONFRONTATION CLAUSE

Fed. R. Evid. 803(8)(A)(ii) excludes from its scope "in a criminal case, a matter observed by law-enforcement personnel." This exclusion was added to what was then numbered as Rule 803(8)(B) — now restyled as 803(A)(ii) — on the floor of the House of Representatives. Like many floor amendments to pending legislation, this one is not worded as precisely as it should have been. The discussion on the floor of the House when the clause was added reveals that its purpose is to avoid "trial by memo book," i.e., to prevent a prosecutor from offering a police officer's investigative report in evidence, without calling the officer to the witness stand. Without a law enforcement exclusionary clause, its sponsors feared, a defendant might be denied the opportunity, guaranteed in the Sixth Amendment Confrontation Clause, to confront and cross-examine his accusers.

All well and good: a prosecutor should not be permitted to offer an investigator's surveillance report instead of calling the investigator as a witness. But the law enforcement exclusionary clause, as written, prohibits a good deal more. For one thing, it denies the prosecutor the right to offer such reports even if the investigator *does* testify. Second, it appears to exclude *all* law enforcement reports of "matters observed," even simple, objectively verifiable, non-investigative administrative or ministerial matters. Third, although the legislative history of the clause makes it clear that it was intended to restrict only a prosecutor,[12] the clause as it is written prohibits the defendant, as well as the prosecutor, from offering a surveillance report prepared by "law enforcement personnel."[13]

Application of the law enforcement exclusionary clause raises the following issues.

1. *Defining "law enforcement personnel."*

This term obviously includes any official who has the power to make an arrest. On the federal level, this will include, among others, FBI, DEA and U.S. Treasury agents, and officials within the Department of Homeland Security who have such authority (e.g., customs and immigration officials). It includes state and city police; campus police at public universities; and, probably, town and village constables. Courts have held that it does *not* include officials such as a Federal Reserve staff assistant or a city housing inspector, who are not responsible for criminal law enforcement and whose agencies are not closely associated with criminal law enforcement.

Courts disagree as to whether forensic technicians (who examine drugs, weapons, etc. at a crime laboratory) are "law enforcement personnel." Most courts apparently hold that a medical examiner, coroner or pathologist who performs an autopsy is not a "law enforcement personnel."

2. *Routine law enforcement reports of a non-adversarial nature.*

Several courts have carved an exception to the exclusionary clause to allow a prosecutor to use such reports. Examples: a report by a customs inspector that a car with a particular license plate crossed the Mexican-American border on a particular night (all such numbers are routinely recorded); a report by a U.S. Marshall that he served a court injunction on a union leader; a report by members of the Royal Ulster Constabulary that rifles of specified make, model and serial numbers were found in Northern Ireland on a particular date.

3. *Confrontation Clause.*

---

[12] The Representatives who discussed the issue on the floor of the House spoke only about precluding a prosecutor from offering an investigator's report without calling the investigator.

[13] You might wonder: if the clause was so poorly written, why didn't the Advisory Committee clean it up when it restyled the rules? Answer: the restyling project was directed to make no *substantive* changes, but only to make the existing rules easier to understand. To make a substantive change would invite controversy and might delay or derail the restyling project.

Prior to *Crawford v. Washington*, many federal and state courts admitted a wide variety of reports under what was then Rule 803(8)(B) — now restyled as Fed. R. Evid. 803(8)(A)(ii) — which might now have to be classified as testimonial. Examples include: lab reports of substances tested for the presence of controlled substances; certifications that intoxylizers, breathalizers and similar devices were tested and found to be accurate; reports of the results of intoxylizer or breathalizer tests performed on motorists suspected of drunk driving; and even those portions of an autopsy report in which the doctor describes the physical condition of the body, its wounds, etc. In *Melendez-Diaz v. Massachusetts*, 129 S.Ct. 2527 (2009), the Supreme Court held that an affidavit by a laboratory analyst, that evidence seized from the defendant contained cocaine, was testimonial. *Melendez-Diaz* is discussed in § 9:50. Related issues are discussed in §§ 9.51–9.53.

4. *Admissibility of report if witness testifies.*

Assuming a police chemist or crime lab technician falls within the category of "law enforcement personnel," if she testifies at trial, there is no hearsay or Confrontation Clause reason to exclude her lab report: her presence at trial gives the defendant the right to confront and cross-examine her.[14]

5. *Use of "law enforcement reports" by the defense.*

Several courts, adhering to what Congress meant rather than what it said, have admitted such reports when offered by the defense.

6. *Use of Fed. R. Evid. 803(6) in lieu of Fed. R. Evid. 803(8)(A)(ii). See § 9.49.*

§ 9.46   FED. R. EVID. 803(8)(A)(iii): "FACTUAL FINDINGS"

Fed. R. Evid. 803(8)(A)(iii) provides as follows:

The following are not excluded by the rule against hearsay, regardless of whether the declarant is available as a witness:

(8) *Public Records.* A record or statement of a public office if:

(A) it sets out: ...

(iii) in a civil case or against the government in a criminal case, factual findings from a legally authorized investigation; ...

Fed. R. Evid. 803(8)(A)(iii) provides that if a government expert or agency has investigated and submitted a report on a matter, the portion of the report setting out the "factual findings" of the individual or group that conducted the investigation is admissible over a hearsay objection. In *Beech Aircraft v. Rainey*, 488 U.S. 153, 170 (1988), the Supreme Court, applying what was then numbered Fed. R. Evid. 803(8)(C) and is now Fed. R. Evid. 803(8)(A)(iii), unanimously held that the provision includes not only objectively verifiable factual conclusions, but also diagnoses, opinions, and

---

[14] The defendant might still object, per Fed. R. Evid. 403, that since the chemist or technician has already testified about the results of the lab tests, admitting her report would be "needlessly presenting cumulative evidence."

reports that state conclusions as to cause, fault and blame. In *Rainey*, a Navy lieutenant commander was assigned to investigate the crash of a Navy training flight which killed the instructor and student pilot. The Court held that the lieutenant commander's conclusion — that the probable cause was pilot error — was admissible in a wrongful death action brought against the manufacturer of the plane by the husband of the flight instructor and by the wife of the pilot trainee who died in the crash.

In essence, this means that instead of (or in addition to) calling expert witnesses to give their opinions about certain events, a litigant can introduce a government agency's report into evidence as proof of what happened or why.

Federal courts have upheld admissibility of government agents' or agencies' factual findings in a variety of settings. Examples:

- In a personal injury suit arising out of a collision between a truck and an auto, an accident report prepared by a police officer, concluding that the auto had probably run the red light.

- In suits alleging discrimination in housing, employment or education, investigative field reports and factual findings made by hearing examiners, concluding that a defendant did, or did not, discriminate.

- In a products liability action against a tampon manufacturer, epidemiological studies prepared by the Centers for Disease Control analyzing the statistical relationship between tampon use and incidence of toxic shock syndrome (even though the raw data was based upon interviews, questionnaires, and reports submitted to CDC by individual patients, doctors, and state health officials).

- In litigation against tobacco companies, reports by the Surgeon General, concluding that cigarette smoking causes cancer.

Fed. R. Evid. 803(8)(A)(iii) does not require, nor does it necessarily permit, introducing an entire report into evidence. It only speaks about the admissibility of specific factual findings that the office or officer reached as a result of the investigation.

Note, too, that the factual findings of government offices and agencies are admissible in civil litigation regardless of whether that office (or any government office) is a party.

Fed. R. Evid. 803(8)(A)(iii) has a major restriction: a prosecutor may not use the rule. *See* § 9.49.

For the sake of consistency, the basic Fed. R. Evid. 803(6)-803(8) outline is used to set out the requirements and issues.

1. *Original source of information.* Fed. R. Evid. 803(8)(A)(iii) does *not* require that a public agency or officer have first-hand knowledge of the events or conditions in question. Quite often, after all, an investigation is not begun until after the events to be investigated have already occurred, and those assigned to investigate it could not possibly have first-hand knowledge. Absence of first-hand knowledge by the government investigator is not a basis to exclude a factual finding per Rule 803(8)(A)(iii), so long as the investigation was

properly conducted by people with the necessary knowledge and experience to evaluate the information they gathered.

2. *"Record."* The evidence must be in some physical (or physically reproducible) form: paper, tape, computer disk or hard drive, etc.

3. *"Public office."* The "factual finding" must be one made by a governmental body, not a private company or individual. If a public office accepts a "private" factual finding after a careful evaluation of it, on the other hand, it logically should fit within Fed. R. Evid. 803(8)(A)(iii).

4. *Making the record: time, duty, "regularity."* The factual finding must be one that "result[s] from a legally authorized investigation." There is no "regularity" requirement; Fed. R. Evid. 803(8)(A)(iii) covers reports of temporary investigative agencies created for the sole purpose of investigating a particular matter, as well as reports of established agencies acting in accord with routine practice. Timeliness is relevant only to the extent that it affects trustworthiness.

5. *Keeping the record.* Fed. R. Evid. 803(8)(A)(iii) imposes no explicit requirements in this regard.

6. *Permissible contents: "factual findings from a legally authorized investigation."* See examples listed supra.

7. *Multiple hearsay.* An agency's "factual finding" may properly be based heavily on hearsay, so long as the investigation was sufficiently trustworthy. See § 9.47.

8. *Procedure for admission. See* § 9.40.

9. *Trustworthiness clause. See* § 9.47.

10. *Sixth Amendment Confrontation Clause. See* § 9:50–9.53.

11. *Law enforcement exclusionary clause. See* § 9:49.

§ 9.47   RULE 803(8)(A)(iii): AND THE TRUSTWORTHINESS CLAUSE

It is important to understand several aspects of the application of the trustworthiness clause to a government report's factual findings.

1. Quite often the factual findings of a government office's report will be based in part on inadmissible evidence. In his investigation into the crash in *Beech Aircraft v. Rainey*, discussed in § 9.46, Lieutenant Commander Morgan interviewed other pilots and students who witnessed some of the events of that day, and took hearsay statements from them. He probably read reports of technicians who examined the wreckage. Perhaps he spoke to other pilots familiar with that particular type of plane, and even some who had previously piloted the very airplane that crashed. None of this is a basis to exclude his factual finding; in fact, it demonstrates that he did a thorough job investigating the crash.

In essence, Rule 803(8)(A)(iii) is based on the assumption that the person or group conducting the investigation are *experts*, who have the training and knowledge and experience to evaluate all of this information properly.

2. This does not mean that the entire report, inadmissible hearsay and all, is admissible in evidence! Fed. R. Evid. 803(8)(A)(iii) only admits relevant *factual findings*, not an entire report. The jury is informed that a government agency (or an employee of that agency) conducted an investigation into a particular matter; then the offering party introduces those aspects of the factual finding that are relevant to the law suit.

3. When a report's factual finding is offered into evidence, the judge's role is a carefully limited one. The judge may evaluate the finding's *trustworthiness*, but not its *credibility*, because credibility is an issue that is left to the jury to evaluate.

Let me guess — you're wondering: "Trustworthiness,' but not 'credibility'? Don't those words mean more or less the same thing?" Well, yes, they do — in normal, everyday English. But in this corner of the law they have fairly precise, and somewhat different, definitions.

If the adverse party challenges the trustworthiness of a factual finding, the judge may evaluate *whether the investigation was conducted in a trustworthy manner.* Did the investigator(s) follow appropriate procedures? Did they speak (or attempt to speak) to the people likely to have useful knowledge about the manner being investigated? Did they examine appropriate documents? Where appropriate, did they consult outside experts? Did they give everyone who had a stake in the outcome an opportunity to submit information or evidence? Did they have adequate training and experience to evaluate all the information they gathered?

If the investigation was conducted in a trustworthy manner, the judge cannot exclude the factual finding, unless the report contains no plausible evidence supporting it.[15] A judge may *not* exclude the finding, merely because, after reading the report, the judge would have reached a different conclusion. Nor may a judge exclude the finding, merely because the judge doubts the accuracy or truthfulness or significance of some of the information relied upon by the officer or group who prepared the report. These issues go to the finding's *credibility.* It is up to the jury, not the judge, whether to accept the factual findings as true, and how much weight to give to those findings.

5. The Advisory Committee Note on Fed. R. Evid. 803(8) discussed at some length the application of the trustworthiness clause to Fed. R. Evid. 803(8)(C), which is now

---

[15] [If you haven't studied burdens of proof, perhaps you should skip this footnote.] The judge's role in assessing the admissibility of a factual finding offered per Fed. R. Evid. 803(8)(A)(iii) is akin to what the judge does when, after a party ("X") rests, opposing counsel ("Y") moves for a directed verdict. In that situation the judge must view the evidence in a light most favorable to party X, and then ask herself: *could* a rational jury find for X? If the answer is "yes" — and it most often is — the judge denies party Y's motion for a directed verdict and submits the case to the jury. Similarly regarding Rule 803(8)(A)(iii): assuming the underlying investigation was conducted in a trustworthy manner, the judge asks herself: viewing the evidence in the report in a light most favorable to the factual finding, does the evidence rationally support that finding? If the answer is yes — and it usually is — the judge must deny the adverse party's challenge to the report's trustworthiness, admit the report's relevant factual findings into evidence, and let the jury decide how much weight to give those findings.

restyled as Fed. R. Evid. 803(8)(A)(iii). This discussion demonstrates that the judge's focus should be on the methods employed during the investigation, not the factual findings themselves:

> Factors which may be of assistance in passing upon the admissibility of evaluative reports include:
>
> (1) the timeliness of the investigation;
>
> (2) the special skill or experience of the official [conducting the investigation];
>
> (3) whether a hearing was held and the level at which conducted;
>
> (4) possible motivational problems suggested by *Palmer v. Hoffman*. [For a discussion of *Palmer*, see § 9.35.]
>
> Others no doubt could be added.
>
> The formulation of an approach which would give appropriate weight to all possible factors in every situation is an obvious impossibility. Hence the rule, as in [Fed. R. Evid. 803(6)], assumes admissibility in the first instance but with ample provision for escape if sufficient negative factors are present.[16]

The final point made in the Advisory Committee Note bears repeating. Once the party offering the evidence establishes that a factual finding in a report was made by a government office or employee (federal, state, local or foreign) "from a legally authorized investigation," it should be admitted unless the adverse party can point to or prove "sufficient negative factors" to overcome the presumption of trustworthiness.

§ 9.48 QUESTIONS

Question 1. P brings a personal injury action against D Manufacturing Company, alleging that he suffered injuries when he slipped and fell on an oil slick as he and his wife were walking along the sidewalk in front of D's factory. D denies liability and also contests P's claim of serious injury. At trial, P offers in evidence a report filed by DL, an attendant in the ambulance that responded to P's wife's call for help. The report contains the following statements.

> *(1) Metropolitan Hospital Ambulance # 14 was dispatched at 9:21 a.m. on 7/7/99 in response to a report of an injury in front of 1509 Westminster Lane. Arrived at 9:40.*
>
> *(2) Injured person (P) was lying on the sidewalk near a large oil spot.*
>
> *(3) P complained of intense back and leg pain.*
>
> *(4) P states he slipped and fell on the oil.*

D objects that the report is hearsay. P cites Fed. R. Evid. 803(8). Ruling?

---

[16] Advisory Committee Note to Fed. R. Evid. 803(8)(C), now restyled as Fed. R. Evid. 803(8)(A)(iii).

Ans. First, we need to know whether "Metropolitan Hospital" is a public or private hospital. If it is a private hospital, admissibility should be analyzed under Fed. R. Evid. 803(6). If it is a public hospital, the judge should rule as follows:

1. Paragraph 1 is admissible under Fed. R. Evid. 803(8)(A)(i). The fact that the ambulance was dispatched to, and arrived at, 1509 Westminster is a record of the "activities of the office" — i.e., of the public hospital.

2. Paragraph 2 is admissible under Fed. R. Evid. 803(8)(A)(ii), assuming the ambulance attendant is required by hospital regulations to describe (i.e., to observe and record) the existing circumstances when he arrived at the scene of an injury.

3. Paragraph 3 is admissible under Fed. R. Evid. 803(8)(A)(ii), assuming the attendant is required to learn what he can about the nature and extent of the injured person's injury. Note, by the way, that Paragraph 3 involves multiple statements: P's statement to the attendant, and the attendant's act of recording P's statement on the form. P's statement is covered by Fed. R. Evid. 803(3) and 803(4); Fed. R. Evid. 803(8)(A)(ii) covers the attendant's recording of P's statement.

4. Paragraph 4 is more problematic. Like paragraph 3, it involves double hearsay. The attendant very likely is expected to take a statement, if possible, as to how the injury occurred; thus, his act of recording P's statement is covered by Fed. R. Evid. 803(8)(A)(ii). P's statement may or may not be admissible under Fed. R. Evid. 803(1) or 803(4). (Paragraph 4 is *not* the attendant's "factual finding" as to what happened; it is simply a record of what P claimed.)

Question 2. P alleges that D Corporation, her former employer, denied her a promotion and fired her, because she spurned the sexual advances of X, her immediate supervisor. In compliance with Title VII of the Civil Rights Act of 1984, P's attorney filed a complaint with the Equal Employment Opportunity Commission (EEOC), which referred it to the appropriate State Civil Rights Commission (SCRC), which in turn assigned the matter to Y, an SCRC caseworker. Y, a recent college graduate who had majored in psychology, separately interviewed P and X, and submitted a report in which he concluded:

> "Without question, there had been a personality clash between P and X. After reviewing all the facts, however, it is clear to me that X did not make unreasonable sexual advances to P and that D Corporation had valid business reasons for not promoting, and for firing, P."

Not satisfied with this result, P's attorney files a Title VII suit in Federal District Court. After P presents her evidence and rests, D Corporation seeks to introduce Y's report to the SCRC to prove that P had not been unfairly discriminated against on the basis of sex. Is Y's report admissible, over a hearsay objection, under Fed. R. Evid. 803(8)(A)(iii)?

Ans. First of all, D Corporation cannot introduce the entire report. Rule Evid. 803(8)(A)(iii) allows into evidence only a report's factual findings.

At first glance, the factual findings appear to be admissible. Caseworker Y's conclusion is (in the language of Fed. R. Evid. 803(8)(A)(iii)) a "factual finding[] from a legally authorized investigation." It is therefore admissible, unless "the sources of information [or] other circumstances indicate lack of trustworthiness." Thus, to keep it out, P will have to attack the report's trustworthiness per Fed. R. Evid. 803(8)(B).

An attack on trustworthiness should include consideration of the factors discussed in the Advisory Committee Note and the Senate Judiciary Committee Report:

(1) The timeliness of the investigation. Let's assume that Y began his investigation soon after getting the assignment, and did not waste significant time before he finished it. That's a plus for the trustworthiness of the report and Y's findings of fact.

(2) The special skill or experience of the official [conducting the investigation]. Since Y just recently graduated from college, he cannot be particularly experienced. Chalk up a factor for P. The fact that he was a psychology major is perhaps a plus for D, but not necessarily a big one.

(3) Whether a hearing was held and the level at which conducted. This factor looks at the investigation itself. How thorough was it? Did it utilize procedures that seem fair and thorough? Y's "investigation" does not seem too impressive: all he did was interview the two principals in the case, P and X. Other than P and X, he apparently did not interview other employees who could have provided useful insights as to how X behaved toward P. He did not examine D Company's records or his own agency's files to determine if there had been other sexual harassment complaints against X, or other sexual discrimination complaints against D Company. It's hard to see how this "procedure" supports a conclusion that the investigation was conducted in a trustworthy manner.

(4) Possible motivational problems [of the investigating officer or agency]. Examine Y's conclusion again: "X did not make unreasonable sexual advances to P." His choice of words implies that Y considers it acceptable for a male supervisor to make sexual advances to a female subordinate, so long as those advances don't become "unreasonable." This suggests, at the very least, a subconscious bias against P's claim, which undermines the presumption of an impartial investigation.

If I were the judge, I would exclude the report.

§ 9.49   803(8)(A)(iii) LAW ENFORCEMENT EXCLUSIONARY CLAUSE: ATTEMPTS TO LIMIT ITS SCOPE

Fed. R. Evid. 803(8)(A)(iii) explicitly states that it may be used only "in a civil case or against the government in a criminal case." The plain language of the rule mandates, therefore, that a prosecutor in a criminal case cannot use the rule. The intent is clear: If the government wants to offer evidence of a government agent's "factual finding," it must put that agent on the stand, thereby assuring that the defendant has the opportunity, guaranteed by the Sixth Amendment, to confront and cross-examine the agent. Thus, for example, a prosecutor should not be permitted to offer a government chemist's lab report in evidence, at least without calling the chemist.

Prior to *Crawford*, however, many federal and state courts developed ways to limit the impact of this language. Some held, for example, that the typical drug case lab report involves steps that are so routine and uncontroversial, and require so little actual judgment, that the conclusions are not "factual findings" banned by Rule 803(8)(A)(iii)'s pre-styled predecessor, Rule 803(8)(C), but merely "matters observed" per Rule 803(8)(B), the pre-styled predecessor for Rule 803(8)(A)(ii) — and that the analysts who conduct such analyses are not "law-enforcement personnel." Other courts held that although a prosecutor may not offer such reports under Rule 803(8), he or she may offer them under Rule 803(6), despite the apparent intent of Congress to preclude the use of 803(6) in such cases.[17] For three decades, some federal courts approved various end-runs around the exclusionary clause of what is now 803(8)(A)(iii) with regard to the results of narcotics analysis, intoxylizer tests, latent fingerprints, DNA tests, etc.

In *Melendez-Diaz v. Massachusetts*, 129 S.Ct. 2527 (2009), the Supreme Court held that an affidavit by a laboratory analyst, that evidence seized from the defendant contained cocaine, was testimonial. Thus, even if a court categorizes such a report as a "matter observed" per Rule 803(8)(A)(ii) — previously Rule 803(8)(B) — or as a business record per 803(6), the prosecutor must call the lab analyst as a witness in order to establish that the substance in question contained contraband, if the defense asserts a Confrontation Clause objection. *Melendez-Diaz* is discussed extensively in the next several sections.

In *Bullcoming v. New Mexico*, 131 S.Ct. 2705 (2011), the Court reaffirmed its holding in *Melendez-Diaz*. See § 9.53, infra.

Autopsies. Some courts have handled autopsies in a particularly clever way. If the doctor who performed the autopsy is no longer available to testify, his or her physical descriptions of the body, its age, injuries, etc. are admitted as "matters observed" per Fed. R. Evid. 803(8)(A)(ii). The prosecutor then calls another doctor to the stand, who expresses an opinion as to the cause of death (or other contested issue) based on the first doctor's observations. Courts are divided as to whether this approach survives *Melendez-Diaz*. The Supreme Court may address this case in *Williams v. Illinois*, mentioned in § 9.53, infra.

§ 9.50 RULE 803(8)(A)(iii) AND THE CONFRONTATION CLAUSE: *MELENDEZ-DIAZ*

In the aftermath of *Crawford* (see § 6.6 et seq., *supra*), courts re-examined the ways in which they had limited the law enforcement exclusionary clause in Fed. R. Evid. 803(8)(A)(iii). Some courts concluded that such reports (or findings within such

---

[17] As a general rule, a party can overcome a hearsay objection by satisfying any provision of Fed. R. Evid. 803 or 804 she chooses; as long as the evidence meets the requirements of any one provision, it is irrelevant that the evidence fails to meet the requirements of other provisions. For example, if a statement satisfies Fed. R. Evid. 803(3) (state of mind), it is admissible over a hearsay objection even if it does not also satisfy Fed. R. Evid. 803(1), 803(2), 803(4), 804(b)(1), etc. But if a prosecutor can use Rule 803(6) to avoid the exclusionary clauses in Rules 803(8)(A)(ii) & 803(8)(A)(iii), then those clauses have effectively been nullified. This is obviously not a result Congress could have intended.

reports) were testimonial, and therefore excluded by the Confrontation Clause, unless the prosecutor called the analyst. Other courts, seizing on Justice Scalia's dictum in *Crawford* that business records are not testimonial (*see* § 9:36), reasoned that since public records are a kind of business record, they are not testimonial either.

In *Melendez-Diaz v. Massachusetts*, 129 S.Ct. 2527 (2009), the Court held that an affidavit by a laboratory analyst, stating that evidence seized from the defendant contained cocaine, was testimonial. Justice Scalia, writing for a 5-4 majority, held that such affidavits implicated "core concerns" of the Confrontation Clause, because they were intended as a substitute for testimony at trial. The majority (at least 4 of them, anyhow; Justice Thomas' opinion is discussed later in this section) made it clear that its rule will apply to *all* forensic reports, not just drug analyses. (In dictum, for example, the Court stated that coroner's reports — which presumably includes autopsies — are testimonial.)

The dissent argued that the lab report wasn't really accusatory evidence; it was an objective conclusion reached by someone who did not witness the crime and had no stake in the outcome. The majority vehemently (and, I think, correctly) rejected this. In defending its insistence that the prosecutor must call the "analyst" as a witness, the majority pointed out that there were lots of ways an analyst might deliberately or accidently get the results wrong, and cited a recent study by the National Academy of Sciences that documented numerous cases of false or faulty forensic reports in criminal cases. Unless the prosecutor was required to call the analyst as a witness so the defense could cross-examine him or her, it would often be impossible for the defense to explore whether such irregularities occurred.

Justice Kennedy dissented, joined by Chief Justice Roberts and Justices Breyer and Alito. In essence, he predicted that the Court's decision would cause untold problems trying drug cases, and cases involving forensic science generally, for no good purpose.

§ 9.51   WHO DOES THE PROSECUTOR HAVE TO CALL AS A WITNESS?

The *Melendez-Diaz* majority says that the prosecutor has to call the "analyst"; the dissent suggested that the decision might also require the prosecutor to call the person who did routine maintenance on the equipment, and anyone in addition to the analyst who prepared the evidence for testing, and also the lab supervisor. The majority replied that the person who maintained the machine probably wouldn't have to testify (see § 9.43). It is also unlikely the prosecutor would have to call the supervisor; after all, unless the supervisor actually watched the analyst do the analysis, the supervisor could not testify to anything much, anyway.

§ 9.52   MUST THE PROSECUTOR CALL THE ANALYST, OR MERELY MAKE HIM AVAILABLE TO THE DEFENSE?

In *Melendez-Diaz*, the state argued that the prosecutor shouldn't have to call the analyst; it merely had to make the analyst available so the defense could call the analyst as a witness if she wanted to. The majority explicitly rejected that argument. The majority pointed out that the illicit nature of the substance was an element of the crime Melendez-Diaz was charged with; thus, if the state was going to rely on a lab report to prove that element, it had to call as a witness the person who performed the analysis recorded in the report.

§ 9.53   RULE 803(8)(A)(iii) AND THE CONFRONTATION CLAUSE: *BULLCOMING v. NEW MEXICO*

In *Bullcoming v. New Mexico*, 131 S.Ct. 2705 (2011), the Court again considered the application of the Confrontation Clause to forensic lab reports. *Bullcoming* involved a blood sample tested for alcohol, rather than a forensic test for drugs. The facts in *Bullcoming* differed from those in *Melendez-Diaz* in several additional respects.

> 1. At trial the prosecutor announced that Caylor — the analyst who had unsealed the container, prepared the sample, put the sample into the gas chromatograph machine, and recorded the results on the lab form — had recently been put on unpaid leave by the lab (reason unspecified). Instead, a state lab scientist, Razatos (apparently someone with more impressive credentials, although the Court does not say so explicitly), would testify to the lab's equipment and procedures and authenticate Caylor's report. (Razatos, however, had not observed any of Caylor's actions with regard to the test of Bullcoming's blood sample.) The trial judge permitted Razatos' testimony over the defendant's Confrontation Clause objection. Thus, unlike *Melendez-Diaz*, in which the prosecution merely introduced the report itself, the state called an expert to testify (generally) about the forensic procedures involved.

> 2. The form Caylor signed was simply a lab form certifying the procedures followed and the result obtained, not an affidavit.

> 3. The actual analysis was performed by a machine, not by a human being.

The Court again, dividing 5–4, held that allowing Razatos to introduce Caylor's report violated the Confrontation Clause. As to the factual differences mentioned in the previous paragraph, the Court, per Justice Ginsburg, held:

> 1. To satisfy the Confrontation Clause, the state had to call the technician who actually prepared the sample and inserted it into the machine, or someone (e.g., a supervisor) who watched him do so. Razatos' testimony was not an adequate substitute.

> 2. Whether the report was an affidavit or not, it was still testimonial, because it was prepared with the purpose of proving a fact that would be offered in evidence at trial.

3. The Confrontation Clause is not satisfied merely because the actual analysis was performed automatically by a machine, rather than by a human being, because the technician involved had to perform several rather technical steps in preparing the sample for the machine. (The Court cited reports detailing human errors that invalidated numerous reports generated by a similar machine in a different state's laboratory.)

Justice Sotomayor wrote a concurring opinion, which Justice Kagan signed, which (among other things) "emphasiz[ed] the limited reach of the Court's opinion." Among other things, she stressed:

1. Razatos, the supervisor, had neither supervised nor witnessed any aspect of Caylor's analysis of the sample. Thus, the Court did not address how much connection with an analysis a supervisor would have to show in order to be able to testify.

2. "[T]his is not a case in which an expert witness was asked for his independent opinion about underlying testimonial reports that were not themselves admitted into evidence." Justice Sotomayor pointed out that Fed. R. Evid. 703 sometimes permits an expert to express an opinion based on facts or data that themselves are inadmissible. "We would face a different question if asked to determine the constitutionality of allowing an expert witness to discuss others' testimonial statements if the testimonial statemetns were not themselves admitted as evidence." The Supreme Court will consider this issue in *Williams v. Illinois*, opinion below 939 N.E.2d 268 (Ill. 2010). Oral argument is scheduled for December, 2011. When the Supreme Court decides *Williams*, I will post an analysis of it on the webpage given on p. iv of this book.

3. The State did not merely introduce machine-generated results, such as a printout from a gas chromatograph; it also introduced Caylor's statements, which included his transcription of a blood alcohol concentration, apparently copied from a gas chromatograph printout, "Thus, we do not decide whether ... a state could introduce (assuming an adequate chain of custody foundation) raw data generated by a machine in conjunction with the testimony of an expert witness." Id. at 2722–2723.

The four dissenting Justices, per Justice Kennedy, made the same points in *Bullcoming* as they did in *Melendez-Diaz*, but also strongly suggested they were willing to reverse *Crawford*.

Stay tuned ...

§ 9.54 QUESTION

Question 1. On June 15, 1990, Victim's body was found in an intermediate state of decay. Dr. K, an assistant coroner in the county, performed an autopsy, and concluded that Victim died of a severe beating sometime between May 29 and June 2nd. Police pursued several leads, but they petered out until 2006, when JHS, a jail house snitch, told the authorities that back in 1991, D told JHS that he had killed Victim.

The state can offer circumstantial evidence that D lived in the same community as Victim until June 4, 1990, when D reported for basic training at a U.S. Navy post about 1,000 miles away; D can prove conclusively that he did not leave the post until sometime in July. D is charged with murder, but the state cannot possibly convict D unless it can offer acceptable proof that Victim died *before* June 4.

The obvious way of offering evidence of when V died would be to call Dr. K. Unfortunately, Dr. K died in 2003. And unlike many forensic reports which can be repeated if necessary, an autopsy cannot simply be repeated by another doctor. The state therefore offers Dr. K's autopsy in evidence. D objects: Hearsay! Confrontation Clause!

Ans. First we will discuss the hearsay issue; then the Confrontation Clause issue.

Hearsay. A doctor's conclusions as to the cause and approximate date of death certainly appear to be "factual findings" per Fed. R. Evid. 803(8)(A)(iii); but the law enforcement exclusionary clause of that rule says a prosecutor cannot use it.

So perhaps the state will try to introduce only the photographs and physical descriptions of the body dictated by Dr. K when he performed the autopsy, and have another doctor, Dr. L, testify that based on her review of that material, she is of the opinion that Victim died between May 29 and June 2. By offering only those portions of the autopsy report in which Dr. K reported what he observed as he performed the autopsy, as "matters observed" per Rule 803(8)(A)(ii), the state argues, it is avoiding Rule 803(8)(A)(iii).

D still objects, arguing that Dr. K, an assistant coroner, was, in essence, "law enforcement personnel."

Let's assume the court overrules this second hearsay objection, concluding that the coroner's office is not a law enforcement agency. (Most courts so hold, with regard to Coroners, Medical Examiners and similar offices.)

Confrontation Clause. Is an autopsy report "testimonial"? Recall the 18th century definition of "testimony" which Justice Scalia quoted in *Crawford (see* § 6.7): "[a] solemn declaration or affirmation made for the purpose of establishing or proving some fact." If that phrase does not describe a doctor's autopsy report describing a corpse, its condition, etc., then somebody is playing games with the English language.

Justice Scalia, in *Melendez-Diaz v. Massachusetts*, 129 S.Ct. 2527 (2009), said in dictum that a coroner's report (which is pretty much the equivalent of an autopsy) is testimonial. Clearly, therefore, Dr. K's report, stating his conclusion as to the date of death, is not admissible over a Confrontation Clause objection. This is probably also true of the descriptive portions of his report. Unless the autopsy was videotaped, therefore, Dr. L. would not be able to rely on any portion of Dr. K's report to form her own opinion as to the date of death.

Which would mean that D could not be prosecuted, because unlike some forensic reports, it is often impossible to have someone else re-do an autopsy many years later. (Either the body was embalmed, or the body was allowed to decay naturally. In either case, it would no longer be possible to examine the body decades later and determine the approximate date of death, which was the key issue in the case on which this problem was based.) Therefore, so, applying the Confrontation Clause to the autopsy report will enable D quite literally to get away with murder — assuming, that is, that he is in fact the murderer.

It is possible that *Bullcoming* will shed some light on this dilemma. If so, you can read about it on the web site: http://law.cua.edu/Fac_Staff/FishmanC/studentguide tohearsay.cfm.

§ 9.55 RULE 803(9): RECORDS OF VITAL STATISTICS

Fed. R. Evid. 803(9) provides as follows:

The following are not excluded by the rule against hearsay, regardless of whether the declarant is available as a witness:

(9) *Public Records of Vital Statistics.* A record of a birth, death, or marriage, if reported to a public office in accordance with a legal duty.

[Prior to December 1, 2011, the rule read as follows:

Rule 803. The following are not excluded by the hearsay rule, even though the declarant is available as a witness:

(9) Records of vital statistics. Records or data compilations, in any form, of births, fetal deaths, deaths, or marriages, if the report thereof was made to a public office pursuant to requirements of law.

The Federal Rules of Evidence were rewritten solely to make them easier to understand; the Advisory Committee did not intend to make any substantive change in the Rules. The text of the old rule may remain useful in reading court decisions that precede the revision of the rules. Thus, this edition of the Student's Guide provides the text of both the new and the old version of each relevant provision of the Federal Rules of Evidence.]

The familiar twin considerations of necessity and reliability justify this provision. It is often difficult to find a witness who was present and recalls a birth, death or marriage that took place many years earlier; and, at the same time, it is unlikely that someone would deliberately falsely report such information.

To secure admissibility of a properly authenticated record (*see* Article IX of the Federal Rules), the offering party need show only that a state or local law required someone to report the birth, death or marriage to a public office, and that the report was made in a way that complied with that law.

Issues sometimes arise as to whether Fed. R. Evid. 803(9) covers only the basic details of the event itself (e.g., date and place of a person's birth; date and place that two people were married; date and place of a person's death), or also includes statements in the document as to the underlying circumstances. If the document is being offered in evidence at a trial in which an underlying circumstance is in dispute (e.g., the identity of the newborn's father, or the cause of deceased's death), most scholars argue that statements in the document about such matters should be admissible only if it is clear that the person who provided the information had a reliable basis for it (e.g., the doctor who attended the deceased as he was dying, or the one who performed the autopsy, would have a reliable basis for making a statement as to cause of death).

There is almost no case law applying this provision, and none that I know of discussing how the Confrontation Clause would apply to such a document.

§ 9.56 RULE 803(10): ABSENCE OF PUBLIC RECORD OR ENTRY

Fed. R. Evid. 803(10) provides as follows:

The following are not excluded by the rule against hearsay, regardless of whether the declarant is available as a witness:

(10) *Absence of a Public Record.* Testimony — or a certification under Rule 902 — that a diligent search failed to disclose a public record if the testimony or certification is admitted to prove that:

(A) the record or statement does not exist; or

(B) a matter did not occur or exist, if a public office regularly kept a record or statement for a matter of that kind.

[Prior to December 1, 2011, the rule read as follows:

Rule 803. The following are not excluded by the hearsay rule, even though the declarant is available as a witness:

(10) Absence of public record or entry. To prove the absence of a record, report, statement, or data compilation, in any form, or the nonoccurrence or nonexistence of a matter of which a record, report, statement, or data compilation, in any form, was regularly made and preserved by a public office or agency, evidence in the form of a certification in accordance with rule 902, or testimony, that diligent search failed to disclose the record, report, statement, or data compilation, or entry.

The Federal Rules of Evidence were rewritten solely to make them easier to understand; the Advisory Committee did not intend to make any substantive change in the Rules. The text of the old rule may remain useful in reading court decisions that precede the revision of the rules. Thus, this edition of the Student's Guide provides the text of both the new and the old version of each relevant provision of the Federal Rules of Evidence.]

Fed. R. Evid. 803(10) can be used to prove two related facts: that a record does not exist, or that an event did not occur. Fed. R. Evid. 803(10) is to public records what Fed. R. Evid. 803(7) is to business records. The necessity for such a rule is clear. Without such a rule it would be difficult for the government to prove, for example, that a defendant failed to comply with laws requiring submission of certain documents (e.g., an income tax return) or information (e.g., draft registration). Similarly, suppose in 2012, it is important to determine whether a child was born in a public hospital in 2000. The only practical way to try to prove that no such birth occurred would be to show that there is no indication of such a birth in the hospital's records.

To use Fed. R. Evid. 803(10), a party must:

1. establish that a particular public agency regularly made and preserved records of the kind of fact or event in question; and

2. prove that the records of the public agency in question contain no mention or reference to the occurrence of the event or existence of the fact in question.

The nonexistence of a record can be proved in either of two ways:

1. An official of the agency can testify that a diligent search failed to locate such a record or entry.

2. An official in that office can submit a written certification in accordance with Fed. R. Evid. 902 that a diligent search of the office's files failed to locate such a record.

To exclude the certificate or testimony, the adverse party would then have to persuade the judge that the office in question did not regularly make and keep such records, or that the search for the record in question was not diligent.

Dictum in *Melendez-Diaz v. Massachusetts*, 129 S.Ct. 2527 (2009) states that in a criminal case, where the prosecutor had to prove the absence of a public record or entry, she would have to call as a witness the public official who did the record search. If she sought to prove the absence of a record via a certification per Rule 902, the defendant's Confrontation Clause objection would be sustained. Id. at 2539. This certainly makes sense: a certificate prepared specifically to be used as evidence in court certainly fits the definition of "testimonial."

Chapter 10

RULE 803: THE "REGARDLESS OF WHETHER THE DECLARANT IS AVAILABLE AS A WITNESS" EXCEPTIONS: MISCELLANEOUS EXCEPTIONS RULES 803(11)–803(23)

§ 10.1 INTRODUCTION

This chapter covers a hodgepodge of miscellaneous hearsay exceptions. Most are very rarely used.

§ 10.2 RULE 803(11): RECORDS OF RELIGIOUS ORGANIZATIONS

Fed. R. Evid. 803(11) provides as follows:

> **The following are not excluded by the rule against hearsay, regardless of whether the declarant is available as a witness: . . .**
>
> **(11)** *Records of Religious Organizations Concerning Personal or Family History.* **A statement of birth, legitimacy, ancestry, marriage, divorce, death, relationship by blood or marriage, or similar facts of personal or family history, contained in a regularly kept record of a religious organization.**

[Prior to December 1, 2011, the rule read as follows:

> Rule 803. The following are not excluded by the hearsay rule, even though the declarant is available as a witness:
>
> (11) Records of religious organizations. Statements of births, marriages, divorces, deaths, legitimacy, ancestry, relationship by blood or marriage, or other similar facts of personal or family history, contained in a regularly kept record of a religious organization.

The Federal Rules of Evidence were rewritten solely to make them easier to understand; the Advisory Committee did not intend to make any substantive change in the Rules. The text of the old rule may remain useful in reading court decisions that precede the revision of the rules. Thus, this edition of the Student's Guide provides the text of both the new and the old version of each relevant provision of the Federal Rules of Evidence.]

This exception simply restates an exception long recognized by the common law. Statements contained in such records are considered trustworthy because generally there is little motivation to fabricate such records.

Much of the information covered by Fed. R. Evid. 803(11) is also covered by Fed. R. Evid. 803(6). Either rule, for example, could be used to introduce the regularly made and kept records of a church, synagogue, or mosque as evidence that M and F were married there on a particular date. In one respect, though, Fed. R. Evid. 803(11) is somewhat broader. It also covers a "statement of . . . legitimacy, ancestry, relationship by blood or marriage, or other similar facts of personal or family history" recorded in the record, even though no one who participated in making the record had first-hand knowledge of that information. For example, the religious organization's record of the wedding could very well include information as to when M and F were born, and their parents' names. In subsequent litigation, this record is admissible, not only to prove that the wedding took place (if that should be an issue), but also, for example, as proof of M's birth date or of F's mother's maiden name (assuming this information is recorded in the record). Presumably, M and F supplied this information, even though neither had first-hand knowledge of it. (You don't have first-hand knowledge of your birth date, for example; you were there, of course, but the odds are that you don't remember being born, and even less likely that you remember checking the calendar as someone was cutting your umbilical cord. You know your birthday only because your parents told you.)

§ 10.3   RULE 803(12). MARRIAGE, BAPTISMAL, AND SIMILAR CERTIFICATES

Fed. R. Evid. 803(12) provides as follows:

The following are not excluded by the rule against hearsay, regardless of whether the declarant is available as a witness: . . .

(12) *Certificates of Marriage, Baptism, and Similar Ceremonies.* **A statement of fact contained in a certificate:**

(A) made by a person who is authorized by a religious organization or by law to perform the act certified;

(B) attesting that the person performed a marriage or similar ceremony or administered a sacrament; and

(c) purporting to have been issued at the time of the act or within a reasonable time after it.

[Prior to December 1, 2011, the rule read as follows:

Rule 803. The following are not excluded by the hearsay rule, even though the declarant is available as a witness:

(12) Marriage, baptismal, and similar certificates. Statements of fact contained in a certificate that the maker performed a marriage or other ceremony or administered a sacrament, made by a clergyman, public

official, or other person authorized by the rules or practices of a religious organization or by law to perform the act certified, and purporting to have been issued at the time of the act or within a reasonable time thereafter.

The Federal Rules of Evidence were rewritten solely to make them easier to understand; the Advisory Committee did not intend to make any substantive change in the Rules. The text of the old rule may remain useful in reading court decisions that precede the revision of the rules. Thus, this edition of the Student's Guide provides the text of both the new and the old version of each relevant provision of the Federal Rules of Evidence.]

To survive a hearsay objection, the party offering the document must show:

1. That the person who performed or conducted the ceremony also filled out the certificate (which satisfies the requirement that declarant had first-hand knowledge of the information contained in the certificate).

2. That that person was authorized by law or by the rules of a religious organization to perform the act in question.

3. That the certificate was apparently filled out "at the time of the act or within a reasonable time after it."

If the ceremony was performed and the certificate was prepared by a public official (e.g., a judge), an official seal will suffice to make the certificate self-authenticating; otherwise, the party offering the document must authenticate it through witnesses or circumstantial evidence.

§ 10.4   RULE 803(13): FAMILY RECORDS

Fed. R. Evid. 803(13) provides as follows:

The following are not excluded by the rule against hearsay, regardless of whether the declarant is available as a witness: . . .

(13) *Family Records*. A statement of fact about personal or family history contained in a family record, such as a Bible, genealogy, chart, engraving on a ring, inscription on a portrait, or engraving on an urn or burial marker.

[Prior to December 1, 2011, the rule read as follows:

Rule 803. The following are not excluded by the hearsay rule, even though the declarant is available as a witness:

(13) Family records. Statements of fact concerning personal or family history contained in family Bibles, genealogies, charts, engravings on rings, inscriptions on family portraits, engravings on urns, crypts or tombstones, or the like.

The Federal Rules of Evidence were rewritten solely to make them easier to understand; the Advisory Committee did not intend to make any substantive change in the Rules. The text of the old rule may remain useful in reading court decisions that precede the revision of the rules. Thus, this edition of the Student's Guide provides the text of both the new and the old version of each relevant provision of the Federal Rules of Evidence.]

An attorney could have a long and happy career as a litigator without ever having to use this provision. Still, who knows? If, some day, an inscription on the container holding someone's cremated remains is your only proof that your client is the testator's son, and is therefore entitled to a share of the estate (that your client is, in other words, owed on a Grecian urn), it is nice to know you can overcome your opponent's hearsay objection. In a situation involving controversy over a marriage, birth, or death, this provision accords entries in a family Bible or genealogy or the like the same status as the official records of a public agency or religious organization.

§ 10.5   RULE 803(14): RECORDS OF DOCUMENTS AFFECTING AN INTEREST IN PROPERTY

Fed. R. Evid. 803(14) provides as follows:

The following are not excluded by the rule against hearsay, regardless of whether the declarant is available as a witness: . . .

(14) *Records of Documents That Affect an Interest in Property.* The record of a document that purports to establish or affect an interest in property if:

(A) the record is admitted to prove the content of the original recorded document, along with its signing and its delivery by each person who purports to have signed it;

(B) the record is kept in a public office; and

(C) a statute authorizes recording documents of that kind in that office.

[Prior to December 1, 2011, the rule read as follows:

Rule 803. The following are not excluded by the hearsay rule, even though the declarant is available as a witness:

(14) Records of documents affecting an interest in property. The record of a document purporting to establish or affect an interest in property, as proof of the content of the original recorded document and its execution and delivery by each person by whom it purports to have been executed, if the record is a record of a public office and an applicable statute authorizes the recording of documents of that kind in that office.

The Federal Rules of Evidence were rewritten solely to make them easier to understand; the Advisory Committee did not intend to make any substantive change in the Rules. The text of the old rule may remain useful in reading court decisions that precede the revision of the rules. Thus, this edition of the Student's Guide provides the text of both the new and the old version of each relevant provision of the Federal Rules of Evidence.]

This provision assures that records relating to property will be admissible over a hearsay objection if those records are maintained according to state law.

§ 10.6   RULE 803(15): STATEMENTS IN DOCUMENTS AFFECTING AN INTEREST IN PROPERTY

Fed. R. Evid. 803(15) provides as follows:

> **The following are not excluded by the rule against hearsay, regardless of whether the declarant is available as a witness: . . .**
>
> **(15) *Statements in Documents That Affect an Interest in Property.* A statement contained in a document that purports to establish or affect an interest in property if the matter stated was relevant to the document's purpose — unless later dealings with the property are inconsistent with the truth of the statement or the purport of the document.**

[Prior to December 1, 2011, the rule read as follows:

> Rule 803. The following are not excluded by the hearsay rule, even though the declarant is available as a witness:
>
> > (15) Statements in documents affecting an interest in property. A statement contained in a document purporting to establish or affect an interest in property if the matter stated was relevant to the purpose of the document, unless dealings with the property since the document was made have been inconsistent with the truth of the statement or the purport of the document.

The Federal Rules of Evidence were rewritten solely to make them easier to understand; the Advisory Committee did not intend to make any substantive change in the Rules. The text of the old rule may remain useful in reading court decisions that precede the revision of the rules. Thus, this edition of the Student's Guide provides the text of both the new and the old version of each relevant provision of the Federal Rules of Evidence.]

This provision covers documents relating to personal property (bills of sale, receipts, and the like) as well as real property.

The rule imposes three requirements:

1.   The statement must "purport[] to establish or affect an interest in property."

2.   The statement must be "relevant to the document's purpose," i.e., the document was drawn for the purpose of defining or changing someone's interest in the property. If so, the document is admissible —

3.   ". . . unless later dealings with the property are inconsistent with the truth of the statement or the purport of the document."

The underlying theory of this provision is that statements in "dispositive documents," i.e., documents that apparently define who owns or controls an interest in property, are not made (or signed) until all those with an interest in the property are satisfied that the document is accurate.

Fed. R. Evid. 803(15) includes not only statements directly relating to the property ("X hereby sells Blackacre to Y for the following consideration"), but related statements of fact as well (". . . executed on X's behalf by Z, attorney at law, pursuant to power of attorney granted by X to Z on . . ."). Unlike Fed. R. Evid. 803(16) (*see* § 10.7, infra), there is no requirement that the document be of any particular age.

§ 10.7   RULE 803(16): STATEMENTS IN ANCIENT DOCUMENTS

Fed. R. Evid. 803(16) provides as follows:

The following are not excluded by the rule against hearsay, regardless of whether the declarant is available as a witness: . . .

(16) *Statements in Ancient Documents.* A statement in a document that is at least 20 years old and whose authenticity is established.

[Prior to December 1, 2011, the rule read as follows:

Rule 803. The following are not excluded by the hearsay rule, even though the declarant is available as a witness:

(16) Statements in ancient documents. Statements in a document in existence twenty years or more the authenticity of which is established.

The Federal Rules of Evidence were rewritten solely to make them easier to understand; the Advisory Committee did not intend to make any substantive change in the Rules. The text of the old rule may remain useful in reading court decisions that precede the revision of the rules. Thus, this edition of the Student's Guide provides the text of both the new and the old version of each relevant provision of the Federal Rules of Evidence.]

The rationale for this rule is simple: necessity. Such documents are often the only way to offer proof of facts from a period sufficiently long ago that there may no longer be witnesses available who have first-hand knowledge and present memory to testify. The likelihood of trustworthiness derives from two sources: the first-hand-knowledge requirement, and the probability that the documents and statements involved were made before the current controversy arose.

The provision changes the common law "ancient document rule" in two ways. First, the common law rule overcame only authentication objections (*see* Fed. R. Evid. 901(b)(8)), not hearsay objections. Second, it required that the document in question be at least 30 years old, not 20.

Any kind of document can qualify (a diary, newspaper article, minutes from a corporate board meeting, private correspondence, etc.) as long as it otherwise satisfies the rule.

§ 10.8   RULE 803(17): MARKET REPORTS, COMMERCIAL PUBLICATIONS

Fed. R. Evid. 803(17) provides as follows:

The following are not excluded by the rule against hearsay, regardless of whether the declarant is available as a witness: . . .

(17) *Market Reports and Similar Commercial Publications.* **Market quotations, lists, directories, or other compilations that are generally relied on by the public or by persons in particular occupations.**

[Prior to December 1, 2011, the rule read as follows:

Rule 803. The following are not excluded by the hearsay rule, even though the declarant is available as a witness:

(17) Market reports, commercial publications. Market quotations, tabulations, lists, directories, or other published compilations, generally used and relied upon by the public or by persons in particular occupations.

The Federal Rules of Evidence were rewritten solely to make them easier to understand; the Advisory Committee did not intend to make any substantive change in the Rules. The text of the old rule may remain useful in reading court decisions that precede the revision of the rules. Thus, this edition of the Student's Guide provides the text of both the new and the old version of each relevant provision of the Federal Rules of Evidence.]

If someone wants to know the price at which XYZ Corp. stock closed at the end of yesterday's trading, she would probably turn to the stock exchange listings in today's daily newspaper or the paper's web page. If you need someone's address and phone number, you would look it up in the phone book. A stamp collector or trader interested in ascertaining the value of a rare postage stamp would look in a catalogue published by a well-respected philately company.[1] Because people have enough confidence in such reports and publications to rely upon them in their personal and professional lives, they should be considered reliable enough for use as evidence in court. Fed. R. Evid. 803(17) so provides.

§ 10.9   RULE 803(18): LEARNED TREATISES

Fed. R. Evid. 803(18) provides as follows:

The following are not excluded by the rule against hearsay, regardless of whether the declarant is available as a witness: . . .

(18) *Statements in Learned Treatises, Periodicals, or Pamphlets.* **A statement contained in a treatise, periodical, or pamphlet if:**

---

[1] Some people have become rich by collecting stamps, thereby proving false the old adage, "Philately will get you nowhere."

(A) the statement is called to the attention of an expert witness on cross-examination or relied on by the expert on direct examination; and

(B) the publication is established as a reliable authority by the expert's admission or testimony, by another expert's testimony, or by judicial notice.

If admitted, the statement may be read into evidence but not received as an exhibit.

[Prior to December 1, 2011, the rule read as follows:

Rule 803. The following are not excluded by the hearsay rule, even though the declarant is available as a witness:

(18) Learned treatises. To the extent called to the attention of an expert witness upon cross-examination or relied upon by the expert witness in direct examination, statements contained in published treatises, periodicals, or pamphlets on a subject of history, medicine, or other science or art, established as a reliable authority by the testimony or admission of the witness or by other expert testimony or by judicial notice. If admitted, the statements may be read into evidence but may not be received as exhibits.

The Federal Rules of Evidence were rewritten solely to make them easier to understand; the Advisory Committee did not intend to make any substantive change in the Rules. The text of the old rule may remain useful in reading court decisions that precede the revision of the rules. Thus, this edition of the Student's Guide provides the text of both the new and the old version of each relevant provision of the Federal Rules of Evidence.]

As a rule, evidence relating to specialized fields of knowledge must be offered through expert testimony; a party is not permitted to use a treatise or scholarly article to prove facts. In a medical malpractice suit, for example, if plaintiff wants to offer proof of the symptoms of and recommended treatment for a particular disease, he cannot simply read an excerpt from a medical treatise; there is too great a risk that the jury, comprised of lay people who are not knowledgeable about the disease, may not fully understand the discussion of it in the treatise and may be unable to accurately apply that discussion to the facts in the case.

Thus, to offer specialized knowledge in evidence, a party must call an expert witness, who can explain the information to the jury, can relate it to the facts of the case, and thereafter can be cross-examined by the other party. Fed. R. Evid. 803(18) provides that once an expert testifies, either side may, subject to several requirements, introduce relevant statements from treatises, scholarly articles, and the like, to explain or impeach the expert's testimony.

The rule imposes the following requirements and restrictions.

1. An *expert* witness must testify.

2. The treatise, article, etc. must be "established as a reliable authority" in the area of knowledge in question. Showing that the treatise, article, etc. is a

"reliable authority" can be done in several ways, discussed *infra*.

3. The witness must cite the treatise on direct examination or be questioned about statements contained in the treatise while being cross-examined.

4. The statements from the treatise can be read into the record, but the book, article, pamphlet (or whatever) cannot be received as an exhibit.

The operation of the rule can be divided into two scenarios: use by the expert on direct examination, and use by the opposing party on cross.

1. Use by the expert witness during direct examination.

In a medical malpractice suit, X v. Y, X calls Dr. W as an expert. The rules governing expert testimony are spelled out in Article VII of the Federal Rules; suffice it here to say that, in explaining his testimony, Dr. W can testify that he relied on a treatise by ABC, which, he testifies, is recognized as a "reliable authority" in the medical field. Where appropriate, Dr. W can read relevant passages of the treatise as part of his testimony.

2. Use to cross-examine the expert.

Suppose the ABC treatise contains statements that contradict Dr. W's testimony. Y's attorney wants to ask Dr. W: "Isn't it a fact that the ABC treatise says, and I quote: . . . [reads quoted passage] . . . Doesn't that contradict what you testified to on direct?" She may do so, without first having to lay a foundation that the ABC treatise is "recognized as an authority in the field," because Dr. W, in his direct examination, already did so.

Suppose further that a different treatise, the DEF treatise, also contains statements that disagree with Dr. W's testimony. Y's attorney may use these statements, too, to cross-examine Dr. W, but first she must establish that the DEF treatise is "recognized as an authority in the field." This can be done in any of several ways.

1. *Ask Dr. W.* "Doctor, are you familiar with the DEF treatise? . . . Is it recognized as an authority in the field?" If Dr. W says "Yes," the requirement is satisfied.

2. *Previous testimony of another expert.* If another expert has already testified at this trial that the DEF treatise is recognized as an authority in the field, that witness (Dr. Z) has already satisfied the requirement, and Y's attorney can use DEF to cross-examine Dr. W. (Dr. W can, of course, answer that *he* doesn't recognize DEF as an authority in the field.)

3. *Judicial notice.* Y's attorney can ask the judge to take judicial notice that the DEF treatise is a recognized authority. (Judicial notice is covered in Article II of the Federal Rules; suffice it here to say Y's attorney shouldn't make such a request unless she has first studied Article II and has the necessary evidence to support her request.) If the judge takes judicial notice that the DEF treatise is recognized as an authority in the field, Y's attorney can use the DEF treatise to cross-examine Dr. W.

4. *Subsequent testimony of another expert.* Alternately, Y can later call another expert witness, who testifies that the DEF treatise is treatise recognized as an authority in the field. Thereafter, Y can recall Dr. W for cross-examination using the DEF treatise.

§ 10.10 RULE 803(19): REPUTATION CONCERNING PERSONAL OR FAMILY HISTORY

Fed. R. Evid. 803(19) provides as follows:

The following are not excluded by the rule against hearsay, regardless of whether the declarant is available as a witness: . . .

(19) *Reputation Concerning Personal or Family History.* A reputation among a person's family by blood, adoption, or marriage — or among a person's associates or in the community — concerning the person's birth, adoption, legitimacy, ancestry, marriage, divorce, death, relationship by blood, adoption, or marriage, or similar facts of personal or family history.

[Prior to December 1, 2011, the rule read as follows:

Rule 803. The following are not excluded by the hearsay rule, even though the declarant is available as a witness:

(19) Reputation concerning personal or family history. Reputation among members of a person's family by blood, adoption or marriage, or among a person's associates, or in the community, concerning a person's birth, adoption, marriage, divorce, death, legitimacy, relationship by blood, adoption, or marriage, ancestry, or other similar fact of his personal or family history.

The Federal Rules of Evidence were rewritten solely to make them easier to understand; the Advisory Committee did not intend to make any substantive change in the Rules. The text of the old rule may remain useful in reading court decisions that precede the revision of the rules. Thus, this edition of the Student's Guide provides the text of both the new and the old version of each relevant provision of the Federal Rules of Evidence.]

The theory underlying this provision is that information about a person's family status that is widely enough known to be "common knowledge" is reliable enough to overcome a hearsay objection, even if no one can be identified who has first-hand knowledge of it. Thus, C, a 25-year old woman, may testify that her parents were married to each other, even though she was not yet born or conceived when the wedding supposedly took place and she never saw a copy of their marriage certificate.

To qualify as valid "reputation" testimony under Fed. R. Evid. 803(19), the party offering the testimony must lay the same foundation as would be required to admit reputation testimony under Fed. R. Evid. 404(a)–405(a) or 608(a). In the previous paragraph, C's testimony that her parents referred to each other as husband and wife, that they celebrated a particular date as their anniversary, and everyone in the community regarded them as married to each other, would establish the required foundation.

See also Fed. R. Evid. 804(b)(4) ("Statement of personal or family history"), § 11.43–11.45.

§ 10.11   RULE 803(20): REPUTATION CONCERNING BOUNDARIES OR GENERAL HISTORY

Fed. R. Evid. 803(20) provides as follows:

The following are not excluded by the rule against hearsay, regardless of whether the declarant is available as a witness: . . .

(20) *Reputation Concerning Boundaries or General History.* A reputation in a community — arising before the controversy — concerning boundaries of land in the community or customs that affect the land, or concerning general historical events important to that community, state, or nation.

[Prior to December 1, 2011, the rule read as follows:

Rule 803. The following are not excluded by the hearsay rule, even though the declarant is available as a witness:

(20) Reputation concerning boundaries or general history. Reputation in a community, arising before the controversy, as to boundaries of or customs affecting lands in the community, and reputation as to events of general history important to the community or State or nation in which located.

The Federal Rules of Evidence were rewritten solely to make them easier to understand; the Advisory Committee did not intend to make any substantive change in the Rules. The text of the old rule may remain useful in reading court decisions that precede the revision of the rules. Thus, this edition of the Student's Guide provides the text of both the new and the old version of each relevant provision of the Federal Rules of Evidence.]

This is another "common knowledge" exception to the hearsay rule. Reliability is assumed because in order to qualify, the party offering the evidence must establish, first, that the belief in question is sufficiently widespread to constitute "reputation," and second, that the belief was firmly established before the "controversy" that is the subject matter of the present lawsuit arose.

§ 10.12   RULE 803(21): REPUTATION AS TO CHARACTER

Fed. R. Evid. 803(21) provides as follows:

The following are not excluded by the rule against hearsay, regardless of whether the declarant is available as a witness: . . .

(21) *Reputation Concerning Character.* A reputation among a person's associates or in the community concerning the person's character.

[Prior to December 1, 2011, the rule read as follows:

> Rule 803. The following are not excluded by the hearsay rule, even though the declarant is available as a witness:
>
> (21) Reputation as to character. Reputation of a person's character among associates or in the community.

The Federal Rules of Evidence were rewritten solely to make them easier to understand; the Advisory Committee did not intend to make any substantive change in the Rules. The text of the old rule may remain useful in reading court decisions that precede the revision of the rules. Thus, this edition of the Student's Guide provides the text of both the new and the old version of each relevant provision of the Federal Rules of Evidence.]

This provision assures that if reputation testimony is admissible under Fed. R. Evid. 404, 405 and 608(a), its hearsay character will not require its exclusion.

At common law, only evidence of a person's reputation in his or her residential community was admissible. Fed. R. Evid. 803(21) recognizes that in contemporary society many individuals reside, work, recreate, worship, etc. among different "communities" or groups of associates, and hence eliminates reliance on only the person's geographic residential community for reputation evidence.

§ 10.13 RULE 803(22): JUDGMENT OF PREVIOUS CONVICTION

Fed. R. Evid. 803(22) provides as follows:

> **The following are not excluded by the rule against hearsay, regardless of whether the declarant is available as a witness: . . .**
>
> **(22) *Judgment of a Previous Conviction*. Evidence of a final judgment of conviction if:**
>
> > **(A) the judgment was entered after a trial or guilty plea, but not a nolo contendere plea;**
> >
> > **(B) the conviction was for a crime punishable by death or by imprisonment for more than a year;**
> >
> > **(C) the evidence is admitted to prove any fact essential to the judgment; and**
> >
> > **(D) when offered by the prosecutor in a criminal case for a purpose other than impeachment, the judgment was against the defendant.**
>
> **The pendency of an appeal may be shown but does not affect admissibility.**

[Prior to December 1, 2011, the rule read as follows:

> Rule 803. The following are not excluded by the hearsay rule, even though the declarant is available as a witness:

> (22) Judgment of previous conviction. Evidence of a final judgment, entered after a trial or upon a plea of guilty (but not upon a plea of nolo contendere), adjudging a person guilty of a crime punishable by death or imprisonment in excess of one year, to prove any fact essential to sustain the judgment, but not including, when offered by the Government in a criminal prosecution for purposes other than impeachment, judgments against persons other than the accused. The pendency of an appeal may be shown but does not affect admissibility.

The Federal Rules of Evidence were rewritten solely to make them easier to understand; the Advisory Committee did not intend to make any substantive change in the Rules. The text of the old rule may remain useful in reading court decisions that precede the revision of the rules. Thus, this edition of the Student's Guide provides the text of both the new and the old version of each relevant provision of the Federal Rules of Evidence.]

In litigation that occurs subsequent to a person's conviction for a crime, the law can treat the conviction in any of several ways.

1.   In some circumstances, the prior conviction is treated as conclusive under the doctrine of res judicata, either as a bar or as collateral estoppel. This use of prior convictions is not covered in the Federal Rules of Evidence; it is governed by constitutional principles that have nothing to do with hearsay.

2.   The prior conviction may be treated as substantive evidence, i.e., as proof (which the fact-finder in the subsequent trial may accept or reject) that the convicted person in fact did what she was convicted of doing, i.e., that she engaged in certain conduct with a certain mental state. Assume, for example, that F was convicted in 2005 of forging Y's name to a check. Several years later, in a trial totally unrelated to the 2005 forgery, a litigant might offer the fact of F's conviction to prove that in 2005 F signed another person's name to a check with the intent to defraud.

     If offered for this purpose, F's prior conviction constitutes a "statement" by the judge or jury (see *infra*) that F forged the check in 2005 with the intent to defraud. If the conviction satisfies the requirements of Fed. R. Evid. 803(22) (not all convictions do), the fact that the prior conviction is hearsay does not require exclusion of the conviction.

     The adverse party can still object that the evidence is irrelevant, or is inadmissible character evidence, or violates Fed. R. Evid. 403. Fed. R. Evid. 803(22) covers only the hearsay objection.

3.   The prior conviction may be used for the limited purpose of impeaching a witness's (or a hearsay declarant's) character for truthfulness. This use of a prior conviction is regulated by Fed. R. Evid. 609.

4.   Some prior convictions are not admissible or usable for any of these purposes.

The use of a prior conviction as substantive evidence in subsequent litigation (the second category mentioned *supra*) involves hearsay, because when a judge or jury in a criminal trial convicts the accused of a crime, it is making a *statement*: "I, the judge (or, we, the jury) find Defendant F guilty of the crime of — ."

In fact, in finding a defendant guilty, the judge or jury is really making several statements. For example, suppose F is indicted for robbing a liquor store at gunpoint at 12th and Elm at 11 p.m. on June 1. To find F guilty, the jury must conclude (1) that F was in the liquor store at 12th and Elm at 11 p.m. on June 1, (2) that she had a gun, and (3) that she used the gun to force W1, the store clerk, to empty the register and give her the money. All three points are, as Rule 803(22)(C) puts it, "facts essential to sustain the judgment" that F committed that liquor store robbery.

Suppose now Plaintiff files a lawsuit against F — or against someone else! — and needs to offer evidence of one of the "numbered" facts in the previous paragraph. One way plaintiff can do so is offer evidence of F's robbery conviction, even though that conviction is hearsay, so long as that conviction satisfies the requirements of Fed. R. Evid. 803(22). Such a conviction is considered highly reliable, because we expect that someone would fight criminal charges that are untrue, and because the prosecutor's burden of proof in a criminal case is so heavy (guilt must be established beyond a reasonable doubt).

Note that only *convictions* are admissible to prove "any fact essential to sustain the judgment." *Acquittals*, by contrast, are *not* admissible in subsequent litigation as proof that the criminal defendant did *not* do what he was charged with. This is because an acquittal is not a finding that the defendant is innocent of the charge; it is only a finding that a reasonable doubt exists as to the defendant's guilt.

Application of Fed. R. Evid. 803(22) imposes the following requirements and raises the following issues:

1. *The nature of the crime.* Only convictions for felonies (i.e., crimes punishable by death or imprisonment in excess of one year) fit within the provision. Misdemeanors (crimes punishable by one year or less) do not.

    Note that the rule does not require that the convicted person *actually receive* a sentence of death or imprisonment in excess of one year; it suffices that he or she *could have* received such a sentence.

2. *Manner of conviction.* The conviction comes within the rule only if it came after trial, or as the result of a guilty plea. Convictions by pleas of nolo contendere do not fit within Fed. R. Evid. 803(22).[2]

3. *Use of conviction in subsequent litigation.* Fed. R. Evid. 803(22) overcomes a hearsay objection only if the prior conviction is being offered in evidence "to prove any fact essential to sustain the judgment."

4. *Use in civil litigation and by the defense in criminal trials.* Civil litigants and criminal defendants may use a conviction under Fed. R. Evid. 803(22) "to prove any fact essential to sustain the judgment" regardless of who the convicted

---

[2] A "nolo" plea is one in which a judge permits a defendant to say, in essence, "I acknowledge that the prosecutor would be able to introduce evidence that I committed the crime, and I agree to having a judgment of conviction entered against me for that crime, but I do not admit that I committed the crime."

person was. The convicted person could be one of the litigants, or a witness, or anyone else.

5. *Use by the prosecutor in a criminal trial.* A prosecutor may use a conviction under Fed. R. Evid. 803(22) "to prove any fact essential to sustain the judgment" only if the person who was convicted in the prior case is also the defendant in the current case.

6. *Pendency of an appeal.* If an appeal of the conviction is pending, the party adversely affected by the evidence may inform the jury of that fact, but the fact that a case is on appeal does not affect admissibility of the conviction.

§ 10.14 QUESTIONS

Question 1. A man and a woman entered a liquor store at 12th and Elm at 11 p.m. on June 1. The man pulled a gun and ordered W1, the liquor store clerk, to empty the cash register into a sack that the woman was holding.

A minute or two after the robbers left the store, W2, who lives nearby, saw a dark-colored Taurus speed up Elm Street and sideswipe a Plymouth Voyager parked on Elm between 14th and 15th Streets, doing substantial damage. W2 can testify that the first three letters of the Taurus's license plate are "VCF."

M and F are subsequently charged with the robbery. According to Department of Motor Vehicle records, F at the time owned a Taurus, with license number VCF-123. W3, a neighbor of F, will testify that F's car was dark brown. F is arrested; M is a fugitive. F goes to trial for the robbery and is convicted. Although robbery carries a maximum possible sentence of fifteen years, because this is her first offense, she has made considerable progress toward kicking her crack cocaine habit, and the judge is a bit of a softy anyway, she is sentenced to five years, all but the first six months of which is suspended, followed by five years probation.

Thereafter, P, the owner of the Plymouth Voyager, sues F for the damage to his vehicle. In the civil trial, P seeks to prove that F was convicted of the liquor store robbery.

a. How is this relevant?

'**Ans.** It is relevant because it establishes that F was in the vicinity of P's vehicle at the date and time that P's vehicle was damaged, and was in a hurry to get away from that vicinity as quickly as she could; this, in turn, makes it more probable than it would be without that evidence that it was F (and F's Taurus), and not anyone else, who sideswiped P's vehicle.

b. Procedurally, how should P seek to offer proof of F's conviction?

Ans. F's conviction is recorded in an official court record. P can therefore subpoena a copy of that record, which can be authenticated under one of the provisions of Fed. R. Evid. 902. P should also subpoena a copy of the indictment and the pleadings, which will contain the details involved (day, time, place, and manner in which the crime was committed).

c. If F interposes a hearsay objection in the civil suit, is her conviction admissible under Fed. R. Evid. 803(22)?

Ans. Apply the Fed. R. Evid. 803(22) issue-requirement checklist.

1. *The nature of the crime.* Robbery is punishable by up to fifteen years, so F's conviction qualifies, even though F was sentenced to only six months' actual imprisonment.

2. *Manner of conviction.* F was convicted after trial, which satisfies Fed. R. Evid. 803(22).

3. *Use of F's conviction in current litigation.* To convict F of the robbery, it was "essential to sustain the judgment" finding her guilty that the jury concluded, beyond a reasonable doubt, that she was in the liquor store at Elm and 12th at 11 p.m. on June 1. Therefore, her conviction may be offered as a basis from which the jury in the civil case can infer that she was in the vicinity of Elm and 14th-15th shortly after 11 p.m., when time P's Voyager was sideswiped.

4. *Use in civil litigation . . .* P may offer F's conviction against F.

5. *Use by prosecutor . . .* not applicable.

6. *Pendency of appeal.* F can offer evidence that she is appealing her conviction, in the hopes that the jury will disregard the implications of her conviction.

Question 2. Change the facts slightly. Assume that the brown Taurus, license number VCF 123, was owned, not by F, but by G, a friend and neighbor of F's. Witnesses at F's criminal trial testified that G had lent F her car for Memorial Day weekend (May 30–June 2).

After F is convicted of robbery, P sues G, not F. (State law provides that the owner of a vehicle is responsible for any damage or injury caused by someone driving the car with the owner's consent. Fortunately for all concerned, G's auto insurance insures her against liability for damages caused by anyone to whom G lends her car.) At the trial of the civil case, P offers in evidence the fact of F's conviction for robbery. Admissible, over G's hearsay objection?

Ans. Yes. The analysis of issues 1–3, and 5–6 from the checklist is identical to that in question 1c. The only difference is that, here, P is using F's conviction as evidence against *G*. In civil litigation, this is explicitly permitted by the rule.

Question 3. Some time after F is convicted, police apprehend M, and his case goes to trial. At M's trial, W1 testifies that M "looks like" the man with the gun, but admits that it's been so long he can't be sure. He easily identifies F as the woman participant. Next, the prosecutor calls witnesses who testify that M and F were living together at the time of the robbery.

a. Now the prosecutor wants to prove that F was convicted of being the woman participant in the robbery. How is this relevant?

Ans. If F was the female participant in the robbery, this has some tendency to make it more likely that M, with whom she was living at the time, was the male participant.

b. Is F's conviction admissible against M, if M interposes a hearsay objection?

Ans. No. This question illustrates issue 5 on the list of issues and requirements. Unlike a civil litigant (see question 2), a prosecutor cannot make evidentiary use of F's conviction against anyone but F.

Question 4. Suppose, a month after F was convicted, the prosecutor develops evidence that F sold drugs to an undercover agent in the same neighborhood on June 2 (the day after the robbery for which she was just convicted). At the trial for the June 2 drug sale, the prosecutor offers evidence of F's conviction for the June 1 robbery, as evidence that since F was in the neighborhood on June 1, she was probably still in the neighborhood on June 2. Is evidence of the conviction admissible?

Ans. Evidence of the conviction is admissible over a hearsay objection, per Fed. R. Evid. 803(22). Again our focus is on issue 5 of the checklist, but here the prosecutor satisfies the rule, because the prosecutor is offering evidence of F's conviction against F.

Even though the prosecutor can overcome a hearsay objection, however, there are other bases on which F can object. First of all, its relevance — to suggest that since F was committing a robbery in the neighborhood on June 1, she was probably still in the neighborhood on June 2 — is something less than overwhelming. Second, if you have already studied Rule 404(b), you recognized that F has a very strong objection that the robbery conviction is inadmissible "bad woman inference" character evidence at the drug sale trial. Given weak relevance and the risk the jury will draw the "bad woman inference," an objection based on Rules 403 and 404(b) should be sustained.

§ 10.15   RULE 803(23): JUDGMENT AS TO PERSONAL, FAMILY OR GENERAL HISTORY, OR BOUNDARIES

Fed. R. Evid. 803(23) provides as follows:

The following are not excluded by the rule against hearsay, regardless of whether the declarant is available as a witness: . . .

(23) *Judgments Involving Personal, Family, or General History or a Boundary.* **A judgment that is admitted to prove a matter of personal, family, or general history, or boundaries, if the matter:**

(A) was essential to the judgment; and

(B) could be proved by evidence of reputation.

[Prior to December 1, 2011, the rule read as follows:

Rule 803. The following are not excluded by the hearsay rule, even though the declarant is available as a witness:

(23) Judgment as to personal, family or general history, or boundaries. Judgments as proof of matters of personal family or general history, or

boundaries, essential to the judgment, if the same would be provable by evidence of reputation.

The Federal Rules of Evidence were rewritten solely to make them easier to understand; the Advisory Committee did not intend to make any substantive change in the Rules. The text of the old rule may remain useful in reading court decisions that precede the revision of the rules. Thus, this edition of the Student's Guide provides the text of both the new and the old version of each relevant provision of the Federal Rules of Evidence.]

Under this provision, if litigation in the past (whether civil or criminal) resulted in a judgment relating to any of the subjects discussed in Fed. R. Evid. 803(19) or 803(20), that judgment is admissible as proof of any fact "essential to the judgment." For a discussion of the phrase "essential to the judgment," see § 10.13.

Rule 803(24)

This rule has been transferred to Fed. R. Evid. 807. Case law interpreting Fed. R. Evid. 803(24) is now applicable to Fed. R. Evid. 807.

Chapter 11

RULE 804: EXCEPTIONS TO THE RULE AGAINST HEARSAY — WHEN THE DECLARANT IS UNAVAILABLE AS A WITNESS

§ 11.1 INTRODUCTION

A major difference distinguishes Fed. R. Evid. 804 from Fed. R. Evid. 803. As we have seen, in Rule 803, the declarant's availability or unavailability has no effect on the statement's admissibility (*see* § 8.1). The exceptions to the hearsay rule set out in Rule 804(b), by contrast, may be used *only* if the offering party can first show that the declarant is unavailable, as that term is defined in Rule 804(a).

Thus, to use a Rule 804 exception, the party offering the statement in evidence must:

(a) Show that the declarant is unavailable, by satisfying the judge that the *declarant* fits within one of the provisions of Rule *804(a)*; and

(b) Satisfy the judge that the *statement* fits within one of the provisions of Rule *804(b)*.

The traditional rationale for imposing the "declarant unavailable" requirement is that, unlike statements fitting within the Rule 803 exceptions which are (theoretically, at least) considered "just as good" as live, sworn testimony,[1] statements fitting within the Rule 804(b) exceptions are considered less desirable than live, sworn testimony. Such statements are therefore admitted over a hearsay objection only if the declarant is unavailable to testify at trial.

Rule 804(b) contains five exceptions to the hearsay rule which apply in more-or-less precisely defined situations.

---

[1] If you have a particularly good memory, you may be thinking: "Doesn't this contradict what Fishman said in § 9.8, that Fed. R. Evid. 803(5) "is considered a less-preferred substitute for testimony . . ."? Well, yes, it does. But then again, Rule 803(5) is anomalous anyhow: it is the only Rule 803 exception that *requires* the declarant to be available. *I* didn't put the "recorded recollection" exception in Rule 803, the Advisory Committee did. So blame the Advisory Committee for the inconsistency, not me. (If you have no idea what this footnote is about, feel free to ignore it; it is unlikely to be on the exam.)

PART A:
DEFINING "UNAVAILABLE": RULE 804(a)

§ 11.2   FED. R. EVID. 804(a): "DECLARANT UNAVAILABLE"

Rule 804(a) provides as follows:

(a) Criteria for Being Unavailable. A declarant is considered to be unavailable as a witness if the declarant:

(1) is exempted from testifying about the subject matter of the declarant's statement because the court rules that a privilege applies;

(2) refuses to testify about the subject matter despite a court order to do so;

(3) testifies to not remembering the subject matter;

(4) cannot be present or testify at the trial or hearing because of death or a then-existing infirmity, physical illness, or mental illness; or

(5) is absent from the trial or hearing and the statement's proponent has not been able, by process or other reasonable means, to procure:

(A) the declarant's attendance, in the case of a hearsay exception under Rule 804(b)(1) or (6); or

(B) the declarant's attendance or testimony, in the case of a hearsay exception under Rule 804(b)(2), (3), or (4).

But this subdivision (a) does not apply if the statement's proponent procured or wrongfully caused the declarant's unavailability in order to prevent the declarant from attending or testifying.

[Prior to December 1, 2011, the rule read as follows:

Rule 804. Hearsay Exceptions; Declarant Unavailable

(a) Definition of unavailability. "Unavailability as a witness" includes situations in which the declarant —

(1) is exempted by ruling of the court on the ground of privilege from testifying concerning the subject matter of the declarant's statement; or

(2) persists in refusing to testify concerning the subject matter of the declarant's statement despite an order of the court to do so; or

(3) testifies to a lack of memory of the subject matter of the declarant's statement; or

(4) is unable to be present or to testify at the hearing because of death or then existing physical or mental illness or infirmity; or

(5) is absent from the hearing and the proponent of statement has been unable to procure the declarant's attendance (or in the case of a hearsay exception under subdivision (b)(2), (3), or (4), the declarant's attendance or testimony) by process or other reasonable means.

A declarant is not unavailable as a witness if exemption, refusal, claim of lack of memory, inability, or absence is due to the procurement or wrongdoing of the proponent of a statement for the purpose of preventing the witness from attending or testifying.

The Federal Rules of Evidence were rewritten solely to make them easier to understand; the Advisory Committee did not intend to make any substantive change in the Rules. The text of the old rule may remain useful in reading court decisions that precede the revision of the rules. Thus, this edition of the Student's Guide provides the text of both the new and the old version of each relevant provision of the Federal Rules of Evidence.]

Before a litigant can introduce a hearsay statement via one of the exceptions codified in Fed. R. Evid. 804(b), he or she must persuade the judge that the declarant is unavailable, i.e., that the declarant falls within one of the definitions of unavailability codified in Rule 804(a). Note that the rule is concerned with the declarant's unavailability *as a witness*, not his or her *physical* availability or unavailability. Someone who is present in the courtroom and on the witness stand is still "unavailable" as a witness if he or she comes within 804(a)(1), (2) or (3).

In accordance with Fed. R. Evid. 104(a), the judge, not the jury, decides whether the witness is "unavailable." Also pursuant to Rule 104(a), the judge may consider inadmissible evidence (out of the jury's hearing) in deciding the unavailability issue.

The final paragraph of Rule 804(a) codifies the common-sense rule that a litigant cannot improperly cause a declarant's unavailability and then rely on that unavailability to satisfy Rule 804(a).

§ 11.3   RULE 804(a)(1): PRIVILEGE

Rule 804(a)(1) provides:

> **(a) Criteria for Being Unavailable. A declarant is considered to be unavailable as a witness if the declarant:**
>
> **(1) is exempted from testifying about the subject matter of the declarant's statement because the court rules that a privilege applies;**
>
> ...

A detailed discussion of testimonial privileges is far beyond the scope of this book. This section will highlight a few of the issues that may arise.

As a rule, a party can establish a declarant's unavailability as a witness on grounds of privilege only if the party calls the declarant as a witness and attempts to question her under oath, and the witness properly asserts either one of the common law evidentiary privileges, a privilege recognized under Fed. R. Evid. 501, or her Fifth

Amendment privilege against self-incrimination. Under some circumstances, however, a judge could properly accept a lesser showing of unavailability (for example, an affidavit signed by DL attesting that, if called, she will assert her Fifth Amendment privilege).

The judge generally will resolve privilege issues while the jury is absent from the courtroom. The judge need not automatically accept the declarant's claim that she is legally privileged not to testify. For example, someone who was convicted of a crime and never appealed the conviction (or whose appeal was denied) can no longer plead the Fifth if asked about the crime itself. Thus, the judge should deny the claim of privilege and order the witness to testify in such a case. If the witness disobeys the order, she may be held in contempt of court, and incarcerated without a trial until she agrees to testify or until the trial ends, whichever comes first. (Such refusal would render the witness unavailable under Rule 804(a)(2).)

A judge may not be able to make an intelligent decision as to whether information is privileged unless she knows what the information is. In *United States v. Zolin*, 491 U.S. 554, 565–566 (1989), the Supreme Court held that in some circumstances, the judge may require the witness to disclose the allegedly privileged information *in camera* before deciding whether the privilege (in that case, the attorney-client privilege) applies.

Remember, too, that a witness' claim of privilege may be valid as to some questions or some subjects but not as to others. Consider the privilege with which you will be dealing with your entire professional life: the attorney-client privilege. That privilege obliges you not to disclose the *confidential* conversations you have with a client in the context of the attorney-client relationship; the privilege does not extend to conversations or conduct that occurs outside the attorney-client relationship. If you are L's attorney on business matters, you cannot be compelled to testify that she admitted to you that she bribed someone in order to get a contract for her business. But if L mentioned to you that she was dating a man named Y, you could be compelled to testify about what she told you about him, because that knowledge did not come to you *within* the attorney-client relationship.

§ 11.4   RULE 804(a)(2): REFUSAL TO TESTIFY

Fed. R. Evid. 804(a)(2) provides:

(a) Criteria for Being Unavailable. A declarant is considered to be unavailable as a witness if the declarant: . . .

(2) refuses to testify about the subject matter despite a court order to do so; . . .

A "refusal to testify" situation sometimes arises when a witness has asserted a privilege under Rule 804(a)(1), the judge concludes that the privilege does not apply, and the witness persists in refusing to answer questions. Another common scenario is the refusal of a reluctant state or government witness to testify against a partner (or superior) in crime. If the witness refuses to answer, the judge should order the witness to do so, and warn the witness that continued refusal will result in being held in contempt.

§ 11.5   RULE 804(a)(3): LACK OF MEMORY

Fed. R. Evid. 804(a)(3) provides:

(a) Criteria for Being Unavailable. A declarant is considered to be unavailable as a witness if the declarant: . . .

(3) testifies to not remembering the subject matter; ...

On March 1, 2010, DL/W attended a meeting. A few days later he told Z what happened at the meeting. Now, in 2011, in lawsuit X v Y, X's attorney calls DL/W as a witness and asks: "What happened at that March 1, 2010 meeting?" DL/W says, "I really don't remember."

X's attorney should first attempt to refresh DL/W's recollection, for example by showing the witness a writing or other object (*see* Fed. R. Evid. 612; §§ 9.2-9.3) and, if that doesn't work, should utilize Rule 803(5) if material exists that satisfies that Rule. If this does not succeed, the attorney may then attempt to introduce DL/W's out-of-court statement, invoking any other Article VIII provision she can satisfy. If the prior statement was given under oath at a proceeding, for example, the attorney may be able to admit it pursuant to Fed. R. Evid. 801(d)(1)(A), if the court agrees that DL/W's current protestation of lack of memory is "inconsistent" with the former statement. *See* § 4.10.

Another option that may be available to X's attorney is to invoke Rule 804. If the judge is satisfied that DL/W truly cannot remember, she can declare the witness "unavailable" per Rule 804(a)(3). If the judge is convinced that DL/W is lying when he claims lack of memory, she can order the witness to testify or hold him in contempt, as outlined in the previous section. If the witness continues to refuse, he is unavailable per 804(a)(2). In either case, this entitles Y's attorney to call Z as a witness and have Z testify about DL/W's statement to him — but only if DL/W's statement to Z falls within one of the hearsay exceptions listed in Fed. R. Evid. 804(b).

§ 11.6   RULE 804(a)(4): DEATH, ILLNESS, INFIRMITY

Fed. R. Evid. 804(a)(4) provides:

(a) Criteria for Being Unavailable. A declarant is considered to be unavailable as a witness if the declarant: . . .

(4) cannot be present or testify at the trial or hearing because of death or a then-existing infirmity, physical illness, or mental illness; . . .

This provision is basically self-explanatory. The burden is on the party seeking to introduce the prior statement to establish the declarant's death, illness or infirmity.

§ 11.7   RULE 804(a)(5): ABSENT FROM THE HEARING

Rule 804(a)(5) provides:

> **(a) Criteria for Being Unavailable. A declarant is considered to be unavailable as a witness if the declarant: . . .**
>
> > **(5) is absent from the trial or hearing and the statement's proponent has not been able, by process or other reasonable means, to procure:**
> >
> > > **(A) the declarant's attendance, in the case of a hearsay exception under Rule 804(b)(1) or (5); or**
> > >
> > > **(B) the declarant's attendance or testimony, in the case of a hearsay exception under Rule 804(b)(2), (3), or (4).**
> >
> > **But this subdivision (a) does not apply if the statement's proponent procured or wrongfully caused the declarant's unavailability in order to prevent the declarant from attending or testifying.**

It is simple common sense that someone is "unavailable" to testify if his whereabouts are unknown. The same is true if the declarant is outside the jurisdiction of the court (i.e., cannot be subpoenaed) and is unwilling to appear voluntarily.

Even so, civil procedure rules allow litigants to depose an out-of-jurisdiction declarant. Lawyers cannot compel W to travel from Texas to testify at a civil trial in California; but the attorneys can obtain a court order in Texas requiring W to submit to a deposition in Texas. The deposition would then be admissible under Fed. R. Evid. 804(b)(1), assuming it satisfied that Rule's requirements.

The final sentence of in Rule 804(a)(5) provides that, if a party offers a hearsay statement under Rules 804(b)(2), 804(b)(3), or 804(b)(4) and relies on declarant's absence from the hearing under Rule 804(a)(5) to establish his unavailability, to satisfy Rule 804(a)(5) the party must show, not only that she was unable to "procure the declarant's attendance," but also that she was unable to depose him to "procure the declarant's testimony."

PART B:
RULE 804(b): THE EXCEPTIONS

§ 11.8   RULE 804(b): OVERVIEW

The five hearsay exceptions found in Fed. R. Evid. 804(b) have two requirements in common. First, each requires that the offering party establish that the declarant is unavailable to testify pursuant to Rule 804(a). Second, each requires that the declarant had first-hand knowledge of what she spoke of in her statement.

Each of the Rule 804(b) exceptions also has its own list of additional requirements and issues that must be addressed.

1. Former Testimony

§ 11.9   RULE 804(b)(1)

A witness (WPP)² testifies at a proceeding of some kind (a trial, deposition, preliminary hearing, grand jury proceeding, congressional hearing, coroner's inquest, police department disciplinary hearing, etc.). Later, the testimony that WPP gave at that prior proceeding is relevant at a different proceeding, but WPP is no longer available to testify. Therefore, one of the parties in the new proceeding offers the transcript of WPP's former testimony in evidence. Should WPP's former testimony be admissible, even though, when offered at a new proceeding, it is hearsay? Or would admitting the testimony give one party an unfair advantage over his adversary?

The answer depends upon whether the examination of WPP at the former proceeding was sufficiently similar to what would occur if WPP were available to testify at the current proceeding. If so, then the rights of all of the parties to the current litigation should be adequately protected, and WPP's former testimony should be admissible. The question is, how much similarity should be required?

At common law, former testimony was admissible only if: (1) all parties at the former proceeding were identical with all parties at the current proceeding; and (2) the issues at the former and the current proceeding were also identical. Only then, the reasoning went, could we be sure that the examination of WPP at the prior proceeding adequately mirrors what would have happened if WPP had been available at the current proceeding.

Many judges and scholars, though, protested that this required more similarity than was necessary to assure fairness, and often resulted in the exclusion of evidence that was quite trustworthy. In enacting Fed. R. Evid. 804(b)(1), Congress sought to accommodate these views. The Rule directs that sufficient similarity (and therefore fairness) exists so long as: (1) the issues relating to WPP's testimony at the current proceeding are the same as they were at the prior proceeding; (2) *the party against whom the former testimony is now offered* (or in civil cases, that party's "predecessor in interest") was a party to the former proceeding; and (3) at the prior proceeding, that party had an *opportunity and similar motive* to examine WPP the way it would examine WPP now if WPP were available.

Fed. R. Evid. 804(b)(1) provides:

b) The Exceptions. The following are not excluded by the rule against hearsay if the declarant is unavailable as a witness:

(1) *Former Testimony.* Testimony that:

(A) was given as a witness at a trial, hearing, or lawful deposition, whether given during the current proceeding or a different one; and

---

² I use "WPP" as short for "witness at the prior proceeding."

(B) is now offered against a party who had — or, in a civil case, whose predecessor in interest had — an opportunity and similar motive to develop it by direct, cross-, or redirect examination.

[Prior to December 1, 2011, the rule read as follows:

Rule 804. Hearsay Exceptions; Declarant Unavailable

(b) Hearsay exceptions. The following are not excluded by the hearsay rule if the declarant is unavailable as a witness:

(1) Former testimony. Testimony given as a witness at another hearing of the same or a different proceeding, or in a deposition taken in compliance with law in the course of the same or another proceeding, if the party against whom the testimony is now offered, or, in a civil action or proceeding, a predecessor in interest, had an opportunity and similar motive to develop the testimony by direct, cross, or redirect examination.

The Federal Rules of Evidence were rewritten solely to make them easier to understand; the Advisory Committee did not intend to make any substantive change in the Rules. The text of the old rule may remain useful in reading court decisions that precede the revision of the rules. Thus, this edition of the Student's Guide provides the text of both the new and the old version of each relevant provision of the Federal Rules of Evidence.]

Testimony that satisfies Rule 804(b)(1) is considered an acceptable substitute for "live" testimony because it has most of the attributes of "live" testimony: the declarant was under oath, and each party had an opportunity to examine the witness (i.e., to conduct direct or cross-examination). The missing factor is that the fact-finder cannot observe declarant's demeanor while testifying.

Rule 804(b)(1) imposes the following requirements and raises the following issues.

1. *First-hand knowledge.* It must be apparent that WPP, the witness whose former testimony is now being offered, had first-hand knowledge of the facts he or she testified to (except when first-hand knowledge is not required, as, for example, where the witness was testifying as an expert).

2. *Unavailable.* The offering party must show that WPP is currently unavailable, per Rule 804(a).

3. *Nature of prior proceeding.* So long as the prior proceeding was sufficiently formal to qualify as a "trial, hearing, or lawful deposition," it meets the "proceeding" requirement, whether it was a prior proceeding in the same case, or in a different case.

4. *Identity of adverse party.*[3] Former testimony is admissible against a party only if it "(B) is now offered against a party . . . — or, in a civil case, [a]

---

[3] Recall that the term "adverse party" is legalese for "the party who will be adversely affected if the evidence is admitted," or, less technically, "the party against whom the evidence is now being offered." See § 2.3.

predecessor in interest . . ." This language creates a different test depending on whether the case is criminal or civil.

a. *Criminal trials.* A prosecutor can offer former testimony against a defendant pursuant to 804(b)(1) only if the defendant was a party in the prior proceeding. Similarly, a defendant can offer former testimony against the federal government only if the federal government was a party in the former proceeding.

b. *Civil litigation.* A civil litigant can satisfy the "identity of adverse party" requirement so long as one of the following requirements is met:

(i) The adverse party (against whom the prior testimony is now being offered) was a party at the prior proceeding; or

(ii) A party at the prior proceeding was the adverse party's "predecessor in interest." How "predecessor in interest" should be defined is a question of some controversy (*see* § 11.16).

5. *Motive to examine.* The issues at the prior proceeding must have been similar enough to those in the current proceeding to assure that the adversely affected party's treatment of WPP at that proceeding is an adequate substitute for how the adverse party at the current proceeding would treat WPP now, if WPP were available (*see* § 11.11).

6. *Opportunity to examine.* The procedures and other circumstances at the prior proceeding must have been such to give the adverse party an adequate opportunity to examine WPP on direct, cross- or redirect examination (*see* § 11.12).

7. *Offering the testimony.* Almost always, former testimony is offered in the form of a transcript, which must be authenticated in accordance with Fed. R. Evid., Art. IX. If no transcript is available, someone who was present and recalls what WPP said can testify, "Here's what I recall WPP said while he testified, . . ."

8. *Objections.* Suppose objections should have been made at the prior proceeding, but weren't? Suppose a proper objection was made, but WPP's testimony was nonetheless allowed to stay in the record? (*See* § 11.14.)

9. *Other rules.* Keep in mind that prior testimony may be offered under Article VIII provisions other than 804(b)(1), including, in appropriate circumstances, Rules 801(d)(1)(A), 801(d)(1)(B), 801(d)(2)(A), 803(5), and 807, and may be used to refresh a witness' memory under Rule 612. *See* § 11.18.

10. *Sixth Amendment Confrontation Clause.* Former testimony that satisfies Fed. R. Evid. 804(b)(1) automatically satisfies the Confrontation Clause. *See* § 11.19.

§ 11.10 QUESTIONS

Question 1. Cars driven by Sturm and Drang collide in an intersection, and Sturm sues. At trial, Sturm calls Angst, who testifies that he saw Drang run a red light and crash into Sturm's car. The jury finds for Sturm, but an appellate court remands for a new trial. At the second trial, Sturm offers a transcript of Angst's testimony; Drang makes a hearsay objection; Sturm responds by citing Fed. R. Evid. 804(b)(1). Ruling?

Ans. Objection sustained. Sturm has made no showing that Angst is unavailable to testify at the second trial.

Question 2. Sturm offers an affidavit from his investigator, attesting that Angst has sold his home and moved to Tierra del Fuego, and told the investigator over the phone that he does not want to return and testify. Sturm again offers a transcript of Angst's first-trial testimony. Ruling, if Drang again makes a hearsay objection?

Ans. Overruled. Following the issue outline:

1. *First-hand knowledge.* Angst's former testimony ("I saw . . .") satisfies this requirement.

2. *Unavailability.* The investigator's affidavit satisfies Rule 804(a)(5) (look up Tierra del Fuego in a world atlas), unless the adverse party can prove that Angst is still available.

3. *Nature of prior proceeding.* Almost any kind of prior proceeding will do. A prior trial certainly satisfies the "proceeding" requirement.

4. *Identity of adverse party.* Drang was a party at the first trial, where Angst testified; she is a party again at the current trial.

5. *Motive to examine.* The issue about which Angst testified at the first trial (who ran the light) is the same as at the second. Drang presumably had just as much reason (i.e., a "similar motive") to discredit Angst's testimony at Trial # 1 as she has at Trial # 2. (See § 11.11.)

6. *Opportunity to examine.* Unless the judge at the first trial improperly restricted Drang's chance to cross-examine Angst, Drang has no basis to object here.

7. *Offering the testimony.* Sturm need only offer a certified copy of the trial transcript, or call the stenographer, or satisfy Fed. R. Evid., Art. IX in some other way.

§ 11.11 "SIMILAR MOTIVE"

Fed. R. Evid. 804(b)(1) requires that the adverse party had a "similar motive" to examine the witness at the prior proceeding. In other words, at the prior proceeding, the party against whom the former testimony is now being offered (or its "predecessor in interest") must have had a motive to develop the testimony of WPP ("witness at the prior proceeding"), on direct or cross-examination, similar to the motive the adverse party would have now in the current proceeding, if WPP was now available to testify.

A number of factors must be considered to determine whether that "similar motive" existed:

1. *Factual issue.* The key factual issues on which WPP's former testimony is now being offered must have been important issues at the former proceeding as well: did Drang run the red light (*see* § 11.10, question 1); did CPA boast to WPP1 about how he was cheating V (*see* § 11.13, Q. 1–5, *infra*). If the key issues at the prior and present proceedings are different, however (*see,* § 11.13, Q. 7), the former testimony should not be admitted.

2. *Same side.* The adverse party must have been on the same side of those factual issues at the former proceeding as it is now in the current proceeding. If subsequently discovered evidence has forced the party to change its cause of action or defense, so now it wishes to prove certain facts it previously sought to disprove, it is unlikely that it had the same motive to develop WPP's testimony at the former proceeding as it would now.

3. *Comparative importance of the issue at the two proceedings.* Even assuming the former testimony passes the first two tests, some courts are sympathetic to a party's objection that it did not have a "motive to develop the witness's testimony" at the former proceeding if the issue just was not as important then as it is at the current proceeding. The test must turn not only on whether the questioner is on the same side of the same issue at both proceedings, but also on whether the questioner had "a substantially similar degree of interest in *prevailing* on that issue i.e., "whether the party resisting the offered testimony at a pending proceeding had at a prior proceeding an interest of *substantially similar intensity* to prove (or disprove) the same side of a substantially similar issue."[4]

A number of factors may affect whether the adverse party had "a substantially similar degree of interest" at the two proceedings:

a. *The nature of the proceedings.* If the former and current proceedings were both trials, there is a substantial likelihood that the "degree of interest in prevailing" was the same at the first trial as it would be at the second. If the former proceeding was of a less significant kind — a grand jury proceeding, a deposition, a preliminary hearing in a criminal case — this weighs against sufficient "similarity of motive to develop" the witness's testimony. But this is *not* a dispositive factor, because courts often *do* admit preliminary hearing or deposition testimony.

b. *The burden of proof at the two proceedings.* In a grand jury or at a preliminary hearing, a prosecutor need only establish probable cause of a defendant's guilt; at trial, the burden is to prove guilt beyond a reasonable doubt. Thus, the prosecutor may not have as strong a motive to cross-examine and impeach an adverse witness at those earlier proceedings, particularly if doing so would reveal information or sources of information best kept hidden until trial. Similarly, a defense attorney at a preliminary

---

[4] *United States v. DiNapoli,* 8 F.3d 909, 912–914 (2d Cir. 1993) (en banc) (emphasis added).

hearing generally knows in advance that the judge will find probable cause. As a result, many defense attorneys simply try to get state witnesses to testify in as much detail as possible. This serves two purposes. First, it enables the defense to conduct some discovery of the state's case;[5] second, the more a state witness testifies at a preliminary hearing, the greater the likelihood that his trial testimony will contain inconsistencies about which the defense attorney can cross-examine him.

§ 11.12 "OPPORTUNITY"

So long as the adverse party had a reasonable opportunity at the prior proceeding to conduct direct, cross- or redirect examination similar in scope to what would be permitted at trial, the "opportunity" requirement is satisfied. Perhaps a major development intervening between the time of the former testimony and the current proceeding might overcome the rule's bias toward admissibility: the adverse party could argue that the changed circumstances makes the motive to develop WPP's testimony different, or that she never had an opportunity to develop WPP's testimony in light of the new development. But if the adverse party at the prior proceeding chose for *tactical* reasons not to examine the witness as extensively as she would now like, she will simply have to live with her choice.

§ 11.13 QUESTIONS

Question 1. V, a businessman, sued CPA, his former accountant, claiming CPA embezzled company funds. During pretrial discovery, V, in accordance with the Federal Rules of Civil Procedure, deposed WPP1, who had been living with CPA while CPA worked for V. WPP1 testified that CPA had boasted to her about how he was cheating V.

At trial, V offers the transcript of WPP1's deposition into evidence. CPA objects: hearsay. V responds: Fed. R. Evid. 804(b)(1). Ruling?

Ans. Sustained. V has made no showing that WPP1 is unavailable.

Question 2. Out of the hearing of the jury, V calls W2, his investigator, who testifies that he has learned that an anonymous benefactor gave WPP1 $20,000, which WPP1 is spending on a world cruise that set sail a few days before trial started. V again offers WPP1's deposition transcript. CPA objects: hearsay. Ruling?

Ans. Overruled. First, WPP1 is unavailable, per Rule 804(a)(5). (If I had to guess, I'd say WPP1's "mysterious benefactor" was probably CPA, who is better off by her absence — she isn't around to testify against him. Thus, the final clause of Rule 804(a) does not apply here because WPP1's absence was not procured by *V*, the party now proffering WPP1's former testimony.) Second, WPP1's former testimony satisfies Rule 804(b)(1).

---

[5] Unlike civil cases, in which litigants routinely depose all of the witnesses before trial, in federal courts and in most state courts, there is comparatively little discovery in criminal cases.

Note, by the way, that technically, this is a triple-hearsay issue. CPA made statements to WPP1; WPP1 testified at the deposition; the stenographer wrote down what WPP1 testified to. But P can easily overcome each level of hearsay:

a. *CPA's statement to WPP1.* CPA's statement to WPP1 isn't hearsay at all; it is an opposing party's statement per Rule 801(d)(2)(A).

b. *WPP1's former testimony.* WPP1's former testimony fits within Rule 804(b)(1):

1. *First-hand knowledge.* WPP1 testified at the deposition that she heard what CPA said, i.e., had first-hand knowledge of the words CPA spoke.

2. *Unavailability.* Rule 804(a)(5).

3. *Prior proceeding.* WPP1's testimony was given at a "lawful deposition" given in connection with this case.

4. *Identity of adverse party.* CPA was a party to the litigation when WPP1 was deposed; he is a party now.

5. *Motive to examine.* A pretrial deposition is conducted primarily for discovery, but arguably CPA had as powerful a motive to cross-examine WPP1 at the deposition as he would now at trial, if WPP1 were available.

6. *Opportunity to examine.* There are no meaningful restrictions on direct and cross-examination during pretrial depositions.

c. *Stenographer to transcript.* As to the final level of hearsay (the stenographer's act of recording WPP1's deposition testimony): if CPA is unwilling to stipulate to its accuracy and admissibility, V need merely call the stenographer or some other "qualified witness" to have the transcript authenticated as the stenographer's business record, under Rule 803(6).

Question 3. A jury returns a judgment for V. Thereafter, CPA is indicted for embezzlement. The prosecutor calls WPP1 (who is back from her extended sojourn abroad) as a witness. WPP1, proudly displaying a wedding band, says, "I refuse to testify against my husband," and produces a wedding certificate showing that she and CPA were married a week before the criminal trial began. The prosecutor offers WPP1's deposition transcript from the earlier civil ligation. CPA objects: hearsay. Ruling?

Ans. Overruled. Even though this is a criminal case and the prior litigation was a civil suit, the situation here is really quite similar to the previous question. Our analysis of issues 2-5 differs slightly from that in Question 2, but this does not change the outcome:

2. *Unavailability.* Most jurisdictions recognize a privilege which entitles a person not to testify against his or her spouse. WPP1 is therefore unavailable pursuant to Rule 804(a)(1).

3. *Prior proceeding.* WPP1's testimony was given at a deposition in a civil case, while the current trial is a criminal prosecution. This is not a problem, however; Rule 804(b)(1) explicitly includes, within the former testimony

exception, testimony given "at a . . . lawful deposition, . . . given during . . . a different [proceeding]."

4. *Identity of adverse party.* The parties aren't completely identical in this problem, the way they were in the previous problems. The deposition was taken in the case V v. CPA, but is now being offered in the case U.S. v. CPA. This is no bar to admissibility, though, because the rule only requires that the party *against whom* the testimony is offered (in this case, CPA) must have been a party at the prior proceeding.

5. *Motive to examine.* Even though the ultimate issues at the civil and criminal cases are somewhat different (civil liability v. guilt), as far as what WPP1 testified about, the issues are the same: did CPA make the statements WPP1 said he made, or was WPP1 fabricating to get back at him for jilting her? Thus, CPA's motive to cross-examine (and impeach) WPP1's testimony at the time of the deposition is probably the same as it would be now if she were a government witness at the criminal trial.

CPA can argue, with some plausibility, that a civil litigant's motive to cross-examination for *discovery* purposes at a pretrial deposition is very different than would be a criminal defendant's motive at trial. The underlying issue in each case was the same, however — did CPA embezzle money from V or not, and, as to WPP1, was she telling the truth or lying about what CPA allegedly said to her about it. Unless CPA can demonstrate some fundamental unfairness about using the transcript, a judge is likely to admit it, rather than force the prosecutor to forego the evidence altogether. And given that it was the defendant's own action (in marrying WPP1) that rendered WPP1 unavailable, CPA should not expect a judge to be overly sympathetic.

In fact, the prosecutor might have an interesting argument that by marrying WPP1, he forfeited his right to assert a hearsay objection, as per Rule 804(b)(6) (*see* § 11.50).

By the way, even though her marriage to CPA gives WPP1 the privilege to refuse to testify at CPA's trial, this in no way effects the admissibility of statements WPP1 made prior to their marriage.

Question 4. Police seize several kilograms of cocaine from an apartment, and arrest Tenant, the tenant, and Alsupp, Tenant's alleged supplier. At a pretrial motion to suppress, challenging the search and seizure, Tenant takes the stand and testifies that (among other things) Alsupp paid half of Tenant's rent in exchange for Tenant letting Alsupp use the apartment as a stash pad. Alsupp does not cross-examine.

The judge denies the defendants' motion to suppress, and Tenant pleads guilty. At Alsupp's trial, the prosecutor offers Tenant's suppression hearing testimony against Alsupp, who makes a timely hearsay objection. Ruling?

Ans. Sustained. The prosecutor has not demonstrated Tenant's unavailability.

Question 5. The prosecutor calls Tenant as a witness, but Tenant tells the judge, "I don't want to testify, because I'm afraid for my family." Does this suffice to establish Tenant's unavailability?

Ans. No. To be "unavailable" even though he is on the witness stand, Tenant must validly claim a testimonial privilege (Rule 804(a)(1)), or "persist in refusing to testify . . . *despite a court order to do so*" (Rule 804(a)(2)). The prosecutor must ask the judge to order Tenant to testify; only if Tenant still refuses is he "unavailable."

Question 6. Pursuant to the prosecutor's request in Question 5, the judge orders Tenant to testify. Tenant testifies fully about his own involvement with the apartment and the cocaine, but when the prosecutor asks him "Who brought the cocaine to the apartment?" Tenant responds, "I don't remember." He gives this same answer to all similar questions about who his supplier was. When asked, "Do you know this man sitting here?" (i.e., Alsupp), he again responds, "I don't remember." Does this establish Tenant's "unavailability"?

Ans. Yes, finally: Rule 804(a)(3). Even though Tenant has testified with regard to part of the "subject matter" of his testimony at the motion to suppress, his professed inability to recall other important details renders him "unavailable" as to those details.

Question 7. Now that we've finally shown Tenant to be unavailable, is his suppression hearing testimony admissible against Alsupp?

Ans. No. The facts in this problem satisfy all but one of the requirements of Rule 804(b)(1). If you don't already know which one, re-read Q. 4. If you have taken the basic criminal procedure course, recall what you learned about "standing" to challenge a search and seizure.

The key issue here is requirement # 5, *motive to examine* — specifically, Alsupp's motive to cross-examine at the suppression hearing vs. his motive do to so at the trial. At a motion to suppress, the legal issue is very different than it is at trial. In particular, a defendant must demonstrate his standing to challenge the legality of the search. Often this requires a defendant to offer evidence *connecting himself to the contraband and to the place where it was seized.* Thus, at the suppression hearing, Alsupp had absolutely no reason to impeach Tenant's testimony, because, in the context of a suppression hearing, Tenant's testimony *helped* Alsupp establish his right to challenge the legality of the search of the apartment.

At Alsupp's trial, by contrast, Alsupp wants to *challenge* any evidence the government offers tending to connect him to the apartment or the cocaine. Tenant's suppression-hearing testimony connecting Alsupp to the apartment and the drugs, which was so helpful to Alsupp at the hearing, is now very damaging to Alsupp at trial. Alsupp's motive to cross-examine Tenant at trial, therefore, would be very different than it was at the suppression hearing.

Objection sustained.

Question 8. In a breach of contract trial, Rhapsody v. Blue, Rhapsody called Ms Clara Nette, expecting her to testify that Rhapsody complied with his contractual obligation to deliver 500 class-A midget widgets to Blue. To Rhapsody's surprise, though, Ms Nette testified that the midget widgets Rhapsody delivered were of inferior quality and didn't meet contract specifications. Flustered, Rhapsody's attorney floundered a bit, asked a few clumsy and ineffectual questions, and muttered,

"Nothing further." Delighted, Blue proclaimed, "Your Honor, we have no questions of this obviously truthful witness."

It becomes necessary to retry the case. At the second trial, Blue offers a transcript of Ms Nette's first-trial testimony. Rhapsody objects: hearsay. Blue responds: Rule 804(b)(1). Ruling?

Ans. Sustained. Blue has not shown that Ms Nette is unavailable.

Question 9. Blue submits an affidavit from Ms Nette's doctor attesting that she is unable to testify. Does this suffice to show that Ms Nette is unavailable? If so, is Ms Nette's testimony now admissible under Rule 804(b)(1)?

Ans. Yes; and yes. Ms Nette is unavailable per Rule 804(a)(4). The judge has discretion to accept such an affidavit, or even a simple letter, as proof that a witness is unavailable.

This question differs from the preceding ones because here, *Rhapsody* called the witness at the first proceeding, while *Blue* is offering the testimony at the new proceeding. This is no bar to admissibility, however. Go through the checklist again. The key issues are:

4. *Identity of adverse party.* Rhapsody was a party at the prior trial; he is a party at this one.

5. *Motive to examine.* Ms Nette's testimony related to the same issue at each trial: whether Rhapsody complied with his contractual obligations.

6. *Opportunity to examine.* Even though Rhapsody conducted direct examination of Ms Nette at the first trial and would be cross-examining Ms Nette if she testified at the second trial, this is no bar to admissibility. Rule 804(b)(1) requires that the party against whom the testimony is now being offered (i.e., Rhapsody) "had an opportunity and similar motive to develop the testimony by direct, cross- or redirect examination." Rhapsody had his opportunity; he just blew it.

Rhapsody may argue that he didn't really have the opportunity, because he was taken by surprise. Similarly, Rhapsody may argue that he didn't really have the same motive in Trial #1 as he would in Trial #2: having called Ms Nette as his own witness in Trial #1, he decided as a matter of tactics to get her off the stand as quickly as possible, whereas if Blue called Ms Nette in the second trial, Rhapsody would go at her, hammer and tongs. Rhapsody has a legitimate complaint here: the tactical situation *is* rather different.

But the judge has to make a choice here: if she saves Rhapsody from the impact of his own tactical decisions, she deprives Blue of valuable evidence not otherwise available. In all likelihood, Rhapsody's objection will be overruled.

§ 11.14 OBJECTIONS

Can the party against whom the prior testimony is now being offered object to portions of the transcript, if objections could have been made at the prior proceeding, but were not?

The best, and prevailing, approach divides such objections into two categories:

(1) Objections that go to *substantive* evidence issues, such as those addressed in Articles IV, V, VII and VIII of the Federal Rules — i.e., objections that go to whether the offering party should be allowed to offer the *content* of the evidence — may be made for the first time at the new proceeding at which the former testimony is being offered.

(2) Objections that go primarily to *procedure or form*, in contrast (leading questions, unresponsive answers, answers more in the form of opinion than fact), cannot be made at the current proceeding if they were not made at the prior proceeding.

The rationale for making this distinction is that the first category addresses whether the evidence is inadmissible per se; no one would be unfairly disadvantaged if inherently inadmissible evidence is excluded from the new proceeding. On the other hand, objectionable aspects of evidence falling into the second category probably could have been corrected at the prior proceeding if a timely objection had been made, so it is unfair to exclude it at the new proceeding.

§ 11.15 QUESTIONS

Question 1. At a civil negligence trial Sweet v. Sour, Sweet offers the following passage from a transcript of the direct examination of an eye witness, Ms Jones, at a pretrial deposition. Assuming all the requirements of Rule 804(b)(1) have been satisfied, what issue may the adverse party nevertheless raise, and how should the judge rule?

Q.   Miss Jones, when you first saw the red car, it was halfway up the block, is that right?

A.   Yes.

Q.   And you noticed immediately that it was weaving from side to side as it approached the intersection?

A.   Yes.

Ans. The attorney asked leading questions.[6] This would be entirely proper if the Q&A had been during cross-examination, but it is generally impermissible to ask leading questions on direct examination. *See* Fed. R. Evid. 611(c). The first paragraph of this question stated that this Q&A occurred during direct examination. Thus, the

---

[6] A "leading question" is one which clearly indicates the answer the questioner hopes to receive. Under some circumstances (but not all), a question may also be leading if it must be answered "yes" or "no."

questions were improper. Nevertheless, this objection goes to form, not substance. Objection overruled.

Question 2. Direct examination of Ms Jones continued:

Q.   What happened when the red car neared the intersection?

A.   Well, Charlie told me later that it started to slow down but then picked up speed again as the light turned red.

Ans. What Charlie told Ms Jones is hearsay; unless Sweet can convince the judge that "Charlie's" statement to the witness comes within a hearsay exception, it should be excluded. A hearsay objection will be sustained.

Question 3. Direct examination continues:

Q.   What did the blue car do as the light changed?

A.   I saw that the red car was definitely going too fast.

Ans. The answer is unresponsive to the question — the question was about the blue car, but Ms Jones testified about the red car. But if counsel had asked Ms Jones, "What if anything did you notice about the red car," Ms Jones would have been permitted to testify that she saw the red car being driven too fast: she had first-hand knowledge and the information is relevant. Thus the problem with her testimony in Q.3 is merely one of form or procedure. Objection overruled.

Question 4. Sour, the defendant in the case, also testified at a pretrial deposition, during which Sweet cross-examined Sour as follows:

Q.   Did you try to settle this thing without going to court?

A.   Well, I figured, —

Q.   Didn't you offer my client $500 if he'd forget the whole thing and not sue you?

A.   Yes, I did. I didn't realize he was gonna make a federal case out of it.

Assume that Sour has since suffered a stroke and is physically unable to testify. Sweet offers this portion of Sour's deposition transcript into evidence, citing Rule 804(b)(1) and, for that matter, Rule 801(d)(2)(A), as well. What objections should Sour's attorney assert; how should the judge rule?

Ans. Even though this Q&A satisfies both Rule 801(d)(2)(A) and Rule 804(b)(1), those rules only overcome a hearsay objection. Sour should, instead, object that the evidence should be excluded per Fed. R. Evid. 408, which generally excludes evidence of attempts to compromise pending or potential lawsuits. Objection sustained.[7]

---

[7] In the real world, Sour's attorney probably would object solely on Rule 408 grounds, and would not bother making a hearsay objection, because she would know that the hearsay objection would be overruled. If you get a question like this on an evidence exam, however, you should discuss both issues, hearsay and Rule 408. Explain that although Rules 801(d)(2)(A) and 804(b)(1) each overcome the hearsay objection, the evidence is nevertheless excluded by Rule 408.

§ 11.16 "PREDECESSOR IN INTEREST"

The original Advisory Committee draft of Rule 804(b)(1) would have admitted former testimony so long as the party against whom it was offered, or a party "with motive and interest similar" to his, had an opportunity to develop the witness' testimony at the former proceeding. The House Judiciary Committee rejected this language, reasoning:

> [I]t is generally unfair to impose upon the party against whom the hearsay evidence is being offered responsibility for the manner in which the witness was previously handled by another party. The sole exception to this, in the Committee's view, is when a party's predecessor in interest in a civil action or proceeding had an opportunity and similar motive to examine the witness.

Congress amended the draft of Rule 804(b)(1) to reflect the House Committee's position. Courts have taken a variety of approaches to interpreting the "predecessor in interest" clause.

1. The "privity" approach

One approach is to read the phrase "predecessor in interest" in the traditional, narrow sense of privity. Under this interpretation, X would be Y's "predecessor in interest" in a lawsuit only if Y "inherited" the suit from X. Examples:

- Parent brought a breach of contract action against Z. After pretrial depositions, Parent died, and Child, Parent's executor, continues the lawsuit on behalf of Parent's estate. Child is Parent's "successor in interest"; Parent was Child's "predecessor in interest." Thus, Parent's handling of depositions, etc. is attributable to Child for purposes of Rule 804(b)(1).

- M Co. and Ax, Inc. merged, to form MAX Corp. Shortly before the merger, a lawsuit brought by P against M Co. resulted in a judgment. After the merger, that judgment was reversed, and a new trial was ordered. This time, P is suing MAX Corp., because MAX now "owns" not only M's assets but also its potential liabilities. M was MAX's predecessor in interest; hence, the manner in which M's attorneys examined witnesses in the previous litigation is now attributable to MAX Corp.

2. The "community of interests" approach

Some courts, by contrast, have substantially ignored the clear congressional intent to limit "predecessor in interest." The leading example is *Lloyd v. American Export Lines, Inc.*, 580 F.2d 1179, 1185 (3d Cir.), *cert. denied*, 439 U.S. 969 (1978). In *Lloyd*, the Third Circuit essentially nullified Congress' revision of the Advisory Committee draft of Rule 804(b)(1), by defining the phrase "predecessor in interest" to mean "community of interest." Alvarez and Lloyd were crewmen on a ship operated by American Export. They fought, and each sued American Export, each alleging that the company negligently failed to protect him from the other. The two civil suits were consolidated into one case for purposes of trial.

Prior to the trial of these civil actions, however, the Coast Guard brought a proceeding against Lloyd, charging Lloyd with assaulting Alvarez. At the Coast Guard hearing, Lloyd testified, and was cross-examined by counsel for the Coast Guard, about the fight and other relevant matters. (Neither Alvarez nor American Export were parties at the Coast Guard proceeding.)

Lloyd subsequently disappeared, so only Alvarez' suit against American Export went to trial (although the case retained the formal title, "*Lloyd v. American Export Lines, Inc.*"). American Export sought to offer in evidence Lloyd's testimony at the Coast Guard hearing. Alvarez interposed a hearsay objection; American Export cited Rule 804(b)(1). The trial judge sustained the objection. The trial judge reasoned, first, that because Alvarez — the "adverse party" against whom Lloyd's testimony was now being offered — had not been a party to the Coast Guard proceeding, he had had no opportunity to cross-examine Lloyd; and second, that the Coast Guard was not Alvarez' "predecessor in interest"; therefore, Lloyd's prior testimony did not satisfy Rule 804(b)(1).

The Third Circuit reversed. The Coast Guard, the court pointed out, had the same goal in cross-examining Lloyd at the earlier hearing as Alvarez would have to cross-examine Lloyd if Lloyd were available at the civil trial. The main issue in each case, after all, was whether the altercation was Lloyd's fault or Alvarez'; the Coast Guard was attempting to place the blame on Lloyd at the hearing, just as Alvarez would try to do at trial. Because Alvarez and the Coast Guard shared a sufficient "community of interest," the Third Circuit reasoned, the Coast Guard was Alvarez' "predecessor in interest" for purposes of Rule 804(b)(1).

One judge concurred in the result in *Lloyd*, but accused the *Lloyd* majority of ignoring the intent with which Congress revised the original draft of Rule 804(b)(1). He also pointed out that because the Coast Guard did not represent Alvarez, its attorney's choice of issues, tactics and strategy might differ substantially from those Alvarez might use at trial.

3. The "formal ties" approach[8]

Some courts have attempted to define a middle ground between strict "privity" and "community in interest," permitting former testimony to be offered against a party in the current trial so long as that party had some formal ties with a party who in the prior proceeding had a "similar motive" to develop the witness's testimony, even if those formal ties were not enough to amount to common-law privity. Suppose, for example, a case goes to trial: XYZ v. Smallcorp, Inc. Ms Small is Smallcorp's chief executive officer and majority stock holder. At that trial, XYZ calls Twain as a witness. Twain testifies about a meeting she had with McBride, Lambert, Brooks and Dunn.

Later on, Ms Small brings a law suit against MNO Co. The lineup:

Prior trial:	XYZ	v	Smallcorp, Inc.
Current trial:	Ms Small	v	MNO.

That same meeting is relevant at the current trial. MNO establishes that Twain is no longer available, then offers Twain's testimony from XYZ v. Smallcorp against Ms

---

[8] By "formal ties," I do *not* intend any reference to what men wear with tuxedos.

Small. Ms Small objects that she was not a party to the first trial, and that the former testimony exception therefore does not apply. Some jurisdictions have suggested that in such a case, even though no privity relationship exists between Smallcorp, Inc. and Ms Small, the formal ties between them are strong enough to satisfy the "identity of adverse party" requirement.

Which of these three approaches should you discuss, if confronted with a quiz or exam question that raises the "predecessor in interest" issue? Whichever one (or two or three) your professor tells you to apply, naturally. (I tell my students to apply all three: "If this jurisdiction applies the 'privity' approach, the judge should . . . If it applies the 'community of interest' approach, the court should . . . If it applies the 'formal ties' approach, the court should . . .' ")

§ 11.17 QUESTIONS

Question 1. Several cars collide when a tractor-trailer overturns on an interstate highway. P1 suffers a bruised shoulder; her car sustains $1200 in damages. P2, in another auto, is terribly burned and will require intensive medical treatment for the rest of his life.

P1 and P2 each sue Transit Co., which owned and operated the truck. The key issue is whether Transit's truck overturned because Transit's driver failed to pay attention, as plaintiffs claim, or, as Transit insists, was the truck suddenly cut off by a red sports car, forcing Transit's driver to swerve suddenly to avoid crushing that car but tragically, to overturn and involve several other vehicles.

P1 retains Newbie, an attorney fresh out of school (not *your* school, but your cross-town or cross-state rival). Newbie brings an action against Transit in state court seeking $5,000 for pain, suffering, expenses and lost wages. Meanwhile, P2's family has retained Oldpro, a leading personal injury attorney; Oldpro files an action in federal district court seeking $14 million in actual and punitive damages. Thus:

In state court: P1 (represented by Newbie) v Transit
In federal court: P2 (represented by Oldpro) v Transit

Because Newbie has very few cases while Oldpro is juggling a heavy calendar, P1's action moves a bit more quickly than P2's. At a pretrial deposition, Newbie deposes WPP1, Transit's driver, and WPP2, an apparently impartial eyewitness. Newbie's inexperience is apparent throughout the proceeding, but Transit, who is anxious to do the right thing if it doesn't cost too much, ultimately settles with P1 anyway.

Shortly thereafter, WPP1 dies and WPP2 quits his job to fulfill a lifelong ambition to backpack from Lisbon to Tierra del Fuego.[9] When P2's case comes to trial, Transit offers the deposition testimony from P1's suit; P2 objects on hearsay grounds. Ruling?

Ans. Applying the § 11.9 checklist:

---

[9] Do you think he'll succeed? (Check a map.)

1. *First-hand knowledge.* It seems clear that WPP1 and WPP2 both had first-hand knowledge of how the accident developed.

2. *Unavailable.* WPP1 and WPP2 are both unavailable.

3. *Nature of prior proceeding.* It does not matter that the prior proceeding was a pretrial deposition in a state case and this is a federal trial, so long as the other requirements of Fed. R. Evid. 804(b)(1) are satisfied.

4. *Identity of adverse party.* This is the essential issue: was P1 the "predecessor in interest" to P2?

> Under Rule 804(b)(1) as the House Judiciary Committee intended it to be applied, the objection would be sustained. Although P1 and P2's claims arose out of the same accident, they are involved in completely separate lawsuits. There is no privity between P1 and P2; therefore P1 was not P2's "predecessor in interest," and the deposition testimony of WPP1 and WPP2 in the deposition of P1 v Transit is not admissible in P2 v Transit.

> Nor are there any "formal ties" between P1 and P2; the only thing they had in common was the misfortune of being involved in the same accident. Thus, the deposition testimony of WPP1 and WPP2 in P1 v Transit is not admissible in P2 v Transit.

> Under the *Lloyd* approach, however, P2's hearsay objection would be overruled. The factual issue in P1's suit was the same as in P2's suit (i.e., what caused Transit's driver to swerve, resulting in the tractor-trailer overturning). P1's interest in developing the testimony of WPP1 and WPP2 is the same as P2's interest: to cast doubts on Transit's version of events and if possible substantiate plaintiffs' theory. Therefore, according to *Lloyd*, P1 *was* P2's "predecessor in interest," and P2 is stuck with Newbie's clumsy and ineffectual attempt to examine WPP1 and WPP2.

5. *Motive to examine.* The issues at the P1 v Transit deposition and the P2 v Transit trial are the same: whether the accident was proximately caused by Transit's driver's negligence. This requirement is satisfied.

6. *Opportunity to examine.* P1 had an unrestricted opportunity to depose WPP1 and WPP2.

Thus, the admissibility of the depositions WPP1 and WPP2 gave in P1 v Transit depend entirely on how the court interprets "predecessor in interest."

§ 11.18   OTHER RULES AND EXCEPTIONS

Students sometimes assume that, if a party offers in evidence testimony that was given at a prior proceeding, Fed. R. Evid. 804(b)(1) is the *only* hearsay exception that can apply. Do not make this mistake. Even if that prior-proceeding testimony does not satisfy Rule 804(b)(1), the offering party can nevertheless overcome a hearsay objection if it satisfies any other Article VIII provision, such as Fed. R. Evid. 801(d)(1)(A), 801(d)(1)(B), 801(d)(2)(A)–(E), 803(5).

§ 11.19   SIXTH AMENDMENT CONFRONTATION CLAUSE

Former testimony is by definition "testimonial." Nevertheless, any former testimony offered in a criminal case that satisfies Fed. R. Evid. 804(b)(1) automatically satisfies the Confrontation Clause. In *Crawford*, the Court said that a testimonial statement could be admitted against a defendant (a) if the declarant was no longer available, and (b) the defendant had a prior opportunity to confront and cross-examine the declarant about the statement. This is precisely what Rule 804(b)(1) requires.

2. Statement Under Belief of Impending Death ("Dying Declarations")

§ 11.20   INTRODUCTION

The law has long recognized a hearsay exception, in homicide cases, for dying declarations. A declarant who knew he was about to die could be trusted to tell the truth about who had caused his soon-to-be-mortal injury, the reasoning went, because no one would be so foolish as to die with a lie on his lips, thereby condemning his soul to eternal damnation or, at least, an extensive stay in purgatory. The exception applied only if the declarant in fact died, and the defendant was on trial for killing the declarant.

Today we are much more knowledgeable about human nature,[10] and furthermore, many people are skeptical about the existence of a soul or life after death. The law nevertheless has retained the dying declaration exception. As the Advisory Committee put it, "While the original religious justification for the exception may have lost its conviction for some persons over the years, it can scarcely be doubted that powerful psychological pressures are present"[11] — pressures which, we hope, produce, even in a nonbeliever, a powerful impulse to speak only the truth.

§ 11.21   RULE 804(b)(2): STATEMENT UNDER BELIEF OF IMPENDING DEATH

Fed. R. Evid. 804(b)(2) provides:

(b) **The Exceptions. The following are not excluded by the rule against hearsay if the declarant is unavailable as a witness: . . .**

(2) *Statement Under the Belief of Imminent Death.* **In a prosecution for homicide or in a civil case, a statement that the declarant, while believing the declarant's death to be imminent, made about its cause or circumstances.**

[Prior to December 1, 2011, the rule read as follows:

---

[10] We *think* we are much more knowledgeable, anyway.

[11] Advisory Committee Note to Fed. R. Evid. 804(b)(2), 56 F.R.D. 183, 326.

(b) Hearsay exceptions. The following are not excluded by the hearsay rule if the declarant is unavailable as a witness: . . .

(2) Statement under belief of impending death. In a prosecution for homicide or in a civil action or proceeding, a statement made by a declarant while believing that the declarant's death was imminent, concerning the cause or circumstances of what the declarant believed to be his impending death.

The Federal Rules of Evidence were rewritten solely to make them easier to understand; the Advisory Committee did not intend to make any substantive change in the Rules. The text of the old rule may remain useful in reading court decisions that precede the revision of the rules. Thus, this edition of the Student's Guide provides the text of both the new and the old version of each relevant provision of the Federal Rules of Evidence.]

The following is an outline of requirements and issues that may arise when applying Rule 804(b)(2), including several changes from the rule's common law antecedent.

1. The declarant (DL) must have had first-hand knowledge of the facts asserted in his statement.

2. The declarant must be unavailable, as defined in Rule 804(a).

3. DL must have believed his death was imminent and certain at the time he made the statement.

4. The statement must have concerned the cause or circumstances of [what DL believed to be] his imminent impending death.

5. *Use in civil litigation.* In civil litigation (e.g., in a personal injury suit for damages), a litigant may use Rule 804(b)(2) *even if DL did not in fact die*, so long as DL is "unavailable" under 804(a).

6. *Use in criminal litigation.* Either a prosecutor or a defendant may invoke the exception, but only in a "prosecution for homicide." *See* § 11.23.

7. *Sixth Amendment Confrontation Clause.* The post-Crawford status of "dying declarations" is uncertain. *See* § 11.24.

§ 11.22   SATISFYING THE REQUIREMENTS

Often the statement itself will provide the necessary proof that DL had first-hand knowledge of the facts asserted in the statement and believed that death was certain and imminent. Back when I was growing up and western (cowboy) movies and TV shows were as big as *Law and Order, CSI*, "reality" shows, talent shows, and pro football combined,[12] you could watch a scene like this a couple of times a month:

Lance comes upon his friend Jim lying on the ground, hand clutched to his stomach.

---

[12] This was before cable, the Internet, video games (or for that matter, video *tape*), computers or FM radio. Most communities had, maybe, 5 TV stations or fewer.

Lance: Jim! What happened?

Jim: I know I'm a goner; not even a miracle could save me now. It was that low-down varmint Clyde what done it. He walked up behind me, tapped me on the shoulder, and when I turned around to face him he just smiled and unloaded his six-shooter in my belly. Tell Lu-Ann I always loved her. Tell her I never blamed her for loving you more'n she loved me —

(As Jim dies, his head cradled in Lance's arms, the camera catches the conflicting emotions on Lance's face — sorrow at the loss of his friend, a grim determination that Clyde will be brought to justice, and wonderment at learning that Lu-Ann, whom he had secretly loved since they were children, might actually love him too.)

Clyde is charged with murdering Jim,[13] and the prosecutor calls Lance to testify as to Jim's last words. Jim's statement satisfies each of the Rule 804(b)(2) requirements:

1. Jim saw who shot him, so he had first-hand knowledge of the what he told Lance.

2. Jim is dead, which establishes his unavailability.

3. He believed his death was imminent and certain ("I know I'm a goner").

4. The statement concerned the cause of his impending death.

5. (Civil litigation: not applicable).

6. The statement therefore should be admitted in a prosecution of Clyde for killing Jim, although Clyde could, if he wanted, exclude the portion of Jim's statement relating to Lu-Ann, since that statement does not "concern the cause or circumstances of what [Jim] believed to be his impending death."

These requirements can also be satisfied in other ways. For example:

Lance: Jim, Doc says you can't hold on much longer. Tell me who did this to you and I swear I'll see him hang for it!

Jim: I didn't see who done it. I didn't know anybody else was there! But then I heard somebody behind me. One of his boots squeaks real loud. I was 'bout to turn around to see who it was when BAM! he shot me in the back. . . . Find the varmint with a boot that squeaks real loud, Lance! He's the one —

In this variation, Lance's statement to Jim ("Doc says you can't hold on much longer") establishes that Jim was aware that death was certain and imminent; and while Jim was unable to identify the perpetrator, his statement demonstrates first-hand knowledge that the man who shot him in the back wore a very squeaky boot. When Lance notices, a few days later, that Wily Landgrabber, who had been

---

[13] In the movie or TV show, of course, Clyde met his well-deserved end in a shootout on main street. Usually Lance was the one who out-drew and out-shot him; occasionally it was Lu-Ann, who came to the rescue after Clyde managed unfairly to get the jump on Lance. But this book is about hearsay, not 1950's popular entertainment, so I have to deviate from the usual script.

attempting to force farmers like Jim off their land, has a squeaky boot, Jim's dying declaration becomes admissible circumstantial evidence that Landgrabber is the killer.

§ 11.23   "UNAVAILABILITY"; "PROSECUTIONS FOR HOMICIDE"

In every "dying declaration" case I can recall reading, the facts fit a pattern like the two scenarios in the previous question: the declarant is dead, and the defendant is charged with killing him. But Fed. R. Evid. 804(b)(2) as written can be interpreted somewhat more broadly. Suppose, for example, D is charged with viciously assaulting V1 and V2. V1 died instantly, but V2 remained conscious; when an ambulance arrived, he gasped to the emergency medical technician (EMT): "I know nothing can save me; D was the one who killed us," and then lapsed into a coma. D is now on trial for the murder of V1 and the attempted murder of V2 (who is still in a coma; or who, perhaps, made a remarkable recovery, everything considered, but can recall nothing about the events in question). The rule, as written, would allow the prosecutor to use V2's statement to the EMT: although declarant V2 is alive, he is unavailable, per Fed. R. Evid. 804(a)(4) (if he is in a coma) or 804(a)(3) (if he has amnesia as to the assault), and the trial is a "prosecution for homicide," even though the victim in question is V1, not the declarant.

§ 11.24   SIXTH AMENDMENT CONFRONTATION CLAUSE

In his majority opinion in *Crawford v. Washington*, Justice Scalia, while discussing the history of the Confrontation Clause and hearsay exceptions that existed at the time of its ratification, commented: "[T]here is scant evidence that exceptions were invoked to admit *testimonial* statements against the accused in a *criminal* case." In a footnote, Justice Scalia acknowledged:

> The one deviation we have found involves dying declarations. The existence of that exception as a general rule of criminal hearsay law cannot be disputed. [Citing various 18th and 19th Century authorities.] Although many dying declarations may not be testimonial, there is authority for admitting even those that clearly are. [Citing sources.] We need not decide in this case whether the Sixth Amendment incorporates an exception for testimonial dying declarations. If this exception must be accepted on historical grounds, it is *sui generis.*[14]

We have no clear indication yet how lower courts will ultimately respond to this language. One could reasonably conclude that all dying declarations are admissible over a Confrontation Clause objection, whether they are testimonial or not; or that testimonial dying declarations must be excluded by the Clause.

If you are confronted with a dying declaration on a quiz or exam, then, the safest approach is to apply the § 6.10 Confrontation Clause check list. Assume it is a criminal case, and that the statement satisfies Fed. R. Evid. 804(b)(2) and is offered for the

---

[14] *Crawford*, 541 U.S. at 54 & n 6.

hearsay purpose of proving who killed the declarant. That takes us through ¶¶ C. We can also skip over ¶¶ D–G, and reach:

¶ H. Is the statement testimonial?

In discussing this issue, state the arguments on both sides. If the statement was made to someone other than a police officer, D must argue that a statement made by someone who knows (or believes) he is about to die, accusing D of being the killer, certainly fulfills the description of " '[a] solemn declaration or affirmation made for the purpose of establishing or proving some fact' " and is therefore testimonial (see § 6.7). If the statement was made in response to police questioning, P will argue, per *Davis v. Washington* and *Michigan v. Bryant*, that the statement was made in "emergency" circumstances and therefore was not testimonial.

Next, still discussing the testimoniality issue, you should add that Justice Scalia, in dictum, speculated that (testimonial) dying declarations, because of their unique history, might be exempt from the Confrontation Clause. Then again, they might not. Finally, with regard to ¶¶ I–L, apply the checklist.

§ 11.25 OTHER HEARSAY EXCEPTIONS

Any time a fact pattern appears to require a discussion of Fed. R. Evid. 804(b)(2), you should also consider whether the facts also require discussing Fed. R. Evid. 803(2) ("excited utterance") and, particularly, Fed. R. Evid. 804(b)(5), the "forfeiture by wrongdoing" exception covered at the end of this chapter.

§ 11.26 QUESTIONS

Question 1. D is on trial for murdering his wife, DL. The state has presented evidence that DL became violently ill on May 20. She was rushed to the hospital and, after several days on the critical list, seemed to be recovering, only to suffer a relapse on June 1; she died on June 3. The state presents forensic evidence that her death was caused by ingestion of arsenic, together with related medical complications. Next, the prosecutor calls W1, a nurse who cared for DL in the hospital. W1 will, if permitted, testify:

DL said, "If I die, tell the police it was my husband. He poisoned the bottle of bourbon I keep behind the hat boxes on the shelf in my closet!" Would this testimony be admissible under Rule 804(b)(2), if D interposes a hearsay objection?

Ans. No. Although DL's statement to W1 satisfies the second and fourth requirements (DL is unavailable and the statement concerns the cause of her subsequent death), it is does not satisfy the first or third requirement. It is doubtful that she had actual *knowledge* that someone poisoned the bourbon, let alone who; the statement sounds more like speculation than a recitation of something she observed. Moreover, the evidence does not show that DL believed her death was certain and imminent; she said "*If* I die," not "*When* I die."

Question 2. P sues for personal injuries suffered when a moving vehicle struck him as he was crossing the street. No one saw the incident, and P suffers from partial amnesia and can no longer recall anything about it. An ambulance attendant will testify that, as P was being rushed to the hospital, he kept muttering, "I'm not gonna make it, I'm not gonna make it. It was a green SUV, Indiana plates, XYZ — I couldn't see the rest. Oh, no, why did this have to happen now, when the Cubs are about to win the World Series![15] I'm not gonna make it. . . ." Does Rule 804(b)(2) overcome D's hearsay objection?

Ans. Perhaps. P will argue that each of the Rule 804(b)(2) requirements are satisfied:

1. P had first-hand knowledge of the facts he asserted — he saw the style, color and partial plate of the vehicle that struck him.

2. Even though P is alive, because he can no longer remember what happened, he is "unavailable" (*see* Rule 804(a)(3)).

3. At the time, P believed his death was imminent and certain ("I'm not gonna make it. . . .").

4. The statement concerned the cause of what P believed to be his imminent demise.

5. Rule 804(b)(2) may be used in civil litigation even though P is still alive.

D will argue, on the other hand, that P's comment about the Cubs suggests that P was not really convinced of his impending death: someone who is about to die wouldn't be worried about a mere sporting event (although, to a diehard Cubs fan,[16] this argument is a sure loser).

A judge could go either way.

3. Statements Against Interest

§ 11.27   RULE 804(b)(3)

Fed. R. Evid. 804(b)(3) provides as follows:

(b) The Exceptions. The following are not excluded by the rule against hearsay if the declarant is unavailable as a witness:

(3) *Statement Against Interest.* A statement that:

(A) a reasonable person in the declarant's position would have made only if the person believed it to be true because, when made, it was so contrary to the declarant's proprietary or pecuniary interest or had so great a tendency to invalidate the declarant's claim against

---

[15] This is a baseball reference. The Chicago Cubs last won a World Series in 1908, and haven't even been in one since 1945, a record of ineptitude among professional sport franchises surpassed only by the French Army, whose losing streak stretches back several centuries.

[16] If you recognize the name "Steve Bartman," you may qualify.

someone else or to expose the declarant to civil or criminal liability; and

(B) is supported by corroborating circumstances that clearly indicate its trustworthiness, if it is offered in a criminal case as one that tends to expose the declarant to criminal liability.

[Prior to December 1, 2011, the rule read as follows:

(b) Hearsay exceptions. The following are not excluded by the hearsay rule if the declarant is unavailable as a witness:

(3) Statement against interest. A statement which was at the time of its making so far contrary to the declarant's pecuniary or proprietary interest, or so far tended to subject the declarant to civil or criminal liability, or to render invalid a claim by the declarant against another, that a reasonable person in the declarant's position would not have made the statement unless believing it to be true. A statement tending to expose the declarant to criminal liability and offered to exculpate the accused is not admissible unless corroborating circumstances clearly indicate the trustworthiness of the statement.

The Federal Rules of Evidence were rewritten solely to make them easier to understand; the Advisory Committee did not intend to make any substantive change in the Rules. The text of the old rule may remain useful in reading court decisions that precede the revision of the rules. Thus, this edition of the Student's Guide provides the text of both the new and the old version of each relevant provision of the Federal Rules of Evidence.]

The justification for this provision is that a person is unlikely to say something that is against her own best interests (i.e., that might later be used against her), unless what she says is true. The key to this exception is that the statement must have been against the declarant's own interests *at the time she made the statement.*

At common law, the "statement against interest" exception included only statements against the declarant's financial ("pecuniary and proprietary") interests. Rule 804(b)(3) also includes statements that would have a negative effect on a potential civil law suit, and statements which tend to expose the declarant to criminal prosecution.

It is best to approach Rule 804(b)(3) as if it was three separate rules. The first covers declarations against financial, proprietary, litigational or penal interest in *civil* cases; this use of the Rule is comparatively rare. The second covers a criminal defendant's use of the declarant's statement against penal interest as evidence of the defendant's innocence, as where a declarant says, in words or substance, "D did not commit that crime, *I* committed it." The third covers a prosecutor's use of a declarant's statement against penal interest as evidence of the defendant's guilt, where a declarant says something that tends to incriminate himself and also tends to incriminate the defendant.

First, though, let's focus on one aspect of the rule that is common to all three situations.

§ 11.28 "BELIEVED IT TO BE TRUE"

It is worth noting that Fed. R. Evid. 804(b)(3)(A) varies the usual formula for hearsay exceptions. The explicit or implicit requirement found in most exceptions, that the declarant have first-hand knowledge, is replaced by the requirement that the declarant *"believed [the statement] to be true."* As a general rule, of course, the fact that a declarant believed that what he said is true is, by itself, not enough to guarantee trustworthiness. With regard to Rule 804(b)(3), however, trustworthiness supposedly is assured from the fact that, in the context and setting in which the declarant said it, the statement itself is seriously dis-serving, not self-serving.

§ 11.29 USE IN CIVIL LITIGATION; "INTERESTS" INCLUDED WITHIN THE RULE

When used in civil litigation, application of Fed. R. Evid. 804(b)(3)(A) imposes the following requirements and raises the following issues:

1. Declarant either had first-hand knowledge, or at least believed that what he said was true.

2. Declarant must be unavailable, as defined in Rule 804(a).

3. *"Interests" included within the Rule.* The Rule covers only pecuniary, proprietary, litigational and penal interests. Statements contrary to other "interests" are not admissible within the exception.

4. *"So contrary . . . so great a tendency . . ."* The statement need not be unequivocally dis-serving; it suffices that it was sufficiently "contrary" to declarant's pecuniary or proprietary interest, or was sufficiently "contrary" to declarant's litigational or penal interest. Remember that we must determine whether it was against the declarant's interest at the time he made the statement. This depends upon the factual context in which the statement was made. *See* § 11.30.

5. *Individual declaration or narration as a whole.* In *United States v. Williamson*, 512 U.S. 594, 602–604 (1994), the Supreme Court held that when a prosecutor offers a statement that was against the declarant's penal interest as evidence against a different defendant, it is necessary to examine each declaration within an utterance to determine whether it was sufficiently against the declarant's interest, rather than considering the declarant's narrative as a whole. Courts have applied this approach to the meaning of "statement" to other aspects of Rule 804(b)(3), and to hearsay statements in general. See § 11.38.

6. *Relationship to other rules.* Rule 804(b)(3) is sometimes confused with Rule 801(d)(2), "admissions of party opponent." *See* § 11.31.

A statement acknowledging a debt ("I owe X $5,000") could be against declarant's pecuniary interest, as could a statement acknowledging that a debt has been paid ("Y has paid me everything he owes me"). A statement acknowledging non-ownership of real or personal property could be contrary to proprietary interest ("I don't own the

Porsche, I borrowed it from my brother-in-law"). § 11.32 **Q. 1** offers an example of a statement tending to expose declarant to civil liability. A statement conceding contributory negligence would tend to "invalidate the declarant's claim against someone else . . ."

The Advisory Committee proposed that Rule 804(b)(3) also include statements that tended to "make [declarant] an object of hatred, ridicule, or disgrace." Congress, however, rejected this language, reasoning that such statements simply lack sufficient indicia of reliability.

§ 11.30 "AGAINST INTEREST"; STATEMENTS THAT ARE BOTH SELF-SERVING AND DIS-SERVING

Fed. R. Evid. 804(b)(3) is based on the assumption that people do not make statements which they know are damaging to themselves unless they strongly believe that the statements are true. Thus, to fit within the Rule, a statement must have been dis-serving, not self-serving, when the declarant made it. This requires the judge to examine the factual context in which the statement was made. If a statement appears on its face to be dis-serving, it is safe to assume it was against the declarant's interest unless the party against whom it is offered can persuade the judge otherwise. DL's statement, "I owe X $5,000," appears to be dis-serving (and therefore appears to fit within Rule 804(b)(3), assuming the Rule's other requirements are satisfied), because declarant is acknowledging a debt. But if DL made the remark during a dispute over whether she owed X $5,000 or $10,000, her statement was actually self-serving, and could not satisfy Rule 804(b)(3).

Statements sometimes contain self-serving *and* dis-serving elements. A motorist, for example, might say after a collision, "I admit I was doing 65 in a 55 mph zone, but the other guy must have been doing 90!" The statement is dis-serving in part ("I admit I was doing 65") but its overall thrust is self-serving. In such cases, where the dis-serving and self-serving parts of the statement are easily severable, the judge can simply redact the self-serving aspects and allow in only the dis-serving parts (unless, of course, the self-serving part of the statement satisfies some other provision of Article VIII). If the judge believes this would unfairly advantage one side over the other, however, she can exclude the entire statement.[17] Where it is impossible to redact the self-serving part, the judge must assess whether, overall, the statement was more dis-serving or self-serving when the declarant made it, and rule accordingly.

---

[17] After the judge rules that only the dis-serving part of the statement comes within an exception to the hearsay rule, the adverse party can still argue that other portions of the statement should in fairness be admitted, too. If the statement was oral, the adverse party will cite the common law "rule of completeness." (You either have, or will, study that rule in connection with *Beech Aircraft v. Rainey*, 488 U.S. 153, 170 (1988).) If the statement was written or recorded, the adverse party can also cite Fed. R. Evid. 106.

§ 11.31   CONTRASTING RULE 804(b)(3) AND RULE 801(d)(2)

It is important not to confuse Rule 804(b)(3), "statement against interest," and Rule 801(d)(2)(A)–801(d)(2)(D), "an opposing party's statement." Under 801(d)(2), we focus only on who made the statement and who is now offering it in evidence: the statement qualifies whether it was self-serving, dis-serving, or neutral, so long as:

> (a) The declarant who made or adopted the statement is now a party to the litigation, or was an agent, when he made the statement, of someone who is now a party to the lawsuit; and

> (b) The statement is being offered by the other party (i.e., the declarant's opponent, or the declarant's principal's opponent) in the lawsuit (*see* §§ 5.4, 5.20, 5.24).

Under Rule 804(b)(3), by contrast, it is irrelevant whether the declarant had any relationship to any of the parties to the current lawsuit, and either party to the lawsuit can invoke the Rule. Instead, the Rule requires that:

> (a) The Declarant either had first-hand knowledge, or at least believed that what he said was true;

> (b) The declarant must be unavailable to testify at trial; and

> (c) The statement must have been against the declarant's pecuniary, proprietary, or litigational (or penal) interest *at the time he made the statement.*

§ 11.32   QUESTIONS

Question 1. On June 1, P brings his car to be serviced by DSS, a service station. X, a mechanic, is assigned to work on the brakes. On June 3, X quits his job. On June 5, the brakes on P's car fail, and P is seriously injured. On June 6, X learns of P's accident. "That might be my fault," X tells W, a friend. "I was drunk that day and probably botched the job." P sues DSS, alleging that X's failure to properly service the brakes caused the brake failure and P's injuries. At trial, P calls W to testify about X's statement. DSS objects: hearsay.

a. Is X's statement to W admissible against DSS under Rule 801(d)(2)(D)?

Ans. No. By the time X made his statement on June 6, he was no longer an employee of DSS, because he quit on June 3.[18] (*See* § 5.24; see also § 5.26 **Q.** 3).

b. Is X's statement to W admissible against DSS under Rule 804(b)(3)?

Ans. No. P has offered no evidence that X is now unavailable.

c. P calls an investigator who testifies that he has searched high and low for X, but that no one has seen him for several months and that he left no forwarding address. Is X's statement to W admissible against DSS now under Rule 804(b)(3)?

---

[18] Remember: when a professor includes dates in a quiz or exam question, they are almost always important.

Ans. Yes. X had first-hand knowledge of whether he was drunk and of whether he completed the job; he is also unavailable. His statement had a significant "tendency to . . . expose the declarant to civil . . . liability" because P could have sued him, as well as DSS. Hence, it is unlikely "a reasonable person in [X']s position" would have made the statement unless he "believed it to be true." (See Fed. R. Evid. 804(b)(3)(A).)

Question 2. Pyre's store burns to the ground, and she files a claim with FIC, her insurance company, seeking to recover the value of the building, the inventory that she claims was destroyed, and other assets. FIC refuses to pay, alleging that Pyre hired Flame to burn the building down. Pyre sues FIC to collect on the policy.

At trial, after Pyre rests, FIC calls Flame, but Flame, asserting his Fifth Amendment privilege, refuses to answer any questions. FIC next calls W, a long-time friend of Flame, who will, if permitted, testify that a few days after the fire, Flame told W, "Pyre hired me to torch her store. A couple of firemen got hurt fighting the fire. I feel real bad about that." (W acknowledges that he decided to come forward and testify after he heard about the $25,000 reward FIC offered to anyone who could prove that the fire was caused by arson.) Is Flame's statement admissible per Rule 804(b)(3)?

Ans. Apply the issue checklist.

1. *Declarant's first-hand knowledge or belief.* Flame presumably had first-hand knowledge as to whether Pyre in fact hired him to burn the building.

2. *Declarant's unavailability.* Flame is unavailable per Rule 804(a)(1).

3. *"Against interest."* Flame's statement to W was against his penal interest: it tended to expose him to prosecution for arson. Rule 804(b)(3) permits a civil litigant to use a declarant's statement against penal interest.

4. *"Tendency to expose . . ."* Even though Flame assumed his friend W would not repeat what he said, Flame had to know there was a possibility that W would do so.

Note that there is nothing dis-serving about *W's* decision to testify: he hopes to reap a $25,000 reward. But W is not the declarant, Flame is. The "against interest" requirement is satisfied so long as it was against the *declarant's* (Flame's) interest to make the statement at the time he made it, even if it is very much *in* the witness's best interest to repeat the statement at trial. In fact, it could well be that W is lying. But W will testify and be cross-examined, and the jury can assess W's truthfulness for themselves.

As you will see shortly, there are several complications that must be addressed when either a *prosecutor or a criminal defendant* seeks to use a declarant's declaration against penal interest in a criminal case. These complications do not apply, however, if a plaintiff or defendant seeks to use such a statement in a *civil* case.

§ 11.33   DECLARATIONS AGAINST PENAL INTEREST: USE BY DEFENDANT IN CRIMINAL CASES

When a defendant seeks to use a declarant's statement against penal interest (such as "D didn't commit the crime, *I* did") as evidence of his own innocence, the following issues must be addressed:

1. Declarant either had first-hand knowledge, or at least believed that what he said was true.

2. Declarant must be unavailable, as defined in Rule 804(a).

3. "Interests" included within the Rule: Penal interest is recognized by the Rule.

4. *"Tends . . . against interest."* The statement need not be unequivocally dis-serving; in other words, it need not be a flat-out admission of guilt. It suffices that the statement had a sufficiently "great . . . tendency . . . to expose the declarant to . . . criminal liability" that the declarant would not have said it unless he believed it to be true. Remember that we must determine whether it was against the declarant's interest at the time he made the statement. This depends upon the factual context in which the statement was made.

5. *Trustworthiness requirement.* Fed. R. Evid. 804(b)(3)(B) requires that the statement must be "supported by corroborating circumstances that clearly indicate its trustworthiness . . ." (*see* § 11.34).

6. *Individual declaration or narration as a whole.* In *United States v. Williamson,* 512 U.S. 594, 602–604 (1994), the Supreme Court held that when a *prosecutor* offers a statement that was against the declarant's penal interest as evidence against a different defendant, it is necessary to examine each declaration within an utterance to determine whether it was sufficiently against the declarant's interest, rather than considering the declarant's narrative as a whole (*see* § 11.38). Courts tend to apply this approach to the meaning of "statement" to other aspects of Rule 804(b)(3) as well.

§ 11.34   THE "TRUSTWORTHINESS" REQUIREMENT

A lone gunman shot and killed X, and D was indicted for the crime. At trial, after the prosecutor presents her case, D offers an alibi defense, but D's attorney senses the jury is not buying it. Just as things look their darkest, D calls a surprise witness, W. "I was hangin' out a couple of months ago," W testifies, "tellin' my friend Eddie how worried I was about D gettin' indicted, when Roger Overnout, this guy I know from the neighborhood, says, 'D didn't kill X; he couldn't have, 'cause *I* killed X.' " When the prosecutor makes a hearsay objection, D's attorney informs the court that Overnout is unavailable — he died of a drug overdose three weeks ago. D's attorney argues that Overnout's statement is therefore admissible under Rule 804(b)(3) as a statement against Overnout's penal interest.

This is an example of a statement "that tends to expose the declarant [Overnout] to criminal liability" (to quote from Rule 804(b)(3)(B)). Evidence of this kind is ridiculously easy for a defendant or his associates to manufacture. All it takes is someone (W) who is willing to invent a conversation with someone else who "confessed" to the crime D is charged with — preferably someone else who, like Mr. Overnout, is not available to deny having made the incriminating statement. That is why Rule 804(b)(3)(B) requires the defendant to show that the statement "is supported by corroborating circumstances that clearly indicate its trustworthiness."[19] Unless the judge is satisfied that the defendant sufficiently demonstrated the trustworthiness of the statement, it does not satisfy the exception, and is inadmissible hearsay.

This leaves us with three questions. First, *who* must be "corroborated"? Second, what factors do courts look to in assessing trustworthiness? Third, how much corroboration is enough?

1. Whose trustworthiness should the trial judge assess?

Hearsay evidence usually involves the credibility of at least two people — the witness and the declarant.

(1)   Is the *witness*, i.e., the person who claims to have heard the statement, testifying truthfully and accurately? In other words, was there, as W claims, a declarant; did he make a statement; and if so, is W accurately repeating what the declarant said?

(2)   The *declarant.* Assuming W is telling the truth, (i.e., there was a declarant and he made the statement W will testify to), was declarant's statement truthful and accurate?

Fed. R. Evid. 804(b)(3) clearly requires the judge to exclude the statement unless the defendant can show that it "is supported by corroborating circumstances that clearly indicate *[the statement's]* trustworthiness." This focuses on the statement and, to an extent, on the credibility of the *declarant.* The credibility of the *witness*, on the other hand, is almost always considered strictly a jury issue, and although a few early decisions read the rule as permitting the trial judge to exclude the statement if she thought the witness was lying about whether the statement was made, most courts reject this approach, reasoning that a *witness's* credibility is a jury issue.

2. Assessing "trustworthiness of the statement"

The last sentence of the Rule directs that the defendant must demonstrate that the statement "is supported by corroborating circumstances that clearly indicate its trustworthiness." In assessing trustworthiness, some courts look only at the statement itself and the circumstances surrounding the making of the statement; others also consider whether the *content* of the statement (i.e., what the declarant said) has been *corroborated* by other evidence.

a. When, where, to whom the statement was made

---

[19] At common law, such statements were inadmissible, because the "declaration against interest" exception to the hearsay rule covered only statements against the declarant's pecuniary or proprietary interest. The Advisory Committee and members of Congress wrangled considerably over whether to include declarations against penal interest within Rule 804(b)(3).

The circumstances surrounding the making of the statement can tell us a lot about whether it is likely to be true. Suppose Q is charged with burglarizing a school and stealing, among other things, several computers. (The crime received a great deal of publicity.) At trial, Q wants to call YW, a young woman. She will, if permitted, testify:

> I had a date with this guy Z, and he was trying to persuade me to invite him up to my apartment. I was looking for a polite way to make him go away, so I said I had to get up early the next morning to go shopping for a new computer. Z started stroking my arm and whispered, "I'm the guy who broke into the school last week and stole all the computers."

The relevance of YW's testimony is clear: if Z committed the burglary, Q didn't. In assessing the trustworthiness of Z's statement, a judge may reasonably consider the likelihood that a man might not be entirely truthful when trying to persuade a young woman on a first date to . . . well, you can complete the sentence.

By contrast, suppose X and D are arrested for a bank robbery committed several days earlier in which X committed the actual robbery while D drove the getaway car. After being given the *Miranda* warnings, X admits, "Yeah, that was me who robbed the bank. But listen, D had no idea what I was doing. He's just some poor schmoe I talked into giving me a ride. He thought I was just going into the bank to make a deposit."[20] The circumstances surrounding this statement make it appear to be reliable for at least three reasons:

(1)   Unlike Z's statement in the previous paragraph, this statement does not merely "tend" to expose the declarant to criminal liability; it is an outright confession of guilt to the police. The greater the likelihood the statement *will* hurt the declarant, the more reliable it probably is.

(2)   Unlike Z's statement in the previous paragraph, X apparently has nothing at all to gain by making the statement.

(3)   If, as X said, D was no more than a casual acquaintance, then we can discount the possibility that X was falsely exonerating D out of loyalty, friendship or fear. Therefore, if D is charged with being X's accomplice, the circumstances under which X made his statement exculpating D have strong indications of trustworthiness.

b. The declarant

This might include a variety of factors. Was DL physically capable of doing what (according to W) DL said he did? Is such behavior characteristic of DL, or highly unlike him? Did DL have a reputation for truthfulness, or for lying a lot? Did DL have a particular motive to commit the crime?

c. The contents of the statement

---

[20] As you recall from your criminal law course, to convict D of being X's accomplice in robbing the bank, it is not enough for the prosecutor to prove that D in fact helped X commit the robbery by driving him away from the bank; the prosecutor must also prove that D did so knowing and intending to help X commit the crime.

The general plausibility or implausibility of the statement is obviously a relevant consideration.

d. Extrinsic corroboration or contradiction

Some courts also look to whether the defendant has offered "extrinsic" corroboration (i.e., evidence), independent of the statement itself, that tends to corroborate its truth. In the school burglary example, suppose Q, the defendant, calls several witnesses to testify that a few days after the burglary, Z, who had no previous known access to computers, went around offering to sell several computers, of the same kind taken from the school, at a ridiculously low price. This requires us to look at Z's statement to YW in a new light. What might otherwise be seen as just an attempt by Z to impress YW with a false promise now looks a great deal more credible.

On the other hand, if several eye-witnesses describe the burglar as being between 5'6" and 5'9" and Z is 6'5", this extrinsic *contradiction* of Z's statement might weigh heavily *against* its truthfulness.

3. How much corroboration?

The defendant must offer some evidence supporting the truth of the declarant's statement. As to how much, the only clear answer is "more than a little." The legislative history makes it clear, for example, that the mere fact that the defendant takes the stand and denies committing the crime is insufficient corroboration to secure admissibility of the (alleged) declarant's (alleged) self-incriminating, defendant-exculpating statement.

§ 11.35 QUESTIONS

Question 1. Consider again the scenario in § 11.34 **Q. 1**: A lone gunman shot and killed X, and D was indicted for the crime. At trial, D calls witness, W. "I was hangin' out with some guys a couple of months ago," W testifies, "tellin' my friend Eddie how worried I was about D gettin' indicted, when Roger Overnout, this guy I know from the neighborhood, says, 'D didn't kill X; he couldn't have, 'cause *I* killed X.'" When the prosecutor makes a hearsay objection, D's attorney informs the court that Overnout is unavailable — he died of a drug overdose three weeks ago. D's attorney argues that Overnout's statement is therefore admissible under Rule 804(b)(3) as a statement against Overnout's penal interest. What kind of corroboration would suffice to secure admission of the statement Overnout allegedly made to W?

Ans. *W's testimony* that Overnout made the statement could be corroborated (if such corroboration is deemed necessary) if "friend Eddie" also testifies that he heard Overnout make the statement, or if other witnesses testify that they heard Overnout make similar statements. But the rule actually focuses on the trustworthiness of declarant Overnout's statement.

The *circumstances surrounding the making of the statement.* Assuming (as I do) that the judge is not permitted to evaluate *W's* credibility — in other words, assuming the judge must (at least outwardly) accept that W is telling the truth about what Overnout said, and leave assessment of his credibility to the jury,— we have a bit of a mixed bag. Overnout probably did not expect his statement to be used against him, which tends to detract a bit from the trustworthiness of the statement. On the other hand, he knew that W was a friend of D's, so presumably he realized there was some risk that W might go to the authorities and accuse Overnout to get D off the hook. A judge might decide this is enough, but it would certainly be within judicial discretion to hold that it is not.

The contents of Overnout's statement might be sufficiently corroborated by some combination of the following. (a) A witness testifies that she saw Overnout near the scene of V's murder shortly before V was killed. (b) Evidence demonstrates that Overnout had a motive to kill V, or that a strong enmity existed between V and Overnout. (c) Overnout was arrested in possession of an item of property that other witnesses placed in V's possession shortly before V's death (assuming the circumstances of V's death suggest V was robbed by his killer).

No particular formula applies; the ultimate question is whether D has introduced enough direct or circumstantial evidence to "clearly indicate" that Overnout's statement (that he, not D, killed V) was "trustworthy."

Question 2. Drago and Viper had feuded for months. Shortly before midnight on the evening of June 1, on Girard Avenue between 14th and 15th Streets, things came to a head: they had words, they pushed and shoved each other, and finally Drago shot and killed Viper. Charged with murder, Drago pleaded self-defense, insisting that he pulled and fired his own pistol only after Viper had pulled a gun and pointed it at him. Several people can attest that Viper owned, and often carried, a pearl-handled.32 caliber revolver. Unfortunately for Drago, no revolver was found on Viper or at the scene.

On July 1, in a different part of the city, someone robbed a branch of the First City Savings and Loan. A few days later, X was arrested for the robbery, and was interrogated by Detective W. X confessed to the robbery. As part of the confession, X told Detective W that he found the gun he used in the robbery. "I picked it up off the street about a month ago right after a guy got shot on Girard near 15th Street."

At Drago's murder trial, Drago calls X as a witness; but X, who has since pleaded not guilty in his robbery case, asserts his Fifth Amendment privilege. Drago therefore calls Detective W, hoping to elicit testimony relating X's statement.

a. How is X's statement relevant in Drago's murder trial?

Ans. From X's statement, it is reasonable to infer that X picked up a handgun off the street shortly after Drago shot and killed Viper. This tends to make Drago's self-defense claim more believable, because it explains why the gun, which Drago claims Viper pointed at him on June 1, was not found at the scene. Therefore, it has some tendency to make it more likely that Viper pulled a gun on Drago, and Drago shot Viper in self-defense.

b. The prosecutor makes a hearsay objection. Is the testimony admissible under Rule 804(b)(3)(B)?

Ans. Apply the list of requirements and issues:

1. *First-hand knowledge.* X, the declarant, presumably has first-hand knowledge of where he found the handgun.

2. *Unavailability.* X is unavailable, pursuant to Rule 804(a)(1).

3. *Interest.* "Penal interest" is recognized by the Rule.

4. *"Against interest."* Although X's statement about finding the gun did not in and of itself incriminate him (unless he is in a state that requires all handguns to be registered), it is so closely connected with his confession to the robbery which clearly *was* against his penal interest that it satisfies this requirement.

This situation differs from the typical defense use of Rule 804(b)(3)(B), because here the declarant's statement incriminates him in a crime different from the one Drago is accused of. But in and of itself, this is no bar.

5. *Trustworthiness*

a. *Circumstances surrounding the making of the statement.* A post-*Miranda* confession is a fairly reliable "circumstance," particularly where the declarant has nothing to gain from telling where he obtained the gun and has no known relationship to Drago that might prompt him to lie on Drago's behalf.

b. *Contents of the statement.* It would be useful if Drago could find some extrinsic corroboration of X's statement. For example, if X (or a witness in the bank) testified that the gun X used to rob the bank was "fairly small in caliber, with a white handle," and other witnesses described Viper's handgun the same way, that might well suffice. But extrinsic corroboration is not a prerequisite, it is only a factor to consider.

c. *Declarant credibility.* X's lack of any apparent motive to lie about where he got the gun strongly supports his credibility here.

d. *Witness credibility.* This probably should not be a factor at all, but if it is, it is unlikely that Detective W, who can testify about the statement, would, or even could, make up such a detailed lie. The odds are pretty substantial that the officer is telling the truth when he testifies that X made the statement.

§ 11.36 DECLARATION AGAINST PENAL INTEREST: USE BY PROSECUTOR

When a prosecutor seeks to use a declarant's self-incriminating statement against the defendant in a criminal trial, the following issues are presented:

1. Declarant must have had first-hand knowledge, or at least believed that what he said was true.

2. Declarant must be unavailable, as defined in Rule 804(a).

3. *"Interests" included within the Rule*: Penal interest is recognized by the Rule.

4. *"Tendency . . . to expose the declarant to civil or criminal liability.* The statement need not be an outright confession; it suffices that it "tends" to be against the declarant's penal interest. A 1994 Supreme Court decision, *Williamson v. United States,* 512 U.S. 594, 599 (1994), defined the word "statement" in a way that will sometimes make it difficult to satisfy this requirement (*see* § 11.38).

5. *Relationship to other rules.* At least two other rules should be considered, as well as Rule 804(b)(3), whenever a prosecutor offers a declarant's self-incriminating statement in evidence against a defendant: the co-conspirator exception, Rule 801(d)(2)(E), and the "second-party *Hillmon*" aspect of Rule 803(3) (*see* § 11.40).

6. *Sixth Amendment Confrontation Clause.* See § 11.39.

7. *Trustworthiness.* See § 11.41.

§ 11.37 "AGAINST INTEREST"

Narco is arrested for narcotics trafficking. After *Miranda* warnings, Detective Washington shows Narco photographs of Narco handing drugs to an undercover officer; he also plays tapes of Narco's drug-related conversations. He reminds Narco that, given his two prior felony convictions, if Narco goes to trial he faces life without parole. But, Washington adds, if Narco confesses, and names his supplier, maybe the D.A. will cut him a break. "O.K., O.K., you got me good," Narco replies, "that's me all right. I've been dealin' pretty regular for the last couple of months. I get my stuff from this guy named Connection. Now about this break you mentioned. . . ."

Connection is subsequently indicted. When the prosecutor calls Washington to testify about what Narco said, Connection makes a hearsay objection, and the prosecutor cites Rule 804(b)(3). Ruling?

Objection sustained. When Narco made his statement to Washington, he did so hoping to help himself by currying favor with the authorities. Hence, from Narco's perspective, his statement was self-serving, rather than against his interest.

The basic point is that the fact that someone admitted that he had committed a crime does not, by itself, satisfy the "against interest" requirement. You must examine the factual context in which the statement was made. If Narco made his admission (incriminating Connection as well as himself) as part of a deal with the authorities, or in the hopes of striking such a deal, the statement cannot satisfy Rule 804(b)(3). And even if the authorities were not involved, if it appears that Narco hoped he might gain more than he would lose by making the statement, it may not satisfy the "against interest" requirement.

§ 11.38　*WILLIAMSON*: INDIVIDUAL DECLARATION OR NARRATION AS A WHOLE; "COLLATERAL" STATEMENTS

In *United States v. Williamson*, 512 U.S. 594 (1994), police caught a man named Harris with 19 kilograms of cocaine in the trunk of his car. He told the police several different versions of how he came to possess the drugs; in each version he admitted knowing the cocaine was in the trunk and claimed that it belonged to Williamson. At Williamson's trial, the Government called Harris as a witness, but he refused to testify even after being granted immunity. The trial court then allowed a police officer to testify about Harris' final statement at Williamson's trial, per Rule 804(b)(3). The Supreme Court unanimously held that Harris's allegations against Williamson should not have been admitted, but left more confusion than clarity as to how the rule it enunciated should be applied in subsequent cases.[21]

The basic issue was, how should a court read the word "statement" in Rule 804(b)(3)? In essence there are two choices:

(1) The first is to assess the declarant's narrative as a whole. If, on the whole, the declarant's narrative was against the declarant's penal interest, then it qualifies under Rule 804(b)(3). Although clearly exculpatory (self-serving) portions should be redacted, neutral collateral declarations within the narrative could be admitted along with the clearly self-inculpatory portions.

(2) The second approach to the general policy question is to examine each individual declaration (assertion) within the narrative. Only those declarations that were against the declarant's interest qualify under Rule 804(b)(3); collateral neutral declarations as well as exculpatory (self-serving) declarations within the narrative must be excluded.

A six-justice majority, per Justice O'Connor, concluded that Congress intended that when applying Rule 804(b)(3) to a prosecutor's use of a declarant's statement against penal interest, a court must examine each declaration within a narrative to determine whether that particular declaration was sufficiently against the declarant's interest, rather than considering the declarant's narrative as a whole. Only those individual declarations within the narrative that were self-incriminating qualified as being against the declarant's penal interest. Exculpatory, mitigating and even neutral declarations within the narrative are not against the declarant's penal interest, the majority held; therefore they would not qualify for admission under Rule 804(b)(3).

Williamson requires us to address two questions:

1. Does the holding apply only to cases in which a prosecutor relies on Rule 804(b)(3) to offer a declarant's statement against penal interest against another defendant; or does it apply to all statements offered under Rule 804(b)(3) (i.e., in civil cases and in criminal cases when the defendant, rather than the

---

[21] Today, of course, in light of *Crawford*, we would immediately recognize Harris' statements as testimonial and, unless the prosecutor could find a way around the Confrontation Clause, Harris' testimony would be inadmissible on that ground.

prosecutor is offering the statement)?

Courts have tended to apply *Williamson* to all uses of Rule 804(b)(3); indeed, to all hearsay statements, regardless of the exception under which they are being offered.

2.   Under what circumstances will a declarant's statement against interest be admissible against someone else?[22] Lower court consensus seems to be that if DL makes a non-testimonial statement acknowledging that he and Narco committed a particular crime, the fact that DL named Narco as the other criminal is self-incriminating as to DL, rather than a "collateral, neutral" fact which must be redacted.

§ 11.39   SIXTH AMENDMENT CONFRONTATION CLAUSE

Crawford v. Washington has dramatically decreased the frequency of prosecutorial use of Fed. R. Evid. 804(b)(3), because statements made by a suspect being interrogated by the police will (except perhaps in highly unusual circumstances) always be classified as testimonial, and therefore inadmissible against a non-declarant defendant. Suppose W1 notifies police that he just saw two men breaking into an office building at 2 a.m. The burglars manage to escape before the police arrive, but fingerprint evidence leads the police to M. PO arrests M and gives him *Miranda* warnings. M waives his rights and says, "I knew it was stupid of me to forget my gloves. You got me, fair and square." Even when offered a deal, however, M refuses to name his accomplice. Eventually, however, the police arrest D and charge him with being the other burglar.

M's statement is clearly against his penal interest: he confessed to a felony. Therefore, it might well satisfy Fed. R. Evid. 804(b)(3). And, even though he refused to name D as his accomplice, this statement might be very useful to the state in D's trial. Suppose, for example, W2 and W3 testify that they saw M and D together at a bar from 11:30 the night before until about 1:30 the morning of the burglary, and W4 and W5 testify that they saw M and D together at an all-night diner at about 2:40 a.m. This supports the inference that M and D were together the entire period between 11:30 p.m. and 2:40 a.m. Therefore, evidence that M admitted to being one of the burglars would strongly support the inference that D was the other burglar.

Because M's statement to the police was testimonial, however, it would not be admissible at D's trial.

§ 11.40   RULE 804(b)(3); RULE 801(d)(2)(E); RULE 803(3) ("SECOND-PARTY *HILLMON*")

From a prosecutor's perspective, Rule 801(d)(2)(E) and Rule 804(b)(3)'s declaration against penal interest provisions are closely related, because *each permits a prosecutor to offer a declarant's statement, which tends to incriminate the declarant, as*

---

[22]   Justices Scalia and O'Connor offered a number of examples, but most of those examples would now be categorized as testimonial and inadmissible for that reason.

evidence of a non-declarant defendant's guilt. The same is often true for "second-party *Hillmon*" statements, in jurisdictions that recognize that variation on Rule 803(3).

Turn back to §§ 5.31-5.35 and review the prerequisites a prosecutor must satisfy to admit a statement under Rule 801(d)(2)(E).

You will recall that the prosecutor must establish five prerequisites and satisfy an important procedural requirement:

1. A conspiracy in fact existed.

2. The declarant was a member of the conspiracy.

3. The non-declarant defendant, against whom the statement is being offered, was a member of the conspiracy.

4. The statement was made "during" the conspiracy.

5. The statement was made "in furtherance" of the conspiracy.

Now examine the final sentence of Rule 801(d)(2): "The statement must be considered but does not by itself establish . . . the existence of the conspiracy or participation in it under (E)." In other words, the prosecutor must offer *corroborating evidence*, independent of the statement itself, as to the first three requirements; the statement is admissible only if it and the corroborating evidence satisfy the judge by a preponderance of the evidence that the prerequisites have been met.

In essence, the five requirements of Rule 801(d)(2)(E), and the additional corroboration requirement are imposed to assure that the statement is sufficiently reliable to satisfy the policies underlying the hearsay rule.

Suppose NB is on trial for being a major drug supplier. The prosecutor calls W1 to testify that SD1, a low-level street dealer, once boasted to him, "I can get you all the heroin you want, cause me and NB, we're real tight; he gives me all the merchandise I can handle." If the prosecutor relies on Rule 801(d)(2)(E), she cannot admit the statement unless she can establish all five prerequisites, and corroborate the first three.

Suppose instead the prosecutor cites Rule 804(b)(3)?

As originally enacted, Rule 804(b)(3) did not require a *prosecutor* to offer "corroborating circumstances" that "clearly indicate [the statement's] trustworthiness." However, in 2010, the Rule was amended to apply the corroboration requirement equally to the prosecutor and to the defense: any time either party seeks to use Rule 804(b)(3)(A), that party must satisfy the trustworthiness requirement.

Now re-read § 8.20, covering "second-party *Hillmon*" statements. In a jurisdiction that recognizes that doctrine, such statements must satisfy the following requirements:

1. The statement must be one in which the declarant expressed an intent to do something with the defendant.

2.   If offered to prove that the *defendant* later in fact committed the act with the declarant, the prosecutor must offer evidence independent of the statement that *corroborates* it (i.e., that tends to show that the defendant in fact did what the declarant claimed he and the defendant intended to do).

The corroboration requirement is imposed because without it, such a statement simply would not be sufficiently reliable to satisfy the purposes underlying the hearsay rule. Suppose, in the same drug trial, the prosecutor calls W2 to testify that SD2, another street dealer, told him, "NB and I are going to pick up 20 kilos of pure tomorrow." As we have just seen, she cannot use Rule 801(d)(2)(E) to admit SD2's statement against NB unless she can corroborate the existence of a conspiracy relationship between NB and SD2. She cannot use 803(3) second-party *Hillmon* unless she offers evidence tending to corroborate that in fact NB and SD2 picked up those two kilograms. Similarly, she cannot use 804(b)(3)(B) unless she can corroborate SD2's statement.

§ 11.41   GUARANTEES OF TRUSTWORTHINESS

The same factors listed in § 11.34, for assessing the trustworthiness of a declarant's statement against penal interest offered by a defendant as exculpatory evidence, apply when a prosecutor offers a declarant's statement against penal interest as evidence of the defendant's (as well as the declarant's) guilt.

§ 11.42   QUESTIONS

Question 1. Two days after a bank robbery, BF told G, his girlfriend, "Willie Sutton[23] and I pulled that bank job they made so much noise about on the TV news the other night. We cleared $20,000 each!" May G, who by now is BF's *ex*-girlfriend,[24] testify as to this statement as a government witness at BF and Sutton's joint trial for committing the robbery?

Ans.

a. G's testimony clearly is admissible against BF: Rule 801(d)(2)(A).

b. Admissibility against Sutton is doubtful.

(1) Rule 801(d)(2)(E)

The judge should not permit the prosecutor to rely on this Rule. Putting aside for a moment whether there is any evidence corroborating the

---

[23] Willie Sutton was a notorious bank robber who, between the 1920's and 1950's, robbed approximately 100 banks. He was convicted several times and, although he escaped from prison more than once, he spent roughly half his adult life in prison. When asked later in life why he robbed so many banks, he allegedly said, "Because that's where the money is." (He denied saying it, and accused the reporter of making it up.) The *Wikipedia* bio of him is worth reading.

[24] When I was a prosecutor, it surprised me at first how often criminals boasted to their girlfriends about their crimes, then treated them shabbily and dumped them. After a while, the only surprising thing about this pattern was that the criminals were surprised at how willing and even eager their ex-girlfriends were to testify against them.

existence of a conspiracy, or Sutton and BF's involvement in it, a robber's boast to a girlfriend is not "in furtherance" of the conspiracy; moreover, it appears that the conspiracy to rob the bank was over when BF bragged to G about it, so BF's statement to G was not "during" the conspiracy, either.

(2) Rule 803(3) — second-party *Hillmon*

Putting aside whether there is any corroborating evidence, the statement cannot satisfy Rule 803(3) because it looks backward to the past, not forward to the future.

(3) Rule 804(b)(3). Applying the checklist from § 11.36:

1. BF has first-hand knowledge of whether he and Sutton were the bank robbers.

2. Since BF is a defendant, the government cannot call him as a witness; to do so would automatically violate BF's Fifth Amendment privilege. Therefore BF is unavailable per Rule 804(a)(1).

3. Penal interest is recognized by the rule.

4. BF's statement that he himself was one of the robbers clearly was against his own penal interest; and even though BF also had a self-serving reason to make the statement — to play the "big man" to his girlfriend — courts universally agree that in this sort of situation, the against-penal-interest aspect of the statement is the dominant one.

Sutton can argue that, parsing BF's statement assertion-by-assertion per *Williamson*, BF's statement that *Sutton was the other robber* does not, in and of itself, have any apparent tendency to incriminate BF. Thus, his naming Sutton as his partner might be viewed as a "collateral, neutral" declaration outside the scope of the rule. If so, the most the prosecutor could use would be a redacted version: G could testify, "BF told me he was one of the robbers." But most courts have rejected the notion that *Williamson* automatically excludes a statement in which the declarant names the defendant as another perpetrator in the crime.

5. Other rules: Fed. R. Evid. 801(d)(2)(A), 801(d)(2)(E) and 803(3) have already been considered.

6. Sixth Amendment Confrontation Clause: a boast a man makes to his girlfriend clearly is not testimonial.

7. Trustworthiness. There is nothing particularly trustworthy about the circumstances surrounding the making of this statement, and there is no evidence of extrinsic corroboration of it. On this ground the statement should be excluded.

Question 2. Suppose a few days after BF dumped G, she went to the police and told them what he had told her — including that BF had also told G, "I used my sawed-off shotgun and Sutton used his pearl-handled .45-caliber pistol." Suppose further that press reports about the robbery had not specified what weapons the robbers used, but several witnesses had described them as a sawed-off shotgun and a pearl-handled .45. When G comes to court to testify at trial, is BF's statement admissible against Sutton?

Ans. Rule 801(d)(2)(E) or Rule 803(3) second-party *Hillmon* still do not help the prosecutor, for the reasons outlined in the previous answer.

As to Rule 804(b)(3):

> Issues 1–6: the analysis under these facts is identical to the analysis in **Q 1.**

> 7. As to trustworthiness, however, the prosecutor has a much better argument — assuming a judge is permitted to look at extrinsic corroboration in assessing trustworthiness.

>> a.   That BF had "insider information" about the type of guns used by the robbers greatly enhances the trustworthiness of BF's (declarant's) statement. Thus, we no longer need be as concerned that when BF claimed to have been one of the robbers, he was lying to G to impress her.

>> b.   The fact that G knew the kinds of guns the robbers used also makes it very difficult for Sutton (or BF, for that matter) to claim that G was lying on the witness stand to get back at BF for dumping her. Thus, this tends to corroborate the *witness's* credibility, too.

Question 3. Reconsider § 11.32 **Q. 1** (the faulty brake job question). If the *Williamson* assertion-by-assertion requirement applies to Rule 804(b)(3) in civil cases, is X's statement still admissible against DSS?

Ans. Yes. X's statement is directly dis-serving only to himself. It becomes relevant against DSS only through the tort law doctrine of *respondeat superior.* This poses no *Williamson* problem.

Question 4. Reconsider § 11.32 **Q. 2** (the arson case). An indictment is filed charging Pyre and Flame with arson. At this criminal trial, is W's testimony about Flame's statement admissible?

Ans.

a. W's testimony as to Flame's statement is admissible against Flame per Rule 801(d)(2)(A).

b. Regarding its admissibility against Pyre, under Rule 804(b)(3):

1. Flame had first-hand knowledge of whether he set the fire and who paid him to do so.

2. Flame is unavailable per Rule 804(a)(1).

3. Flame's admission that he burned the building clearly was against his penal interest.

4. Does Flame's naming of Pyre satisfy *Williamson*, or is Pyre's identity as the person who paid Flame merely a "collateral, neutral" fact? Most courts hold

that in this kind of situation, it was against Flame's penal interest to name Pyre.

5. Relationship to other rules: Neither Rule 801(d)(2)(E) nor Rule 803(3) second-party *Hillmon* admit Flame's statement against Pyre, because the statement was not in furtherance of any conspiracy and was backward looking.

6. Confrontation Clause: Flame's statement of remorse to a friend is not testimonial.

7. Trustworthiness:

(a) Circumstances surrounding the making of the statement. Suppose W testifies that he and Flame have long been good friends and that they regularly confided in each other, that W noticed after the fire that Flame began acting depressed and distracted, and that Flame told W about setting the fire only after W coaxed and nudged him to "tell me what's eating you." A judge might reasonably conclude that this offers sufficient "guarantees of trustworthiness."

(b) Extrinsic corroboration. (1) Suppose a fire insurance company salesman testifies that Pyre significantly increased his fire insurance just a few weeks before the fire. (2) Officials at companies that supplied Pyre with merchandise testify that Pyre had a great deal of difficulty selling their goods. (3) Other witnesses testify that they saw Pyre moving her most expensive merchandise and a few prized personal belongings out of the building the night before it burned. (1) and (2) suggest that Pyre had a powerful motive to hire someone to burn down her building. (3) tends to suggest that Pyre expected her building to burn down. This is the kind of evidence that would lend extrinsic circumstantial corroboration to Flame's statement.

4. Statement of Personal or Family History

§ 11.43   RULE 804(b)(4)

Fed. R. Evid. 804(b)(4) provides as follows:

(b) The Exceptions. The following are not excluded by the rule against hearsay if the declarant is unavailable as a witness:

(4) *Statement of Personal or Family History*. A statement about:

(A) the declarant's own birth, adoption, legitimacy, ancestry, marriage, divorce, relationship by blood, adoption, or marriage, or similar facts of personal or family history, even though the declarant had no way of acquiring personal knowledge about that fact; or

(B) another person concerning any of these facts, as well as death, if the declarant was related to the person by blood, adoption, or marriage or was so intimately associated with the person's family that the declarant's information is likely to be accurate.

[Prior to December 1, 2011, the rule read as follows:

> (b) Hearsay exceptions. The following are not excluded by the hearsay rule if the declarant is unavailable as a witness:
>
> > (4) Statement of personal or family history. (A) A statement concerning the declarant's own birth, adoption, marriage, divorce, legitimacy, relationship by blood, adoption, or marriage, ancestry, or other similar fact of personal or family history, even though declarant had no means of acquiring personal knowledge of the matter stated; or (B) a statement concerning the foregoing matters, and death also, of another person, if the declarant was related to the other by blood, adoption, or marriage or was so intimately associated with the other's family as to be likely to have accurate information concerning the matter declared.

The Federal Rules of Evidence were rewritten solely to make them easier to understand; the Advisory Committee did not intend to make any substantive change in the Rules. The text of the old rule may remain useful in reading court decisions that precede the revision of the rules. Thus, this edition of the Student's Guide provides the text of both the new and the old version of each relevant provision of the Federal Rules of Evidence.]

The Rule covers statements concerning two closely related subjects: statements by the declarant involving his own "personal history," and statements by a declarant involving someone else's "family history."

§ 11.44   RULE 804(b)(4)(A): DECLARANT'S OWN PERSONAL HISTORY

The only prerequisites for admissibility are that the declarant must be unavailable, and the statement must relate to his or her "personal history." Note that the exception explicitly requires *no* showing that declarant had first-hand knowledge. The reason is simple: while most people "know" who their parents, grandparents, aunts, uncles, cousins, etc., are, and "know" how they are related to each of them, it is the rare person indeed who was present at his own conception[25] or has first-hand knowledge of his own birth, let alone those of his parents, grandparents, and most other relatives. As to many such matters, first-hand knowledge is simply impossible to acquire; hence the Rule does not require it.

Unlike its common law antecedent, Rule 804(b)(4)(A) does not require that the statement must have been made before the controversy arose that resulted in the lawsuit.

---

[25] Offhand, I doubt you could name even one.

§ 11.45 RULE 804(b)(4)(B): STATEMENT CONCERNING FAMILY HISTORY OF ANOTHER

This Rule imposes three requirements: the declarant must be unavailable; the statement must relate to the family history of another person (which may include the circumstances of his death); and declarant must have been either legally related to the other person, or must have been "so intimately associated with the person's family that the declarant's information is likely to be accurate." As with Rule 804(b)(4)(A), first-hand knowledge is not required.

Rule 804(b)(4)(B) differs from its common law predecessor in two respects. First, like Rule 804(b)(4)(A), 804(b)(4)(B) does not require that the statement must have been made before the controversy arose which resulted in the lawsuit. Second, Rule 804(b)(4)(B) expands the common law exception by including statements made by non-relatives who are "intimately associated with the other's family"; the family doctor or lawyer, for example, or a longtime neighbor or friend. (The party offering the statement has the burden of establishing that the declarant had an intimate enough association with the family "that the declarant's information is likely to be accurate.")

Note that even if this degree of intimacy cannot be shown, the statement may still win admission under Rule 803(19), which covers reputation as to personal or family history. See § 10.10. Similarly, if the statement is in a document or record of some kind, it may be admissible as a business or public record, see §§ 9.20-9.52, a family record (Rule 803(13), see § 10.4), a baptismal or similar certificate (Rule 803(12), see § 10.3), an ancient document (Rule 803(16), see § 10.7), or under other hearsay provision.

5. Deleted Rule 804(b)(5)

§ 11.46 "OLD" RULE 804(b)(5)

As originally enacted, Rule 804(b)(5) consisted of a residual exception provision, identical to Rule 803(24). Both have since been transferred to Rule 807. Case law interpreting and applying old Rule 804(b)(5) is still relevant in applying Rule 807. After this provision was eliminated from Rule 804, the number 804(b)(5) was recycled to cover the completely different provision discussed in §§ 11.47 et. seq.

6. Statement Offered Against a Party Who Wrongfully Caused the Declarant's Unavailability

§ 11.47 RULE 804(b)(6)

In 1997, a new provision was added to Fed. R. Evid. 804(b), entitled "forfeiture by wrongdoing."

Fed. R. Evid. 804(b)(6) provides as follows:

(b) The Exceptions. The following are not excluded by the rule against hearsay if the declarant is unavailable as a witness:

(6) *Statement Offered Against a Party Who Wrongfully Caused the Declarant's Unavailability.* A statement offered against the party that wrongfully caused — or acquiesced in wrongfully causing — the declarant's unavailability in order to prevent the declarant from attending or testifying.

[Prior to December 1, 2011, 804(b)(6) read as follows:

> (b) Hearsay exceptions. The following are not excluded by the hearsay rule if the declarant is unavailable as a witness:
>
> > (6) Forfeiture by wrongdoing. A statement offered against a party that has engaged or acquiesced in wrongdoing that was intended to, and did, procure the unavailability of the declarant as a witness.

The Federal Rules of Evidence were rewritten solely to make them easier to understand; the Advisory Committee did not intend to make any substantive change in the Rules. The text of the old rule may remain useful in reading court decisions that precede the revision of the rules. Thus, this edition of the Student's Guide provides the text of both the new and the old version of each relevant provision of the Federal Rules of Evidence.]

Thus, if a party bribes or threatens or kills a declarant, or hires or encourages someone else to do so, or "acquiesces" in such conduct, that party has in essence waived a hearsay objection as to that declarant's hearsay statements. The provision codifies a rule that emerged in the case law over the past two decades, mostly in criminal cases, and a principle the Supreme Court had recognized in the 19th Century.

The rule is not restricted to criminal cases. A civil litigant could use it; theoretically so could a defendant in a criminal case. It was added to the rule, however, primarily to help prosecutors, and virtually all of the cases discussing the rule involve a prosecutor's invocation of it. Accordingly, in the discussion that follows, I am assuming that a prosecutor is offering a declarant's statement in evidence and claims that the defendant has forfeited the hearsay objection per this provision. But remember: your professor could give you a quiz or exam question in which a civil litigant or criminal defendant might seek to use this hearsay exception.

The requirements specified in Fed. R. Evid. 804(b)(6) are as follows:

1. *Unavailability.* The exception applies only if the declarant in fact is unavailable to testify, as "unavailability" is defined in Rule 804(a).

2. *"Caused" declarant's unavailability.* Defendant's conduct, or the conduct of another in which defendant "acquiesced" (see issue 3), "caused" the declarant's unavailability as a witness. *See* § 11.49.

3. *"Acquiesced."* The Rule covers not only active procurement of wrongdoing, but also "acquiescence" in such wrongdoing. *See* § 11.49.

4. *Wrongdoing.* The prosecutor must establish that the conduct in question constitutes "wrongdoing." *See* § 11.50.

5. *Intent to cause the declarant's unavailability as a witness.* In addition to showing that the wrongdoing *in fact* "caused" the declarant's unavailability as a witness, the prosecutor must also establish that the defendant's *intent* was to cause the declarant's unavailability as a witness. *See* § 11.54.

In addition, the Rule raises these additional issues:

6. *Sixth Amendment Confrontation Clause. See* § 11.51.

7. *Burden of proof; procedure. See* § 11.53.

§ 11.48 A DOMESTIC VIOLENCE SCENARIO

The issue arises with some frequency in domestic violence cases, and occasionally in organized crime and street gang cases, as well as miscellaneous crimes.

Here is how an all-too-typical domestic violence might develop. Someone calls 911: "It sounds like the guy in apartment 4B is beating up his wife again! You'd better send the police, and an ambulance!" Police arrive five minutes later. A badly bruised and beaten woman (W) is sitting in the kitchen. Asked what happened, she tells the officers that H, her husband, beat her up. Asked "where is he now," she replies, "he's in the bedroom." The officers arrest H and charge him with felonious assault. Other officers (or an ambulance, if necessary) take W to the hospital, where her bruises are photographed, and she is treated. W signs a statement for the police, describing what H did to her.

By the time the case goes to trial, however, W refuses to testify, or claims that she tripped and fell and lied to get H in trouble for some reason (say, because she thought he was cheating on her, or the like). According to the *Davis* and *Hammon* decisions, all of W's statements accusing H of the assault are testimonial (see § 8.10), and *Michigan v. Bryant* does not really undercut those decisions (see §§ 8.12–8.14).[26] Thus, if W recants or refuses to testify, it may be impossible for the state to survive the defendant's motion for a directed verdict at the close of the state's case.

In § 11.53 I'll discuss how the forfeiture rule might apply in such a case.

§ 11.49 "CAUSED" OR "ACQUIESCED"

Caused. To satisfy this requirement, the prosecutor must prove that the defendant engaged in conduct which caused the declarant's unavailability, i.e., the defendant did something which resulted in the declarant's falling within one of the provisions of Fed. R. Evid. 804(a). Evidence that the defendant killed, bribed, frightened, or persuaded the declarant not to testify will satisfy this requirement. The term "cause" also includes active encouragement.

To show causation, a prosecutor need not establish that the defendant himself killed the declarant, or threatened, bribed (etc.) the declarant into silence. If the prosecutor

---

[26] It is possible that *Giles v. California* indicates a willingness of a majority of the Court to reconsider the rule established in *Davis* and *Hammon* (see § 8.11), but that's just speculation.

can establish that someone else did so at the defendant's instruction or as a result of the defendant's encouragement, that also establishes that the defendant "caused" the declarant's unavailability.

Acquiesced. It also suffices to show that the defendant "acquiesced" in such wrongdoing by another. To "acquiesce" is "to accept or comply tacitly or passively." Consider:

> If an underling says to an organized crime boss about to stand trial, "It would be a real shame if X [the key government witness] had an accident" and the boss shrugs, does this constitute "acquiescence" to the underling's implied suggestion that he kill the witness?

> If a lawyer in civil litigation tells a client, "I'll try to persuade Y [plaintiff's key witness] not to testify," does this constitute the client's "acquiescence" in the lawyer's subsequent bribery?

If a lawyer bribes the witness or an underling kills a witness without first getting at least the client's tacit, passive acquiescence, however, the hearsay exception probably does not apply.

§ 11.50   "WRONGFULLY"

Certain conduct clearly qualifies as wrongful: murder, assault, threats, bribery. If a party arranges for someone to offer the declarant a lucrative job out of the country so the declarant will not be around to testify, this also probably qualifies as "wrongful," even if the declarant is unaware that his good fortune was prompted by the party in the impending litigation. Occasionally, though, it may be questionable whether conduct that prevents a declarant from testifying can be classified as "wrongful."

Suppose, for example, a defendant in a criminal case *marries* the government's key witness, so he can assert the privilege (recognized in some jurisdictions) of preventing his wife from testifying against him. Is this "wrongful"?

If H in the domestic violence scenario tells W he's very sorry, and begs her to forgive him, and agrees to go to counseling, and as a result, W decides not to testify against him, is this "wrongful"?

Suppose X, who knows that he and Y are being investigated, tells Y, "Don't worry, the same law firm that represents me will represent you — and I'll foot the bill for both of us." Suppose further that Y's lawyer urges Y not to cooperate and to plead the Fifth if called to testify against X. Is this "wrongful"?

If you are presented with a scenario like the lasts three, make sure your answer (a) specifies that, to invoke Fed. R. Evid. 804(b)(6), the prosecutor would have to establish that the defendant's conduct was "wrongful"; (b) argue both sides of the issue as well as you can; and (c) take your best guess as to how a court would rule. If I had to decide, I'd probably rule that none of them are "wrongful," although I waver back and forth about the third one.

§ 11.51   CONFRONTATION CLAUSE: *GILES v. CALIFORNIA* — THE INTENT REQUIREMENT

In *Davis v. Washington*, the Supreme Court acknowledged that its approach to the Confrontation Clause sometimes gave domestic violence defendants an "undeserved windfall" because victims so often recanted, and reminded prosecutors and courts that the forfeiture doctrine was available to prevent this "windfall." In *Giles v. California*, 554 U.S. 353 (2008), the Supreme Court held that to qualify a statement under the forfeiture exception to the Confrontation Clause, a prosecutor had to establish the following:

1. The declarant was unavailable.

2. The defendant engaged in (or, presumably, acquiesced in) conduct that was responsible for the declarant's unavailability,

3. The conduct in question consisted of "wrongdoing."

4. The purpose or intent of that conduct was to render the declarant unavailable to testify against him.

In essence, therefore, the requirements of Fed. R. Evid. 804(b)(6) and the requirements of the forfeiture doctrine exception to the Confrontation Clause are identical.

The case arose when Giles killed his ex-girlfriend, Brenda Avie, by shooting her six times from close range. He was charged with murder. Although she was unarmed at the time, Giles pleaded self-defense, claiming she had engaged in violent, assaultive behavior in the past and had threatened him and his new girlfriend, earlier on the day he shot her, and again at the beginning of their fatal encounter.

To rebut Giles' self-defense claim that Ms Avie had threatened Giles just before he shot her, the prosecutor offered evidence that, three weeks earlier, police, responding to a domestic violence complaint, went to the home Giles then shared with Ms Avie. An officer testified that Ms Avie described how, a few minutes before the officers arrived, Giles had assaulted and choked her and threatened her with a knife. (By the time the police arrived, however, the incident was over and, although Giles was still in the house, he was no longer assaulting or threatening her.) The trial judge allowed the officer to testify.

Although the procedural setting is somewhat complicated, in essence the Supreme Court considered the case as if the trial judge admitted the statement over a Confrontation Clause objection under the forfeiture doctrine. In doing so, the trial judge did not consider whether, when he killed her, Giles' intent was to prevent Ms Avie from testifying against him. By a six-to-three vote, the Court concluded that to satisfy the forfeiture exception to the Confrontation Clause, the prosecutor had to prove to the trial judge that Giles in fact had this intent when he killed her.

In other words, if Giles killed Ms Avie simply because he wanted her to be dead, he did not forfeit his constitutional right to raise a Confrontation Clause objection to the use of her hearsay statements against him.

294   EXCEPTIONS TO THE RULE-DECLARANT UNAVAILABLE   CH. 11

It took four separate opinions, however, to reach this conclusion, and the majority was so fractured that the words "we hold" never appear in the opinion.[1] Moreover, two of the *Giles* majority stated or suggested that perhaps Ms Avie's statements to the officer were not even testimonial, and the three dissenters perhaps hinted along the same lines as well. (See § 8.11.)

Justice Breyer, joined by Justices Stevens and Kennedy, dissented, arguing that it should suffice that the prosecutor show that the defendant *knew* that by killing Ms Avie, he was preventing her from ever testifying against him, whether that was one of his purposes or not.[2]

§ 11.52 *GILES*: RATIONALE FOR THE DECISION

The *Giles* majority based its decision on two primary considerations. First, Justice Scalia concluded that the history of the Confrontation Clause indicated that proof of the defendant's intent to prevent the declarant from testifying was always part of the forfeiture rule. Second, Justice Scalia reasoned that allowing a judge to admit the statement merely based on a judicial finding by a preponderance of the evidence that Giles had killed Ms Avie undercut the prosecutor's obligation to prove a defendant's guilt beyond a reasonable doubt. The dissent, not surprisingly, rejected both of these conclusions.

§ 11.53 BURDEN OF PERSUASION; EVIDENCE TO BE CONSIDERED

The Advisory Committee Note to Fed. R. Evid. 804(b)(6) states that, per Rule 104(a), the party seeking to invoke the exception must persuade the judge of the requirements for the exception by a preponderance of the evidence. In *Giles*, the Court hinted strongly (albeit in dictum) that this same burden of persuasion would apply to the constitutional forfeiture doctrine as well.

As to what evidence a judge can consider in making that judgment, remember that, in ruling on the admissibility of evidence, per Fed. R. Evid. 104(a), "The court must decide any preliminary question about whether . . . evidence is admissible. In so deciding, the court is not bound by evidence rules." Thus, for example, hearsay evidence that would not be admissible at trial to prove the defendant's guilt, would be admissible at a hearing to decide whether the prosecutor satisfied Fed. R. Evid. 804(b)(6). The same is true at a hearing to decide whether the prosecutor has satisfied the forfeiture doctrine exception to the Confrontation Clause.

---

[1] The Court remanded the case back to the California courts. A state judge ultimately excluded Ms. Avie's statements.

[2] As you can probably guess, approximately half the Evidence professors in the United States have published law review articles that attempt to make sense of this remarkably confusing opinion. My own analysis, *Confrontation, Forfeiture, and* Giles v. California: *An Interim User's Guide*, is published at 58 Catholic Univ. L. Rev. 703 (2009). The best part of the article, according to some observers, is a footnote that can be found by the following Westlaw search: da(aft 2008) & Fishman & pancake & "peat moss."

In other words, litigating the admissibility of a statement over a hearsay objection per Rule 804(b)(6), and litigating the admissibility of the statement over a Confrontation Clause objection per the forfeiture doctrine, involve precisely the same issues and permit consideration of precisely the same evidence.

§ 11.54 APPLYING RULE 804(b)(6) AND THE CONFRONTATION CLAUSE FORFEITURE DOCTRINE: DOMESTIC VIOLENCE CASES

In the scenario in § 11.48, here is how the case might play out.

W refuses to testify against her husband; she tells the police and prosecutor that she hurt herself falling down stairs and lied to the police because she was angry at H. This would appear to preclude the prosecutor from using W's testimonial verbal statement to the police when they questioned her in her home, or her testimonial signed statement at the police station.

Suppose, however, that at a hearing to determine the admissibility of these statements, the prosecutor calls M, W's mother, who testifies, "W told me two weeks ago she was afraid if she testified, H would kill her."

W's statement to her mother is hearsay, and it fits no hearsay exceptions: it is inadmissible *at trial*. But, per Rule 104(a), it *is admissible at the Rule 804(b)(6) hearing*. And even if W takes the stand at the hearing and denies ever having said that to her mother, the judge could disbelieve W, believe M, and find, by a preponderance of the evidence, that W's refusal to testify against H was "caused" by H's threats, and that he made those threats with the intent of preventing her from testifying against him. Result: if W refuses to testify at trial, H has forfeited the right to object on hearsay or Confrontation Clause grounds; therefore, the statements *W* statements to the *police*, in her home and at the station house, are admissible against H at his trial as substantive evidence of H's guilt.

But what about a case like *Giles*, where the prosecutor can prove that the defendant killed the victim, but lacks direct evidence that his purpose was, or at least that his purposes included, preventing her from testifying against him? Consider what Justice Souter said in his concurring opinion in *Giles* (an opinion also signed by Justice Ginsberg):

> [T]he element of intention would normally be satisfied by the intent inferred on the part of the domestic abuser in the classic abusive relationship, which is meant to isolate the victim from outside help, including the aid of law enforcement and the judicial process. If the evidence for admissibility shows a continuing relationship of this sort, it would make no sense to suggest that the oppressing defendant miraculously abandoned the dynamics of abuse the instant before he killed his victim, say in a fit of anger.[3]

Justice Souter's phrase "the classic abusive relationship" refers to sociological and

---

[3] Giles v. California, 128 S.Ct. 2678, 2695 (2008), Souter, J., concurring.

psychological studies that describe the "battered woman syndrome" ("BWS") in which a man, by threats and violence, attempts, and often succeeds, in frightening and cowing a woman to the point where she is afraid to leave him, afraid to seek help, or afraid to follow through if she does seek help.[4] In other words, if the prosecutor in a case like *Giles* can prove that the defendant and the homicide victim were in a "classic abusive relationship," this may be enough, without more, to entitle the hearing judge to conclude by a preponderance of the evidence that the defendant killed the victim, at least in part to prevent her from testifying or cooperating with the authorities with regard to his previous abuse of her. And while only Justice Ginsberg signed Justice Souter's concurrence, if we add the three dissenting judges, who don't think intent should be required at all, we have a majority of at least five that would allow the required intent to be inferred whenever the prosecutor can show that the defendant and the victim were in a "classic abusive relationship."[5] Thus, the judge could conclude that the intent requirement of the hearsay and Confrontation Clause forfeiture exceptions have been satisfied, and all of W's statements to the police would be admissible at trial against H.

The Souter approach might also apply in the § 11.48 scenario, where the declarant is still alive, but recants the accusation, claiming instead she fell and hurt herself.

How might the prosecutor prove that H and W were in a "classic abusive relationship"?

Suppose, in the § 11.48 scenario (without W's mother's testimony), at the hearing the prosecutor calls police officers who testify that on two previous occasions, just like the present case, they responded to domestic violence reports at the H-W home. On those occasions, like the present case, W had fresh bruises, and the home showed signs of a struggle (broken glass, overturned furniture, etc.). Each time, W told them that H had beaten her; each time, she later refused to press the charges or to testify against him, without saying why, or by giving a lame-sounding reason. The prosecutor could also call expert witnesses at the hearing to describe BWS, and to express an opinion that H and W were in a BWS relationship. Justice Souter's approach probably would permit the judge, based solely on this evidence, to conclude that W has recanted her most recent accusation because H threatened to beat her even worse if she testified against him. Thus, her oral and written statements to the police would be admissible at H's trial to prove his guilt — even if W refuses to testify, or testifies that she lied to the police and H had nothing to do with her injuries.

---

[4] Experts have subsequently recognized that such relationships exist in other contexts. A battered person relationship can exist in a homosexual relationship. It can also exist where the batterer is a parent, and the victim is a child; sometimes the other way around; sometimes, even, where the wife is the batterer and the husband is the victim. In such cases it is usually referred to as "battered person syndrome."

[5] Justice Scalia also acknowledged something along these lines, although he would demand a bit more than Justice Souter.

§ 11.55   APPLYING RULE 804(b)(6) AND THE FORFEITURE DOCTRINE: AN ORGANIZED CRIME SCENARIO

Now consider an organized crime scenario. Police were investigating a narcotics distribution network known as the Herb Gang, because its members are named Parsley, Sage, Rosemary, Thyme and Oregano. They arrested Oregano, and he agreed to cooperate, and provided detailed statements outlining how the distribution ring operated, and of how Parsley and Sage arranged to kill Rice and Spud, members of a rival drug distribution network. Then Oregano was shot and killed. Later the police arrested Thyme, and, as part of a deal, he agreed to testify against Parsley, Sage and Rosemary. He told the police that Parsley and Sage came to suspect that Oregano had turned informant, and that he was present when Parsley and Sage told Rosemary to kill Oregano. (Thyme's testimony about this is admissible against Parsley, Sage and Rosemary, per Fed. R. Evid. 801(d)(2)(A), 801(d)(2)(B), and 801(d)(2)(E).)

Eventually, Parsley, Sage and Rosemary are indicted for multiple crimes, including drug distribution, the murders of Rice and Spud, and the murder of Oregano. Consider the curious burden of persuasion issues in this case:

a. To *secure admissibility of Oregano's statements* to the police pursuant to Fed. R. Evid. 804(b)(6) and the forfeiture doctrine exception to the Confrontation Clause, the prosecutor must *persuade the judge by a preponderance of the evidence* that Parsley, Sage and Rosemary "caused" Oregano's unavailability by killing him or having him killed, and did so for the purpose of preventing him from testifying against them. In deciding this issue, the judge may consider all admissible evidence against Parsley, Sage and Rosemary — including Thyme's testimony; and, for that matter, may also consider Oregano's hearsay statements, which are not (yet) admissible at trial, that Parsley and Sage arranged two other killings; and any other information the prosecutor has on the subject, even if that other information could never be admitted at the trial.

b. To *convict Parsley, Sage and Rosemary of the murder of Oregano*, the prosecutor must *persuade the jury of their guilt beyond a reasonable doubt.*

In other words, in the same trial, with regard to the same factual issue, there are different burdens of proof to different fact-finders, judge and jury. If the judge is satisfied by a preponderance that Parsley, Sage and Rosemary procured Oregano's unavailability by killing him, and did so for the purpose of preventing his testimony, Oregano's statements accusing them of the murders of Rice and Spud are admissible against them. And even if the jury ultimately acquits Parsley, Sage and Rosemary of killing Oregano, they might still legitimately convict them of killing Rice and Spud, based heavily on Oregano's statements.

Chapter 12

THE "RESIDUAL EXCEPTION": RULE 807

§ 12.1 IN GENERAL

When Congress first enacted the Federal Rules of Evidence, in addition to the more-or-less specific provisions of Rules 803(1)–(23) and 804(b)(1)–(4), it included two identical provisions, Rules 803(24) and 804(b)(5), intended to afford the federal courts a limited amount of flexibility and discretion to admit hearsay which, although not fully satisfying any of the specific exceptions, has "equivalent circumstantial guarantees of trustworthiness" and which satisfies several other substantive and procedural requirements. In 1997 Congress combined these two provisions into an identical new provision, nominated Rule 807. No change in meaning was intended.

Fed. R. Evid. 807, entitled "Residual Exception," provides as follows:

(a) In General. Under the following circumstances, a hearsay statement is not excluded by the rule against hearsay even if the statement is not specifically covered by a hearsay exception in Rule 803 or 804:

(1) the statement has equivalent circumstantial guarantees of trustworthiness;

(2) it is offered as evidence of a material fact;

(3) it is more probative on the point for which it is offered than any other evidence that the proponent can obtain through reasonable efforts; and

(4) admitting it will best serve the purposes of these rules and the interests of justice.

(b) Notice. The statement is admissible only if, before the trial or hearing, the proponent gives an adverse party reasonable notice of the intent to offer the statement and its particulars, including the declarant's name and address, so that the party has a fair opportunity to meet it.

[Prior to December 1, 2011, the rule read as follows:

Rule 807. Residual Exception

A statement not specifically covered by Rule 803 or 804 but having equivalent circumstantial guarantees of trustworthiness, is not excluded by the hearsay rule, if the court determines that (A) the statement is offered as evidence of a material fact; (B) the statement is more probative on the point for which it is offered than any other evidence which the proponent can procure through reasonable efforts; and (C) the general purposes of these rules and the interests of justice will best be served by admission of the statement into evidence. However, a statement may not be admitted under this exception unless the proponent of it makes known to the adverse party sufficiently in advance of the trial or hearing to provide the adverse party with a fair opportunity to prepare to meet it, the proponent's intention to offer the statement and the particulars of it, including the name and address of the declarant.

The Federal Rules of Evidence were rewritten solely to make them easier to understand; the Advisory Committee did not intend to make any substantive change in the Rules. The text of the old rule may remain useful in reading court decisions that precede the revision of the rules. Thus, this edition of the Student's Guide provides the text of both the new and the old version of each relevant provision of the Federal Rules of Evidence.]

For a statement to overcome a hearsay objection pursuant to Rule 807, five conditions must be met; and if a prosecutor seeks to use the exception, the Confrontation Clause must also be considered.

1. The statement must be "offered as evidence of a material fact." Rule 807(a)(2). (*See* § 12.2.)

2. The statement must be "more probative on the point for which it is offered than any other evidence that the proponent can obtain through reasonable efforts." Rule 807(a)(3). (*See* § 12.2.)

3. The statement must have "circumstantial guarantees of trustworthiness" equivalent to the exceptions in Rule 803 and Rule 804. Rule 807(a)(1). (*See* § 12.4).

4. The trial judge must be satisfied that "admitting it will best serve the purposes of these rules and the interests of justice." Rule 807(a)(4).

5. The offering party must give the adverse party advance notice of the intent to offer the statement. Most courts require that the notice specifically refer to the residual exception. This alerts the adverse party to seek evidence to challenge the hearsay's admissibility or to refute it. Despite the seemingly absolute language of the advance notice clause, where the offering party only learned of the evidence during trial (and therefore could not give the required notice), instead of excluding the evidence, courts have given the adverse party a recess, adjournment or continuance to enable it to attempt to counter the evidence.

6. *Sixth Amendment Confrontation Clause. See* § 12.6.

These requirements should be interpreted in light of the legislative history of the residual exception. The Advisory Committee admonished that the residual exceptions "do not contemplate an unfettered exercise of judicial discretion"; the House Judiciary Committee sought to exclude them altogether; the Senate Judiciary Committee reinserted them into the Federal Rules of Evidence, commenting that in doing so, the Committee did "not intend to establish a broad license for trial judges"; rather, the residual exceptions should be reserved for "exceptional circumstances . . . and exceptional cases. . . ."

§ 12.2 "MATERIAL"; "MORE PROBATIVE"

Fed. R. Evid. 807(a)(2) requires that "the statement is offered as evidence of a material fact."[1] Rule 807(a)(3) requires that the statement is "more probative on the point for which it is offered than any other evidence that the proponent can obtain through reasonable efforts." The latter requirement has been the focus of considerable judicial attention. Some generalizations can be drawn from the case law.

1. Courts consider live testimony more probative than hearsay statements. Where a party fails to call an available witness who presumably could testify about the same facts, attempts to offer hearsay through the residual exception are often rejected.

2. Courts tend to be fairly strict in applying the "reasonable efforts" aspects of the requirement: the residual exceptions do not excuse an attorney's laziness.

3. The "reasonableness" of the effort to be required depends to some extent on the importance of the evidence and whether it is offered on a contested issue.

§ 12.3 QUESTIONS

Question 1. D was accused of carnal knowledge of G, a girl less than 16 years old. The case began when G went to SN, her school nurse, and reported what had been going on, and SN reported the matter to the authorities. At trial G testified and was cross-examined, but the jury could not reach a verdict. By the time the case comes up for retrial, G is unavailable: she and her family have moved to a different state. Therefore, the prosecutor seeks to have SN testify about what G told her. When D makes a hearsay objection, the prosecutor cites Rule 807. Ruling?

Ans. The objection should be sustained. G's testimony at the first trial, admissible under Fed. R. Evid. 804(b)(1), is more probative than her statement to SN, because her first-trial testimony was under oath and subject to cross-examination. Even if G's statement to SN satisfies the other requirements of Fed. R. Evid. 807, therefore, it fails to satisfy the "more probative" requirement.[2]

Question 2. P sued five asbestos manufacturers, alleging that exposure to asbestos caused his debilitating lung disease. At trial, after proper advance notice to the defendants, P invoked Fed. R. Evid. 807 to offer in evidence the deposition of Dr. W, who had been a staff physician and consultant for JMC, one of the five companies P

---

[1] The use of the word "material" is probably inadvertent, given the care with which the Advisory Committee eschewed its use elsewhere in the Federal Rules of Evidence (*see* Advisory Committees' Note to Fed. R. Evid. 401, discussing the definition of "relevant evidence"); probably "relevant" is what was intended. Some scholars argue, however, that the word "material" was chosen deliberately to indicate that more than mere relevance is required to justify using the residual exception.

[2] G's statement to SN might nevertheless be admissible in part per some other hearsay exception, such as Fed. R. Evid. 803(4).

was suing. Dr. W's deposition, which focused primarily upon what the asbestos industry knew about the health hazards of asbestos at various points in time, had been taken prior to the trial of a different lawsuit brought by a different plaintiff against JMC; Dr. W died shortly after she had been deposed.

All five defendants in the current case interpose a hearsay objection. Ruling?

Ans. As to JMC, overruled under Rule 804(b)(1). The issue in P's suit is the same as in the prior suit; JMC had an opportunity and similar motive to conduct direct or cross-examination of Dr. W at the deposition as it would now if she were available.

As to the other four companies, overruled under Rule 804(b)(1) if the court follows the Third Circuit's broad definition of "predecessor in interest." (*See* § 11.16.)

Otherwise, overruled under Rule 807. Even though P could have obtained expert testimony from other witnesses, Dr. W's situation, having been employed as a doctor and consultant for one of the defendants, was particularly probative on the issues of what the industry knew and when it knew it; testimony from an "outside" expert would not have been as probative.

§ 12.4 "CIRCUMSTANTIAL GUARANTEES OF TRUSTWORTHINESS"

No all-purpose checklist or mathematical formula exists to govern the assessment of whether a particular statement has "circumstantial guarantees of trustworthiness" that are "equivalent" to one of the specific exceptions, as required by Fed. R. Evid. 807(a)(1). Courts have considered a variety of factors, including the following:

1. *First-hand knowledge.* As a general rule, this is a "must"; without it, the statement will not qualify, except in highly unusual circumstances.

2. *Was the statement a "near miss"?* Most courts have held that a statement that almost qualifies under a specific provision may need only minor additional "guarantees of trustworthiness" to satisfy the residual exception. Other courts, however, have held that "near misses" should *not* be admitted under the residual exception, lest the residual provision subvert Congressional intent in spelling out the requirements for the specific provisions.

3. *Credibility and condition of the declarant.* Is (or was) she someone likely to be truthful, or not? Is she a clergyperson, law professor, police officer, used car salesman, drug dealer, convicted perjurer . . . ?[3] Was the declarant drunk or under the influence of prescription or illicit drugs at the time she made the statement?

4. *The statement itself.* Does it demonstrate, or at least suggest, that declarant had first-hand knowledge? Is it clear or ambiguous? Is it plausible or implausible on its face?

---

[3] Reasonable people may disagree as to where to rank these professions on the scale of probable credibility (except law professor, which of course tops the list).

5. *When, how, where and to whom the statement was made.* Any number of sub-factors may be relevant:

   a.　Was it made under oath,[4] or under other circumstances giving the declarant a particular motive to speak truthfully; or, to the contrary, did the circumstances give declarant a powerful motive to lie?

   b.　Was the statement dis-serving, self-serving, or neutral?

   c.　To what "audience" was it made — a grand jury,[5] a parent or spouse, a diary, a business associate, a casual acquaintance, a call-in radio program?

   d.　How much time elapsed between the events in question, and the declarant's statement?

6. *Other circumstances surrounding the making of the statement* may be relevant in assessing the probable truthfulness of the statement.

7. *Availability of declarant.* Some courts have considered it very significant if the declarant testifies at trial, on the theory that the oath, cross-examination and the jury's opportunity to watch declarant's demeanor on the witness stand all tend to guarantee trustworthiness of the declarant's earlier out-of-court statement.

8. *Corroboration or contradiction.* Does evidence independent of the statement itself tend to confirm or contradict the statement? Note, though, that while courts may consider extrinsic corroboration in civil cases, the Supreme Court has indicated that this is not permissible when a prosecutor seeks to use the residual exception in a criminal case (*see* § 12.6).

9. *Credibility of witness.* Although the credibility of the witness who will testify that declarant made the statement is usually a question strictly for the jury, some courts have included this factor in the evaluation as well.

§ 12.5　QUESTIONS

Question 1. A few days after a winter storm, several construction workers, including R, the crew supervisor, were sent by their company to make repairs to the roof of a building owned by D Co. The roof was surrounded by a five-foot high wall. The roof could be reached from inside the building through the building superintendent's apartment, or from outside by climbing a flight of stairs. The opening at the top of the stairs was shut with a makeshift gate that had been wired to the wall around the roof.

After the work crew arrived, R had a conversation with S, the building superintendent. A few minutes later R told W, a member of his work crew, "The super says we

---

[4] If it was made under oath, a prosecutor could not offer it under the residual exception, because statements made under oath are by definition testimonial. But a criminal defendant or civil litigant could offer such a statement under the residual exception.

[5] See the previous footnote.

can't go through his apartment, because he's afraid we'll track mud all over his carpets; and he won't let us take down the gate, because he lets his dog run around on the roof and if we take down the gate the dog might get down the stairs and run away." Thus, the only way the men could get on and off of the roof was to climb over the fence at the top of the stairs. The men worked for several hours. As R was climbing over the fence to get to the stairs at the end of the day, the fence gave way, and R fell to his death.

Mrs. R, R's widow, brought a wrongful death action against D Co., alleging that unsafe work conditions caused R's death; D Co. defended by claiming that R's own negligence (his failure to take down the gate) caused his death. Prior to trial, Mrs. R served notice on D Co. that she planned to elicit testimony about what R had told W about R's conversation with S.

At trial, W testifies that there was a lot of slush and mud on the ground because of the previous day's storm, and also testified that there were dog droppings on the roof. Then Mrs. R seeks to have W testify as to what R told him following R's conversation with S. (S is unavailable at trial.)

D Co. makes a hearsay objection. How many levels of hearsay are there?

Ans. It appears that there are two (S to R and R to W).

As to the first level (S to R), the hearsay objection is easily overcome. Mrs. R can argue, (1) that what S said to R wasn't an assertion of fact, it was a direction or imperative ("You can't go through my apartment"; "you can't take down the fence") (*see* § 2.9); or (2) that because S was D Co.'s building superintendent, what he said is admissible against D Co. under Rule 801(d)(2)(D) (*see* § 5.23).

Thus, only the second level (R to W) poses problems.

Question 2. What rules should Mrs. R cite to overcome D Co.'s hearsay objection?

Ans. The two likely candidates are Rule 803(1), present sense impression, and Rule 807.

Rule 803(1). R's statement to W, in which he repeated what S allegedly had said to him, satisfies most of the requirements quite easily (*see* § 8.2.). R had first-hand knowledge of what S had said; R's statement to W "described or explained" what S had said to R, and also explained how the men would have to get to the roof. The time factor, though, may be a problem. W can't be quite sure how much time elapsed between the R-S conversation and R's statement to W — perhaps five minutes, perhaps 10, perhaps 15. To some courts, that is too much time for Rule 803(1) (which requires that the statement was made "while the declarant was perceiving the event, or immediately thereafter").

Rule 807. Mrs. R easily satisfies the first (advance notice), third (relevance) and fourth ("more probative") requirements. The key is the second: trustworthiness. Of the factors listed in § 12.4, the following are pertinent:

1. *First-hand knowledge.* R had such knowledge of what S had said to him.

2. *Near miss.* See the discussion of Rule 803(1) at the beginning of this answer, addressing this point.

4. *The statement itself.* It was a plausible explanation, by a supervisor to his work crew, of how they would have to get access to the roof and why.

5. *When, where, and to whom the statement was made.* R made his statement to W only minutes after his conversation with S, so it is unlikely he would have forgotten what S said. R had no motive to lie, because following S's instructions made the job more difficult and dangerous.

7. *Availability of declarant.* R is dead and S cannot be found.

8. *Corroboration or contradiction.* The mud and slush on the ground corroborate R's explanation of why S would not let the men enter the roof through S's apartment; the dog droppings on the roof corroborate R's statement as to why S insisted the men could not take down the gate.

Conclusion: R's statement is admissible under the residual exception.

Question 2. In 2006, Fil's father Pater was shot and bludgeoned to death. Fil's relationship with Pater had been tempestuous for many years, and in 2010 Fil was charged with the crime. During the state's case-in-chief, police officers testified that when they first interviewed Fil shortly after the crime, he told investigators of an incident in 2005: he and his father Pater were outside Pater's lake front home, when someone apparently fired a shot at Pater from across the lake; the bullet hit a nearby tree; Pater told him not to mention it to anybody.

Why would the state offer this evidence?

Ans. Perhaps the prosecutor concluded that Fil's story — that someone apparently attempted to kill Pater, yet Pater never reported it and insisted that Fil tell no one about it — was so implausible that the jury would conclude that it was an obviously untrue attempt by Fil to deflect suspicion from himself onto some non-existent stranger.

Question 3. After the officers testified about this statement at trial, Sybil, who had been Pater's girlfriend at the time he was killed, approached Fil's attorney and told him that Pater had told her about the shot that had been fired at him. Fil's attorney now seeks to have Sybil testify about this statement to her by Pater. The prosecutor objects that Pater's statement to Sybil is hearsay. Fil's attorney responds that it should be admitted per Rule 807, and that the advance notice requirement should be waived because he just found out about the statement. The prosecutor argues that the statement is untrustworthy, and strongly suggests that Sybil is lying: Sybil never told either the police or defense counsel about this supposed conversation with Pater until, in violation of a sequestration order,[6] she heard other witnesses mention it during their testimony.

---

[6] If requested by either party, a judge will order that individuals who are likely to be called as witnesses at trial must be "sequestered," i.e., must not be in the courtroom to hear the testimony of other witnesses. *See* Fed. R. Evid. 615. It is standard practice for both attorneys to make such a request at the beginning of a trial.

Why is Fil seeking to have Sybil testify?

Ans. Sybil's testimony makes it more probable that the shooting incident actually occurred, which in turn makes it more probable that someone else (i.e., not Fil) hated Pater enough to kill him.

Question 4. How should the judge rule on the prosecutor's hearsay objection?

Ans. Applying the basic Rule 807 checklist:

1. *Material fact.* Whether someone fired a shot at Pater in 2005 is a "material fact," because it suggests that someone (other than Fil) hated Pater enough to want to kill him.

2. *More probative.* Fil has a good argument that Sybil's testimony that Pater told her about the shooting incident is more probative (to prove that the shooting incident occurred) than Fil's statement about it to the police, because, unlike Fil, Sybil has no known motive to make up such a story.

3. Circumstantial guarantees of trustworthiness. Applying the § 12.4 checklist:

1. Pater, the declarant, certainly had first-hand knowledge of whether the shooting incident occurred.

2. *Near Miss?* N/A

3. *Credibility of declarant.* There is nothing to suggest that Pater had anything to gain by making up such a story. (This assumes, of course, that Sybil's testimony, that Pater told her about the shooting incident, is true.)

4. *The statement itself.* The statement is still somewhat implausible. (Events like this don't happen very often!)

5. *When, and to whom, the statement was made.* Sybil and Pater were close to one another, which makes it less likely Pater would lie to Sybil about something so serious.

6. *Other circumstances.* Sybil's proffered testimony does not include any explanation why Pater did not report the matter to the police.

7. Pater, the declarant, is dead, therefore unavailable.

8. *Corroboration.* Fil's statement to the police corroborates Sybil's testimony about Pater's statement to her; Sybil's testimony corroborates Fil's statement to the police.

9. *Credibility of witness (Sybil).* Assuming this is a valid consideration at all (most courts agree it is not): on one hand, Sybil has no apparent reason to make up such a story. On the other hand, the fact that she never told it to the police or to Fil's attorney, until she improperly heard it in the courtroom, is no great endorsement.

In the case on which this problem is based, the trial court excluded "Sybil's" testimony on two grounds. (1) Because the jury had already heard about the shooting incident (when the police testified for the state that Fil told them about it), Sybil's testimony was not "more probative" than what the jury already heard. (2) The judge disbelieved Sybil.

As my answer (above) explains, I think the judge was wrong on both counts. (1) Sybil's testimony, that Pater told her about the shooting incident, has a considerable tendency to make it more probable that the incident actually occurred. (2) It should be up to the jury, not the judge, to assess the credibility of Sybil, the witness. Nevertheless, Minnesota's Supreme Court, in *State v Bolstade*, 686 NW2d 531, 542 (Minn 2004), upheld the trial judge's exclusion of "Sybil's" testimony.

Question 8. So how do I explain why the trial court ruled as it did, and the state supreme court confirmed?

Ans. Who knows? Perhaps the trial judge was convinced that Fils was guilty and that Sybil was lying, and decided to exercise his or her discretion in a way that would tilt the case toward the result the judge thought was the right one. (That is not "officially" a proper basis on which a trial judge should exercise discretion, but I strongly suspect it happens from time to time.) And perhaps the state supreme court, reading between the lines, intuited that this is what happened, and trusted the trial judge's judgment on the matter. To paraphrase a sappy line from a tear-jerker novel and movie that was enormously popular in the 1970's, "Having discretion means never having to say you're sorry — unless you are reversed."[7]

§ 12.6 CONFRONTATION CLAUSE; TRUSTWORTHINESS

If a "residual exception" statement is testimonial, it must be excluded on Confrontation Clause grounds, unless the prosecutor can fit it into ¶¶ C, D, E, F, or H of the Confrontation Clause checklist, § 6.10.

The Supreme Court in *Davis v. Washington* indicated that non-testimonial hearsay is no longer subject to a Confrontation Clause objection, *see* § 6.9, and the *Roberts* "trustworthiness" test no longer is valid law in Confrontation Clause cases. Nevertheless, if a prosecutor wants to use Fed. R. Evid. 807, he or she must make a "particularized showing of trustworthiness" in order to satisfy the hearsay exception.

In *Idaho v. Wright*, 497 U.S. 805, 817 (1990), the Supreme Court held that in assessing the trustworthiness of a statement offered by a prosecutor under the residual exception, a court may look only at the statement itself and the circumstances in which it was made; a court may not look at extrinsic corroboration. Wright was charged with assisting her male companion to sexually abuse her 5- and 2-year-old daughters. In considering the admissibility of statements that the younger child made

---

[7] The novel, by Erich Segal, and the movie made from it, is *Love Story*. The opening line is, "What can you say about a twenty-five-year-old girl who died? That she was beautiful and brilliant? That she loved Mozart and Bach, the Beatles, and me?" That pretty much tells you the plot. The "girl" gets to say its most famous line: "Love means never having to say you're sorry." Which, as anyone who has ever truly been in love knows, is absolute nonsense. In reality, love sometimes means saying you are sorry, even when you are convinced you've done nothing to be sorry for — or don't know *what* you are apologizing for. (But this is a book about hearsay, not a treatise on love, so I'd better quit while I'm behind.)

to a pediatrician, the trial court considered, among other things, physical evidence that the child was abused, testimony by the older child that she had seen the male molesting the younger child, and circumstantial evidence suggesting that the abuse occurred while the mother and her companion were in the house with the child. The Supreme Court, per Justice O'Connor, held that it was error for the trial judge to consider any of this evidence. Permitting extrinsic corroboration as proof of a statement's trustworthiness, a 5-to-4 majority concluded, "would permit admission of a presumptively unreliable statement by bootstrapping on the trustworthiness of other evidence at trial," which, the majority concluded, would be "at odds with the requirement that hearsay evidence admitted under the Confrontation Clause be so trustworthy that cross-examination of the declarant would be of marginal utility." Thus, *Wright* is based on the *Roberts* approach to the Confrontation Clause which the Court, a quarter century later, rejected in *Crawford* and *Davis*.[8]

Courts generally hold, however, that extrinsic corroboration or contradiction of a statement's trustworthiness may be considered when a civil litigant, or a criminal defendant, seeks to introduce a statement per Rule 807.

---

[8] In case you're curious, Justice Scalia voted with the majority in *Wright*. Justice Kennedy, the only other member of the Court in Wright who is still on the Court, dissented, pointing out the irony of excluding from consideration an entire class of evidence most likely to establish whether the statement was in fact trustworthy. I'm not going to try to guess what they, or the Court, would do today if they granted cert on a case raising the issue anew.

INDEX

[References are to sections.]

[References are to sections.]

[References are to sections.]

[References are to sections.]

[References are to sections.]

[References are to sections.]